Edward Bulwer Lytton

Speeches of Edward, Lord Lytton

Edward Bulwer Lytton

Speeches of Edward, Lord Lytton

ISBN/EAN: 9783743347830

Manufactured in Europe, USA, Canada, Australia, Japa

Cover: Foto ©ninafisch / pixelio.de

Manufactured and distributed by brebook publishing software (www.brebook.com)

Edward Bulwer Lytton

Speeches of Edward, Lord Lytton

SPEECHES

OF

EDWARD LORD LYTTON

NOW FIRST COLLECTED

WITH

SOME OF HIS POLITICAL WRITINGS

HITHERTO UNPUBLISHED

AND

A PREFATORY MEMOIR BY HIS SON

IN TWO VOLUMES

VOL. II.

WILLIAM BLACKWOOD AND SONS
EDINBURGH AND LONDON
MDCCCLXXIV

CONTENTS OF THE SECOND VOLUME.

REPRINT OF SPEECHES DELIVERED.

ORIGINAL MATTER.

OUTLINES OF SPEECHES INTENDED TO HAVE BEEN DELIVERED.

XX.

A SPEECH

DELIVERED IN

THE HOUSE OF COMMONS,

ON THE 15TH OF JUNE 1855.

On Friday, the 15th of June 1855, the Member for Aylesbury, Mr Austin Henry Layard, moved the subjoined resolution—"That this House views with deep and increasing concern the state of the nation, and is of opinion that the manner in which merit and efficiency have been sacrificed in public appointments to party and family influences, and to a blind adherence to routine, has given rise to great misfortunes, and threatens to bring discredit on the national character." The Member for Herts, Sir Edward Bulwer Lytton, during the discussion which ensued, moved the following amendment—"That this House recommends to the earliest attention of her Majesty's Ministers the necessity of a careful revision of our various official establishments, with a view to simplify and facilitate the transaction of public business ; and, by instituting judicious tests of merit, as well as by removing obstructions to its fair promotion and legitimate rewards, to secure to the service of the State the largest available proportion of the energy and intelligence for which the people of this country are distinguished." The debate occupied two nights, at its close the original motion being rejected by 359 votes to 46. On introducing the amendment, during the first night's discussion the following speech was delivered.

SIR,—I think there has been no question in our time which contains on the one hand a proposition in itself more just and reasonable, and which, on the other hand, is encumbered by more dangerous exaggeration, than that popular demand which

this motion submits to the consideration of the House. That
when the failure of our departments connected with war, after a
forty years' peace, compelled us to turn our eyes to our various
establishments with a more rigid scrutiny, we should find a
great deal that is obsolete in principle, or cumbersome in detail,
and that when we so find it, we should desire to improve and
simplify both the mechanism and its operation, is natural
enough ; but that we should suddenly pervert a matter of business, to which all men might fairly bring their collective experience and dispassionate intelligence, into an irritating inflammatory
attack upon particular classes, seems to me a very grave misfortune—so grave that I think in the first instance we should
try and see what are the causes which have given to a demand,
natural and harmless in itself, such sinister and alarming tendencies. Now, it is very important to look at the date in which
the cry for administrative reform took the shape which it has
now assumed. It was almost immediately after the accession of
the noble Viscount to the place that he now holds. There had
been great calamities and disasters in the due provision for an
army in which the country felt the deepest interest. Parliament,
rightly or wrongly, laid the main fault upon certain Members of
the late Government. This idea was sanctioned by the opinion
of the noble Lord the Member for London, who had implied,
first to the Chief Minister and then to the House of Commons,
that things would come right if one of his colleagues—the noble
Viscount—took the administration of the war out of the hands
of another of his colleagues—the Duke of Newcastle. The
people shared in that belief ; they thought that whatever defects
there might be in the system—however blundering and incapable minor officials might have been—a Minister of greater
vigour would much more promptly remedy the defects and replace the offenders than they could do by any irregular efforts
of their own. They saw in the noble Viscount the personifica-
tion of their own energy and freedom. He came into his present
office backed by a popular enthusiasm almost unequalled since
1757, when the first William Pitt entered on his famous war
Administration. Up to the time of the noble Lord's accession

to office not a word was said out of doors on administrative reform, in that sense which it has now assumed. About two weeks afterwards the whole country rang with that cry. Why? Because the noble Viscount had disappointed the expectations of the country. At the very commencement he seemed to prove that he wanted that decision of character, that firm reliance on his own judgment, and that penetrative foresight, which are the primary qualities that the people demand in a public man on whom for the moment they confer a virtual dictatorship. The motion for the inquiry into the state of our army, which had been carried by so large a majority, was, the noble Viscount himself frankly said, "the main difficulty that stared him in the face ;" yet, so little had been his foresight, that he had not even arranged with his colleagues beforehand what course to pursue with regard to that inquiry, and so little was his decision that he had not even made up his own mind on the subject. At first he proposed to rescind the vote to which he owed his elevation, and compared himself, with a curious infelicity of illustration, to Richard II., who, as history tells us, had indeed appeased the mob by promising to be their leader—but for the sole object of drawing them away from their immediate object and revoking every promise he had made. Finding the House neither coaxed by his blandishments nor convinced by his illustration, the noble Lord suddenly turned round, and jauntily stepped into that terrible breach of the constitution, leaving three of his colleagues on the other side of the wall. The noble Lord thus lost popu- larity by his injudicious resistance, and then impaired the respect which belongs to manly firmness by the levity of his subsequent acquiescence. Now the people have quick instincts in discovering whether their favourites are thoroughly in earnest. They do not go by actions alone, but also by words. There are times when words are things. For instance, Lord Chatham's first military expedition against Rochfort had been a notable failure, yet the public unanimously acquitted him, because they felt that the failure did not arise from his want of earnestness and vigour : and there was something in Lord Chatham's lan- guage, his tone, and moral bearing, which induced them to wait

with confidence for the full development of his designs. But
from the very first day of the noble Viscount's accession, he led
the public to believe—no doubt erroneously—that he was unduly
trifling with the solemnity which they attached to the occasion,
and he met that impatient grief which complained of national
disaster, and feared even national discredit, with an air that
might remind us much more of Lord North than Lord Chatham.
There is another consideration here which is most important,
when we seek to ascertain the causes for whatever is dangerous
and embarrassing in the popular demand which this motion submits to us ; and on this head I put one question to the noble
Lord's most partial supporters.   Did they not welcome his
accession to the head of affairs upon the supposition that his
Government would proffer a striking contrast to that of the
Ministry he succeeded, or rather reconstructed ?   That was the
belief to which the noble Lord owed his elevation.   What was,
then, the surprise of the public when the noble Viscount's new
Minister of War, Lord Panmure, declared, in his inaugural
speech, that "his anxious desire" was—what? to contrast by
his vigour all previous lethargy ?   No—" to do away with the
impression on the public mind that his predecessor had neglected,
or rather had not carried out to the fullest extent, the interests of
the army committed to his charge ? "   Carried out to the fullest
extent the interests of an army at that instant rotting away from
disease, which was without food, without shelter, without clothing, and with hospitals in a state that made humanity shudder ?
Why, if this were the fact—if in Lord Panmure's opinion the
Duke of Newcastle had carried out to the fullest extent the interests of the army, why on earth did you change the Duke of
Newcastle for Lord Panmure ?   Sir, in all other respects, the
public were disposed to do justice to the Duke of Newcastle ;
his own touching defence had secured to him much respect and
sympathy.   All dispassionate men were willing to acknowledge his
humanity, his application, his honesty of intention, to hope that
he would serve his country hereafter in some other department.
The only fault they found in him was that fault which placed the
noble Viscount where he is—namely, that for some cause or

another the Duke of Newcastle had not carried out the interests of the army. And when my Lord Panmure openly declared that this belief was a mistake, and that, in fact, he meant to follow in the steps of his predecessor—and when, simultaneously, the language and bearing of the noble Viscount destroyed all the previous enthusiasm in his favour—then suddenly broke out this cry—the middle class rose up and said, " It is no use trusting to Ministers, one set is as bad as another ; the affairs of the country at a time when its very existence may be at stake are managed by the conventional courtesies of a drawing - room clique ; we must make a sweeping change, not in Ministers, but in the whole system of administration, and take the functions of a trifling and effeminate Executive into our own uncompromising hands." That, Sir, was the mode in which this cry arose ; and for all that is dangerous in the cry the noble Viscount is thus responsible. Then, indeed, when the country was roused into resentment, when public meetings threatened to take the whole matter out of their hands,—then, but not till then, the Government seemed to be dimly conscious that something more was expected from them than pleasant jokes and flattering epitaphs upon the defunct predecessors they had slain and buried, and the noble Viscount rose to avert the gathering storm —by what ? by an announcement of official arrangements recommended by a Committee of the House more than twenty years ago—pressed last year by the right hon. Member for Buckinghamshire, but pressed vainly, on the Cabinet of which the noble Viscount had been one of the leading members, and improving in no particular upon such reforms as we should equally have had if Lord Aberdeen had been still at the head of affairs and the Duke of Newcastle still Minister of War. Well, then, I pause to put this direct question to the noble Viscount and his colleagues—did you reconstruct yourselves into a new Government only to carry out the projects and measures of the last one ? If so, how deeply has the noble Lord the Member for London injured the Duke of Newcastle, and how egregiously have you duped the expectations of the people ! If, on the other hand, you tell me, " No, we came in to contrast

the late Government with improvements and ideas of our own,"
I ask you what is meant by these grateful eulogies on the Duke
of Newcastle, and I entreat you to distinguish your improvements and your ideas from those which the Duke of Newcastle
was forbidden to develop by the denunciation of his own colleague ! Thus, Sir, the Government at length produced the
mouse that their own mountain had not conceived. And do
you think that these stale and plagiarised reforms, embodying
not one proof of inventive sagacity, not one original conception,
and, strange to say, leaving that department which the noble
Viscount himself declared had the most broken down, I mean
the Commissariat, precisely the department in which all reforms
are indefinitely postponed—do you think that these will suffice
to silence the new cry which is startling the country and threatening to usurp altogether our constitutional powers of legislation?
It is not enough that the late Government launched us into a
war without any definite plan or adequate preparation, but you
—not Lord Aberdeen's Cabinet—you, the noble Viscount's
Government, have exposed us to a far worse danger from the
vague and restless discontent which an appearance of trifling
and frivolity has engendered, than we have to apprehend from
all the armaments of Russia. We have cause, indeed, to be
thankful to Providence for our late successes ; for what would
have been the consequences to our whole political and social
system if some serious defeat to our arms, some indelible stain
upon our national honour, had, in the ferment of public feeling,
been suddenly added to the minor calamities of barren victories
and wasted valour ? Do you not see, in the direction which this
movement for administrative reform has unhappily taken, the
germs of danger to something more important than the existence of any individual Government, something more deeply
rooted into our system than aristocratical ascendancy ? The
danger is to the fundamental principles of representative institutions. I do not think that those who are now so fiercely
agitating against the influences of party and of Parliament are
aware of the logical consequences to which their agitation may
lead. I am sure the hon. Member for Aylesbury is not, or he

would be the first to condemn what he now approves. Talk
thus loosely, yet thus fiercely, against the influences of party.
The influences of party are the sinews of freedom. Party and
freedom are twins, united at the birth by a ligament which is
nourished from the life-blood of both, and if you divide the ligament you kill the twins. Oh, yes, without the influences of
party you might, indeed, have able and efficient men in your
bureaux—England will never want such men under any system!—
but you will have exchanged the nerve and muscle of popular
government for the clockwork machinery which belongs to
despotism! But, Sir, to judge by the language out of doors, it is
not meant to clear away the obstacles that beset the career of a
clerk in a public office—no, it is meant to make the Queen's
Government, make the Ministers of the nation, independent of
the influences of party,—in other words, of the opinions of
Parliament. That is the only way in which I can interpret the
language we hear out of doors—that there must be an entirely
new administration of the country perfectly free from the influences of party—why, Sir, if it is meant that the Crown is to
appoint to the higher offices of State, free from the influences of
party and from the opinions of Parliament, the Crown would
become as absolute as it was in the time of the Tudors; and if
these agitators against Parliament say, "Oh, no, we do not
mean that; we mean that the people are to dictate to the Crown,
according to their ideas of merit, who are to be the Ministers
of State, through other channels than Parliamentary parties,
through patriotic associations and audiences accustomed *plausu
gaudere theatri.*" I tell them that they would root out the durable institutions of liberty to make room for the deadly ephe-
merals of Jacobin clubs. But if they say, "Oh, no—we mean
neither one nor the other," what do they mean—they who are
attacking Parliament—except to bring Parliament into contempt,
and to trust the chance of a substitute to the lottery of revolutions? But let the House inquire if the Government is not in
some degree responsible for the loud cry which has been raised
against family patronage and party influence? Can you deny
that it has ever been the peculiar characteristic of the Whigs

when in office to concentrate power as much as possible within
their own narrow and exclusive coteries, and to make a marked
distinction between the great body of their supporters and the
highbred materials from which they construct their Cabinets ?
So far as that goes, I think the hon. Member for Aylesbury has
proved his case. Your Cabinets have been one colossal instance
of family patronage. You trace your map of office as the
Chinese trace the map of the world. The Chinese draw a
square ; in that square they describe a circle, which fills up all
the space except the four little corners. The circle is the Celestial Empire of China, and the four little corners are assigned
to the miserable remnants of mankind. So when you come into
power you describe round Downing Street your circle ; in that
circle you place the sacred family of Whigs—that is the Celestial
Empire ; and to the four little corners you banish the herd of
your supporters. Now it is because ever since the Whigs came
into office, more than twenty years ago, the public have seen
this exclusive principle, this preference of family connections,
applied to the more conspicuous departments of the State, that
therefore now, when national disasters tend to magnify every
abuse, and some abstract cause is to be found for every grievance, there has risen up this cry against the governing classes,
and a persuasion, which I do you the justice to say is much
exaggerated, that you apply the same system of favouritism to
all the ramifications of official power and distinction. The
belief is exaggerated—the exaggeration is dangerous ; it tends
to shake the basis of our social system ; but for that exaggeration
and for that danger you are responsible, because in the composition of your Cabinets you have, one after another, installed
a combination of families and privileged houses like a sacred
caste, and have contrived to sour, to chill, and to alienate the
energy, the intellect, the enthusiasm, of that class of your supporters in whom the people can recognise their own hardy
children ; while you mortify the pride of a numerous gentry
with birth as ancient as your own, but who happen not to be
allied to your houses, nor partially naturalised to your coterie
by having been disciplined in its drawing-rooms. Sir, I will

grant most readily that the noble Viscount, in seeking to form
the materials of his Government, was much less to blame for
family exclusiveness than Whig Ministers have been before
him. I believe that he did honestly desire to extend the range
of selection. In the selection, for instance, of a right hon.
Gentleman opposite (Mr Horsman) to the important post of
Chief Secretary for Ireland—a post which requires the union of
courtesy and firmness, of ready powers in debate, with comprehensive knowledge of mankind—the noble Viscount has, to my
mind, been most fortunate and judicious. But parties, like
kings, are punished for the faults of their predecessors ; and
what the people resent is this, that the very nature of the party,
or rather the coterie, which the noble Lord represents, has compelled him still, notwithstanding a few exceptions, to retain in
the map of his Cabinet that general preponderance of the old
Celestial Empire which is out of all reasonable proportion to the
rest of the world. At the bottom of all this agitation that which
I see most clearly is this—that the public are tired of Governments purely Whig, and that, sooner or later, the doom of that
oligarchy will be sealed. Long ago Mr Burke said, " The Whigs
had never a majority in the country, but they obtained their
ascendancy by dexterous management." We know in our time
what that management has been ; it consists in saying to the
Radicals, " Support us, or you will let in those horrible Tories;"
and in whispering to us Conservatives, " Bear with us, or those
horrible Radicals will upset the country." I think that device
is now pretty well worn out. Well, then, I distinguish between
the dangerous elements which have been added to the question
of administrative reform and the reform itself. For the dangerous elements I arraign the Government—for the reform I am a
cordial advocate. You must, as soon as possible, take this
question out of the hands of agitators, and turn it to safe directions in the hands of statesmen. Exactly a parallel case arose
towards the end of the American war, when the cry throughout
the country was for economical reform, coupled with an attack
on the power of the Crown ; now the cry is for administrative
reform, coupled with an attack upon the predominance of the

aristocracy. In both instances the country felt that its resources had been wasted, and feared its character was tarnished:
it sought to trace the causes to a tangible origin, and in both
instances believed it found that origin in the abuse of patronage.
By a timely—and, because timely, a moderate — reform the
Rockingham Administration contented the people and averted
all danger from the Crown. By the same means—though I hope
the reform will be more extensive—you may again content the
people and relieve the aristocracy from unmerited censure.

Sir, it is not my intention at present to touch at all upon the
vast but intricate question of military reform. I am convinced
that you will do much better to keep that question apart from
the administrative reform connected with the civil service, and
entertain it in a different debate; and it is to the civil service
that I shall confine myself. Sir, the elaborate and able speech
of the hon. Member for Aylesbury has saved me from inflicting
on you quotations from the Reports of our various offices, which
Reports I have studied with great care. Those Reports allow
us to take it for granted that administrative reform is imperatively necessary, since there is not one of those offices in which
that reform is not urgently enforced by those who are the best
judges of it; and I shall content myself with this short extract
from the Report on our general civil service :—" All who have
had occasion to examine its constitution with care, have felt
that its organisation is far from perfect, and that its amendment
is deserving the most careful attention. It would be natural to
expect that so important a profession would attract into its
ranks the ablest and most ambitious of the youth of the country;
that the keenest emulation would prevail among those who had
entered it; and that such as were endowed with superior quali-
fications would rapidly rise to distinction and public eminence.
Such, however, is by no means the case. Admission into the
civil service is indeed eagerly sought after; but it is for the
unambitious, and the indolent or incapable, that it is chiefly
desired. Those whose abilities do not warrant an expectation
that they will succeed in the open professions, where they must
encounter the competition of their contemporaries, and those

whom indolence of temperament or physical infirmities unfit for
active exertions, are placed in the civil service, where they may
obtain an honourable livelihood with little labour, and with no
risk; where their success depends upon their simply avoiding
any flagrant misconduct, and attending with moderate regularity
to routine duties; and in which they are secured against the
ordinary consequences of old age, or failing health, by an arrangement which provides them with the means of supporting
themselves after they have become incapacitated."

I have made a short summary of the principal reforms suggested for the existing imperfections. They are, the establishment of a primary, and of, perhaps, periodical examinations,
and those for the highest situations should be on a level with
the highest description of education; a more judicious regulation
of the principle applied to salaries; the adoption of honorary
rewards and distinctions; the bestowal of all the places and
prizes in the service on those who belong to it; accountability
by records of individual and reports of departmental service;
and, in short, the general regulation, not only that merit
should be the rule for promotion, but that there should be
legitimate occasions to test that merit, and increased facilities
for its rise. In looking over all the evidence on the subject,
and weighing all the objections made to these recommendations,
I have convinced myself that the reforms proposed by the various Commissions are sound and judicious, but that they require
a vigour the Government have not yet shown in arranging the
details into a systematic whole, and an honest determination,
not yet evinced, to encourage the workings of such reforms, and
a generous vigilance of ministers in the discernment of merit in
their own departments. We shall be told that the Government
have done much, and are doing still more, in the way of amendment and reform. I will tell the Government why I am not
satisfied to rest simply on that declaration. In the first place,
I cannot compliment the right hon. Member for the University
of Oxford on his share in the Order in Council. I think your
mode of examination under that Order a complete evasion of all
the real questions at issue. The objects sought by the Com-

mittee on the Reorganisation of the Civil Service, and by all
genuine reformers of that service, are to obtain the largest available amount of energy and intelligence ; first, by fair competition, and next, by all professional inducements. Now, I say
that your Order in Council frustrates these objects. By that
Order in Council you did not widen the range of candidates.
You may have improved the examinations to a certain extent,
but you still retain that which reformers specially desire to
correct throughout the whole civil service—the character of a
close borough ; and you do not increase the inducements to
candidates of talent to enter the service, by assuring them of
professional rewards ; for the Order in Council enables the
chiefs of departments to nominate persons to office who have
not been in the civil service, and who have been distinguished
only in other pursuits, without undergoing any examination
whatever. On the one hand you invite men to submit themselves to a severe examination ; and, on the other hand, you
prepare them to have men who have never been in the public
service set over their heads. Thus, I say, that by this Order in
Council you sanction the two worst abuses of which all your
official reports complain. When I look at the minutes of answers
made by the heads of departments to the reports on their own
offices, I see in them nothing more than a servile acquiescence
in detached suggestions, without the slightest indication that
those great officers of State have mastered the subject for themselves, without one original conception or proof of constructive
faculty ; while they all exhibit the same indolent and desultory
spirit, and affect to deliberate when in reality they only dawdle.
Now, this is precisely what I object to. I would rather you
left things alone. You cast a slur on what exists without being
prepared to replace it. You strip off the roof and let in the
rain, not only before a new covering is ready, but while you are
still undecided whether you will use slates or tiles. This is one
of the cases in which reform ought not to be slothful and vacillating, but prompt and decisive, because as long as you leave the
public servants of any department uncertain what is to become
of them, you deprive them of all energy and good-heart. I

believe that one reason of the Duke of Newcastle's failure was, that you placed him at the head of establishments which lay effete and paralysed under sentence of death. Hesitating reforms unsettle; decided reforms reconstruct. And I am convinced, also, that any general rules you may adopt to excite emulation and encourage merit should be applied simultaneously to all establishments, and that the reform in one should not be contrasted by the abuse in others. For instance, what could be so unwise, at a time when the eyes of the public are fixed on you with so keen a scrutiny, as to announce a very proper but a very rigid examination for the vacancies in the senior practical class at Woolwich Academy, and proclaim in the newspapers of the very same day that three of the best places in the public service, that of Director-General of Stores, Director-General of Contracts, Assistant-General of the Army Clothing Department, were bestowed upon gentlemen who, whatever their merit, are less connected with those departments than they are with yourselves, and therefore appear to the uninstructed public audacious specimens of that very favouritism which your reforms affect to abolish? Let me again impress upon you that it is not enough to subject young candidates to a rigorous examination, to decoy into the public service the rising energy and talent of the country, unless you set before them all the lawful prizes of the profession, and convince them that not one such prize shall be abstracted from their ambition, and bestowed upon gentlemen who, however able, are not connected with the service. If the public service is to be really a profession, it ought to be as monstrous to give one of the great prizes in that service to a man who has not been actively distinguished in it, as it would be to give a clever lawyer the colonelcy of a regiment, or a gallant officer the Mastership of the Rolls. I am more alarmed than I can well express at the state of things out of doors, and I am most desirous, for the sake of satisfying the country, and allaying all disaffection, that the Ministry should frame a scheme which they can openly bring before this House, and so inform the country exactly what they are doing, and intend to do.

Sir, I cannot vote for the motion of the hon. Gentleman the

Member for Aylesbury—not, he may be sure, from disrespect to himself, but because, looking at his motion in connection with its supporters out of doors, I cannot sanction an influence quite apart from the question of Administrative Reform, which I conscientiously believe to be unsound in principle and perilous in the consequences to which they would lead. But I am desirous, not only for my own sake, but that of many gentlemen on both sides of the House, to have an occasion of recording our votes in favour of the simple question of Administrative Reform. For this reason I have not framed the Amendment I propose in a party spirit ; my remarks may have been under that influence : my Amendment shall be free from it. My hon. friend * has referred to a lovely passage in Tasso, and says that I would smear the bowl with sweets that the child may swallow the medicine. No ; I present the medicine as it is. He adulterates the medicine with the bitterness of unnecessary gall. Not the least dangerous part of the agitation out of doors, which it was scarcely worthy of a distinguished Member of Parliament and a distinguished scholar to countenance, is the attempt of certain persons to disparage the character of this House. Acting as I do with a minority, it might be more consistent with the passions of party to connive at that depreciation, and insinuate that it is the fault of the tribunal when we cannot carry our cause. But I say, from the bottom of my heart, that the longer I have lived, and the more familiar I have become with books or with mankind, the more deeply the patriotic spirit and the intellectual eminence of this House of Commons are impressed on my convictions. And during my experience of more than twenty years in the records of your proceedings, I can recall no time in which this House was ever more worthy of the confidence and respect of the country, whether for the ability which by all sections of opinion has been displayed, or, as I solemnly believe, for the personal incorruptibility of its Members as a body, or for that zeal for the welfare of the country which, whether you have assailed or supported Ministers, posterity will acknowledge to have been your prevailing motive. It is not at

* Mr Layard.

such a time that a mere form of words, which some of us cannot accept, should alienate the affections of the people from this palladium of their liberties; and in order that every Member, no matter what his politics or party, who cannot accept the motion now before us, may have the opportunity of recording a vote which he can vindicate to his constituents and justify to his conscience, I submit to you this proposition, which you will pardon for its temperance if it obtains the object of conciliating your approval.

XXI.

A SPEECH

DELIVERED IN

THE HOUSE OF COMMONS

ON THE 16TH OF JULY 1855.

ON Monday, the 16th of July 1855, the Member for Herts, Sir Edward Bulwer Lytton, moved in the House of Commons :

" That the conduct of our Minister in the recent negotiations at Vienna has, in the opinion of this House, shaken the confidence of the country in those to whom its affairs are intrusted."

The Minister therein referred to, anticipating the submission of this Resolution to the House, suddenly announced to the Commons, in the course of an explanatory harangue, that he had resigned. The original motion was eventually withdrawn in consequence of this resignation, but not until after it had given rise to a lengthened and animated discussion. It was immediately after the Minister's startling announcement of his resignation that the following speech was delivered.

SIR,—If I understand correctly the allusions of the noble Lord * towards the end of his speech, it is not before the phalanx of a hostile party that he retires from office. That is true. It is before the sense of the country, evinced in the desertion of his own followers. But do those followers deserve the lofty taunt of the noble Lord ? No, Sir; it is not, as he implies, that they forsook him because his fortunes waned or wavered, but because

* Lord John Russell.

he deviated into a path which seemed to leave behind it the honour of his country. The noble Lord has a second time in one campaign left the field upon the eve of contest, and in doing so he has entered at such length into a vindication of his previous conduct, that I trust the House will not consider it ungenerous or vindictive in me, if I also vindicate some of those reasons which have induced me, and those who support me in this motion, to think that the conduct of the noble Lord was such as to shake the confidence of the country in those who administer its affairs. Under the altered circumstances of the case, however, I shall make my statement as temperately as may be consistent with the requisite proof that it was not upon light grounds that we brought forward a charge against a man so eminent, and against a Government so justly entitled to the indulgence of compassion. What, Sir, on Thursday last, was the position of the noble Lord and of the Government who then so boldly accepted our challenge, and who have since selected as a victim for sacrifice the very champion whom they then armed at all points for encounter? The position of the noble Lord on Thursday last was this, and he must pardon me if I state it frankly, because in the whole course of his speech, he does not seem to have understood how that position is viewed by his countrymen. Here was a great and distinguished statesman, who had held the office of Chief Minister of the Crown, who was sent to Vienna to negotiate terms of peace, or to report to us honestly the necessity for continued war. Under what circumstances was he selected? He had just before broken up a Government by his own solitary desertion—a desertion so sudden, and accompanied by a denunciation of two of his colleagues so startling, that it was without parallel in the records of this House. But it was not without an excuse. What was the excuse? Why, that upon a question involving the fate of armies he could not, as an honest man, conceal his sentiments, and rather than do so he left his associates whom he could not defend. Well, that is a very noble excuse; and in saying so, I do not desire to imply a sarcasm.

Lord JOHN RUSSELL : I beg the hon. Baronet's pardon. What

I said was, that I could not oppose the motion for inquiry, not that I could not defend their conduct. There was no question about defence.

Sir BULWER LYTTON: I have not the least objection to the change of terms; and as I now understand the noble Lord he left his former office, in the Earl of Aberdeen's Administration, because he could not oppose the motion for the appointment of the Sebastopol Committee; but does he forget all the observations which he made in explanation of the course he then took? Does he forget the charges, or at least the strong insinuations, which he made against the Duke of Newcastle and the Earl of Aberdeen? Surely, if the noble Lord's explanation at that period was rightly conceived, it informed us that he was com-pelled to retire, and to break up the Government of which he was so eminent a member, because of his distrust of the warlike capacities of his colleagues. He says he could not resist inquiry. Inquiry into what? National disasters; ascribed to what? To the want of competent vigour either in the chief Minister or the Minister of War. This was his excuse for not suppressing his sentiments. I say again, a noble excuse, but an excuse that required the uniformity of an inflexible political creed. Well, then, this statesman is sent to Vienna; he apparently fails in his object; he returns; a suspicion gets abroad that the noble Lord is inclined to favour the proposals of the Austrian Government. That suspicion is mentioned in this House on the 24th of May, and the noble Lord rises to make a speech to dispel that suspicion, to vindicate the breaking-off of negotiations, and the continuance of the war; and although the noble Lord does not refer to the Austrian proposals at all, he does in that speech, which I do not think he has successfully defended to-night, speak with marked disdain of the propositions which embodied that main principle of naval counterpoise which, we have since learned, the Austrian propositions contained. He says, "After I had left Vienna another proposal was made, which my right hon. Friend the Member for the University of Oxford* seems to think offered a security—namely, to leave the treaty of 1841 as

* Mr Gladstone.

it now is; but when Turkey is menaced, to enable her to call the fleets of her allies to her assistance." "I own," said the noble Lord, "I can see very little security in that proposal." The noble Lord then proceeded triumphantly to argue in favour of the absolute necessity of limiting the power of Russia in the Black Sea. He denounced the idea of guarding against that force by any counterpoise in the ships which the Western Powers might station in those waters; he pointed out the costly and preposterous folly of our being there, to use his own words, "perpetually defending Turkey" (all arguments that apply equally against the Austrian proposals then locked within his breast); and, finally, he wound up with a spirited imitation of that famous philippic in which Demosthenes inflamed his country against Macedon, by dilating on the corruption which penetrated every council hall and the ambition which threatened every civilised State. The general impression then was, that that speech of the noble Lord was somewhat extravagant in its zeal. But we, who advocated the vigorous prosecution of the war, pardoned that extravagance for the sake of its high spirit; we said, "Here, at all events, is one man who is thoroughly in earnest for the prosecution of the war." Suddenly there appeared in the public prints the circular of the Austrian minister, in which Count Buol states that this very statesman had not only inclined to a peace upon the terms proposed, and which he had appeared to us indignantly to scout, but that he had actually promised to lay before his Government definite proposals for peace so framed, and to back those terms in the Cabinet with all his power. The thing seemed incredible; but the question on Friday week was put to the noble Lord, and he then rises, confirms the statement, and informs the House that he had brought back propositions of peace which he did conscientiously recommend as likely to end the war "with honour to the allied Powers, and on terms calculated to afford security for the future," and that, thus thinking peace both possible and honourable, he did, nevertheless, when the question was formally brought before this House, while the peace in question was being actually discussed by the Cabinet, abuse the station he took from the favour

of his Sovereign, and the confidence the people placed in his
honesty and truth, and join with his colleagues to urge us to
sacrifice the best blood of England in a war that he deemed no
longer necessary, and to disdain the peace that he himself recommended. Now, Sir, what made the political conduct of the
noble lord still more disingenuous—I request his pardon for the
word—is, that subsequently to the 24th of May, namely, on the
6th of June, when the expediency of peace through the inter-
vention of Austria was again discussed, the right hon. Baronet
the Member for Carlisle * alluded plainly to the report that the
terms of peace suggested by Austria had been favoured by the
French envoy, that the Emperor of the French actually proposed
them to the English Government, and that it was the English
Government that prevented the acceptance of those terms.

The noble Lord replied to that speech, and evading all distinct
reference to the Austrian proposal, he left the House, the country,
and the great Powers of Europe, under the impression that our
illustrious ally would have sanctioned terms of peace which
were utterly disdained by the lofty spirit of the noble Viscount
and the united chivalry of his Cabinet. Now, let the House
mark the inconsistency and want of faith in the noble Lord.
On Friday week what was the noble Lord's excuse for his preference of peace? Why, that Russia was so powerful! And
what was the excuse of the noble Lord on the 24th of May for
his preference of war? Why, that Russia was so powerful! So
that the excuse of the noble Lord for peace and his excuse for
war was literally the same. And what was the apology of the
noble Lord on Friday week for having suppressed his real sentiments, and stilled his conscientious convictions? Why, forsooth,
if he told the truth he might have damaged the Government.
But what was the noble Lord's apology for destroying the Government some months ago? Why, that as an honest man he
could not suppress his sentiments or still his conscience. Does
he think that this mockery of our common-sense can be endured
—does he think that this English Parliament would accept, and
that this Christian people would endorse, a bill drawn upon

* Sir James Graham.

human life under fraudulent pretences? It is only those who hold that the war is necessary, and that no honourable peace could be obtained upon the basis proposed, who have a right to call upon the country to make every sacrifice of its blood and treasure. But can any excuse of Cabinet compromises justify .the statesman who was sent forth to negotiate a peace, and who feeds the flames of war with the very olive branch which he brought back from his mission? Oh, is it you—I declare that I speak more in sorrow than in anger—is it you, whose brief and touching allusion to your past services deserved louder cheers than it received—is it you, whose labours and whose genius have so honoured your name that we feel every stain upon it as a national calamity—is it you who have taken from the people of England power and dignity for twenty years—is it you who could call upon your countrymen to send their children to a slaughter which you deemed unnecessary, and advise your Sovereign to jeopardise her sceptre rather than endanger that feeble and rickety thing you call a Government, and of which you told us last Friday week we ought to be the more tender because it had lost the favour of the people? Sir, the noble Lord said that the Executive was weakened by popular distrust; and I tell the Government that the weakness and the distrust both arise from that belief in your insincerity and vacillating purpose, of which on Thursday last the most signal proof was the appearance of the noble Lord upon that bench (the Ministerial). The noble Lord complained that our counsels were unstable. How could they be other than unstable when the noble Lord represented in the Cabinet the very element of instability? The noble Lord rebuked the people for their distrust of public men, while, in the same breath, he told them on Friday week that insincerity on a question affecting life and death was a duty he owed to the public service. The noble Lord then said, "See the circumstances of the time." The circumstances of the time require either peace in earnest or war in earnest. And I say you cannot have peace in earnest if your negotiator accepts terms upon one day which he shrinks from the responsibility of adhering to on the next. With what face could the Govern-

ment have appealed to the ardour of the people so long as the
noble Lord remained in office to paralyse, by his acknowledged
sentiments, the war which he sanctioned by his official vote?
But the noble Lord said, "I am misrepresented; it is not because
I thought this peace safe, honourable, or expedient on the 1st of
May, when I brought those proposals back from Vienna—it is
not because I still think that at that time peace might be safe,
honourable, or expedient, that I am bound to think so now."
That is the argument of the noble Lord; "and then," said the
noble Lord, on Friday week, in a tone so languid that it might
have disheartened Achilles, that "the only chance of peace now
is in a vigorous prosecution of the war." But does not the noble
Lord see that though that last revised and corrected edition of
his opinions disqualifies him from becoming a member of a Peace
Administration, yet that it does not in the slightest degree
amend his position as a Minister of the Government pledged to
the carrying on of the war? For, if the noble Lord tells us that
the object of the war could have been attained in May, it is in
vain that he appeals to the military ardour of the people in July.
What progress would a recruiting sergeant have made through
the country with the cheering cry, "Fight, my boys, for your
Queen and country. Think of Alma and Balaklava. Never
mind a cannon-ball nor a wooden leg if you obtain this glorious
result—that if Russia shall hereafter be at liberty to send eight
ships of war to the Black Sea, Old England shall have the privilege of sending four." Now, I say, that when a Minister so
recently as May had approved of the principle of the Austrian
peace propositions, he is not a fit Minister to carry on the war
in July. What are the reasons which, in the noble Lord's mind
rendered a certain proposition for peace honourable and expedient in May, which are not equally good in favour of such a peace
in July? "We have gained some victories," he says; "our army
is in a better state." Good arguments these if we were at war
for dominion, none if we are at war for definite objects of justice.
I deprecate this sliding-scale of homicide, which is to go up and
down with every fluctuation in the market of blood. But, as I
understood the noble Lord, he said that in the position in which

England and France was, he did not think he would be acting prudently in resigning. With an eye solely to that position, I think the reverse. For, as to France, did he not place our counsels at variance with the French? He brings back a peace from Austria, proposes it and retains office; the French negotiator brings back the same peace, proposes it and is dismissed. This is not all—the French Emperor has declared Austria imperatively bound by her engagement to share in our hostilities; but the noble Lord some days ago, in the very teeth of Lord Clarendon, said he considered that Austria might be excused from her fulfilment of that engagement. So that, as long as the noble Lord remained in the Cabinet, you possessed a Minister in whom Russia could find her excuse, Austria her justification, France a dissentient from her policy, and England the condemnation of her war.

I understood the noble Viscount on Thursday last to say, that the Government were prepared to stand or fall together. And, indeed, the old Parliamentary principle that one Minister of the Cabinet does not stand alone—that all are equally worthy of praise or censure—applies with peculiar force to the present case. For the House will remember that, when we were discussing the conduct of the noble Lord in these negotiations, and while we were yet in the dark as to the Austrian proposals, the noble Viscount, as chief Minister, emphatically declared his cordial approval and admiration of his envoy and colleague. And yet the sole practical result of that mission was the sketch or idea of peace which the Cabinet was at that moment debating. While, if any blame was subsequently to be attached to the noble Lord, including his speech on Friday week, the chief Minister of the Crown shared the responsibility, since he saw in that speech no cause to invite the resignation of his colleague. Nay, on Friday week the noble Viscount defended what some other Member has harshly called the duplicity displayed in that speech by confounding it with the ordinary concessions upon ordinary questions which one Minister makes to his colleagues, and treated a vital difference of opinion upon peace and war with as much levity as if it were a disagreement in the details of a

Beer Bill. Now, Sir, I will take the liberty of telling the noble
Viscount, that there are two parties in this House who have
some reason to suspect, that among the many accomplishments
and rare talents of the noble Viscount, the rude frankness of
sincerity does not bear a prominent place as respects the part he
has taken in these transactions. I mean, first, the party that
advocates the Austrian peace ; and, secondly, the party that advocates the vigorous prosecution of the war. The House will
remember that immediately upon the formation of this Cabinet
the noble Viscount gave a pledge, in answer to a question from
the right hon. Baronet the Member for Carlisle, that he would
adhere to the foreign policy of Lord Aberdeen with regard to the
war. Well, Sir, those who consider that that policy wanted the
requisite vigour have a right to complain that he had given a
pledge so opposed to the expectations of those who assisted in
raising him to his present position. On the other hand, those
distinguished adherents of Lord Aberdeen's Government—who
best know what Lord Aberdeen's policy was—have some right
to complain that the noble Viscount had given that pledge rather
too lightly, when they see him reject terms which his own envoy, who left the Aberdeen Government from the want of vigour
in the administration of the War Department, had not only
assented to, but promised to support in the Cabinet with all his
power. Now, Sir, I have looked carefully through this correspondence before us, and I confess my astonishment is increased
that the noble Lord the Member for London did not resign his
office as Minister of the Crown, within a week after he returned
with his propositions from Vienna. This correspondence also
justifies my continued distrust in the Government in consenting
to act with the noble Lord in the counsels of the Crown. For
these papers show that during the latter period of the negotiations at Vienna, the noble Lord was at direct variance with the
noble Earl our Minister for Foreign Affairs ; and that the noble
Lord had agreed to a peace founded upon a basis which the
noble Earl the Minister for Foreign Affairs had already declared
to be inadmissible, impracticable, and dishonourable. To the
very first suggestion of the noble Lord—which was called an

Austrian proposal, but which, in fact, emanated from our English envoy—Lord Clarendon writes word, on the 18th April, what appears in that suspicious form called an extract:— "We think that the limitation of the Russian fleet should be absolute, and that it would be made too conditional by the plan which you propose. We must avoid, as much as possible, the system of counterpoise, the objections to which you have explained fully to the Austrian Government." Well, then, what does the noble Lord do? Why, the noble Lord matures that plan that was considered so objectionable, and bases it upon the principle of a counterpoise. He does not return from Vienna until he has promised the Austrian Minister to introduce this proposal to the Cabinet when he arrives in London. The noble Viscount who succeeded Lord Aberdeen in the Government, on the express ground that all dissension upon the question of peace or war should cease, deems that dissension in the Cabinet of no consequence, so long as it is concealed; and when it is found out, he declares that the concealment of the opinion of the noble Lord, to use his own words, "is highly becoming the elevated position of his noble friend."

I am quite willing to accord to the Government all the praise which they are entitled to claim. I am willing to say, so far as Lord Clarendon is concerned, that there is a frank, hearty, and English tone in all his despatches. And I would willingly extend to the noble Viscount the praise I so cordially bestow on Lord Clarendon? But then, though Lord Clarendon in these despatches represents himself—and of course the majority of the Cabinet—the noble Viscount does more than represent a majority. He is First Minister of the Crown, and he alone is responsible for the unanimity of his Cabinet. He alone is responsible if there be a minority at variance with the majority. And therefore, if the noble Lord does cordially approve the sentiments of Lord Clarendon, how could he have expressed an approbation, equally cordial, of the negotiator and colleague whose opinions so flatly contradict those which Lord Clarendon expresses? One may suppose that the noble Viscount could not have been so indifferent to the success of the negotiations as never himself to

have written to the negotiator. Yet, not one letter from the
noble Viscount appears in this correspondence. (Ironical cheers
from Ministers.) Yes ; I understand that cheer. You say the
Secretary for Foreign Affairs was the right person to communicate officially. True ; but the noble Viscount, in fairness to the
country, and in justice to himself, might have extended this
publication beyond the formality of strict routine, and inserted
some of the admirable letters he no doubt addressed to the perplexed conscience of his noble friend. The noble Lord's earlier
speeches had not been so free from levity, from ambiguity, but
what some persons were ill-natured enough to doubt the consistent earnestness of his sincerity. (" No, no !") He might disdain justification for himself, but to justify himself would have
been to strengthen the Government and assure the unquiet mind
of the country. But do Gentlemen who cry " No, no," doubt if
there was any cause to suspect that the noble Viscount ever
hesitated as to the Austrian terms ? Very well, let us see.
Observe : the Earl of Westmoreland communicates to the English Government the last Austrian proposal, which was received
in London on the 19th of May. Now, Lord Clarendon almost
invariably answers communications on the following day they are
received by him. It, however, appears that the noble Earl does
not answer these communications until ten days afterwards—
namely, the 29th of May. Now, I should like to know what
occurred in the interval. Why, from the hesitating tone of the
English Government, and more especially of the noble Viscount,
my right hon. friend the Member for Buckinghamshire * was
induced to bring forward a Motion upon the ambiguity of their
language and the uncertainty of their conduct. During those
ten days Ministers were deliberating upon those proposals in
their Cabinet. We, too, were discussing the Resolutions of my
right hon. friend in Parliament. And Lord Clarendon was evidently instructed not to reply to Count Buol's propositions until
you [the Government] had ascertained the sense of the House of
Commons. The judgment of the House being taken, it left the
Government no option but to continue the war. With these

* Mr Disraeli.

facts before us, I think it is a fair inference that the noble Lord (Lord J. Russell) does not stand alone in his opinions in the Government, and that Lord Clarendon is not the spokesman for the entire Cabinet. It was not until the temper of the House of Commons compelled you to renounce the ambiguity of your language and uncertainty of your conduct that these Austrian proposals were rejected.

Sir, the noble Lord the Member for the City of London has misunderstood something I said upon a former occasion in regard to the Austrian alliance. On that occasion I made a distinction between the alliance of Austria and the friendship of Austria. I said that I was desirous of the friendship of Austria, but that I did not care for her alliance. At this moment I would really rather be without it. In the first instance, I believe that such an alliance would necessarily produce a schism between England and France. Even now, Austria, as a mediator, makes a proposal of peace, which France rejects and which induces you to hesitate—the mere entertaining of which almost broke up the Government. Now, suppose the same thing to occur again when Austria becomes our ally, with power to raise her voice in the general counsels of the united nations. Suppose, then, that France accepts this Austrian proposal. Suppose that the English people will not allow the British Government to accept it. You would, under such circumstances, fulfil the prediction of the hon. Member for the West Riding of Yorkshire (Mr Cobden). You would stand alone in the struggle, with exhausted finances, and the remnant of disheartened armies. Surely some gain would come of this war if we could convince the world that England and France united in arms are quite sufficient to check any aggression on the dominion of her neighbours on the part of Russia. But if you choose to lay down the doctrine that France and England are not sufficient without the aid of Austria;—if you must, as the noble Lord says, bring all the other European combinations to back the two Western Powers,—your successes, if you succeed to the utmost, will not diminish the moral power of Russia; her very concessions will become glorious to her, and she can say to Turkey, say to the East, say to the existing world and to future ages, "France and England united have shown themselves no match for me, and it required all the combined armaments of reluctant Europe to restrain my ambition within the boundaries of my lawful realm. Such a combination cannot readily occur again; the combination is momentary, my ambition is eternal." I would simply repeat what I said on a former occasion. I value the friendship of Austria. I would even be indulgent to her weakness. I would not entrap her into reluctant engagements. I would not take a single step to bring about an alliance with her, unless she felt that she could embark in it with a hearty sense of her own interests. If, however, you desire to have Austria neither your ally nor your friend, surely you could not take a better course to effect that object than to allow a Member of the Cabinet to promise her his support of her definite proposal for peace, and afterwards to join with his colleagues that the proposal should be rejected.

One thing, however, is clear; we cannot afford the ridicule of Europe consequent upon these constant Cabinet scandals—we cannot allow the great name of England to be thus frittered away. Let us have peace even upon Austrian terms, and let us hope that the energies of our commerce may atone for the failure of our arms; or let the Ministers and the people join with one heart and one soul to carry on this war to a speedy and triumphant end, by the earnestness of their purpose and the worthiness of their preparations. Are you so united? Is Lord Clarendon the spokesman of the entire Cabinet? I should like to hear the expression of opinion on the part of other Members of the Cabinet besides the noble Viscount. There are Gentlemen in the Government who have not as yet expressed their opinion upon the nature of the war or the propositions for peace. What are the opinions of the Chancellor of the Exchequer? What are the opinions of the First Lord of the Admiralty? Are all the Members of the Government united upon this subject? Again I ask, is Lord Clarendon the spokesman of a united Cabinet? ("Hear, hear!") I am glad if it be so; but you told us the same thing in the month of May last, when we now know that the noble Lord the Member for London was dividing your

counsels, and it is my impression, and that of the country, that
the noble Lord did not stand alone in those opinions. I am,
however, willing to give you all the benefit of the doubt. The
noble Lord's retirement from office has so far effected my object,
that if it has not cancelled what I presume to call his errors, it
has at least prevented for a time any injury which those errors
would inflict on the public service. There is something, however, which I think ought to be more lasting than any peace,
and more glorious than any war—I mean, that high standard of
public integrity, without which nations may rot, though they
have no enemies, and with which all enemies may be defied.
On Friday week that standard was debased to the ignoble reasons
by which expediency seeks to justify dissimulation. You, the
representatives of the people—I desire not to make it the triumph of a party—be it the triumph of the House of Commons
—you have once more raised that standard to its old English
level; and in now asking your leave to withdraw my Motion, I
congratulate you on having so successfully asserted that vital
element of all free Governments which is lost the moment you
divorce from the national counsels the recognition of that public
virtue which demands that our actions shall not, with a cynical
audacity, give the lie to our convictions. All the objects we
have had in view have been thus effected, except the mere party
object of replacing one Government by another. But what Englishman, at such a crisis, would suffer that object to be paramount in his thoughts ? I am willing that the Government
should not be removed, but I warn them that they will remain
under the vigilant surveillance of public opinion ; and it is yet
to be seen whether the sacrifice of a man who had been trusted
by his country and revered even by his opponents, until in an
evil hour, when on two previous occasions he might have retired
from office with honour, you induced him to consult your temporary interests rather than the dignity of his own imperishable
name—it remains to be seen whether that sacrifice has really
removed the only obstacle to the earnestness of your purposes
and the unity of your counsels.

XXII.

A SPEECH

DELIVERED IN

THE HOUSE OF COMMONS

ON THE 1ST OF MAY 1856.

ON Monday, the 28th of April 1856, the Member for Enniskillen, Mr James Whiteside, moved in the House of Commons a resolution to the effect—
"That, while this House feels it to be its duty to express its admiration of the gallantry of the Turkish soldiery and of the devotion of the British officers at the siege of Kars, it feels it to be equally a duty to express its conviction that the capitulation of that fortress and the surrender of the army which defended it, thereby endangering the safety of the Asiatic provinces of Turkey, were in a great measure owing to the want of foresight and energy on the part of Her Majesty's Administration."

A discussion thereupon arose which lasted three nights, the member for Dorsetshire, Mr Henry Ker Seymer, on the second evening, moving as an amendment—

"That it is not expedient to offer any judgment as to the causes and the consequences of the capitulation of the fortress until the House has an op-portunity of considering the terms of the treaty of peace and the Protocols of the Conferences recently held at Paris."

Upon a division, the amendment was rejected by 451 votes to 52, the original motion being lost afterwards by 303 votes to 176. The second adjournment of the debate having been moved by the member for Hert-fordshire, Sir Edward Bulwer Lytton, upon the opening of the third night's discussion, the following speech was delivered.

SIR,—After the discussion which has taken place on the Orders of the Day, I feel it becomes me to assure the House, and more especially those hon. Gentlemen to whom my motion for the adjournment of the debate from Tuesday last has occasioned inconvenience, how wholly unconscious I was at the time that the motion would have been opposed by the noble Viscount (Viscount Palmerston). I had no personal wish to gratify in moving the adjournment; it was not my intention then, nor is it now, to address the House at any great length; I was urged to make that motion by several hon. Gentlemen whose wish to prolong the discussion was entitled to respect. I looked to the opposite benches; I saw that many of the Members most accustomed to adorn our debates had not yet spoken, though they had been pointedly appealed to. I looked to the Treasury bench; only one Cabinet Minister, the Chancellor of the Exchequer, had addressed us, and that at an hour when the House was so empty that few indeed had been able to profit by his elaborate defence of the Government, or the interesting memoir of the Turkish loan by which that accomplished historical critic relieved the dreary chronicle of the decline and fall of Kars. At half-past twelve o'clock I had, therefore, considered that the adjournment had become a matter of course, and I never was more surprised and vexed than when I found that a second time in my life— and this time, at least, innocently—I had occasioned to the noble Viscount a degree of angry excitement, which, whether genuine or simulated, overcame for the moment his ordinary urbanity and polish.

Sir, the best amends I can make for my unintentional offences is to condense as much as possible what I have to say, and deal as little as I can with familiar extracts from this book. Indeed, I would chiefly confine myself to what I hope will be fair replies to the arguments of hon. Gentlemen opposite. Sir, the hon. Gentleman the Member for Aylesbury (Mr Layard), who commenced by saying that he could make a much better defence for the Government than they had made for themselves, appeared to rest much of that defence upon an exaggerated estimate of the charge which was brought against them. He said—"He thought they had committed serious mistakes, but that it was unfair to assert that the fall of Kars was solely attributable to the want of foresight and energy on the part of the

British Government alone. That proposition entirely passed over the French Government, which, after all, might have had some share of responsibility for that event." Sir, this Resolution does not exclusively ascribe the fall of Kars to the English Government. If it did, fair is fair; and the Resolution would not have my vote. But the question is, Whether, among other causes, the want of energy and foresight on their part did not, in great measure, contribute to that disaster? The hon. Gentleman speaks of France. I may touch upon that point later. But here, in the meanwhile, is a Correspondence between an English Government and an English Ambassador as to the due support to be given to an English Commissioner from the date of September 1854, to the date, we will say, of June 1855; and in all this France is not a consulting party. This Commissioner had been sent to Asia not only to report on the state of disorganisation in which our Government already knew that the Turkish army had long been, but to use all means at his disposal to ameliorate its condition; and this very book is published to show that the English Government and the English Ambassador between them failed to place at his disposal any adequate means whatsoever. That fact, whether or not the fault entirely rests with the Turkish Administration, the Government takes the greatest pains to establish from January 11, 1855, when Lord Clarendon writes to Lord Stratford, "that little has been sent to Kars, with the exception of some ball cartridges," to the date of the fall of Kars, November 21 (four days before the capitulation), when Lord Clarendon writes the letter which provokes so severe a comment from my hon. and learned friend the Member for Enniskillen (Mr Whiteside)—"That that neglected garrison will at least have the satisfaction of knowing that their sufferings troubled the sleep and repose of the Turkish Ministers, who, in default of all ordinary measures of relief, never ceased to pray for their safety and success." And now, Sir, the question is, Whether there were not other Ministers besides the Turkish whose repose that neglected garrison might have troubled, and whom the default of all ordinary measures of relief might have inspired, not only with the piety of prayer, but the humility of repentance? The hon. gentleman the Member for Aylesbury referred to the despatches of Lord Clarendon with great praise; and my hon. and learned friend the Attorney-General, as well as the hon. Member for Leominster (Mr J. G. Phillimore) seemed to think those despatches a sufficient proof of the energy and foresight of the Government. Nay, the Attorney-General said, what more could they do? Sir, in much of the praise bestowed on these despatches I heartily concur. I think many of them excellent. I will go further and say that if despatches alone could have saved Kars, Lord Clarendon would have saved it. But if one thing should be more clear than another to the excellent understanding of those hon. gentlemen, it is that despatches alone and letter-writing, of whatever kind, were wholly insufficient for the purpose, and that the inventive genius of the English Government should have devised some other mode for the relief of Kars and the security of Asia. It is perfectly true that Lord Clarendon faithfully reports to Lord Stratford, General Williams's complaints. He wants cavalry, he wants artillerymen, he wants reinforcements, ammunition, provisions—above all, he wants money; and Lord Stratford, with all his faults, very fully explains that for all these purposes the state of the Sultan's revenue is wholly inadequate; and very lucidly shows that corruption and peculation, having been the habit for generations of an Eastern Government, cannot be reformed in a day, no matter how sincerely the Porte may desire it—cannot be reformed in time for you to rely on that reformation for the safety and defence of Kars. Lay what blame you will on the inherent vices of the Turkish administration, still one fact comes clear from this correspondence, and that fact the Chancellor of the Exchequer has failed to grapple with. It is said, as to reinforcements in the spring, you could not withdraw men from the Crimea. Granted. But if men you had not, money you had; and a moderate sum of English money placed at General Williams's absolute disposal would, in spite of all the abuses of oriental lethargy and corruption, have thrown into Kars ammunition and provisions sufficient to defy and outlast the Russian blockade. For how did

Kars fall at last? Not for want of men; it had at the time of
the capitulation a much larger proportional force than the be-
sieging army. Every one knows that Kars was conquered by
famine. We are told that the Russian general would have
raised the siege when Omar Pasha entered Georgia, if he had
not learnt from an Armenian spy that there were not more than
a fortnight's provisions in the garrison. But while England was
cheerfully taxing herself to the utmost to save his dominions
to the Sultan, not a shilling of her money goes to the aid of the
English general who is holding the fortress on which those dominions and—not indeed in the opinion of the hon. and learned
Member for Kilkenny (Mr Serjeant Shee) but of Omar Pasha—
the safety of the Turkish capital itself may depend. For, says
Colonel Simmons in a despatch to General Simpson, July 12,
" The Government inform Omar Pasha if Kars should fall there
is no force to prevent the Russians marching directly upon
Constantinople," and Omar Pasha credits that information.
Surely the Chancellor of the Exchequer might have been a little
more in the confidence of the Secretary of State for War, and
he would then have told us with that unvarnished severity of
candour with which he does sometimes tell us very disagreeable
truths: "I am about to raise several millions for the vigorous
prosecution of the war; by-and-by there may be a Turkish loan
to consider, but I can tell you, for your comfort in the meanwhile, that not one sixpence of your money will go to General
Williams in defence of the great key of Asia Minor; which, indeed," says the Chancellor of the Exchequer, with an easy confidence I should not have expected from so grave an intellect,
"if lost, the easiest military operation would be all that was
needed to recapture." Permit me to ask the Chancellor of the
Exchequer, not as a military but as a financial authority, whether
it would not have been much cheaper to save Kars than to recapture it? But, if there be some valid reasons, which the
Chancellor of the Exchequer has wholly failed to show, why
you could not place English money directly at the disposal of
your English Commissioner and General, what is the strange
reason set up by the right hon. gentleman against application

to Parliament for a grant expressly for the relief of Kars? Why, that the amount would have been contemptible. Apply to Parliament for £100,000 or £200,000! A Chancellor of the Exchequer could not so degrade his financial dignity. There was something respectable in the lavish subsidies we granted to foreign nations in the French war, but to come to Parliament for £100,000 or £200,000 was below the dignity of a Chancellor of the Exchequer. Sir, the answer is obvious. It is not the sum given, it is the use to which it is to be applied, that it becomes a statesman to consider. And if Dr Sandwith is right in saying that, had General Williams had absolute control (or for "means of control" we must say plainly "funds") in the special question of the commissariat, Kars would have been saved—if that be true, the simple question for the House would have been, what sum would suffice for that purpose? "But," said the Chancellor of the Exchequer, "we must have had the same securities for that grant as for the larger loan, and been subject to the same delays." No; if you had been freed from the joint guarantee of France, and in earnest for the relief of Kars, the country would have forgiven you if you had made the grant as an advance in anticipation of any loan afterwards required, and all tedious securities for the moment might have been dispensed with or deferred. Where there's a will there's a way. But if you would neither give the money direct to General Williams nor apply for a special grant for the provisioning and relief of Kars, why, when you learnt, in 1854, that the Turkish revenues were so inadequate, could you not have come to the House with that or some similar proposition in the spring, and not deferred it to creep through the Legislature in August, when its application could be no longer of the slightest assistance to that garrison? Sir, the Attorney-General said, in his terse and argumentative speech, that a reproach on that score could not well come from those who had opposed the Turkish loan in July. That may be a good House of Commons argument, but it is not an argument to common-sense. Sir, I was not in the House at the time of that debate. I had paired off for the rest of the session. If I had been present I should

have voted for the loan; but on referring to the debate, I find
that the objections made were not against the principle here at
stake—the relief of Kars—but to the joint guarantee with
France; and I appeal at once to the candour of the noble Viscount (Viscount Palmerston), and I ask him whether, if, in the
spring, the Government had come to this House and said frankly,
upon the information they possessed, but of which this House
was wholly ignorant, that, without such pecuniary aid to Turkey,
Kars might be lost, and with that loss the honour of the British
name be tarnished and Constantinople left defenceless—I ask
him, I say, whether the conduct of gentlemen on this side the
House in the prosecution of the war—nay, even the conduct of
the warmest advocates for peace—has been such as to lead him
to suppose that any mere financial objections, though they
might have been temperately stated, would ever have been
urged by us to a hostile division? By one of these modes—
either by sending money directly to the Commission, or by a
grant made expressly for the relief of Kars, or even by a Turkish
loan, with the direct understanding that a portion of it should
go, under the direction of the British Government, to the relief
of Kars—by one or other of these means Kars might have been
easily supplied with arms and provisions. But on the 3d of
August, when Lord Panmure is urging the adoption of the
Turkish loan on the House of Lords, and Lord Ellenborough is
pointedly calling your attention to the distressed state of Kars
and the neglect of the war in Asia, well may my learned friend
the Member for Enniskillen (Mr Whiteside) remind you of Lord
Panmure's reply, "that Turkey in that quarter is well able to
maintain herself." And Lord Panmure says this in the teeth
of these despatches, published to show how utterly helpless in
that quarter Turkey alone then was—in the teeth of Lord
Clarendon's letter to Lord Cowley on the very same day, the 3d
of August, in which Lord Clarendon says, "It is clear, without
assistance the whole Turkish force in Asia must be destroyed or
captured,"—and when it was Lord Panmure, who, in the previous
month, the 16th of July, had rejected the proposals of Turkey to
defend herself, and without having preconcerted any means of

his own by which Asia might be saved. And the hon. gentleman the Member for Aylesbury, who rarely speaks without
some—doubtless just, but—complimentary allusion to his own
peculiar frankness and honesty,—which, indeed, I never before
questioned, which I will not question now,—eulogised that assertion because it is untrue, and thinks a British Minister justified
in deceiving Parliament and the country in order to impose
upon the Russian general a hollow brag, which, in the month of
August, when that general was blockading Kars, could not have
deceived him for a moment. Nay, the hon. gentleman thinks
that Lord Panmure did not go far enough. "If I," said he,
"had been in Lord Panmure's situation, and was asked in August
what was the state of the army in Asia, I should have certainly
said it was immensely strong, and supplied with provisions,
arms, everything, for ten months." Sir, the hon. gentleman
has compared himself, with Homeric simplicity, to a dog upon a
race-course, shouted at by both parties and sometimes whistled
to within the ropes. There is a familiar saying applicable to
those faithful animals, "Brag is a good dog, but Holdfast is a
better." On this side the course we would always whistle to
Holdfast; we must leave it to the other side of the course to
find more enticing allurements for Brag.

Well, Sir, let me now touch upon a point which, though it did
not affect the fall of Kars, still shows that spirit and predisposition on the part of Lord Panmure to which I think the fall of
Kars may be in a great measure ascribed. No sooner does our
Commissioner arrive in Anatolia, than he tells you that from
10,000 to 12,000 men had perished in the hospitals in the previous winter, and asks for a few English surgeons. The Duke
of Newcastle, on whose humanity, at least, there never rested a
stain, promptly replies to that appeal on the 6th of November,
and directs inquiry whether the Turkish Government will consent to place the hospitals at Kars and Erzeroum under the
superintendence of three or four English or French army
surgeons. But when, that complaint not being redressed, Lord
Clarendon, with humanity equal to the Duke of Newcastle's,
encloses, through Lord Wodehouse to Mr Peel, April 16, 1855,

a despatch from General Williams and a medical report from
Dr Sandwith to Lord Panmure, and begs to suggest to his lordship whether it would not be expedient to send out some
surgeons to the Turkish army; what is Lord Panmure's reply,
through Colonel Mundy, April 21—an ominous date, almost
simultaneous with Lord Panmure's frigid despatch of April 12,
in which he had met the request for reinforcements by a languid
recommendation to the Porte " to pay attention to these requirements whenever the more pressing need of the Ottoman troops
elsewhere shall have ceased"? That was was his reply about
troops. What his reply about surgeons? That, "in supplying
the army under Omar Pasha, and the Turkish Contingent, with
a medical staff, he does not see much prospect of being enabled
to send medical aid to the province of Anatolia." True, he
graciously adds, " that he will endeavour to do so to a limited
extent, as soon as he has provided for the other two services."
Yes, as soon as Russian generals save him the trouble, and
Russian surgeons are dressing the wounds of the men to whom
Russian magnanimity is kinder than English care! Talk of
foresight! When you sent General Williams to ameliorate the
condition of the Turkish army, the necessity of European medical
aid was the first requisite to foresee. Talk of energy! When
that medical aid was imperatively required, and again urgently
pressed, why, an advertisement in the 'Times,' offering good
remuneration to young surgeons, would have brought you applications by the hundred. At that very time, as a Member
of Parliament, I was beset with requests from young medical
students to obtain them employment in the Crimea. You say
that the Turkish Government is alone to blame for not attending
to the requests of your Commissioner ; and here, when your Commissioner sends a request direct to you, backed by the Foreign
Minister to the Secretary for War, for what is entirely under
his own control, the laziest Pasha in all Asia could not have
treated that request with more supreme indifference. And while
you are laying the whole blame on the Government of the Porte,
do not forget that that Turkish Administration, with all its
oriental languor and institutional defects, had achieved vast

things without the mighty aid you sent to its defence in Asia. When it stood alone, before you came to denounce its deficiencies without supplying them by adequate resources of your own— when no jealousies of the foreign Christian obstructed its action and divided its responsibilities—it coped gallantly with the might of Russia. What is your aid, and what its result ? " Oh," says the Attorney-General, " we took 20,000 Turkish soldiers into English pay." Yes, and when those soldiers are wanted for the defence of Kars they cannot budge a step. In the spring, general Williams writes that if he is to have no aid from the Allies he shall require in all 20,000 Turkish soldiers for reinforcement. You have taken these 20,000 Turkish soldiers to yourself—that is the reason why they cannot be sent to Kars. This is your aid, and this is its result. And now there is an assertion made by the Chancellor of the Exchequer which compels me to enforce on you the practical mischief that was effected by the doubtful position and equivocal authority assigned to General Williams — nominally a commissioner, in reality a general; nominally under the orders of the Turkish commander, but the Turkish commander instructed by your ambassador to defer to the advice of General Williams. Well may Omar Pasha place in that luminous memorandum, page 272, of this book, among the foremost causes of the misfortunes that had befallen the army in Asia, that its general was not invested with full powers. " But," says the Chancellor of the Exchequer—and the Attorney-General has said it before him—"the Government cannot be blamed because they did not furnish General Williams with an authority that could only emanate from the Porte." Certainly not; but you are to blame if you left his position doubtful in the eyes of English officials. I don't excuse Lord Stratford for neglect in correspondence ; I don't accept the defence set up for him ; but enough has been said on that score by others, and it is not the general practice of this House, nor the true principle of the constitution, to saddle all this blame on the absent diplomatist—not here to defend himself—when we have before us the Government who, constantly grumbling at his ill success, still maintain him in his post. Nor will I even

blame them for doing so. All I say is, that those who heap all
the blame on the agent do not understand the English constitution if they acquit the employer.

But I must again remind you, since it has not been answered,
that Lord Stratford, stung by the complaints of General
Williams, writes to you on February 19th, 1855: "It is desirable that I should be made acquainted with the extent of
General Williams's powers on the spot, with the degree to which
he is independent of the Commander-in-Chief, how far it is
thought expedient by her Majesty's Government that I shall
insist upon obedience to his demands without reference to any
doubts entertained of their expediency either by the Porte or
by me."

To these questions, which gave you so good an occasion to
strengthen General Williams by defining and enforcing the
authority of one who had proved so worthy of his charge, no
answer whatever appears in this book. The Attorney-General
says, that after your rebuke there was no lack of punctuality in
correspondence on the part of Lord Stratford; that is not the
case; so little is he affected by the rebuke that, so late as May
1st, 1855, General Williams writes to Lord Stratford: "Several
weeks ago I addressed your lordship on the necessity of my
having authority direct from Constantinople to take an active
part and have a decisive voice in the purchase of provisions for
this army; but although Lord Panmure has expressed his sentiments on this vital point, I have not received a line in allusion
to it from your Excellency."

These applications are on the subject of provisions;—they
receive no answer, and it is for want of provisions that Kars
falls in November. You may say that the energy of General
Williams surmounted the neglect of the ambassador, and that
by his individual exertions he gets provisions enough into Kars
to last for four months; but you are informed by his despatches
that unless relief be sent before then, the perspective of Kars
must end in the vanishing point of starvation. And this brings
us to the camp at the Crimea, and shows that it was your omis-
sion more stringently to enforce the authority of General

Williams, which appears to have been yet more injurious to his weight in the camp of the Crimea than in the Ottoman Porte— that it proved fatal to the rescue of Kars at the very moment when the fate of that garrison was the most imminent ; for when, on July 15, Omar Pasha addresses the allied generals and admirals for the adoption of his plan of relieving Kars by an army of diversion, his note is written in consequence of infor- mation contained in a despatch from General Williams to Lord Raglan, dated Kars, June 23 ; but the allied generals refuse to give any opinion, on the ground that they " have no information from their respective ambassadors at the Porte to lead them to suppose that the affairs of Asia are in the precarious state in which Omar Pasha, from the information he had received from his Government, believed them to be." Yet Omar Pasha founds his representations on the despatch of your own Commissioner to your own General-in-Chief; and so little weight have you given, in your headquarters in the Crimea, to the hero who is defending Asia, that even an opinion is delayed upon the alleged absence of that information which your ambassador had not given—which your Commissioner had given—and the only man who attended to it is the General of the Porte, which you accuse of indifference to the fate of Asia and disrespect to the representations of your Commissioner ! And it is you who sneer at the apathy and sloth of the Government of the Porte ! Why, when at last, in the month of June, it is clear that there must be some plan to succour and reinforce the garrison of Kars, does that plan first proceed from your energy and foresight ? Do you send to this lazy Divan from your European councils of war a profound premeditated scheme, with all its preparations complete ? No ; it is from the Porte and its generals that the first scheme emanates, and it finds you prepared with nothing but objections. Just as you let the war drift to the Crimea, so you had let it dribble into Armenia. Unwarned by the past calamities, exactly on the same principle which allowed you to land in the Crimea without tents, without knapsacks, without winter provisions, without an army of reserve, you throw Gene- ral Williams into Kars—you leave him to the mercy of the

corrupt system, the vices of which you know beforehand—you
provide no requisite by which the faults of that system are to
be counteracted; and when an army is proposed to be sent to
his aid, you are not even furnished with a strategy or the conception of one. For if you would refer to your first plan, by
Trebizond, which you hastily proposed, it is clear that that plan
was never premeditated, since you were not aware of any of the
objections which would be made against it. Why was General
Williams at Kars? To defend it from the Russians. Early in
the spring of 1855, preparations for a Russian army had commenced at Gumri. Did it ask the vision of a prophet to know
that that army would besiege Kars,—that, if besieged, an army
of relief or diversion would be required? Did you once think
beforehand what you would do in such a contingency? had
you one scheme for the raising, for the transport, for the movement of such an army? Or did you mean to leave it entirely
to the Porte to effect all these operations? If so, you had no
right to obstruct the operations which the Porte advised. There
seems to me no excuse for the want of some premeditated
scheme of your own. You had Omar Pasha in your own camp.
He was surely as sincere as you for the defence of Asia. You
might have communicated with him from the first in the spring
of 1855; discussed beforehand and settled all the objections
which paralysed you at the last; arranged some plan for a relieving army—whether under him, if he could be relieved from
Sebastopol, or some other general if he could not—some plan to
be adopted if Sebastopol was taken, another if it was not; and
when you allege as an excuse for procrastination in July and
August the necessity of consulting France and obtaining her
consent, that is no excuse if in the month of April or May you
could have consulted with France on some contingent scheme
for a relieving army, to be modified according to varying circumstances, but equally to be acted upon whenever the time arrived,
and so prevented all that scramble and bewilderment of cross
purposes which close this melancholy record with one medley of
hopeless confusion and inevitable disaster. But no; when the
Russians are before Kars you seem as much astounded as if

they had dropped from the moon. Reinforcements, relieving armies, are then really necessary; where are they to come from, where are they to go? Shall they proceed to Trebizond? shall they go by Redout-Kaleh? shall General Vivian take his contingent? how shall Omar Pasha make up the force drawn from the Crimea? I do not pretend to say what plan you ought to have adopted—that is not my province. I have my ideas, like others; but it is not for me, in an assembly which boasts of British officers so distinguished—of one so pre-eminent, whom I now see before me (General Sir De L. Evans)—to point out or criticise a strategy. All I say is, that some strategy or another should have been devised in time, and its necessity not burst upon you by surprise, first communicated to you by a perplexed ambassador, to whom you had never given a hint before as to what plan you would prefer, and finding you without an original conception of your own. A great military authority has said that "a good general may be beaten, but can never be surprised." Surely the same thing should be said of a Minister for War. He should have a choice of plans ready for any probable emergency, but the one or the other, adopted by previous concert with his generals and allies, for prompt action the moment prompt action is suddenly called for.

Then we come to the natural consequence of this preliminary, effete, and impotent correspondence—that indescribable mixture of hurry and torpor, of contradictory orders to and fro, which, in the month of July, prepares us for the catastrophe of November. Dr Sandwith tells us that the meaning of Bashi-Bazouks in English is "spoiled heads." In the month of July we had plenty of Bashi-Bazouks in our councils of war. And if ever that respectable force should want for their war department a spoiled head in perfection, I think we could furnish them with some very eligible candidates. But now, in that month of July, out of this cloud of despatches, emerges the awful form of our Minister for War. All is breathless with expectation. Can Kars be saved? It is the fifth act of the tragedy, and our *Deus ex machinâ* descends. Only there is this difference between him and the *Deus ex machinâ* of the ancient stage; when the god, there, descended from his cloud, it was to solve the difficulties and complete the action ; when our *Deus ex machinâ* descends, it is to increase the perplexities and obstruct the plot. The moment to stir has arrived—the only question is, how to stir, and whom to stir ?—and Lord Panmure takes that brilliant occasion to deliver his oracular essay upon the virtue of caution. " Do not risk," he exclaims, " the honour of the British name and your own reputation by undertaking military operations for which proper bases have not been laid, communications opened, transports provided, and supplies arranged." Why, good heavens, Sir, certainly not. But if all these things were wanting to save Kars, secure the frontier of Asia, and the road to the Turkish capital, in July 1855, after all the warnings these repeated despatches contained—why on earth have we had a Minister for War ? If you are so careful of the honour of the British name, why commit that name to the defence of Kars in September 1854, and in July 1855 not be prepared with any means to preserve it ? For, don't let the Chancellor of the Exchequer flatter himself that English honour was in no way concerned in the fall of Kars. The eyes' of England and of Europe had already turned to the grand image of that English soldier who was there, with his three or four dauntless countrymen, embodying and supporting the renown of his whole nation. General Williams and Kars could no longer be divided. That Englishman was Kars, and Kars was that Englishman—and both together, if saved by your energy and foresight, would have closed this war with a glory, not only to English valour, but your English councils, which would have covered all your blots at Sebastopol. " Organisation," says Lord Panmure, "is as necessary to any army as endurance and valour." Nothing was ever better said. General Williams had the endurance and the valour for the defence of Kars—what has Lord Panmure to say as to the organisation for its relief ? In Dr Sandwith's graphic account of the Russian army before Kars—the soldiers in warm huts with fireplaces, the officers with glazed windows, the admirable wellbeing of the enemy we have been taught to look down upon as comparative barbarians—who could help contrasting those sleek, carefully-provided-for, thriving soldiers, with the famished spectres whom our Government, with all the wealth of England at their disposal, and dropping so lavishly elsewhere from their spendthrift fingers, had left for fifteen months to struggle and to starve—to whose wounds our Secretary for War could give slight hope of medical aid—for whose succour he could devise no plan of relief, until he says, " It is too late even for regret "—until the Russian general (honour to his name!) is shedding tears of generous sympathy for his ill-used and deserted foe—until the population of Kars are crowding round to kiss the departing stirrup of the man who had implored you not to forget him and " the remnant of his army "—until General Williams says, " I am a prisoner," and ought to have added, " and Lord Panmure is the British Minister for War " ?

But it is said that the affair is over—the evil irremediable. The affair is not over. Discredit and its consequences remain. The Chancellor of the Exchequer says that the fate of Kars did not influence the articles of peace. Possibly. But will you deny that if ever again—which Heaven forbid!—we are at war with Russia for the defence of Turkey, that war will come from the Asiatic frontier, in which the fall of Kars has permitted Russia to retain the menace of her forts and garrisons? But are we to hold the doctrine that because the offence is past the offender is to go free ? That is not the line of argument our Government adopts towards the Porte. Their correspondence closes with vehement demands that the Porte should dismiss Selim Pasha from his office—and Selim Pasha is dismissed. Why? The Porte might say, " Kars has already fallen; the affair is over ; the evil irremediable! " What is the fault of Selim Pasha? Procrastination. But if procrastination is to be punished by loss of office, have we no Pashas of our own whose dismissal the Porte in turn might vehemently demand ? The Attorney-General asks, " Make your charges distinct," turns to the despatches, and says triumphantly, " What more could we do ? " One gentleman says all the fault lies with Turkey, another with our ambassador; a third hints at the generals and Government of France. Faults in all these quarters no doubt

there may be. But still, when General Williams applies to you
for what it is in your power to give, nothing is done. He asks,
or implies that he asks, three things : first, money ; second,
medical aid ; third, that you will enforce and extend his authority as much as you can. You don't send the money ; you
don't send the medical aid ; you decline to extend his authority
with your own ambassador when the ambassador invites you
to do it—and you so little enforce that authority in the Crimea,
that your generals refuse to receive his statements as accredited
authority. A fourth thing he asks is assistance from the Allies
in case Kars should be invested. Here, I grant, France may
have thrown some obstacle and delay in the way ; but you have
failed to show that you consulted France long beforehand—that
you asked simply, " Suppose a force, whether European or
Turkish, should be required for the relief of Kars, what shall we
do ? don't let us be left entirely to the chapter of accidents at
the close." Therefore, when it is asked what more could we
have done, I rather ask, what less could you do ? Don't turn to
the despatches for an answer. I grant that you could not write
better. I don't see how you could well act worse.

Just as I think this resolution is, there may be a majority
against it. But I think I read the English hearts of some of
those by whom the majority may be composed. Many,' no
doubt, will vote with you from the conviction that there is no
case against you ; but many will also vote with you from the
loyal affection of party ; many from the reasons so touchingly
urged by the Attorney-General, that, having closed the war with
a peace which has excited so popular an enthusiasm, you have
been enabled to invite both Houses of Parliament to a naval
exhibition, in which your administrative energy and foresight
have left so grateful a recollection on the minds of your applauding guests ; many from a personal admiration for the noble
Viscount—in which admiration I, too, humbly claim to have a
share ; many to keep in the Government, and keep out the
Opposition. But I do not think a majority will be tantamount
to a verdict of acquittal. Ask, in a whisper, any friend who
goes out with you into that lobby—" Don't you think, as a

Government, we showed great foresight, great energy, in the defence and relief of Kars?" I think the chances are, your friend may reply in the same cautious whisper, "If that be your energy and foresight, for Heaven's sake, try in future to imitate Lord Chatham's improvidence and sloth." I would fain separate individuals from the Government. I can do justice to the gallant nature of the noble Viscount. I can give credit to Lord Clarendon's evidently deep but helpless sympathy for his glorious correspondent. His approving letters must have been gleams of sunshine to that great soldier in his hour of trial and desolation. But, thanks to other agencies in the war councils of the Government, if those letters come to cheer and to encourage, they come also to sadden and to doom—they come to the defender of Kars as the false apparitions came to Macbeth— come to glad

> " his eyes and grieve his heart—
> Come like shadows, so depart ! "

Other causes conspired to the fall of Kars. Give to the Government the full credit for them. But tell me in turn, do you not honestly think among the main causes is the want of zeal and comprehension, of energy and foresight, on the part of your Minister for War? Sir, in all Cabinets there must be a division of labour; but since in none there can be a division of responsibility, whatever my respect for individuals, I think the charge against you as a Government has not been rebutted. In almost every letter from General Williams he warns you of evils and dangers; in almost every letter from Lord Stratford he proves to you that against these evils and dangers no reliance is to be placed upon the Ottoman resources alone. On those resources do you continue to rely. Not a step do you take, not a conception do you originate, not a strategy prepare, until you are overwhelmed by the logical consequences of your own improvidence and neglect ; and the stain of the fall of Kars will cling to your memory as a Government as long as history can turn to this book for the record of a fortitude which, in spite of your negligence and languor, still leaves us proud of the English name.

XXIII.

A SPEECH

DELIVERED IN

THE HOUSE OF COMMONS

ON THE 26TH OF FEBRUARY 1857.

ON Thursday, the 26th of February 1857, the Member for the West Riding of Yorkshire, Mr Richard Cobden, moved in the House of Commons a resolution to the effect—

" That this House has heard with concern of the conflicts which have occurred between the British and Chinese authorities in the Canton river ; and without expressing an opinion as to the extent to which the Government of China may have afforded this country cause of complaint respecting the non-fulfilment of the treaty of 1842, this House considers that the papers which have been laid upon the table fail to establish satisfactory grounds for the violent measures resorted to at Canton in the late affair of the Arrow ; and that a select Committee be appointed to inquire into the state of our commercial relations with China."

A discussion arose upon this which lasted four nights, a division being taken early in the morning of Tuesday, the 3d of May. The first part of the resolution having been previously withdrawn, the concluding portion of it was carried by 263 votes to 247—showing a net majority of 16 against the Government. During the first night of the debate the following speech was delivered.

SIR,—Although the right hon. gentleman has spoken with great earnestness, and although he has touched upon a great variety of subjects, I do not think he has succeeded in giving a very satisfactory reply to the powerful arguments of the hon. Member for the West Riding ; and if the House will vouchsafe me its indulgence, I think I may be able to show, without any tedious references to Parliamentary papers, how groundless is the position assumed by the right hon. gentleman. Let me first briefly state the nature of the question before us, and then show, from the wording of the resolution, how little it merits the condemnation of the right hon. gentleman. The two main questions before us, out of which many others incidentally arise, are— first, was this vessel, the Arrow, *bona fide* a vessel belonging to the English nation, according to the plain meaning of the 17th Article of the Supplementary Treaty? and next, if that was the case, were the circumstances attending the alleged outrage on the part of the Chinese authorities, such as to warrant the adoption of the consequent proceedings on the part of the British authorities? The 17th Article of the Supplementary Treaty contains regulations respecting certain small vessels belonging to the English nation. The hon. Member for the West Riding asks, very properly, " How can a vessel that is notoriously Chinese in every stage of its history—that is built, owned, manned, fought for, litigated for by Chinese, with nothing English about it except a mere lad of twenty years of age, who was hired by the Danish Consul as the nominal master—how can that be a vessel belonging to the English nation according to the plain meaning of the 17th Article?" The right hon. Secretary for the Colonies (Mr Labouchere) referred us to the practice we adopt in the Mediterranean. I will presently show the right hon. gentleman that the illustration does not apply. The only mode in which a Chinese vessel could become a vessel belonging to the English nation is by the colonial ordinance, and you might as well by a colonial ordinance attempt to turn a tea-tree into an oak-tree. Your colonial ordinances may bind your own subjects ; but neither a colonial ordinance nor even an Act of Parliament can have the effect of altering the international law with regard to other nations whom such ordinance or Act of Parliament may concern. You refer to the Treaty of Nankin, you put your own construction upon its Articles ; the Chinese have a right to refer to the date of that treaty. And if at the period when the treaty was concluded no class of vessels

similar to the Arrow did belong, or could by any possibility
have belonged, to the English nation, the Chinese are not bound
to allow you a right by subsequent internal regulations to appropriate to the English nation a certain class of ships which by
build and ownership and crew essentially belonged to the Chinese
nation; for a fundamental maxim in the construction of all
treaties, which the noble lord at the head of the Government
will not deny, is that it must be construed by the forms and
usages prevalent at the time the treaty was drawn up and concluded. But, according to the words of the treaty and the usage
in force at its date, no such vessels could by any possibility have
belonged to the English nation. If the Chinese had asked you
while that clause in the treaty was under discussion to define
what you meant by a British vessel, you could only have referred
them to our navigation laws. By our navigation laws, as they existed at the time the treaty was made, every British vessel must
have had a British subject for an owner, and her crew must also
have been three-fourths British subjects. It was not until the year
1854, many years after that treaty was made, that by the Merchant Shipping Act you could have attempted to torture this
Chinese vessel into an English one; and how is it done then?
why, by destroying the vital principle of the Act itself, and
granting to foreigners, not naturalised, the right of ownership
which the Act confines to the subjects of the British Crown.

I now come to the supposed parallel which the right hon.
gentleman has found in the ownerships of vessels in the Mediterranean. The difference between the two cases is this—
there you do not take a vessel belonging to another sovereign,
and you do here. I concede that by the Alien Act of
1847 you may grant naturalisation to every Chinese in Hong
Kong. But then you cannot alter the operation of the law of
nations in their behalf. You cannot, by the law of nations,
give such naturalisation the force of a protection to such natives
in their own country against the independent sovereign whose
natural-born subjects they are. I ask the noble lord—I ask
any hon. member—to tell me whether, if a foreigner gets letters
of naturalisation or protection they will avail him in the country

of the independent sovereign to whom the naturalised subject has belonged. You may naturalise an Austrian, but you cannot give him a passport that will protect him in Austria against the Emperor of Austria, unless Austria has first denaturalised him. I will suppose, then, that the naturalisation of these Chinese aliens had given them rights which would avail them anywhere except in the seas and the empire of China; but it could not give them protection there unless China had denaturalised them or absolved them from their allegiance. This axiom belongs not to law only but to civilisation, and it is founded upon the most obvious principles of reason. For how can you protect the vessels and the subjects of an independent sovereign within his own jurisdiction and domain, and make your laws and customs supersede the laws and customs of the country to which the persons you protect owe an allegiance from which they have never been absolved? How, in a word, can you turn a Chinese vessel into a British vessel, and Chinese subjects into British subjects, without usurping the sovereign rights of the Emperor of China in his own dominions? The only pretext by which this lorcha could be said to be a British vessel is to be found in the 17th Article, which declares that every British vessel shall have a sailing letter or other act of registration, which she is to deliver up to the British Consul on arrival, and which is to be restored when she sails. It is contended that because this vessel had a sailing letter she was unequivocally British. But the article only refers to vessels that are *bona fide* British, and that would be considered British at the date of the treaty. It does not follow that every Chinese vessel which complies with your internal regulations is therefore a British vessel, in spite of the Chinese laws. According to the English law, the Arrow could not have been a British vessel at the time of the treaty; she could not have been so according to the law of nations at the date of the dispute; and she cannot be made English merely by doing something which vessels legally English are required to do. If at the time of signing the 17th Article of the Supplementary Treaty you had said to the Chinese, " We claim the right hereafter to sell all the privileges and protection of the

British flag to vessels belonging to Chinese natives," do you
suppose the Chinese would have acceded to such a demand, or
that England would have renewed the war for the monstrous
privilege of selling the flag of England for fifty dollars? What
was the reason for your claim alleged by the British agents to
the authorities at Hong Kong in the preamble of this precious
ordinance? Why, "That legal trading might be protected, and
illegal trading prevented." What has been the result? In two
instances our flag has been used in protecting smuggling, and in
the present instance it was used to protect a pirate, to the destruction of legal trading by our cannon-balls and shells. To
sum up, then—I say this vessel, belonging to Chinese subjects,
manned by Chinese, and employed in Chinese waters, did not,
at the date of the treaty, belong to the English nation. If you
chose afterwards to call it so by a local ordinance, that might
bind your own subjects, but would not acquire the force of
international law, and would not bind the Chinese, if they had
never agreed to it, which it was clear they never did. It is said
by Wheaton, the most modern authority on international law,
that where a nation alters its existing laws of trade and navigation so as to affect another nation, it may require the Act of the
internal Legislature of the nation so affected in order to procure
the adoption and execution of such alterations; and he instances
the well-known case of the commercial treaty of Utrecht, which
the British Parliament refused to execute, though the treaty
itself had been concluded by the negotiators. It follows from
this, as clearly as one problem of Euclid follows from another,
that if, after a treaty has been concluded, you, as one of the contracting parties, alter your existing law so as to affect the Chinese,
the other contracting party, your alterations will be binding on
your own subjects, but that it will require the legislative power
of China to give those altered laws force and effect in that country.
The whole argument lies in this. If you cannot by the 17th
Article of the treaty call this a British vessel, then you cannot
avail yourselves of the 9th Article, which says, that if any
Chinese malefactor be on board a British vessel, and the Chinese
authorities wish to arrest him, they shall not forcibly enter upon

such British vessel, but shall make application to the British Consul. For that 9th Article applies to British merchantmen, and this is not a British merchantman but a Chinese vessel.

I will, however, grant for a moment the right of this vessel to be considered an English vessel, and then I ask, was the act of the Chinese so inexcusable—was it so outrageous, so insulting to the dignity of this country, as to warrant the terrible revenge that we have inflicted? The right hon. gentleman the Secretary for the Colonies had said that the evidence in the matter is so overwhelming in favour of the British authorities, that he wondered any man could question the course which they have pursued. What is the evidence on this subject? Four persons, two British and two Chinese, have deposed that the British flag was flying at the time the lorcha was boarded, and that it was hauled down. What was the evidence brought before the Imperial Commissioner Yeh? He had not four witnesses, but more than seventy—the soldiers, the mandarins, and the crew, who are computed at the number of sixty, and the twelve sailors whom he took away. If we may suppose, as is natural, that he had received the report of all these persons, he has against our four witnesses seventy witnesses, when he states that the flag was not flying, and could not therefore have been hauled down. We are inclined to believe our own countrymen; that is natural. Yeh is inclined to believe his: is not that natural, also? And is it not the more excusable, because, as the hon. gentleman the Member for the West Riding has observed—and the statement has not been contradicted by the right hon. gentleman— it is the established custom of English vessels in those waters not to have the flag flying until the vessel is under way? But, assuming that the flag was flying, according to the evidence of one of the Chinese, the mandarin who gave the orders for pulling down the flag said, " Why, this cannot be a foreign lorcha ; there are no foreigners on board ; haul down the flag." Grant that the mandarin was wrong ; but still, when he comes in search of a pirate on board a vessel that had been notoriously a pirate ship—which was known to be so to all the Chinese authorities—which was stated to have been employed in the disturbances between the imperialists and the insurgents—and when he does not find a single foreigner there, may he not excusably believe that the flag was fraudulently hoisted? Observe, this is not merely a question of who was right and who was wrong, but whether the Chinese were so outrageously in the wrong as to justify the terrible punishment we have inflicted. Englishmen are not the Dracos of legislation. Every offence with us is not punishable by death. Are we mild philosophers in our domestic legislation, and ruthless exterminators in the enforcement of every questionable point of international law? It would be a monstrous inconsistency if, while we are mitigating, and have for the last thirty years been mitigating, our criminal code, and dealing mildly with offenders who prey upon the very vitals of the State, we should wage a ruthless war—no, not a war, but a wholesale massacre—on our helpless customers at a remote corner of the globe. And what for? Why, to maintain a trumpery ordinance which our own Board of Trade has admitted to be of "very questionable propriety," and which is at direct variance with the Acts of our own Imperial Parliament. It is a complaint against Commissioner Yeh that he will not apologise for the alleged insult offered to our flag. But if you ask Yeh to apologise—if you ask him to acknowledge that he believes the vessel to be Chinese and to belong to the English nation, you ask him to be a traitor to his sovereign and his country, and to admit that the representatives of a foreign sovereign can dictate laws to China. Instead, however, of making any such admission, Yeh holds to his statement that the Arrow is a Chinese vessel; and he hits the right nail on the head, and'is strictly within the limits of international law, when he says so mildly to Sir John Bowring, with a view to prevent disputes in future, "I would be obliged to your Excellency if you would not give an English register to a Chinese ship." I was surprised to hear the Colonial Secretary quote the language of Mr Consul Parkes as something that was remarkably decorous and proper from an official of his rank. Will the House permit me to read a few words from a communication addressed by Consul Parkes to Commissioner Yeh, not for the sake of its proper tone, but on account of its prevarication? Mr Consul Parkes says,—"I have seen clear and conclusive proof of the facts that your Excellency attempts to deny." Attempts to deny! Where, Sir, in all Yeh's correspondence shall we find a phrase so gratuitously insulting as that? It would have been quite as easy and more in conformity with diplomatic usage to say, "Your Excellency is misinformed." Mr Consul Parkes informs Commissioner Yeh that he has seen clear and conclusive proof that the Arrow had an English ensign hoisted and an Englishman on board—facts, he adds, "of which there can be no further doubt or question." Here, Sir, there is more than prevarication—there is positive untruth; for, according to our own evidence, there was no Englishman on board when the Chinese officials reached the vessel —the Englishman did not go on board till after the seizure: so here we have Consul Parkes deposing as to two facts being so clear and conclusive that there could be no doubt or question respecting them, while upon one of those "facts" he goes directly in the teeth of his own evidence. Is Commissioner Yeh so very unreasonable when he refuses to believe him as to the other fact? Lord Clarendon, with somewhat incautious haste, asserts that it was evidently an afterthought on the part of Yeh to say that the Arrow was not a British ship. It is too much to ask Lord Clarendon to condescend to look into the papers concerning any case before him; but if we had a Minister of less commanding capacity who would descend to that drudgery, he would see that, so far from its being an afterthought, Yeh states in his first letter that the Arrow was not an English lorcha. Before the affair of the Arrow, in the case of the two Chinese smugglers whom we took under our protection, the Chinese authorities used exactly the same arguments—namely, that a Chinese vessel cannot be altered into an English vessel; and they not only said that, but acted upon it. The case of our officials is greatly aggravated, when we find Sir John Bowring deliberately stating that this vessel, for which we are committing such havoc of law, of order, of property, and of life, is not legally entitled to our protection. Such is the statement made by Sir John Bowring to Mr Consul Parkes; and yet these officials not only continue to urge their claim upon China, knowing it to be unjust, but they proceed in the deception, step by step, to the bombardment of a city containing 1,000,000 inhabitants. I was not astonished at the thrill of indignation that ran through the House when the hon. Member for the West Riding, with that peculiar and enviable eloquence of his, alluded to the miserable argument that the Chinese did not know the true position of the Arrow. Why, Sir, a falsehood does not exist only in the telling a lie, but in the wilful suppression of truth; and this suppression of truth Lord Clarendon, a Minister of the Crown, does not hesitate to re-echo and approve. In the magniloquent appeal with which the Colonial Secretary concluded his peroration, he talked loftily of vindicating the honour of the nation. The honour of the nation! Sir, prevarication and falsehood have nothing to do with the honour of the English nation; they appertain rather to the honour of an Old Bailey attorney. We have heard a great deal about the dissimulation and duplicity of Russia. How Russia will chuckle at this! Here is a Minister of the Crown, the austere negotiator of the Paris Conference, the rebuker of Russian duplicity, approving colonial agents in the maintenance of a claim which they knew to be illegal, and the assertion of a fact which they knew to be untruth! But another excuse has been advanced. It is said that by the 10th rule of the ordinance the register of the Arrow might continue in force for more than the year for which it was granted. That is not the case, and the argument was not thought of at the time. It never occurred to Sir John Bowring, who had no doubt that the vessel was not entitled to our protection, and it was never mooted until the town had been bombarded. The proviso in the 10th rule, upon which the excuse is founded, refers to the claims of the owner to renew the licence, and not to the continued force and effect of an old register after its expiration. It simply means that if the vessel be detained at sea by unavoidable circumstances, the licence may be renewed, notwithstanding that irregularity; but it does not mean that the force and effect of the licence shall be continued in the interval. If you look at the ordinance, that would be found to be impossible, because no limit as to time is placed during which the vessel might be at sea; and therefore, according to your construction, the vessel might remain out many years and the licence still have force. It is quite clear that Sir John Bowring interprets this part of the ordinance as I do, since he says, " I will consider if the licence can be renewed, but there is no doubt that the vessel's right to protection has expired." Were there ever, then, more miserable special pleas for the defence of violence and fraud ? The right hon. gentleman said that there had been no desire to quarrel with China; but I ask, if the Government had not predetermined upon these hostilities, what better moment could have been chosen to take us out of this affair with dignity than when Lord Claren-don hears that the licence of the vessel had expired ? How well might we have said to the Chinese (retaining the right to this class of vessel if we thought proper) that we had found a tech-nical difficulty in the fact of the expiration of the vessel's licence ; and as it was doubtful whether she was entitled at that time to the British flag, and as we were a nation singularly just, and lived under a Government singularly humane, you, the Chinese, shall have the benefit of the doubt ! Then, if we wished to gain an entry into the city of Canton, we should have had a better claim in our forbearance than we have had in our violence. If, however, we were too candid to own that we could be the least in the wrong—and if it were necessary for the dignity of this country not to suffer the least affront from China, however unin-tentional—then I say that when we captured a Chinese junk, with a valuable cargo, instructions should have been given that that capture was a sufficient reprisal. But, if that was not enough, we might have stopped short after bombarding the Barrier Forts. Good heavens, Sir, it is a stain on the nineteenth century that we hurried on to the shelling of a city, the destruction of its property, the slaughter of its inhabitants, who were disavowing offence and imploring mercy ! And all for what? In order that we may convince these barbarians how unenlightened is their prejudice against foreigners. Then there comes this new feature of the case—the alleged infraction of the Treaty of Canton in not admitting the English into the city of Canton. Now, I am going

to raise the question a little more boldly than it has been raised
by the hon. Member for the West Riding, and I would ask the
noble lord at the head of the Government, than whom no greater
authority exists as to the law of nations, whether, according to
the law of nations, as interpreted by all authorities, the Chinese
Emperor may not feel specially exempt from the fulfilment of this
part of the treaty ?   For the fulfilment of a treaty there are five
conditions : the most essential of the five is, that its fulfilment
shall be practicable and not pernicious to the State and people
of the power that enters into the engagement.   Nothing is more
clearly laid down by Vattel than that proposition.   I need not
quote him to show that where a treaty is not practicable it cannot be fulfilled.   No one wants a Vattel to tell him that ; but on
the latter and more delicate part of the proposition—namely, that
a sovereign may be exempted from fulfilling a treaty where it
proves fatally pernicious to the people he is primarily bound to
protect, Vattel is more worth attention.   He cites the well-known
instance of Louis XII., who was called on by the States-General
of France to break his treaty with the Emperor Maximilian and
the Archduke Philip, on the ground that it was pernicious to the
French people.   Frederick the Great has treated this very critical question with the acute distinctions of a king whom the subject vitally interested.   But he plainly allows the broad fact,
that one sovereign should not and cannot bind another sovereign
to do that which, not being intended at the time, would, if done,
prove destructive to his State or pernicious to his people.   Then
I ask, first, are you sure that the Emperor of China can practically effect your entrance into the city of Canton ?   Secondly,
what are really the powers of the Chinese Emperor over the pro-
vincial city of Canton ?   We know little of the political constitution of China, but it is perfectly clear that it differs essentially
from all modern oriental nations.   When the French Jesuits
went there, they were struck with the similarity of the manners
of the Chinese to those of the ancient Egyptians, and one wrote
a work to prove that China was a colony from ancient Egypt.
I believe a Chinese scholar replied, " Not so, but Egypt was a
colony from China !"   However that be, what most struck the

Jesuits was, that under the forms of despotism there prevailed, as there did in Egypt, a religious respect for the feelings, customs, and habits of the people, which the Chinese Emperor could not venture to transgress. Are you sure, then, that it is in the Emperor's power, or in that of his Viceroy, to enforce our entry into Canton against the will of its population? If he attempted to do so by a violent exercise of prerogative, the attempt might be fatal to him at a time when his empire is rent by rebellion. The Emperor of China has admitted us into every port into which it was possible for him to give us admission, and if he does not admit us into Canton, may it not then be solely because he cannot do so; and might not a violent effort on his part to force us on the inhabitants be fruitless in itself, but more injurious to him than we had ever presupposed? Ought we, then, to insist on what it may not be possible for an ally to grant? No; does not Vattel expressly declare that, "when a treaty, which has been concluded with upright intentions, becomes thus difficult of fulfilment, nothing can be more honourable, more praiseworthy, or more conformable to the histories of international treaties, than to relax the terms of such treaty as far as possible without exposing yourselves to loss and danger"? How much more, then, may we be disposed to do so, when it is not by relaxation, but by rigorously insisting that loss, if not danger to ourselves, is incurred? The right hon. gentleman tells the House that this is not the first time that China has insulted us. But does not Sir John Bowring tell us that, in 1852, before he began to revive the obnoxious claim to enter the city, so far from desiring to insult us, "the Chinese were in a state of unusual tranquillity, and the prejudices against foreigners are gradually subsiding"? That was the happy state of things which he found in 1852, and which he began to disturb in 1854. And the moment in which Sir John Bowring, in his innocent simplicity, becomes animated with the most friendly intentions of entering the city of Canton at all hazards, is that in which we are uniting all the inhabitants against us, and justifying the prejudices which led them to exclude us. The whole of this question was brought in 1849 before the noble Viscount now at the head of the Gov-

ernment. Sir George Bonham was then the representative of
this country in China. I am sure that more admirable despatches
than those written at that time by the noble Viscount on this
subject I have never read. Sir George Bonham fairly put before
the noble Viscount all the bearings of the case. He stated all
the disadvantages that would accrue from our not enforcing that
part of the treaty. All the rubbish we have heard about the Chinese not being sufficiently afraid of our power was urged then
as now ; but Sir George Bonham came to the conclusion that
the advantages of enforcing the treaty would be as nothing compared with the risk and the danger accompanying it : and the
noble Viscount, in one of those admirable despatches which he
wrote to Sir George Bonham, stated distinctly that "it had always
appeared to him to be doubtful whether the right of entering the
city of Canton would be productive of any material advantage
to British residents; while it had been plain that the unrestricted
entrance of British residents into that city might lead to disputes
and collisions between British subjects and Chinese, the consequences of which might be serious." All the advantages to be
gained, then, in the opinion of the noble Viscount and Sir G.
Bonham, could not arise from the indiscriminate entrance into
Canton, be it observed, of the commercial English—no ; that was
deemed to be undesirable on all sides—no ; but only from the
convenience that the English Superintendent and Consul should
have access to the Chinese authorities on special occasions. No
doubt that object was a very desirable one—desirable in 1849,
and desirable now. But in 1849 the noble Viscount said that
that object, however desirable in itself, "was not worth a naval
and military operation ;" and accordingly he resolved not to renounce it, but to suspend it indefinitely, and that for reasons
which apply more strongly at the present day than they did at
that time ; because if ever the treaty was to be enforced by naval and military operations, surely the time to do it was when
the treaty was fresh, and our moral claim had not been weakened
by its having been left in abeyance for eight years. If the main
reason that we did not urge it then was the prejudice which
existed on the part of the inhabitants of Canton, and the noble

Viscount wisely left it until time had softened that prejudice, can we expect that prejudice now to diminish when we have bombarded the city, and every Chinese who has lost a brother or son in the conflict is thirsting for revenge ? The more, therefore, I admire the prudence of the noble Viscount in 1849, the more I am astonished that he should have lent his sanction to a diametrically opposite policy in 1856. Lord Malmesbury no less wisely enforced the precaution which the noble Viscount had laid down; and Lord Clarendon is the first of our Ministers who, listening to the siren voice of Sir John Bowring, has plunged us into the Charybdis. With regard to Sir John Bowring, we all know that he is an able and accomplished man; but he is also a man of enthusiastic temperament, and, like all men of genius, is very desirous of carrying out his own wishes. From the first he was seized by a strong ambition to obtain an entrance into Canton; and although I do not doubt that Sir John Bowring is as humane and honourable a man towards his own countrymen as any amongst us, yet when agents of European Governments come in contact with oriental nations, they are apt to be gradually warped from the straight line of humanity and justice they would adopt at home. It is then that we look to a wise Government to guard against the over-zeal of agents by salutary cautions which foresee and prevent their errors, and by temperate rebuke when the errors are first incurred. When a Government forsakes this duty—when it places before us nothing but unqualified approval of actions like those recorded in the papers laid on our table—all subordinate agents, like colonial superintendents and consuls, vanish from our eyes, and it is only with the Government that we have to deal. Here, then, in my place as a representative of the people, it is the Government that I charge. I charge them with sanctioning an ordinance which, unknown to Parliament, has turned into a dead letter that grand Act of the Imperial Legislature which regulates the whole trade and navigation of the country. I charge them with approving the enforcement of that ordinance by measures that equally violate the laws of nations and the spirit of English honour. I charge them with lending the authority of the Crown to homicide under false pretences, belying the generous character of our country, and offensive to every sentiment of right and justice which our nature receives from Heaven! You tell us it is necessary that China should learn to know our force. It is not true : all these papers tell us that China knows and dreads our force ; and what China doubts is, the friendliness of our intentions and the simple rectitude of our objects. In dealing with nations less civilised than ourselves, it is by lofty truth and forbearing humanity that the genius of commerce contrasts the ambition of conquerors. Talk not of the interests of trade ! Your trade cannot prosper if you make yourselves an object of detestation to those you trade with. You may, indeed, force a road for your merchants to the market-place at Canton over the ruins of the city and the corpses of your customers—you may carry your tariffs at the point of the sword, and surround your factories by armed garrisons and bristling cannon—but I warn you that your trade will fly the place, for commerce recoils from unnecessary bloodshed. *Et udam spernit humum fugiente pennâ.*

XXIV.

A SPEECH

DELIVERED IN

THE HOUSE OF COMMONS

ON THE 18TH OF FEBRUARY 1858.

On Friday, the 12th of February 1858, the First Lord of the Treasury, Viscount Palmerston, moved in the House of Commons for leave to bring in a bill for transferring from the East India Company to the Crown the government of her Majesty's East Indian possessions. The member for Huntingdon, Mr Thomas Baring, thereupon moved by way of amendment, "That it is not at present expedient to legislate for the government of India." A debate arose upon this which occupied three nights, the motion being carried on the morning of Friday, the 19th of February, by 318 votes to 173. During the third night of the discussion the following speech was delivered.

SIR,—It has been made a subject of complaint by the right hon. baronet the First Lord of the Admiralty against my hon. friend the Member for Huntingdon,* that he should have rested his objection to this bill on the score of time. But the right hon. gentleman must be well aware that a measure of this importance brought forward by the head of the Government would be entitled, whatever might be its defects, to be allowed to pass to a discussion of its principle upon a second reading, if there were not something in the season at which it was submitted to our

* Sir Francis Baring.

consideration that was peculiarly unfavourable to its introduction. With regard to the bill itself, which I am not disposed to discuss at this moment at any length, I must say that I think it is at once audacious, incomplete, and unconsidered. It is audacious, inasmuch as it affects the conversion of an administrative body, through which, whatever may have been its faults, every hasty or unwise proposal on the part of her Majesty's Government was sure to be carefully sifted, into a set of irresponsible nominees of the Ministers of the day. It is incomplete, because it does not afford us a single guarantee for that wholesome restraint on a precipitate or a despotic policy that is effected by the system which it is proposed to remove. And it is unconsidered, because even on so simple a point as the mere number of the council which it would establish, every hon. gentleman who has any practical acquaintance with the affairs of India, tells you that is preposterously inadequate for the discharge of the amount of business which the council undertakes to perform. I believe it may be shown, too, that it is unconsidered on a much more important point, because her Majesty's Ministers assert, and I have no doubt honestly believe, that this bill will not increase their patronage ; while I am persuaded that it will appear, when we come to detail, that their patronage will be enormously increased, and increased in a direction that is peculiarly dangerous, because it applies to the class of gentlemen—the class of whom this House of Commons is composed; and the patronage is therefore of a nature which will prove hard to reconcile with our virtuous horror of bribery and corruption. I am not surprised to find that this measure is incomplete and unconsidered, because I do not think that the Government could have had the requisite calmness of temper to devise a complete, safe, and comprehensive measure for the civil administration of India at a time when revolt is still raging—at a time when no man knows or can conjecture how far disaffection has spread or is spreading—at a time when none can know the proper remedies that ought to be applied—and at a time when all our thoughts are, or ought to be, concentrated on the fittest military measures for the support of a handful of our countrymen, amid the dangers that surround them. But the noble Viscount says this cry of time is a stale cry; that it is always said that it is not the right time for change. The noble Viscount is unquestionably the highest authority of any man living as to the right time for change, and I am surprised that so acute a statesman should not be able to distinguish between the mere hollow cry against a time for change, which Mr Bentham classes among the "Fallacies of Delay," and the plain truth that nevertheless there are times which are peculiarly unpropitious to change; a truth which Mr Bentham himself would have been the first to acknowledge, because, though he was a great philosopher, he was also, strange as it may seem, a man of common-sense. But, by the by, after that remarkable chapter of Mr Bentham's on the "Fallacies of Delay" comes his immortal chapter on the "Fallacies of Confusion," in which is explained the fallacy of Ministers making use of the name and authority of the Crown for the purposes of corrupt patronage— a chapter that her Majesty's Ministers have, no doubt, studied with extraordinary diligence and care. But with respect to this objection of delay, what was the answer which the noble Viscount made to his noble friend the Member for the City of London, when he wished to persevere with his scheme of Parliamentary Reform? We all know the life-long attachment of the noble Viscount to the cause of Reform. But what was his answer on that occasion to the noble Lord? It was, "This is not the right time for change." Why was it not the right time for change? Because we were then engaged in a war with Russia. And can this, then, be the right time for a reform in the government of India, when you are engaged in a war with India itself? Yes, said the noble Viscount, this is exactly the time, because we want a system of more vigour and promptitude to deal with the difficulties that surround us. "Only think," says the noble Viscount, "of the waste of precious hours in sending cabs from one end of London to the other. How much more convenient would it be to have one snug little family party round a single table in Cannon Row?" Why do you want this peculiar promptitude and decision? Because you are in a state

of abnormal and temporary difficulty. I object to legislate for
the securities of permanent and normal administration in a time
of abnormal and temporary difficulty. I object to legislate for
the provisions of peace at a time when your thoughts are concentred on the exigencies of war. I grant that war requires
promptitude and decision—but peace requires deliberation and
caution ; and I believe that the slowness produced by the checks
and counter-checks of which the noble Viscount now complains,
have saved the empire from many fatal blunders which would
have been committed by the rashness of a Minister if he had
had no better advisers than the complaisant nominees of himself
and his party—men not like the present Court of Directors,
who have nothing further to expect from the Government, but
men who, if they are of the mark and ability you desire to secure
for your new Board, will be comparatively young and ambitious
—men who will, perhaps, only take their place at your Board
with a view to some higher and more dignified position in India,
and who will thus be stimulated to a discreet acquiescence in
the policy of their Ministerial patron by a lively sense of the
prospective benefits of Ministerial patronage. But I ask
whether, according to the policy you are now pursuing, you are
likely to attain the object you desire ? Do you think that the
advantage of promptitude and vigour, for a special, and, we hope,
temporary occasion, will be obtained by the course you propose
to adopt ? Are not the next few months most critical in regard
to the security and tranquillity of our sovereignty in India ?
And how do her Majesty's Ministers invite us to spend them ?
In conveying to the hesitating courts of the neutral princes of
India our own doubts as to the efficacy of our machinery and
the rectitude of our cause; in apprising rebels that the Ministers
of England admit that our rule was acquired by "rapacity and
perfidy," and is administered by a system cumbrous and feeble
and effete. Is not this the language of the Chancellor of the
Exchequer ; and can you suppose that that language will not be
published, translated, and garbled from one end of India to the
other ? Is this the way to strengthen our government over
those who are doubting whether they should submit to be

governed by us at all? All orientals dislike change — all orientals are suspicious—all orientals believe that the wiser you are, the more in any change you mean to dupe or to injure them ; and therefore, whenever you propose change for orientals, take care that you propose it when your sovereignty is unquestioned —when your rule is calmly predominant. To institute a change in the midst of rebellion, is too often considered but a treaty of compromise with the rebels. Take the language of the Chancellor of the Exchequer—say that our empire was acquired by unqualified rapacity and perfidy—say that it is matter of doubt whether the empire be a boon to England,—and do you not justify rebellion? Accompany the change with the language of the noble Viscount, which has also been repeated by the First Lord of the Admiralty—say that the change is of no importance —say that it affects only the home administration—say that it holds out to India no particular benefit or hope of amelioration —say that it will only make our rule more vigorous, or, as India will construe it, more arbitrary and stern—say that the Company, which you are now constrained to acknowledge has always opposed schemes of conquest, annexation, and religious intolerance, is no longer to be allowed to thwart, to admonish, or to recall a governor-general who may be stimulated by the lust of popularity or of fame to meditate schemes of annexation, conquest, or religious intolerance,—and can you tell me that this may not provoke to rebellion the princes who at this moment remain neutral, or even friendly to our rule? When it is understood in India that you propose to new model the machinery of government in such a manner as to render the governor-general more despotic—when it is understood that a large party in this country is opposed to this scheme, and that months may be spent in discussing it,—and when all this occurs in the very ferment and meridian of disaffection—when the whole population of India is, I will not say hostile to you, but still in that state of oscillation which the hon. and gallant Director * could only describe by an expressive movement of his hand— when the whole state of feeling in that country is so delicate

* Colonel Sykes.

that no prudent man will venture to analyse it,—will you tell me that, at such a moment, the very discussion of a change does not tend to weaken authority, and to provoke resistance? An important paper has been put into our hands to-day, to which I will briefly refer. It is a portion of a despatch from a commissioner of revenue, in which the writer states that many people endeavour to persuade themselves that the natives are not aware of the contents of the English papers, and that, so far as they are concerned, it is immaterial what appears in those publications; but that, he adds, is a great mistake : the English newspapers have for many years been the source to which the natives have looked for news and intelligence; and since the revolt commenced, the greatest anxiety has been manifested to learn what those papers say. Every one who is fortunate enough to get hold of an English paper is called upon to translate it for a large circle of natives; and there can be no doubt that whatever appears in those papers which can in any way serve the purposes of the disaffected, is speedily made known to them by agents in Calcutta or elsewhere. If this be so, who can doubt that these debates will not be extensively translated among the natives ? In England we think little of imprudent speeches. Gentlemen may cheer the Chancellor of the Exchequer when he denounces the founders, and questions the value, of the Indian empire. But what will be thought of such opinions stamped with the authority of the Queen's adviser, by men who are actually rebelling or considering whether they should rebel ? At what period did the necessity for this change flash on the inexperienced mind of the noble Viscount ? For fifty years the noble Viscount has been in the service of his country, one of the most eminent statesmen which this country has ever known. Whatever may happen to him, his name is immortal in the history of this country. Well, but in that interval we have had momentous wars in India; and yet in that interval the evils of what is called the "double Government," or what the right hon. gentleman the First Lord of the Admiralty called the "compound Government," never seemed to occur to the noble Viscount. They never occurred to him at all till—when? Till any check or counter-check whatsoever is extremely inconvenient to the single Government of the noble Viscount. Says the noble Viscount, " Under the present system we have no responsibility—we want more responsibility." The Chancellor of the Exchequer echoed the same plaintive cry—" We want more responsibility." No, you do not want more responsibility ; what you want to obtain is more power—and power not only over the population of India, but over the Parliament of England. When the right hon. gentleman the First Lord of the Admiralty got up, I own I felt a lively interest to know what he would say on this point. I recollect the speech the right hon. gentleman made in 1853. He then said,—" I, as President of the Board of Control, have as much responsibility for whatever happens in my office as the Secretary for the Colonies has for whatever happens in his." I therefore felt a lively interest when the right hon. gentleman got up this evening, to know his opinion. Did he retract ? Did he say that upon reflection he had discovered that the President of the Board of Control was not responsible ? No ; his great object was to show that the present Court of Directors were a dependent body, and therefore, that the President of the Board of Control was actually responsible to Parliament. That was the whole of his argument. But, says the Chancellor of the Exchequer, it is only in stress of weather that the vessel can be proved. The metaphor is not very new ; but, as coming from a gentleman of his solid attainments, any metaphor acquires the grace of novelty. It is only in stress of weather that the vessel can be proved. That is true ; but only just observe the ingenious manner which the Chancellor of the Exchequer has of proving the vessel. He and his friends, who are the temporary passengers, throw overboard the tried and regular crew, and appropriate to themselves the cargo. That is the ingenious mode by which the Chancellor of the Exchequer proves a vessel ! What does he mean by stress of weather ? He means that this is a time of peculiar emergency—a time of mutiny, revolt, and disaffection. Well, let us grant that it is so. But now tell us in what joint has the vessel parted ? In what single instance,

metaphor apart, has the Company failed you? Has it failed
you in a single instance by which it could assist you in putting
down the mutiny or quelling the rebellion? No; it is to the
Company we owe those instances of ability and heroism which
have never been exceeded in the annals of any country in the
world. And is this a moment to annihilate their existence,
and to affix—there is no mincing the matter, for you do affix
upon them in the eyes of India, of Europe—the ignominy of
an abrupt dismissal, not only without a fault, not only without
a trial, but in the midst of acknowledged and imperishable
obligations? And by whom is it done? By that grateful
Administration, whose numberless blots of policy and prudence,
of energy and foresight, that Company has been lavishing the
blood of its best and bravest in the endeavour to efface.
Hitherto it has been the policy of the noble Viscount, and it
is a generous policy, to support his officials, his agents, his em-
ployés, even though they should commit occasional acts of
indiscretion. We are now, for the indiscretion of a couple of
agents at Hong Kong, plunged into a war with China, of which
none of us can conjecture the end—of which very few of us
can conceive the object. But now, in a temporary moment of
clamour, you refuse to stand by a great Company to whom
you owe the acquisition, the preservation of India; and all its
virtues are to be ignored, all its faults exaggerated, and itself
thrust aside from all participation in the glory of restoring
peace and security to an empire which was won by the genius
of its founders, and which is hallowed by the graves of its
martyrs. I have now a word or two to say on the speech of
the First Lord of the Admiralty; but the right hon. gentleman
has so many claims to our respect and regard, he has served
this House and the country with so much ability—and I understand that he has, in much bodily suffering, come down to
the House this evening from a desire to show respect to the
House, and to acquit himself of the charge of inconsistency—
that I think it would be ungenerous in me if I were to triumph
over the weakness of his argument under these circumstances.
I shall content myself, therefore, with observing that the greater

portion of his speech to-night was an inadequate answer to his argument of 1853, and consisted mainly of those reasons for change which he then declared to be such utter rubbish " that no man of sense would answer them." But he thinks he obtained a triumph over my hon. and learned friend the Member for Enniskillen * and other hon. gentlemen on this side of the House. He says that in 1853 the Member for Enniskillen, and others on this side the House, voted in favour of carrying on the government of India in the name and authority of the Crown. Well, why not? I myself think that would be an advantage. I think the right hon. gentleman urged a new and a cogent argument in favour of it, deduced from the increased number of British troops to be henceforth employed in India. I see nothing at all inconsistent with that view in the whole of the speech of the hon. and learned Member for Enniskillen. Nothing can be more obvious than that the Company are the trustees of the Crown ; than that every act that is done in relation to the government of India is at this very moment approved of by the Crown, ratified by a responsible minister of the Crown ; that, in short, such acts are acts of the Crown. Well, then, supposing that to-morrow you were to pass an enactment by which the government of India should henceforth be carried on in the name of the Crown, that would not—and I appeal to any lawyer in the House to say whether I am wrong —that would not necessarily destroy the existence of the Company ; it would not necessarily alter the position of the Board of Control and the Court of East India Directors. I myself am for carrying on the government of India in the name of the Sovereign. But I go much further than that in the way of concession. I grant that it may be inconvenient that the respective places in which the business is transacted should be so far distant from each other as to be an obstacle to the despatch of public business ; I grant that it may be proper that the two bodies should meet either in the same building, or buildings contiguous to each other—although, so far as the question of the preparation of the despatches is concerned, I must do the

* Mr Whiteside.

hon. and gallant gentleman * who commenced the debate this
evening, the justice to say that he made a most admirable answer
to that; but I will, for the sake of argument, suppose that the
history given with reference to the delay of despatches is correct,
and that that which was said by the hon. and gallant Member for Reigate (Sir H. Rawlinson), by the Secretary of the
Board of Control, by the Vice-President of the Board of Trade,
was the fact—granting, I say, that the present mode of communication between the Court of Directors and the Board of
Control is too tedious and prolix, cannot you make all the
necessary improvements without destroying the Company?
That is the point which I wish to impress upon the House.
Granting all the defects of which her Majesty's Ministers complain, I venture to say that, if you had come down to the House
with a simple bill to remedy those defects, you would have met
with no opposition to it. But, Sir, even if I assume, for the
sake of argument, that it is quite right to destroy the Company
—further than that, if I assume that the present is the right
moment for so doing—am I therefore obliged to accept the
substitute which you propose? Am I obliged to accept the
principle of your bill? The hon. and gallant Member for
Reigate himself, although he is going to vote for leave to introduce it, cannot accept the principle of the measure. What!
Did not the hon. and gallant gentleman say that he wished
the council to be independent? Did he not say, " I want the
council to be chosen not by nomination, but upon some principle of election"? But look at the bill. Is not its very
essence nomination? You say that for the Board you constitute
you may obtain some of the most eminent of the existing Court
of Directors. The great inducement held out to this House to
persuade it to accept the measure is this—that you may possibly
obtain for your new council a small portion of that wisdom
possessed by the Court which we are now called upon to abolish.
Sir, I do not believe that the more eminent of the Court of
Directors will condescend to sit as mere Ministerial nominees
at that Board you propose to institute. But grant that they

* Colonel Sykes.

do. Do you mean to say that there is no difference between
a Board which consists of Ministerial nominees, and a Board in
which the same men are animated by the pride of an independent class, and exercise the functions of a responsible body?
Take the twelve most eminent men in this House; place them
in the legislative council of some absolute sovereign, and will
you venture to tell me that they would exhibit the same high-
spirited intelligence; that they would be impressed with the
same pure and noble feeling of grave responsibility by which
they are now distinguished? If you want to govern India by
clerks, call them clerks; and, as clerks, let them be nominated.
If you want councillors, councillors must be free. You will
substitute, you say, for an existent independent council, the
superintendence, the vigilance of Parliament. The noble Lord
condescends to flatter us by saying that it is all very well for
people out of doors to disparage the House of Commons, but
he does not think that any hon. gentleman will get up here and
say that we are not just as wise, just as capable of administering the affairs of India as a set of merchants. Sir, I hope the
members of this House are too manly to accept that species of
adulation. We all know the merits of this illustrious assembly
of which we are so justly proud, we also all know its defects—
there is no man who knows them better than the noble Viscount. If upon any question, however trivial—if upon any
question of foreign policy, not half so important to us as the
affairs of India, not half so delicate to deal with—some hon.
gentleman were to ask a question of the noble Viscount, would
not the noble Viscount rise with more than usual stateliness,
and would he not as good as tell us that we had better attend
to our domestic legislation, and imply that it was not well that
such delicate matters should be handed over to the tender
mercies of a popular assembly? Suppose that this bill passes,
and some young and innocent member, anxious to assert that
vigilant superintendence now held out as so strong and seductive an inducement in favour of this measure, should venture
to put such a question as—What are the intentions of the
Government regarding the Nizam?—what the true state of our

relations with Holkar or Scindia?—do we not know perfectly
well that the noble Viscount would rise in his place and say,
as he said the other night, "that without meaning anything
personal, the question was extremely absurd"? And indeed,
for my part, I own to a wholesome dread of hon. gentlemen
cramming themselves with blue-books, and coming down to the
House with an elaborate speech about Rajahs and Nawabs conceived in accordance with the respective interests of party;
sometimes, as the case may be, to defend some more than
ordinary act of duplicity by which we had annexed a kingdom—
or, on the other hand, to declaim against some measure which
might be necessary to the stern necessities of oriental rule, but
painful to the feelings of an English popular assembly. That
would be dangerous for India; but still more dangerous in its
effects upon the moral character of England, which it cannot
be well to familiarise with all the details of despotism, all the
excuses for arbitrary powers. Before you can judge with dis-
crimination of a policy applied to orientals, you must learn to
orientalise yourselves; you must be familiar with the customs,
the laws, and the manners most at variance with all your own
free institutions; you must know the principles and the forms
of a mythological religion which, I suspect, very few of us can
comprehend, but which is interwoven with the habits, with the
feelings, with the affections, with the daily routine of Hindoo
life. Without some clear perception of the mode in which that
religion influences and colours all the social and moral existence
of Hindoos, how can you even pass an opinion on that administration of justice to which the superintendence of Parliament
is to be involved? You may sanction penalties which, to your
English ideas, will seem mild and equitable, and which, to a
Hindoo, seem the most exquisite torture. And why? Because
such penalties, mild in their operation in this life, may, according to his creed, affect him in the life to come; and, in forfeit-
ing the sacred privileges of his birthright, condemn him to
countless ages of degradation. But you will peaceably escape
this danger. The House will have the wisdom to shun it;
the House will never habitually exercise the superintending

vigilance you commend to it—it will only interfere with the despotism you are about to establish whenever it suits the interest of party to assail a Minister or asperse some illustrious name. But be that as it may, I content myself now with the simple declaration, this is the moment not to legislate, but to arm. This is the moment, above all others, when you should give to that authority which is already established in India, and which has never failed you, all the force, all the power of your own unanimity. This is not a time when you should damp the ardour of England by tracing to perfidy the empire you ask it to defend. Rather should you appeal to the conscience of Englishmen for every aid they can raise and send forth, to protect from carnage and massacre their countrymen, their women, and their children. Your Indian empire has passed through the perils of a mutinous army; do not expose it to the more fatal ordeal of an organised system of favouritism and jobbery. That empire was won by the valour and intellect of the middle classes, of whom you call yourselves the representatives; and it is for you now to determine whether it shall henceforth be jeopardised by official imbecility and Ministerial corruption.

XXV.

A SPEECH

DELIVERED IN

THE HOUSE OF COMMONS

ON THURSDAY THE 8TH OF JULY 1858.

ON Thursday, the 8th of July 1858, the Secretary of State for the Colonies, Sir Edward Bulwer Lytton, introduced into the House of Commons a bill to provide for the government of New Caledonia. This measure resulted in the organisation by him of the new colony of British Columbia. On bringing before the House his motion for the second reading, the following speech was delivered.

SIR,—The bill which I rise to ask the House to sanction, is necessary to the maintenance of law and the preservation of life in the district in which it proposes to establish a Government, and it realises at an earlier period than was anticipated an object which has already entered into the colonial policy of this country. The House is aware that in 1849 the Crown granted to the Hudson's Bay Company the soil of Vancouver's Island, on the condition of establishing a colony there, disposing of the land to emigrants, and defraying its expenses ; at the same time, the Crown reserved a right to resume the land on the expiration of the grant of exclusive trade in 1859. But the Company enjoy in Vancouver's Island no rights of government or of judicature. The government is administered by a Governor appointed by the Crown, with a Legislative Council, and the House of Representatives chosen by the people. The judicature is administered by courts instituted by the Crown, under the special authority of an Act of Parliament, "to provide for the administration of justice in Vancouver's Island." Next year it is the intention of the Crown to resume the soil, and the whole public connnection of the Company with the island will cease. Indeed, my right hon. friend the Member for Coventry,* in his able evidence before the Committee on the Hudson's Bay Company, says, "The sooner the public re-enter into possession, and the sooner they form establishments worthy of the island, and worthy of the country, the better." My right hon. friend proceeds to say—" That this island is a kind of England attached to the continent of America; that it should be the principal station of our naval force in the Pacific; that it is the only good harbour to the northward of San Francisco, as far north as Sitka the Russian settlement; that you have in Vancouver's Island, the best harbour, fine timber in every situation, and coal enough for your whole navy; that the climate is wholesome, very like that of England; the coasts abound with fish of every description;—in short, there is every advantage in the Island of Vancouver to make it one of the first colonies and best settlements of England." But when my right hon. friend was asked by the Committee if he thought it desirable to attempt also at once to colonise the land on the adjacent coast he answered, " No, we should have enough to do in colonising the island." He will not say that now. He knows that since the evidence was given circumstances have arisen which call upon us to place, as soon as possible, the adjacent territory under the safeguard of an established Government, such as this bill will provide. And those circumstances are the discovery of gold-fields, the belief that those gold-fields will be eminently productive, the number of persons of foreign nations and unknown character already impelled to the place by that belief. I need say no more to show the imperative necessity of establishing a Government wherever the hope of gold—to be had for the digging—attracts

* Mr Edward Ellice.

all adventurers and excites all passions. At this moment there
is no Imperial Government at all in the place, for the Governor
of Vancouver's owns no commission on the mainland. Thus
the discovery of gold compels us to do at once what otherwise
we should very soon have done—erect into a colony a district
that appears, in great part, eminently suited for civilised habita-
tion and culture. Before I proceed further, it may be interesting
to the House to give a sketch of the little that is known to us,
through official sources, of the territory in which these new
gold-fields have been discovered. The territory comprehended
in the proposed bill lies between the Rocky Mountains and the
Pacific ; it is bounded on the south by the American frontier
line, 49 degrees of latitude, and may be considered to extend to
the sources of Fraser River, in latitude 55 degrees. It is therefore about 420 miles long in a straight line, its average breadth
about 250 to 300 miles. Taken from corner to corner its greatest length would be, however, 805 miles, and its greatest breadth
400 miles. Mr Arrowsmith computes its area of square miles,
including Queen Charlotte's Island, at somewhat more than
200,000 miles. Of its two gold-bearing rivers, one, the Fraser,
rises on the northern boundary, and flowing south falls into the
sea at the south-western extremity of the territory, opposite the
southern end of Vancouver's Island, and within a few miles of
the American boundary ; the other, the Thompson River, rises
in the Rocky Mountains, and flowing westward joins the Fraser
about 150 miles from the coast. It is on these two rivers, and
chiefly at their confluence, that the gold discoveries have been
made. Hon. entlemen who look at the map may imagine this
new colony to be at such an immeasurable distance from England as to be fatal to anything like extensive colonisation from
this country; but we have already received overtures from no
less eminent a person than Mr Cunard for a line of postal steam-
vessels for letters, goods, and passengers, by which it is calculated that a passenger starting from Liverpool may reach this
colony in about thirty-five days by way of New York and
Panama. With regard to the soil, there is said to be some
tolerable land on the lower part of Fraser River. But the

Thompson's River district is described as one of the finest countries in the British dominions, with a climate far superior to that of countries in the same latitude on the other side of the mountains. Mr Cooper, who gave valuable evidence before our Committee on this district, with which he is thoroughly acquainted, recently addressed to me a letter in which he states, that "its fisheries are most valuable ; its timber the finest in the world for marine purposes ; it abounds with bituminous coal well fitted for the generation of steam. From Thompson's River and Colville districts to the Rocky Mountains, and from the 49th parallel, some 350 miles north, a more beautiful country does not exist. It is in every way suitable for colonisation." Therefore, apart from the gold-fields, this country affords every promise of a flourishing and important colony. In Charlotte's Island, which we include in this new colony, gold was discovered in 1850, but only in small quantities. Here I may perhaps correct a popular misconception. In Vancouver's Island itself no gold has been yet discovered. The discovery of gold on the mainland was first reported to the Colonial Office by a despatch from the Governor of Vancouver's Island, dated April 16, 1856. The Governor had received a report from a clerk in the service of the Hudson's Bay Company at Fort Colville on the Upper Columbia River. Further reports followed in October 1856, testifying to the importance of the discovery. From experiments made in the tributaries of Fraser River there was reason to believe that the gold region was extensive ; the similarity in the geological formation of the mountains in the territory to those of California, induced the Governor to believe that these would prove equally auriferous. Subsequent accounts in 1857 varied as to the quantity of gold obtained, but confirmed generally the opinion of the richness of the mines, especially above the confluence of the Fraser and Thompson Rivers. The Governor writes on the 15th of July 1857, that gold was being discovered on the right bank of the Columbia, and the table-land between that river and Fraser's. On December 29th he ascribed the small quantity found to the want of skill and tools on the part of the natives, who opposed any white men digging. The Indians were especially hostile to the Americans, and opposed their entrance into the country. Great excitement now prevailed in Oregon and Washington territory. An influx of adventurers might be expected in the spring, in which case collisions between the whites and the natives might be expected to occur. As far back as the first discovery in April 1856, the Governor had suggested the system of granting digging licences. The right hon. gentleman the Member for Taunton,* then Secretary of State for the Colonies, pointed out, in a reply (Aug. 4), that it would be abortive to attempt to raise a revenue from licences to dig for gold in that region in the absence of effective machinery of government, and left to the Governor's discretion the means of preserving order. In the exercise of that discretion he issued a proclamation (December 28th 1857), declaring the rights of the Crown to the gold in Thompson's and Fraser's Rivers ; establishing licence fees [of 10s., which, on the 1st of January 1858, he raised to 20s. ; and prohibiting persons from digging without authority from the Colonial Government. But this proclamation has virtually proved a dead letter ; for, in point of fact, the Governor had no legal power to issue the proclamation, or cause it to be respected, he having no commission as Governor on the mainland ; his sole power has been the moral power of his energy, talents, and extraordinary influence over the natives. Indeed, the manner in which he has preserved peace between the white man and the natives is highly to his honour. In a letter from the Governor to the Hudson's Bay Company, March 22, 1858, he trusts that her Majesty's Government would take measures to prevent crimes, and protect life and property, or there would be ere long a large array of difficulties to settle. "A large number of Americans," he said, "had entered the territory ; others were preparing to follow." On the 8th of May in the present year, he states to the Colonial Office that 450 passengers, chiefly gold miners, had come from San Francisco ; that they all appeared well provided with mining tools ; there seemed to be no want of capital or intelligence among them ; that about sixty were

* Mr Labouchere.

British subjects, about an equal number Americans—the rest were chiefly Germans, with some Frenchmen and Italians. And I have here the pleasure to observe that he states, that though there was a temporary scarcity of food and a dearth of house accommodation, they were remarkably quiet and orderly. The Governor then touches on the advantage to the trade of the island from the arrival of so large a body of people ; but he adds significantly,—" The interests of the empire may not be improved to the same extent by the accession of a foreign population whose sympathies are decidedly anti-British. From this point of view the question assumes an alarming aspect, and leads us to doubt the policy of permitting foreigners to enter the British territory *ad libitum* without taking the oath of allegiance, or otherwise giving security to the Government of the country." He states that "the principal diggings at Fraser's and Thompson's Rivers at present will continue flooded for many months, and there is a great scarcity of food in the gold districts ; that the ill-provided adventurers who have gone there will exhaust their stock of provisions, and will probably retire from the country till a more favourable season ; that on the dangerous rapids of the river a great number of canoes have been dashed to pieces, the cargoes swept away, many of the adventurers swept into eternity—others, nothing daunted, pressing on to the goal of their wishes." He again, in a letter to the Hudson's Bay Company, repeats his fears, " how seriously the peace of the country may be endangered in the event of the diggings proving unremunerative, and the miners being reduced to poverty and destitute of the necessaries of life."

I should state that I have also seen private letters recently from San Francisco, giving an account of the extending excitement prevailing there, and of the number of Americans, of other foreigners, and of negroes, preparing to start for Fraser's River. In one letter it is stated that 2000 persons have already left, and 20,000 persons might leave before the end of the summer, if the news continued favourable ; but perhaps the news of the flooding of the waters may for a time retard so copious an emigration. I think I have said enough to convince the House of the neces-

sity of providing at once for the government of a country
threatened by so many disturbing elements. My first care has
been to urge upon my right hon. friend the First Lord of the
Admiralty the necessity of despatching an adequate naval force
in the harbour of Vancouver—sufficient to provide against lawless aggression,—and instructions to this effect my right hon.
friend assures me he has given ; and my next care is to bring in
this bill, which is intended to establish lawful authority and
order. Now, Sir, the Crown of itself could, if it thought proper,
make a colony of this district. But the law officers decided, in
the case of Vancouver's Island, that no Legislature can be established by the Crown, except an elective assembly and a nominative council ; and, considering the very imperfect elements for
such a constitution at such a moment, considering the ordinary
character of gold-diggers, considering that our information as
yet is really so scanty that we are at a loss to constitute even a
council of the most limited number, I think that most hon.
gentlemen will agree that it would not be fair to the grand
principle of free institutions to risk at once the experiment
of self-government among settlers so wild, so miscellaneous,
perhaps so transitory, and in a form of society so crude. This
is not like other colonies which have gone forth from these
islands, and of which something is known of the character of the
colonists. Neither is it like those colonies in which the first
thought of the emigrants is the acquisition of land, and the first
care of the governor those allotments of land, which are the
preliminary of representation. As yet the rush of the adventurers is not for land but gold, not for a permanent settlement
but for a speculative excursion. And therefore, here the immediate object is to establish temporary law and order amidst a
motley inundation of immigrant diggers, of whose antecedents
we are wholly ignorant, and of whom perhaps few, if any, have
any intention to become resident colonists and British subjects.
But where you cannot at once establish self-government, all
sound political thinkers, all friends to that responsibility which
is the element of freedom, will perhaps agree that the next best
thing is to establish a government which shall have as few

COLONY OF BRITISH COLUMBIA.

checks as possible on its responsible functions; which shall
possess unhampered what powers we can give it, to secure the
respect for recognised authority; which shall be clearly for a
limited time, and with the avowed and unmistakable intention of
yielding its sway at the earliest possible period to those free
institutions for which it prepares the way, and which it will
always henceforth be the colonial policy of this country to effect.
I think that all complicated attempts to construct half-and-half
forms of government for such new societies are unsatisfactory.
They only serve to weaken the executive, and to form an excuse
for retarding the completion of popular systems. What, therefore, we propose to do by the bill we now ask the House to read
a second time is, to empower the Crown, for a limited period,
till December 1862, and the end of the Session of Parliament
next ensuing after that time—a period nominally of five years,
though in reality of four—to make laws for the district by Orders
in Council, and to establish a Legislature; such Legislature to
be, in the first instance, the Governor alone; but with power
to the Crown, by itself or through the Governor, to establish a
nominative council and a representative assembly. If, therefore, before the five years expire, there are the elements for a
representative assembly, I cannot doubt that, whoever then may
be the advisers of the Crown, a representative assembly will
cheerfully be given. Sir, there will be some, no doubt, who think
the term of five years too short—who think that the materials
for popular self-government could not be matured at the end of
that term, and that there would be many inconveniences in
coming again to Parliament to renew the powers of the Act.
To these objections I have given the most respectful care, and
I would submit that the larger proportion of the immigrants
attracted by the gold-fields will probably be Americans, accustomed to self-government; that, if you desire to keep them loyal
and contented, you should give them the prospect, at the earliest
possible period, of that representative form of government to
which, in their native country, they have been accustomed; and
that if you desire a strong Government for the preservation of
internal order, no Government we can make, without the aid of

armies, is so strong as that where the whole society is enlisted
in securing respect to the laws which it has the privilege to en-
act, and has no motive to rebel against the authority in which
it participates. And if, which is not impossible, the gold-fields
should prove a delusive speculation, and the principal settlers
should be the steadier class of emigrants—perhaps our own
countrymen, who will rather cultivate the other resources of the
land in its coal-mines, timber, fisheries, and other agricultural
produce—you may have at the end of five years a quiet and
orderly population, well fitted for self-government. Therefore
I think we had better fix the shortest term for the experiment
of a provisional Legislature. With regard to Vancouver's
Island, which has already a free constitution, we do not propose
to annex that island to the new colony. In fact, if the gold-
fields should prove to be really productive, a very large population will rapidly spread over the neighbourhood of the diggings,
which it will be impossible to govern from the distance of several
hundred miles at Vancouver; while, if we extend our view to
the natural destinies of Vancouver as the great naval station to
our only possession on the Pacific side of the whole of America
—a station from which we should carry on a trade with India,
China, the Indian Archipelago, Australia—a trade now carried
on exclusively by the Americans from California—I think we
must allow that the Government of the island would have
enough to occupy its care and attention in developing the true
interests and resources of that single colony. Nevertheless,
difficulties in the severance of the two colonies may be found in
their geographical relation to each other. According to maps,
the maritime access to New Caledonia can be only made facile
and guarded by its command of the noble harbour of Esquivault
at Vancouver's Island; natural circumstances may thus compel
the fusion to which otherwise there may be sound political
objections: we therefore propose to leave the question of annexation open to further experience; and the Act will empower the
Crown to annex Vancouver to New Caledonia, if the Legislature
of the island intimate that desire by an address to the Crown,
under such terms and conditions as may be approved. Mean-

while, as the most pressing and immediate care in this new
colony will be to preserve peace between the natives and the
foreigners at the gold-diggings, so there is nothing in the Act
which impairs the prerogative of the Crown to permit the
Governor of Vancouver to administer also New Caledonia,
should that be absolutely necessary, in the first instance, just as
the Governor of the Cape, which has a free constitution, is also
Governor of the Crown colony of British Kaffraria, holding
separate commissions for each. Our object, in short, has been,
under our very imperfect information, and the uncertainty, as
yet, of the value of the gold-fields, to insure some immediate
Government, and to leave to the Crown all discretional power,
according to the advice it may receive, and suited to the variation of circumstances. I should add that it has been deemed
necessary by the law advisers of the Crown to abolish in the
proposed Act—as was done in the Act for Vancouver's Island,
by the advice of the Committee of Privy Council, in 1848—the
jurisdiction which the courts of Canada claim over civil and
criminal cases in this region. The Crown has power to appoint
magistrates and constitute courts having a concurrent jurisdiction with Canadian courts up to a certain amount. The Canadian jurisdiction is a dead letter ; and though it has subsisted
nominally for nearly forty years, it has never been put into
execution—certainly not in the north-west territories. It is clear,
however, that the concurrent jurisdiction would be attended with
many practical inconveniences, which, in creating a colony, it
will be necessary to remove, as we did remove them for Vancouver's Island. I have now, Sir, stated the substance of the
bill I ask leave to introduce. I have shown, I trust, the necessity of an immediate measure to secure this promising and
noble territory from becoming the scene of turbulent disorder,
and to place over the fierce passions which spring from the
hunger of gold the restraints of established law. If the machinery we propose is simple, it is because the society to which it is
to be applied is rude. But happily, in that new world, the true
sense of the common interest is rapidly conceived, and the capacities of self-government no less rapidly developed. And pro-

bably even before the end of the five years to which I propose
to limit the operation of this Act, the materials for a popular
representation may be found, and the future destinies of this
new-born settlement boldly intrusted to the vigorous movement
of liberal institutions. It may be necessary to observe that,
both as regards Vancouver's Island and this more extensive
territory of New Caledonia, it is not intended over these colon-
ised districts to renew to the Hudson's Bay Company the licence
of exclusive trade, which expires next year. The servants of
the Company will then have in those two colonies no privileges
whatever apart from the rest of her Majesty's subjects there ;
and therefore I was glad to hear the hon. and learned gentleman
the Member for Sheffield (Mr Roebuck) express his opinion that
the present occasion was not a fitting opportunity for raising the
question of which he had given notice. It is desirable to keep
any discussion upon this bill free from the more angry elements
which may be involved in the general question as to the powers
of the Hudson's Bay Company, by virtue of its charter, on the
different districts of Rupert's Land, on the eastern side of the
Rocky Mountains, a question which the hon. Member for Sheffield will have a distinct opportunity to introduce. Sir, I have
wished to keep my statement of the present value and ultimate
importance of this new colony clear from all the exaggerations
which belong to the philosophy of conjecture. I have carefully
abstained from over-colouring our imperfect knowledge as to
the permanent richness of the gold discoveries. Nothing can be
more cruel to immigrants and more dangerous to the peace of
the settlement than to give undue favour to any extravagant
expectations as to the produce of these gold-fields. It is a terrible picture, that of thousands rushing to what is already called
the new El Dorado, influenced by avarice and hope, and finding,
not wealth, but disappointment and destitution—provisions dear
and scanty, and the gold itself meagre in its produce, and
guarded by flooded rivers and jealous Indians. At present,
whatever may be the riches of the discovery, it is fair not to
forget the fact that California exported in the first eight months
from the discovery of its mine 150,000 ounces of gold-dust ;

while the largest amount ascertained or conjectured from Fraser's River since 1856 is not more than 1000 ounces. More rational, if less exciting, hopes of the importance of the colony rest upon its other resources, which I have described, and upon the influence of its magnificent situation on the ripening grandeur of British North America. I do believe that the day will come, and that many now present will live to see it, when, a portion at least of the lands on the other side of the Rocky Mountains being also brought into colonisation and guarded by free institutions, one direct line of railway communication will unite the Pacific to the Atlantic. Be that as it may, of one thing I am sure—that though at present it is the desire of gold which attracts to this colony its eager and impetuous founders, still, if it be reserved, as I hope, to add a permanent and flourishing race to the great family of nations, it must be, not by the gold which the diggers may bring to light, but by the more gradual process of patient industry in the culture of the soil, and in the exchange of commerce ; it must be by the respect for the equal laws which secure to every man the power to retain what he may honestly acquire ; it must be in the exercise of those social virtues by which the fierce impulse of force is tamed into habitual energy, and avarice itself, amidst the strife of competition, finds its objects best realised by steadfast emulation and prudent thrift. I conclude, Sir, with a humble trust that the Divine Disposer of all human events may afford the safeguard of His blessing to our attempt to add another community of Christian freemen to those by which Great Britain confides the records of her empire, not to pyramids and obelisks, but to states and commonwealths whose history shall be written in her language.

XXVI.

A SPEECH

DELIVERED IN

THE HOUSE OF COMMONS

On the 20th of July 1858.

On Tuesday, the 20th of July 1858, the Member for Sheffield, Mr John Arthur Roebuck, proposed, and the Member for Norwich, Viscount Bury, seconded a motion to the effect—"That the privileges of the Hudson's Bay Company, about to expire, ought to be renewed." After some discussion, this motion was eventually withdrawn. During the course of the debate the following speech was delivered by Sir Edward Bulwer Lytton, in his capacity as Secretary of State for the Colonies.

Sir,—It is with some reserve that I approach the great and difficult questions involved in the resolutions of my hon. and learned friend. The Government, as yet, are in the condition of negotiators. Certain distinct propositions, as the right hon. gentleman who spoke last told us, were made to Canada by the late Government with regard to any districts now covered by the charter of the Hudson's Bay Company which she might desire for the purposes of settlement; and whatever cause there may be to suppose that the Canadian Government will reject those proposals, still every motive of policy, as well as of respect to that great colony, would make us desire that any scheme for colonisation in that region may have her sympathy and concurrence. To those propositions we have had no official answer; still, Sir, I own that the probability that they will not be accepted is so notorious, and the interests involved in this question are so great, that I cannot hesitate to state at least the general views by which I venture to think that we ought to be guided. In glancing over the vast regions devoted to the fur trade, which are loosely said to be as large as Europe, the first thought of every intelligent Englishman must be that of humiliation and amaze. Is it possible that so great a segment of the earth under the English sceptre, can have so long been abandoned as a desolate hunting-ground for wandering savages and wild animals? I put aside, for a moment, excuses of soil and climate; it is always presumptuous to decide hastily between man and nature—to say what man may or may not do to conquer those obstacles of soil and climate which nature may raise against him. It is enough for us to cling to the grand principle that civilisation should be left to find its own voluntary channels; that we should not force it, but should take care not to obstruct it. No one can deny that a trade which preserves wild animals, and has a direct interest in excluding civilised men, does obstruct civilisation if it claims territorial rights in any district which civilised men are disposed to cultivate and inhabit. The right hon. gentleman the Member for the University of Oxford (Mr Gladstone) summed up the general evidence before our Committee in the first two of a series of resolutions which he proposed to that Committee: first, that the country capable of colonisation should be withdrawn from the jurisdiction of the Hudson's Bay Company; secondly, that the country incapable of colonisation should be left to that jurisdiction. In the two abstract principles involved in these propositions lies the readiest solution of the gravest difficulties that beset the question; it is the attempt of a practised statesman to effect a compromise by which civilisation may gain all it asks at present, and humanity may not only preserve to the savages scattered over frozen deserts, inaccessible to regular government, the trade on which they depend for existence, but guard them from the terrible demoralisation produced by rival bribes of ardent spirits, and the

strife and bloodshed among themselves, or between themselves
and the whites, which might follow if the administrative machinery which it is the interest of a trading company to establish were destroyed before any effective substitute could be
found. These are the reasons which will weigh upon the Government in considering the renewal of the licence. The Government will certainly not renew the licence over any part of the
Indian territory which promises early settlement; but they reserve for further deliberation whether they will renew it for a
limited period over the more remote and northern regions, taking care that the Crown shall have always the power to withdraw from that licence any land that may be required for the
uses of civilised life; that it shall retain all the imperial rights
to fisheries and mines, and whatever may call forth human industry and enterprise in pursuits more congenial to our age than
that gloomy trade in the skins of animals which seems to carry
us back to a date before the annals of history. Now, although
the renewal of the licence may possibly form a part of any fresh
negotiations with the Hudson's Bay Company for arrangements
respecting the Red River Settlement, yet it ought in principle
to be considered apart from such arrangements, and on its own
merits; in lands held as yet only by the Indians, does the exclusive licence, or does it not, work well for the Indians? The
licence is a question wholly distinct from that of the charter;
the licence gives none of the territorial rights which the charter
assumes—it involves no principle of compensation in case of
any lands which colonists may require, and it ought to be regarded simply as an instrument by which the Government can
effect that safeguard from broil and disorder which in so vast
and profitless a wilderness the Government is not able of itself
to establish. But, whatever doubts may be entertained as to
the second proposition of the right hon. gentleman the Member
for Oxford—namely, that land incapable of colonisation should
be left to the jurisdiction of the Hudson's Bay Company—no one
can dispute the soundness of the first proposition, that the
country capable of colonisation should be withdrawn from that
jurisdiction; and turning our eyes from a trade which, unlike

all other commerce, rests its profits, not on the redemption, but on the maintenance of the wilderness, it must cheer us to see already, in the great border-lands of this hitherto inhospitable region, the opening prospect of civilised life. Already, by the Pacific, Vancouver's Island has been added to the social communities of mankind. Already, in the large territory which extends west of the Rocky Mountains, from the American frontier up to the skirts of the Russian domains, we are laying the foundations of what may become hereafter a magnificent abode of the human race ; and now, eastward of the Rocky Mountains, we are invited to see, in the settlement of the Red River, the nucleus of a new colony, a rampart against any hostile inroads from the American frontier, and an essential arch, as it were, to that great viaduct by which we hope one day to connect the harbours of Vancouver with the Gulf of St Lawrence. This is the district offered to Canada, and I think my hon. and learned friend has good reason to presume that Canada will decline the task of forming it into a colony at her own responsibility and charge. If the answer from Canada be unfavourable, we have two options : either to leave the district, as now, under the jurisdiction of the Hudson's Bay Company, which nothing but absolute necessity would justify; or to take it into our own hands and form a colony, which will, no doubt, one day constitute a confederate part of a great Canadian system, and which might meanwhile, perhaps, be administered by a Government in concurrence with Canada. To this there have been two objections. The first is the presumed expense. This I do not at present anticipate. All healthful colonies should be self-supporting, and I agree with my hon. and learned friend in the general theory he advances with so much eloquence and wisdom. Colonies will be self-supporting in proportion as you leave them to raise their own revenues under free institutions. The second objection is, that such a colony would not be peopled by Canadians ; that, owing to the easier access from the American frontier, the majority of immigrants would be Americans. This objection does not alarm me. In the first place, though the immigrants come from the American territory as the readiest access, it does not follow that

they should all be Americans. Probably large numbers of our
own countrymen, especially the Scotch, would flock there, as well
as Americans; and as for Americans, once settled as British
colonists, it is probable that they would soon identify their national feelings and interests with the land in which they lived,
and the conditions of the Imperial Government. It has been so
already in Canada—it would be so at Red River; because all
history tells us how soon men, if at all of kindred race, take, as
it were, the stamp and colour of the land in which they settle.
We, in this country, are an instance of that truth. No less than
sixteen counties in this kingdom were given up to the immigration of the Danes—and probably the great mass of the population in those counties, more particularly in Yorkshire, Lincoln-
shire, and Norfolk, are of Danish origin to this day; yet in a
very short time they became as heartily English and as hostile
to the Danes of the Baltic as the Anglo-Saxons of Kent. Nay,
even the Normans, despite their pride as a conquering race, despite the difference of language, became in the third generation
as intensely English and anti-French in their national feelings
as if they had been Saxon Thegns. In short, no matter where
men come from, place them in ground covered by the British
flag, overshadowed, though at a distance, by the mild British
sceptre, and they will soon be British in sentiment and feeling.
All that I say on this score is, do not, on account of such jealousies and fears, obstruct civilisation. Here is land fit for settlement; if civilised men will settle in it, let them. Never let
us mind the difficulties of access, soil, or climate. Leave the
difficulties to them. Nature and man will fight their own battle and make their own peace. With regard to the fitness of
the place itself for colonisation, I am contented to take the
opinion of the Hudson's Bay Company themselves; for, in a
letter from the Company to Lord Glenelg, February 10th, 1837,
when asking for a renewal of the license, I find it said,—"The
soil and climate of the country of the Red River Settlement are
favourable to colonisation; that it was intended that this settlement should be peopled by emigrants from Britain, and that
the Company hoped to establish in time a valuable export trade

from thence to the mother country, in wool, flax, tallow, and other agricultural produce." Sanguine hopes, not realised since 1837 under the auspices of the Company, but which may be more rapidly fulfilled when the Company withdraws from the place the shadow of its chilling protection. With regard to the safety of a settlement at the Red River from all ordinary attacks that might be made on it from the American quarter, I have a most satisfactory report from Sir William Eyre, the Lieutenant-General commanding the forces in British North America. He states that "the Red River Settlement consists of about 8000 persons, of whom 2000 are Irish, English, and Scotch; the remaining 6000 all mostly half-breeds. They are generally good shots, skilled in the use of firearms, and good horsemen. A local force or militia, of at least 1000 men, could be easily organised and embodied. . . . The barracks are perfectly habitable, and the post defensible, except against heavy ordnance, which it would be difficult to bring up against it. Norway House is the chief depot of the Company—the position might be made impregnable. All communication between Lake Superior and the Red River is now, according to Sir George Simpson, impracticable for any body of troops. . . . A few individuals might go, but not any force. There is abundance of provisions in the country; no want need be apprehended; water is good—wood abundant. The climate is severe in winter, but healthy at all seasons."

These few extracts may suffice to show that a settlement once established would be safe from danger from without. As regards the fur trade in this district, I need scarcely say, that if you take the land from the Hudson's Bay Company, the monopoly that goes with the land will expire. To attempt to maintain the monopoly there would be impossible, and only give rise to perpetual feuds. In fact, I must be pardoned if I say that there is good reason to believe that that monopoly has practically, in a great measure, ceased to exist in those parts. Major Seton reports from Fort Garry itself,—"The Hudson's Bay Company have long since abandoned in practice their pretensions to exclusive trade in this district and far beyond it." Captain Pallisser

writes word: "That monopoly there is unattainable now and
for evermore; that the people engaged in the illicit trade are
inhabitants of the Indian land, and born on its soil. Most of
them are half-breeds; they are British subjects; and whatever
the rights of the Hudson's Bay Company under the charter,
they think it a very hard case that they should be debarred from
trading in the land of their birth. There appears to be a shadow
of justice in this complaint; but, just or not, the opposition
exists, and nothing short of extirpating the people engaged in it
can ever stop it." Indeed, this report is so far confirmed by
Captain Shepherd himself, on the part of the Hudson's Bay
Company, that he states, in a letter to the Colonial Office,
"That the diversion of the fur trade is carried on by the inhabitants of the Red River Settlement, who, regardless of the
Hudson's Bay Company, conduct an illicit trade in spirituous
liquors and furs in various parts of the country."

I think, therefore, there can be no doubt that, where the
Company yields the land, it must resign the monopoly. It will
be an after consideration by what regulations the trade should
in that case be carried on, so as to maintain order and peace,
and respect that considerate humanity which is due to the Indians. But now comes the difficulty. The land we would thus
dispose of for colonisation is within the charter of the Hudson's
Bay Company; and if that charter be valid, the land belongs to the
Company, but not the monopoly of the trade, except as includes
the right of ownership to keep others off the land. The law
officers of the late Government, men of very high distinction,
consider—"That the Crown cannot now, with justice, raise the
question of the general validity of the charter; but that, on every
legal principle, the Company's territorial ownership of the lands
granted, and the rights incident thereto—as, for example, the
right of excluding from their country persons acting in violation
of their regulations—ought to be deemed valid." While this
opinion of the late law officers remains before us, unexamined
by our own law officers, it would be presumptuous in me to
express any opinion of mine. It is our intention to submit the
question to the most careful and deliberate consideration of our

law officers, and ascertain from them whether, in equity and justice, we could advise the Crown, or recommend to Parliament any mode by which to facilitate a judicial decision upon this venerable title-deed. But I am bound, in justice to the Company, to say that, though it might be very desirable to try the validity of the charter, it is not absolutely necessary to do so for any immediate objects of colonisation. It is but just to the Company to say that it has not hitherto shown itself stubborn or intractable. It does not say, "You shall not have the land which our charter covers." It says, on the contrary, "Take whatever land you please ; Heaven forbid we should stand in the way of civilisation. We are not the fit agents to colonise ; we have not the means for it ; we tried it at Vancouver's, and are glad to get rid of the experiment ; take, then, whatever land you desire within the range of the charter. But"—here comes the critical but!—"we rely on your honesty." In other words, "If you take from us that which we actually possess, without proving that we have not the right to possess it—we are human beings, and we expect some kind of compensation." Seeing all the embarrassments of this dilemma, I cannot but admire the skill with which, in pursuance of the report of our Committee, the right hon. gentleman the Member for Taunton (Mr Labouchere) devised a scheme which was intended to unite the objects we have in view with a temperate conciliation towards the claims of the Company. He proposed to cede this territory to Canada if she would agree to open a line of communication to it, and give satisfactory evidence of her intention to take steps for laying out townships and settling and administering the affairs of these districts ; and as to the Hudson's Bay Company, he proposed to renew its trading licence for twenty-one years over the wilderness not fitted for colonisation ; and that three Commissioners—one chosen by Canada, one by the Imperial Government, and one by the Company,—should consider and report what, under all the circumstances of the case, might be justly payable to the Company in consequence of such contemplated annexation, and in respect of property which they might be required to surrender. Well, if Canada reject these proposals,

our hands are free for fresh negotiations and unfettered action.
Meanwhile, to sum up my answer to the hon. and learned gentleman—first, I think the licence ought not to be renewed except
where civilisation has no requirements and law no other machinery but that of the Company. Secondly, with regard to raising
the question of the validity of the charter, it will be submitted to
our law officers, and we can obviously say nothing one way or
the other till their opinion is received. Thirdly, I grant the
expediency of strengthening our empire in North America by
substituting, and in one connected frontier line, the colonies of
Great Britain for the hunting-grounds of a trading company. It
is my sincere wish and hope that arrangements for that object
may be effected in a spirit of reasonable conciliation to all
parties concerned, and that we may thus lay the foundation of
a civilised community, upon those principles of humanity towards the red man, and of honour and honesty towards the
white, which our civilisation should carry along with it wherever
it extends, as the colonisers of old carried along with them a
fragment of their native earth, and a light from the altar of their
ancient council-hall. The Company have assured us of their
desire to meet the necessities of the case in a spirit of concession,
and I do hope that early next Session we may propose to Parliament arrangements that will receive its approval. In the
object before us we all have a common interest,—to fulfil the
mission of the Anglo-Saxon race, in spreading intelligence, freedom, and Christian faith wherever Providence gives us the
dominion of the soil, and industry and skill can build up cities
in the desert. Sir, hoping that what I have said will satisfy my
hon. and learned friend, at least as to the general views of the
Government, I have only to thank the House for the indulgence
with which it has heard me.

XXVII.

A SPEECH

DELIVERED IN

THE HOUSE OF COMMONS

ON THE 3D OF MARCH 1859.

ON Thursday, the 3d of March 1859, the Member for Maidstone, Mr Charles Buxton, moved in the House of Commons, " That a Select Committee be appointed to inquire into the condition of the West Indies, and the best means of promoting immigration into them." A brief discussion thereupon ensued, the motion being eventually withdrawn.

As Secretary of State for the Colonies, the Member for Hertfordshire, Sir Edward Bulwer Lytton, was especially called upon to take part in the debate ; and it was upon this occasion that the following speech was delivered.

SIR,—Let me, in the first instance, express my sense of the temperance as well as the ability with which the hon. gentleman has introduced his motion. The bearer of his father's name enters into the discussion of all questions that affect humanity with an hereditary title-deed to respect. It is clear that he will preserve that heirloom without a flaw. If I question his views I can equally honour his sincerity. The hon. gentleman has divided the subjects of his inquiry into two heads—the present condition of the West Indian Islands, and the question of immigration. I will take the latter first, for it goes to the core of the question, and I am glad this subject is to be openly dis-

VOL. II.   G

cussed. I take it first on its broadest ground. Sir, I should be dealing unfairly towards those friends of the Anti-Slavery Society whose petitions have been before me, if I did not assume that on principle they are opposed to the whole system of labour immigration which I found established in the West India colonies. On my part, I so sympathise with zeal on behalf of the negro, even where I think those who entertain it misguided and misinformed on details, that I entreat beforehand forgiveness if inadvertently a single word should escape me that may seem to disparage the humanity that I hold in reverence. But I must say, frankly and firmly, that from that system of immigration I am convinced that no Minister, responsible for the welfare of the West India colonies, can depart. Let the House listen to facts and figures, and then say if I am wrong in the convictions I express. The hon. gentleman says that the prosperity which characterises many of the colonies does not arise from immigration alone. No; but where immigration has been continued prosperity has followed. Sir, the experiment of Coolie immigration was first tried in the Mauritius in 1835 or 1836 ; it was then commenced by the planters as private importers of labour. Abuses arose ; the immigration was consequently suspended in 1838. In 1843 the Government took it into their hands, and by the Government it has since been conducted. Now hear the result. Since the experiment there have been introduced into the colony 170,000 persons ; out of these, in 1856, as many as 134,291 were still residents. The effect on the produce of the colony has been this : The sugar crop in 1844 was 70,000,000 lb. ; in 1855, ten years afterwards, it amounted to 238,480,000 lb. That has been the effect on the produce. What has been the effect on the immigrant population ? Three-fourths of those immigrants who returned to India at the end of three or five years brought back with them from 1200 to 50 rupees each; and Sir G. Anderson, who had formerly been a distinguished judge in India, in 1850 reported his opinion in these words—" The immigrant, as a labouring population, is perhaps nowhere in the world in such favourable circumstances." But I may be told that the Mauritius is a special and singular example: is it so ?

Take next the case of British Guiana; into that colony about 23,000 Coolies have been introduced: they do not, as in the Mauritius, form the whole of the agricultural population, but a considerable part of it. The produce of the sugar crop, which in 1841 was little more than 34,000 hogsheads, was in 1855, 55,366 hogsheads. While this was the increase to the wealth of the colony, what was the benefit to the immigrants? Judge by this instance,—In a single ship which left British Guiana last year, 277 Coolies paid into the hands of the authorities as the amount of their savings for transmission to India more than £6000. I turn next to Trinidad. I find in the despatch from the Governor, dated September 26, 1858, that the population returned by the census of 1851 was 68,600; by immigration and the influx of strangers it is now raised to about 80,000. About 11,000 Coolies have been introduced into that island. Now wages in Trinidad are not so high as in British Guiana, but I find that 343 of these labourers on their return to India paid into the hands of the authorities for transmission the sum of £5389, and took with them more than £900. Such has been the gain to the immigrant; what has been the gain to the colony? The imports of Trinidad in 1855 were £554,534—in 1857, £800,830; the exports in 1855 were £387,999—in 1857 there were £1,013,414; and the Governor, in summing up the cause of this sudden and marvellous increase of the surest signs of prosperity, says—" But it is to the stream of immigration, though expensive, and by no means sufficient, which has flowed into the island during the years under review, that it is mainly indebted for the progress it has achieved." Now, turn to the other side, and compare this increase of produce in colonies caused by immigration with the decline of produce in Jamaica, where immigration has been suspended. In Jamaica the produce of sugar for three years after the apprenticeship was 1,812,204 cwts., and during the last three years it has fallen off to 1,244,373 cwts. Now, then, I respectfully ask you who advocate the cause of humanity, who feel with me that humanity belongs exclusively to no colour and to no country—who, if you advocate the cause of the negro, must advocate equally the cause of the Indian—I ask you whether, when we find that more than 200,000 persons left countries in which labour was worth from 2d. to 3d. a-day, where impressment and forced labour exist, where, as was said by the Lieutenant-Governor of Bengal, "the strong universally preyed upon the weak"—left, I say, those countries for British colonies, in which easy labour secures comparative affluence, where the labourer lives under British law, and has at all times access to a British magistrate—I ask you to say whether humanity should bid me arrest that immigration, fling these human beings back to oppression and to famine,— and why? — because their labour benefits our fellow British subjects and saves a British colony from ruin. You object to the system of indentures to a master. Just hear the answer as it is supplied to me by the Immigration Commissioners: "It has, however, been objected that the Coolie, being paid for a certain time under indenture, is in reality in a state of bondage. The answer is that, before the indenture system was established, the Coolies abandoned their work and wandered about the country, and, in many instances in the West Indies, perished miserably from disease and want." Their condition was thus described in August 1859, by Mr Carberry, a stipendiary magistrate in British Guiana, whose sympathies are much more with the Coolies than with the planters. " With the indentures," he says, "the immigrant becomes an useful and industrious member of society. His labour is alike profitable to himself and his master. Without it he too often becomes a wandering mendicant, a nuisance and disgrace to the colony, and finishes his career in the public hospital; in the interest, therefore, of the Coolie himself, the indenture system is necessary." But it is said by the Anti-Slavery Society, there has been great mortality on board the immigrant vessels from Calcutta. Undoubtedly there was in the years 1856-57. But it is fair, while allowing this fact, first to remind the House that the rate of mortality was taken from selected vessels, and that it may be in much accounted for from causes that do not apply to Coolie immigration alone. Take the very worst cases that occurred. In Calcutta ships the average mortality was in the year 1856-57

a little more than 17 per cent ; but in 1847, on board the vessels
that carried the Irish immigrants to America by a far shorter
voyage, the mortality was much the same—about 17 per cent.
Imagine what advantages would have been lost to Ireland, England, and America, if, on account of that melancholy average,
the Irish exodus had been stopped. I hold here recent reports
of the mortality of Coolies from inquiries instituted in India.
The causes are most carefully analysed ; remedies which will
receive the most diligent attention are suggested. The most
searching of all the inquirers, Mr Morant, who is the inspector
of jails and prisons, thus sums up: "I am distinctly and
decidedly of opinion that the great sickness and mortality of
1856-57 need not recur ; that, whether exceptional or not, it can
be prevented by proper care and attention ; and that there is no
need to prohibit the continuance of immigration on grounds either
of humanity or policy." What he thus says is borne out by
facts and figures ; for I have here a return showing the average
of mortality on board Calcutta vessels during the whole eleven
years immigration has taken place. Ninety-four ships have
been sent from Calcutta to the West Indies, and the average
mortality in all these years had been but 6 1-5th per cent ;
while on board thirty-one vessels sent from Madras to the West
Indies that average has been under 2 per cent: and it will be
satisfactory to the House to learn that in the last year there has
been a marked decrease in mortality, both in Calcutta and
Madras ships ; for whereas in 1857-58 the mortality in the first
was 13 per cent, in 1858-59 it has been only 6 1-6th per cent ;
while in the Madras ships in 1858-59 the mortality has been a
seventh part of 1 per cent. Stress has been laid on the Coolie
immigrants in Jamaica. In most of the petitions that have been
before me it is stated to be 50 per cent. What are the facts ?
I find by the last return, August 1858, that the total number of
Coolie immigrants since the immigration began was 4451, and
that the number of those who had died, disappeared, or were
unaccounted for, during those thirteen years, was 1597. I am
told, in fact, that a number of these immigrants chose to re-
emigrate to Panama to work at the railroad, and lost their lives

by that climate ; but that was their own fault. But suppose they all died in Jamaica, calculate that mortality : as taken for the thirteen years, it gives, not a percentage of 50 per cent, but a percentage of only 2 1-6th per cent ; but taking it, as I think you ought, by calculating the average mortality of those who had returned to India during the thirteen years, you only get about 4 per cent. And this is a specimen of the exaggeration by which honest and well-meaning men have been deceived. As to the colonies generally, we find by returns that the average mortality among the Coolies in the Mauritius is a little more than 3 per cent. In British Guiana it is under 4 per cent ; in Trinidad it is returned as so low that I think there must be some mistake, into which I will inquire ; meanwhile, I think I may safely assume it not to exceed 3 per cent. I turn, then, to the second class of argument—namely, that which condemns the present system of immigration as unfair to the Creole. It is said that there is really no scarcity of hands to meet the habitual requirements of the labour-market in the West Indian colonies ; that immigration is an attempt on the part of the planters to beat down the wages of the negroes. But surely it is a sufficient answer to that assertion that the proprietors pay an extra sum to obtain elsewhere the labour which you say they can find more conveniently at home. Is that human nature ? Do men do so even in the West Indies ? Does Barbadoes do so ? No. Barbadoes sends for no immigrants, because Barbadoes has a sufficient population, and that population is eminently industrious. But does the absence of immigration keep up wages ? No. Wages in Barbadoes are lower than those in any of the colonies to which immigration has been admitted. Compare the average wages of Barbadoes even with those at Jamaica, where you say the planter wishes to drive so hard a bargain with the Creole. Wages at Barbadoes since emancipation have ranged at 1s. 1½d. per day to 10d ; at Jamaica they have ranged from 1s. 6d. to 1s. ; and in colonies where immigration is admitted freely, a man, be he Creole or Indian, can obtain by task-work at least 2s. a-day. But is the immigrant a competitor for labour at less wages than are current with the native ? No ; it is provided that the immigrant shall receive as a minimum the current rate of wages paid to an unindentured labourer, and these wages cannot be low, if, as we have seen, they enable the Coolie to return home in a few years with what to him is affluence for the rest of his life. But it is said, " At all events, for this importation of labour the planters should pay exclusively ; the population should not be taxed for the labour that competes with their own." Sir, I grant at once that the planter should pay the greater portion of this expense ; that is a condition which both my predecessors and myself have kept steadfastly in view. And, according to the Jamaica Act, the planters pay two-thirds ; but that is not all. The money applicable for the payment of the first immigration is the sum of £50,000 remaining on the imperial guaranteed loan of £100,000. The repayment of that loan is to be effected by an export duty, and an export duty falls on the producer, that is, the planter. But granted that a portion of the expense does fall on the general community, if the immigration conduces to its prosperity, it may fairly be expected to contribute towards it. Increased prosperity is always followed by increased civilisation ; more money is required for schools, for religious worship, for public works ; every individual in the country rises higher in the scale in proportion as it becomes more prosperous ; is it unjust to call on the Creole to pay something towards what enriches and exalts the country in which we have made him a freeman ? Well, Sir, then I venture to think there are really no grounds for this Committee. So far as the West Indies are concerned, there are no petitions from them demanding this inquiry, nor are there any special measures for their benefit proposed. So far as information is concerned, it is given to you every year in blue-books as numerous and as bulky as the most passionate student of blue-books could desire. And we are now printing for Parliament papers upon nearly all the subjects to which the hon. gentleman has referred. But it must not be supposed that we shrink from inquiry. And I make the hon. gentleman two proposals : 1st, Let him wait till the papers about to be printed for the use of hon. members are on our table ; if he then wants more information, let him specify the

points in which those papers are defective ; if the Government
cannot give it, then let him move for his Committee upon those
points, and we will see if those points do really need a Parliamentary inquiry, in which case we will concede it.   Or, 2dly, if
he insist on a Committee immediately, I will grant it, provided
he thus defines its inquiry—namely, " To inquire into the present mode of conducting immigration into the West Indian
colonies, and the best means of promoting that object." I think
that is fair ; but if he take my advice he will wait for information before he decides on moving for any Committee at all.   Let
me say, in conclusion, a few words to the friends of the Anti-
Slavery Society.   I have fought by their side in my youth, and
now, when I think they have been misinformed, I still believe
that our object is the same—namely, to give complete and
triumphant success to the sublime experiment of negro emancipation.   It becomes them above all men to do their best to
render prosperous the colonies in which slavery has been
abolished.   Every hundredweight of sugar produced by the
immigrant at Jamaica is a hundredweight of sugar withdrawn
from the market of Cuban slaves.   Will slave States follow our
example unless capital flourish under it ?   Can capital flourish
unless it has the right to hire labour wherever labour is willing
to be hired ?   I warn them, that if by any indiscretion of over-
zeal on our part one West Indian colony becomes vitally injured, it is we who shall rivet the bonds of negro slavery wherever it yet desecrates a corner of the earth.

XXVIII.

A SPEECH

DELIVERED IN

THE HOUSE OF COMMONS

ON THE 22D OF MARCH 1859.

ON Monday, the 21st of March 1859, the Chancellor of the Exchequer, Mr Disraeli, moved the second reading of the Bill to Amend the Representation of the People in England and Wales. The Member for the City of London, Lord John Russell, thereupon moved as an amendment—
"That this House is of opinion that it is neither just nor politic to interfere in the manner proposed in this bill with the franchise as hitherto exercised in the counties of England and Wales ; and that no readjustment of the franchise will satisfy this House or the country, which does not provide for a greater extension of the suffrage in cities and boroughs than is contemplated in the present measure." The discussion which arose upon this lasted for seven nights. At length, on the morning of Thursday the 31st of March, the amendment was carried by 330 votes to 291. On the second night of the debate the following speech was delivered.

SIR,—The hon. gentleman who just sat down * has employed in vain much subtlety of argument and great variety of detail. Despite his undeniable talents, despite his industry in collecting and his dexterity in combining materials, whether for attack or for defence, he has failed to obscure the question so clearly put before the House by the right hon. Member for Stroud.† That question is, Will you take into consideration—

* Mr Wilson.   † Mr Horsman.

I say into consideration, for this is all that is now asked—a
moderate measure of reform, which is offered by a powerful
Conservative party with a large concession on their part; or
will you rather wait for that other measure which the hon.
gentleman says should be immediately proposed, which should
be a satisfactory solution to every problem, but which, unhappily, is not before you, of which there is not a glimpse
either in the amendment or even in the speech of the noble
Lord the Member for London, and for which you must calculate the odds that its provisions will be such as to satisfy those
gentlemen who profess what they call Radical principles, and
to satisfy also those other gentlemen who have spent the last
six-and-twenty years in decoying Radical votes and in abjuring
Radical opinions? Of course, if you cannot take the mere
principle of a moderate measure from us—if, as you say, the
country will not accept it—then the question of Reform passes
out of the hands of Lord Derby's Government. But into whose
hands will it pass? Noble lords and hon. gentlemen who are
at this moment so carefully bridging the gangway with a rope
of sand [Sir W. Hayter, who was seated in "the gangway,"
rose up hastily at this allusion, and left the House amid great
laughter] may, by the aid of that experienced personage who
has so abruptly vanished from his place, patch up the quarrels
of years for the division of a night. But grant that they
triumph. Grant that the solemn lecture which has just been
addressed to Lord Derby by the hon. gentleman has its effect,
and that no appeal is made to the country. Grant that you
are in Downing Street to-morrow, will not the quarrels of years
be in Downing Street also? But where will be any Reform
Bill? As my noble friend the Secretary for India justly said
last night, this resolution will answer the noble Lord's purpose
much as the Irish Appropriation Clause answered a similar
purpose in the hands of the same unrivalled destroyer of
Governments; and it may then leave the English suffrage
much as that famous clause left the Irish Church. And
indeed it must have struck all who have listened to this debate,
that, however hon. gentlemen may agree in disapproval of our

bill, they have shown so little agreement as to any other, that some have even taken pains to imply that there ought to be no Reform Bill at all. The hon. Member for Sandwich* said last night that rather than take our measure he would wait— he did not say how long. The hon. Member for Birmingham,† who is always the frankest of men, was somewhat more explicit. He said, a few weeks ago, that in order to have a good bill, he would consent to wait five years. Well, then, why not move an amendment which would get us all out of the dilemma, and which, I am sure, is at the bottom of the hearts of half the reformers opposite? Why not propose as an amendment to this bill that a good bill should be read a second time this day five years? For my part, speaking frankly, I have no super-stitious dread of any of those questions which are raised by the more ardent reformers opposite. Some of those questions I espoused myself many years ago ; one or two of them I still individually favour ; and if on others I have since modified or wholly altered the opinions I then held, I have done so with no uncharitable prejudice against those who believe now what I myself once believed, or may even believe a little more than my political creed ever permitted me to do. But from me, at least, advanced reformers are entitled to respect; and I know that in arguing the case with them I argue it not with the mob-leaders of fifty years ago. I argue it with gentlemen of refined education, and some of whom have proved the independence of their character by the loss of their seats, rather than yield to what they held to be the mistaken judgment of their constitu-ents. I will be fair to them. I ask them, in return, to be fair to me. We will enter on the question not as enemies but as reasoners. Now, when a Government undertakes a Reform Bill, it is impossible to discard the question—what party does that Government represent? Conservatives are free as other men to undertake financial or administrative reforms; and there may be points, both in the management of business and even of policy, in which there is more sympathy between Con-servatives and advanced Liberals than there is between advanced

---

* Mr Knatchbull Hugessen.   † Mr Bright.

Liberals and Whigs. But when it comes to great organic
changes, your own good sense and your instinct of party honour
must tell you that a Conservative Government could not give
the same kind of reform as a Government which represents
your views and is supported by your constituents. An hon.
gentleman who spoke last night said, with great anger, that
this bill was a compromise. Of course it is. We could only
deal with this question as men offering a compromise, in which
we tender concessions on our side and ask concessions upon
yours. What you lose in amount of reform you gain in the
expedition and ease with which some reform at least may be
effected. This is not all; a violent party battle upon Parliamentary Reform, to be fought throughout the length and breadth
of the kingdom, is in itself a great calamity. I remember what
it was before. Lifelong friendships are dissolved, families are
divided. In each town or county, in each section of the community, society is embittered for years; trade and credit are
seriously injured. The metropolis was said to have suffered in
its trade to the amount of £2,000,000 by the agitation of the
great Reform Bill. All those evils, according to your views,
may be counterbalanced by some large triumph for popular
Government such as you would propose. All those evils are
counterbalanced by the amendment of the noble Lord. All
those evils are prevented, and some advantage even to your
views is obtained, if, by passing the second reading of this bill,
you will meet the spirit in which a Conservative party offers
to you the grounds for a compromise. The right hon. gentleman the Member for Stroud, in the course of his weighty and
impressive speech, put our position on grounds I at once accept.
He said a Government, in dealing with Parliamentary Reform,
has these two questions to determine: first, what will the
temper of public opinion enable us to carry—what does public
opinion require? Second, what is the amount of acknowledged evil—what is there for a Government (and I must here
add a Conservative Government) to admit and to remedy?
Sir, I think few will deny that when we undertook the question of Parliamentary Reform public opinion was extremely

apathetic. Doubtless, nine out of ten said loudly, "We must have a Reform Bill;" but eight out of every nine whispered to each other, "Does anybody want one?" Is there a reason why public opinion should have changed on this subject since last year? Look to the state of Europe. During the latter date of our deliberations on reform, war seemed inevitable. True, it is peace to-day; can any man say there will not be war to-morrow? Is this the precise moment suddenly to transfer political power from the middle class, with which, on the whole, it now rests, and by which, on the whole, it has been liberally and usefully exercised, to the wider area of a class, however honest and respectable, still not yet educated up to the mark which England should require in a constituency that is to enable her to confront foreign Powers, not with the force of numbers, but with the majesty of disciplined intellect? Mr Fox once uttered words to this purpose—"What gives England her power in Europe? It can never be numbers; it must be always intellect." Can England represent intellect in Europe, if numbers are to make the law of representation in the House of Commons? And now, Sir, when I hear the Government accused of a want of earnestness and sincerity in dealing with this question, I must venture to ask if no insincerity, no want of earnestness, has been shown by many eminent persons opposite? When it was supposed out of doors that we intended to propose a sweeping and comprehensive measure, many of those eminent persons actually became anti-reformers. Articles appeared in Whig journals that might have been written by Mr Croker. Speeches were addressed to their constituents by Whig members that might have been uttered by Lord Liverpool. I appeal to our own social experience. Were not gentlemen on this side besieged with confidential whispers by gentlemen on the other side, " I hope your Reform Bill will be a very moderate measure; in fact, it cannot be too moderate for public opinion." And now, Sir, because this measure is brought forward by a Government they oppose, those same eminent persons, not contented with censuring its details, declare that it falls far short of their expectations; when if it had gone but a few feet further, if it had but touched the corner of that bench which the noble Lord the Member for London now adorns as a reluctant visitor, they would have said that it left Church and State behind it. Sir, that is very naturally the voice of party. I do not think it is the voice of public opinion; and if public opinion had a glass window to its bosom, we should there see among the better educated classes, on the whole, a preference to our bill, with all its shortcomings, rather than to any bill founded upon the principles which have been set forth in the only public meetings in which our bill has been denounced—principles against which I say nothing. If you want to know what is to be said against triennial Parliaments and vote by ballot, I refer you to the speeches of the noble Lords the Members for Tiverton and London. Well, then, in answer to the first question, What was the temper of public opinion; and when we undertook this bill what did it require? I say the temper of public opinion was listless. I say that it either required a measure quite as moderate as we propose ; or, if you tell us that public opinion has been lately represented in local public meetings, then I say it requires something which is not to be found in the amendment of the noble Lord. It requires something which no Whig Government could propose, and no conceivable Government at this time could hope to carry. I turn to the second question, put by the right hon. gentleman the Member for Stroud,—What was the amount of acknowledged evil? What was there that asked a remedy? Why, Sir, it could not be very large, for the right hon. Baronet the Member for Radnorshire,* with all his scholastic acuteness, did not, in addressing his constituents, appear to discover any evil at all. The evil could not be one very popularly felt, for the hon. gentleman the Member for Birmingham, with all his masculine eloquence, failed to get up an agitation commensurate to his talents and proportioned to his zeal. Still, there were these defects, which candid men upon all sides were disposed to admit. First, some large constituencies were unrepresented. Secondly, some large classes

* Sir George Cornewall Lewis.

did not possess the franchise. We addressed ourselves at once to these. As to the first, we found that the really large towns unrepresented were extremely few. To all those with populations approaching 20,000, we have given members; if we have omitted some that should be represented, prove the case, and it is a fair question of Committee; but reject the bill on account of that amendment, and you leave the towns we enfranchise still unrepresented. Secondly, there were large classes that did not possess the franchise. Now, should we really best obtain the remedy by the principle of the noble Lord's amendment, the lowering of the borough household franchise? No; for we should then equally exclude some of the intelligent and independent persons who live in lodgings, and have no house at all. We believe we have adopted a fair rental at 8s. a-week. Is the rental too high? prove the case— it is a fair question of Committee; but reject the bill on account of that amendment, and you leave those intelligent persons unrepresented. We desired to extend the principle of representation by admitting personal property of all kinds. We wished to bring that qualification down to a scale that might include the artisan if he has given proofs of thrift and foresight by investment in a savings bank. Have we made the amount of that investment too high? prove the case—it is a fair question of Committee; but reject the bill on account of that amendment, and you reject the principle that was honestly meant to include the superior artisan. We found it loudly complained, especially by hon. gentlemen opposite, that in counties there were many respectable persons living in towns and villages not represented, and excluded from a vote as residents in the county; these we resolved to enfranchise. We took the £10 occupier, and we gave him a vote for the county. We did so with large concession on our side. Why? I am not ashamed to say, because our subject, if possible, was conciliation. Do you object to the nature of that proposal as between lands and tenements? prove your case—it is a fair question of Committee; but reject the bill on account of that barren amendment, and I ask you whether this £10 occupier is to be enfranchised by the mere resolution of this House, or whether he is to wait for that other bill, which the right hon. gentleman the Member for Coventry (Mr Ellice) tells you a Liberal Government could not carry against the consent of the Conservatives, and which the right hon. gentleman the Member for Stroud tells you it is more than doubtful whether you could carry at all. I decline to accept the noble Lord's invitation, in the earlier part of his amendment ; I decline to allow the whole scheme of this measure to be judged piecemeal, by a clause which you can alone thoroughly discuss in Committee. Take but one single instance of the unfairness into which we are led, if we are once distracted from all that belongs to the broad outline of the bill on such a subject, into the investigation of details which can only be sifted at a later stage. The Member for Devonport, who preceded me, is an authority in facts and figures—he is a master of detail ; yet even he seeks to prejudice you against the second reading of the bill by an inaccuracy he would not, I am sure, have incurred, had we been in Committee on the clause ; for he said that our mode of dealing with the borough freeholds would create a fluctuating constituency between town and country for the next sixty years. But only allow the bill to go into Committee, and I think we shall be able to show that there will be no such floating constituency, as a voter must select between the two at the first registration. Again, the noble Lord says, " By withdrawing the borough freeholders from the counties, we withdraw the commercial element those freeholders represent." But he forgot to state that we give to the counties more than double the votes by occupiers of the votes withdrawn by the freeholders ; and if these occupiers should be for the most part the inhabitants of towns, they are more likely to be in trade than even the freeholders ; and thus the commercial element is not withdrawn, but probably it is doubled—more than doubled, if you add those who will obtain either the lodger franchise or that derived from personal property. Thus, I say, you cannot judge the whole bill by a single clause. You must compare one part with another. And to analyse the clause you object to would require a debate to itself. Meanwhile, I am contented to leave that part of the general measure to the able defence of my noble friend the Secretary of State for India. I go further, and say that, granting all the force you like to the noble Lord's objections, those objections apply to details you can consider in Committee ; and unless you say it is nothing to enfranchise the large towns now unrepresented—nothing to improve the registration—nothing to enfranchise new classes—nothing to admit the £10 occupier to a vote in counties,—you ought not to reject the second reading of the bill on account of a clause you have a later and a fuller opportunity to discuss. I pass on to the latter part of the noble Lord's amendment, which involves a more important question—I mean the lowering of the borough franchise. The difference between us is, that he would suddenly lower the borough franchise, and we would extend the general franchise of the nation ; while in admitting the principle of lodger franchise, of investments in a savings bank, of education as it advances becoming a qualification in itself, we not only extend the suffrage, but we open vistas for gradual reduction, according to the views to which some of the most thoughtful reformers have inclined more than they have done to the coarse substitute of a £6 or a £5 for a £10 house qualification. Surely education and independence ought to be the characteristics of a liberal suffrage ; surely you gain those much more through the educated persons who hire lodgings, than you do through the persons who are struggling with poverty in a £5 house. Take no very uncommon example : a retired servant, or a broken tradesman, hires a house and lets lodgings ; in those lodgings may live an artist, a banker's clerk, a man of letters, a superior artisan. The one retired servant or the broken tradesman alone has a vote ; the four educated men who lodge with him have none. Will you tell me that their four votes would not be of more value to the constituency in the right choice of a member than the votes of four £5 householders if you added them to the constituency instead ? Now, Sir, so far as regards the mere interest of the Conservative party in this House, I have always said, and I still think, that the lowering of the borough franchise would be no disadvantage to us, and might indirectly be of advantage. No disadvantage, because I take it for granted that the disposition of all the larger towns will be to return candidates of the opposite party. Whether those candidates are returned by a £10 or a £5 constituency could, therefore, in no way affect the balance of party in this House. Indirectly it might be an advantage to us that gentlemen opposite should be chosen by a £5 constituency rather than a £10. And why? Because a party does not depend on its numbers alone; it depends on the dignity, the independence, the education, and, on the whole, the moderate good sense of its representatives. I believe you gain all those qualities better under a £10 constituency than under a £5. I believe the worst enemy an upright reformer can have is not a Conservative gentleman; it is a demagogic adventurer. Once adopt a very low suffrage in your towns, and are you sure that in the present state of popular education the upright reformer would not be often displaced by the demagogic adventurer? That would be your loss; indirectly it would be our gain. Our gain, because you would no longer be the same formidable candidates for power. Violent politicians may make a troublesome and unscrupulous Opposition, but they could never unite to form the Queen's Government. If we wanted to destroy the moral power of your party, we would give you the lowest suffrage you like to ask; because, lower the franchise beneath £10 in counties, lower it to £5, and you would bring our own village labourers into the franchise, and thus place numbers under the influence of property. That would be our gain. But in towns it is different. Lower the franchise in towns, and the lower you go the more you place numbers under the control of ignorance and passion. That would be your loss. But, far from wishing to destroy your party, I consider it essential to freedom that the Liberal party in this House should be always strong; and if I ask you to pause before you lower too much the borough franchise, it is because I am convinced you cannot be always strong if you create a constituency that does not secure to Liberal members the same high standard of integrity and culture. But do not let gentlemen who represent the smaller boroughs credulously believe that you can by any political logic lower the franchise in boroughs without also destroying the smaller boroughs; the two principles must go together. For why lower the franchise in boroughs except to take population more into account, and except to enfranchise a larger number of the superior part of the working class? You cannot, therefore, by your principle preserve the smaller towns to the exclusion of the larger; you cannot pass over the artisans of larger towns, where intelligence is most diffused, in order to enfranchise the artisans of smaller boroughs, with a less rate of wages, and probably a less degree of education. Therefore you cannot separate the two. To lower the borough franchise is to annihilate the smaller boroughs. Are there any members for such boroughs so guileless and lamb-like as to be caught by the noble Lord's ensnaring amendment and seductive tongue? Yes, Sir, there is one, the Member for Sandwich—

> "Pleased to the last he crops his flowery food,
> And licks the hand just raised to shed his blood."

But when those smaller boroughs are destroyed, what then? To what constituencies will they be transferred? Do not think we did not carefully examine that subject. We might have given what is called a more comprehensive, and might have been a more popular measure. We might have swept away 80, 90, 100, 120, boroughs. But, had we done so, it appeared clear to us, as it does to my noble friend who spoke so well last night (Lord Robert Cecil), that the majority of the seats taken from the boroughs ought to be given to the counties. The noble Lord in his last Reform Bill arrived at the same conclusion. If we had done this you would have said, "We undertook a Reform Bill in order to serve our party." We did not do this. We would not, in the present state of Europe, provoke that town and county quarrel which renders always so difficult, and at this time so dangerous, the question of any large redistribution of seats. Having resolved that our measure should be moderate, we resolved that, as between party and party, it should be fair. But whenever you open that question of a wide redistribution, then, on every ground of justice, the counties will ask a larger proportion of seats than they now possess. But grant that you put aside our pretensions; grant that you get the kind of Reform Bill you require, and that this House is swayed and this country governed by a large preponderance of great urban populations with a very low franchise. Sir, let us face that question fairly. It is one far more important than the party battle which the noble Lord's amendment presents to the ardour of some, and forces on the distaste of many who support it. This question—namely, a preponderance of large urban constituencies with a very low franchise—has the deepest interest to us all as well-educated men anxious for the dignity of our councils and the continued power of the House of Commons. Pause for a moment—reflect. What do you seek? What is your object? The increase of popular freedom? Be it so. Popular freedom is not secured by the machinery that returns representatives; its security is in the power the representative assembly will exercise over that highest class of minds which first guide and then consolidate the public opinion of a civilised state. That power must be intellectual, or it has no duration. That power all reforms must tend to increase, or they are worse than worthless. Fatal mistake, if in augmenting the constituency we lower the character of the assembly that represents it! From one end of Europe to the other, freedom is strengthened or enfeebled not by the numbers which bear her into our councils, but in proportion as, once installed amongst us, we preserve or endanger her attributes to confidence and respect. Well, then, the power and dignity of the House of Commons. That is the object, and all reforms are but as means to maintain it. Sir, first let us see what the House of Commons really is. It is not merely a popular assembly, it is a deliberative assembly. It arrogates inquiry, and decides upon all the most complicated questions of policy both at home and abroad. It is this in which it strikingly differs from our free colonies, to which we may accord the most popular suffrage. A colonial legislature is little more than a vestry on a great scale. It does not provide even for its own military defences. It does not touch upon foreign affairs. All those matters belong to the imperial government. It is this, too, in which the House of Commons differs from the popular Assembly of America. In that Assembly foreign affairs are seldom discussed, except when they relate to tariffs or the disposition of public money. Foreign affairs belong by right to the Senate, when they escape from the Select Committee of the Senate to which they are more habitually consigned. And the Senate itself, in discussing the ratification of treaties and public appointments, becomes an executive body, excludes reporters, and sits with closed doors. Even in domestic matters the debates in the American popular Assembly never excite the same interest, nor carry with them the same weight, as the debates in the Senate do. The guiding intellect of America is in her oligarchical Senate, not in her popular Chamber. And why? Because the American House of Representatives is what you would make this House of Commons,—so popular in its constituent elements — so brought down to the level of the masses—that even the masses have small respect for its wisdom; and it is to the Senate that the grand republic looks for deliberate judgment upon the graver matters which involve its honour and affect its national interests. It is not so as yet in England. The brain and the heart of England are still in the House of Commons. The wisest of our people have still a paramount interest in our debates ; the greatest potentates of Europe have still a reverence for your decisions. But once Americanise the House of Commons and you would lose more in the intellectual attributes that create your real power than you could obtain by all the popular vigour you could get through manhood suffrage and electoral districts. One reason for the moderation and dignity which pervade our councils is to be found in this—that we have not as yet, on the whole, lowered our suffrage beyond the fair standard of education which ought to be required from an English voter. I grant that in all the very large towns, even under the present franchise, the suffrage is practically so low that democracy may be said to prevail. But it is the retention of those small boroughs where the franchise, though apparently the same, is really higher, which gives us that calm wisdom and fair intelligence which interposes, as the Member for Devonport has well said, between rival interests—between the agricultural classes

on the one hand, and the great urban populations on the other.
I do not say that this or any other argument would avail to save
those smaller boroughs in proportion as the larger towns grow
up in wealth and importance. But, in the meanwhile, you need
not be in a hurry to get rid of a machinery which adds to the
power of this House by insuring the varied accomplishments of
its members and increasing the number of competitors for the
Government of the country. This advantage I do not think is
to be counterbalanced merely by transferring the seats taken from
smaller boroughs either to counties or to towns already represented, and thus diminishing the number of members who have
nothing but the business of the State to think of. And I do fear,
that whenever that transfer is effected, whenever the smaller
boroughs wholly vanish out of our system, you will realise the
same evil which America has long felt, which our free colonies,
such as Canada and Australia, begin to feel already—namely,
that when only very popular constituencies exist, members become rather delegates than representatives ; men of large property, of refined education, of independent character, decline to
enter into political life, and the popular Assembly ceases to represent, what this House now does, the highest and noblest elements of the general community. Sir, in the curious correspondence between Mirabeau and the Count de la Marcke, in which
the Count was engaged in obtaining Mirabeau's aid to save the
monarchy, Mirabeau said (I forget his exact words, but they are
to this effect) : "You have adopted from aristocracy the most
dangerous of its elements—namely, the influence of money ; you
have adopted from democracy the most fatal of its properties—
namely, the influence of great towns over rural districts." Mirabeau was right. Of all aristocracies, that of money is at once
the most corrupting to popular virtue, and the most timid in
defending institutions. Of all democracies, that of great towns
is most fickle in the choice of its favourites. Freedom has no
surety in popular favourites ; they may begin as the demagogue
—they may end as the tyrant. Freedom has no enemy so fatal
as the favourite, who may push its advancement one inch beyond
the boundaries of order. Mirabeau was right. The monarchy

went. What went with it? Did not liberty go? Monarchy, in one shape or other, was soon restored; monarchy reigns still. Has liberty been restored as well? What killed liberty? The democracy of large towns, and the terror which that democracy itself had of its own excesses. But democracy in France still exists—a democracy of universal suffrage and vote by ballot. Pardon me if I prefer the freedom of which this House, with its tempered suffrage, is still the guardian—a freedom safe, because education controls and property does not fear it. Hon. gentlemen ask, "Are you afraid of the working man?" Certainly not; we country gentlemen, by the nature of our pursuits, by the habits of our lives, are brought of necessity into an intercourse with the village workmen around us, more familiar, more friendly, than can well exist between the employer and the operative in great towns. We are not likely to fear the working man. And for my part I am proud of the English workman, whether he be the simple village peasant, with his homely virtues, or that more agitated, but, amid all his faults, that noble human being, the skilled mechanic of our manufacturing towns, with his thirst for knowledge and his dreams of some political Utopia quite as rational as Plato himself had dreamed before him. But it is one thing to admire the individual, to respect the class he belongs to—one thing to devise modes, by which every individual amongst it who gives proof of intelligence by forethought for the morrow, or who by the investment of earnings, however modest, wins a stake in the preservation of order, shall come welcome and honoured into the franchise—and it is another thing to say that to that class you will intrust all the destinies of England. I would intrust the destinies of England to no single class whatever; but if you admit the working men, as a body, their numbers alone give them a large majority in every constituency, and thus all the education and property of the other classes must be borne down by that class in which education is of necessity the least diffused, and by which all the intricate laws that, if only through political economy, affect the interests of property, must be the most imperfectly understood. And here, Sir, I do complain of the dangerous want of candour with which hon. gentlemen op-

posite have made their appeal to the working class—the noble
Lord the Member for London, and the right hon. Baronet the
Member for Halifax (Sir Charles Wood), both say that the fault
of the bill is, that it does not admit the working class. They
dwell on this objection ; they inflame the working men with the
belief that they shall come into the franchise not by threes and
fours, but by hundreds and thousands ; and then, in the same
breath, they declare that they have no idea of admitting the
numbers whose expectations they so cruelly excite. No, you do
not admit the numbers, but you lay down the principle by which
they must be either admitted or deceived. You would lower the
suffrage on the express principle that it ought to include the working class. Does it do so by the mysterious franchise which the
noble Lord would give, but declines to divulge ? then the evil is
accomplished. Does it not do so ? then you have equally conceded
the principle that must accomplish the evil ; for the workmen excluded by the suffrage you restrict will never rest till they are admitted by the principle you allow. And I venture to predict, when
you talk of our releasing the elements of democracy—and upon
this subject I have heard some of the most deplorable rubbish that
ever was talked by educated men—that whenever the noble Lord
and the Member for Halifax bring forward their measure, and the
workmen as a class find that they do not pour in their countless
multitudes through the door those gentlemen will keep ajar with
a chain across it, there will be among them one cry of angry disappointment. But I may be asked, " Would you never lower the
borough franchise at all, or do you mean to say that the working
class are to be everlastingly excluded ? " To both these questions
I answer, " I make no such assertion." With regard to the borough franchise, I can but place before you, in no hostile spirit, the
reasons why I think you should pause before you insist on any
great reduction ; but I do say, it is your duty to tell us to what
extent you would go. Show us the numbers below the present
£10 constituency which your franchise would give, and then clearly
ascertain whether your constituents desire you to swamp them.
As to the future admission of the working class, I ask not the
noble Lord to give us all the details of the bill that he would pro-

pose ; but I do say, that when a statesman so eminent invites the
agitation of the working class against the measure proposed by the
Queen's Government, he incurs to that working class a very solemn
responsibility ; and he owes it to them, he owes it to his country,
to make clear whether that for which the working class are to
agitate is or is not that which he is prepared to concede. For myself, I cannot but think that at heart I go farther than the noble
Lord ; I go farther than most of the great republican writers, ancient and modern : I go in theory as far as Mr John Mill, and I
would not object to the widest possible suffrage, if you can effect
a contrivance by which intelligence shall still prevail over numbers.
If that be impossible, then I say, at least, the first step towards
anything that approaches to universal suffrage should be something
that approaches to universal education. But this I repeat, that
when you invite the agitation of the working class against this
measure, you should not only tell us what you refuse from us, you
should make it distinct and unequivocal what you would give, and
then let the country decide between the two.   Sir, Lord Plunket,
in one of his great forensic speeches, said—" Time is represented
with the hour-glass as well as the scythe." True ; with the scythe
he mows down—by the aid of the hour-glass he metes the duration of that which he intends to destroy : let me add to Lord
Plunket's grand image—by the aid of the hour-glass Time also
must reckon the moment for that which he designs to construct.
You would borrow from Time the scythe ; have you consulted his
hour-glass? You would mow down this Government and this Reform Bill. Granted. Look at the hour-glass! What Government
and what Reform Bill will you reconstruct? So far as this Government is concerned, I will not defend at this moment its alleged
faults—I will not at this moment ask if it has had no merits; nor
will I, even now, when gentlemen opposite are arrayed against it,
ungratefully forget the patriotic countenance it has received amidst
its earlier but not its greater difficulties. All I would say is, our
intentions in this bill, amidst the general state of England and of
Europe, are not such as to merit the censure of any high-minded
Liberal. I grant the bill is not one which gentlemen below the
gangway would give if it were their task to make one ; but, so far

as the Government is concerned, I ask those very gentlemen, as
men of honour, if Lord Derby's Government had passed a bill according to your models, though you would have accepted the bill,
would you not have despised its authors ?   Should we not have
been traitors to those we represent ?   We should have come into
your camp, not as now, with a fair flag of truce and overtures of
mutual compromise, but with standards trailed in the dust, and
offering up the keys of every fortress which the loyalty of our partisans had confided to our charge.   No ! If a Reform Bill, such as
you desire, must be carried, it is for you to propose it; it is not
for us.   But, before you raise the scythe to mow us down, look
again at the hour-glass !   What is to be the next Government ?
Can it last if the Member for Birmingham and the noble Viscount,
if the Member for Sheffield and the Member for London, do not
sit on the same Treasury bench ?   Can it last if they do ?   In either
case the sands in the hour-glass will be violently shaken.   So much
for this Government.   One moment more to this bill.   It is said
not to be final.   No Reform Bill can be.   The fault you allege is
its merit.   It is its merit if it meets some of the requirements of
the day present, and does not give to-day what you may regret
to-morrow that you cannot restore.   Democracy is like the grave—
it perpetually cries " Give, give ; " and, like the grave, it never returns what it has once taken.   But you live under a constitutional
monarchy, which has all the vigour of health, all the energy of
movement.   Do not surrender to democracy that which is not yet
ripe for the grave.   Gentlemen employ much sarcastic cavil in the
dispute as to what is the main principle of this bill.   I say, as
Lord Macaulay said in the debate on the old Reform Bill, I care
little for technical definitions on that score.   I would not base the
defence of this or of any Reform Bill upon an abstract dogma on
which special pleaders may differ.   I would take that which was
our main object for the backbone and life-spring of the bill.   That
main object, so admirably stated by my noble friend the Secretary
for India, was, irrespectively of party interests, to confirm and extend to the middle class the political power which, during the last
twenty-seven years, they have exercised, so as to render liberty
progressive and institutions safe ; but at the same time to widen

the franchise the middle class now enjoys, so that it may include all belonging to the class who are now without a vote ; and, instead of bringing the middle-class franchise down to the level of the workmen, lift into that franchise the artisan who may have risen above the daily necessities of the manual labourer by the exercise of economy and forethought. The bill therefore, I own it, is emphatically a bill for the middle class. The cause is theirs ; it is not the cause of the aristocrat ; it is not the cause of the Conservative country gentleman, who, of all parties concerned, now tenders the largest concession. The cause is that of the middle class, down to the verge at which the influence of that class would melt away amidst the necessities of manual labour and the turbulence of concentred numbers. If they of the middle class like to abandon that cause, they abdicate their own power, and with it all which has hitherto made the resources of England unshaken amidst the vicissitudes of commerce and the calamities of war. If they honestly think the time has come when it is safe to accept the counter-principle which you advance — namely, that political power should descend to the working class—not knowing, so far as I can judge by the language of popular meetings, where that principle, once adopted, can stop till it reaches manhood suffrage,—then I say with the middle class the responsibility must rest. Meanwhile you in this House will determine whether it is your duty thus abruptly to sign away the influence of that class of which you are still the representatives and trustees,—whether you really secure the title-deeds of their commerce, and take solid guarantees for the safety of their old English freedom, by accepting an amendment which commits you to a pledge to the working class—a pledge which you can never redeem to their satisfaction until you have placed capital and knowledge at the command of impatient poverty and uninstructed numbers.

XXIX.

A SPEECH

DELIVERED IN

THE HOUSE OF COMMONS

On the 26th of April 1860.

On Monday, the 19th of March 1860, the Secretary of State for Foreign Affairs, Lord John Russell, moved the Second Reading of the Bill to Amend the Representation of the People in England and Wales. After a discussion which lasted for six nights, the motion was agreed to without a division. On the fourth night of the debate the following speech was delivered.

Sir,—The debate has hitherto chiefly turned on the quality and nature of the proposed borough franchise. It is evident from the speech of the hon. member who has just sat down,* that this involves a question on which gentlemen opposite have an interest fully equal to our own ; I shall therefore so far imitate his example, that I will endeavour to state my views in a spirit that shall be as free from party bias as I can possibly form and express it; and as I think it very important that we should have clear perceptions of the nature of our dispute, and of the consequences of any mistake we may commit, I will first entreat the House to bear with me for a few minutes, while I try to

* Mr Black.

consider whether, at least, we cannot agree as to some broad principle upon which all good representative systems should be based. Sir, I will assume that every popular reformer, and every sound political thinker, who seeks to estimate the proper standard at which to fix an electoral franchise, must, in abstract theory, start from the same point;—and that point is the *primâ facie* right of manhood suffrage. Where you find a civilised community in which all the members are equally free, and where, by a system of indirect duties, every man is more or less taxed to the support of the State, I can readily understand that every man should consider that he has a *primâ facie* right to vote for those who superintend his affairs and regulate the machinery by which his welfare is controlled. But here, from the origin of all political societies, commences another view of that same question, upon which popular reformers may differ—I do not know if they do—but on which all who are acknowledged to be sound political thinkers are agreed ; and it is this : granting that every man in a free community may thus put forward his claim to the electoral franchise, still every member of a community merges all his individual rights, and many rights much nearer and dearer to him than an electoral franchise, in the paramount consideration how the State itself can be best sustained for the general safety and the social advancement ; or, in the words of the hon. gentleman who has just spoken, how "the greatest happiness of the greatest number" can be secured from attacks without and within, from foreign dangers or its own mistakes, for the longest probable period. The Member for Edinburgh says that he would wish to see established some definite principle by which we might construct our measure, and by which we might test its details. That which he asks has been the object of research to political reasoners for more than two thousand years ; but I think the substance of all that has been said by those whom we hold to be authorities may be found in this very simple definition : a free State will be thus best sustained and advanced by securing to its legislative councils the highest average degree of the common sense of the common interest. For this, intelligence is requisite, but not

intelligence alone; you might have a legislative assembly composed of men indisputably intelligent—nobles, lawyers, priests
—who might honestly believe they used their intelligence for
the common interest, when in fact they used it for their own.
Hence it follows that no one class interest must predominate
over all the others, or the common interest is gone; gone if
that class be the great proprietors—gone if that class be the
working men. But there is this distinction between the working class and every other, that, granting their intelligence
to be equal to that of others, granting that it be not more
likely to be misdirected, still, when it is misdirected, the consequences are, if they are invested with the electoral power that
determines legislation, immeasurably more dangerous both to
the common interest and to their own. For they are the roots
of society, and it is the roots of society that their errors will
affect; while their numbers are so great that their votes could
overpower the votes of all the other classes put together. When
this happens, the instinctive safeguard of the rich is corruption ;
and the instinctive tendency of ambition, if it be not rich, is towards those arts which give dictatorship to demagogues.

The hon. and learned Member for Marylebone has done me
the honour to quote expressions of mine in praise of the labourer
and mechanic. I neither retract that praise, nor the qualification with which it was then accompanied. The working class
have virtues singularly noble and generous, but they are obviously more exposed than the other classes to poverty and to
passion. Thus, in quiet times, their poverty subjects them to
the corruption of the rich ; and in stormy times, when the State
requires the most sober judgment, their passion subjects them
to the ambition of the demagogue. To every man who has read
history, these are not unsupported propositions. The history of
all the old republics is uniform as to their truth; and as in all
those old republics, at least where democracy was established,
vote by ballot was employed, so the same history tells us that
vote by ballot is no cure for the evils. Hence it is that those
eminent writers on the Liberal side who have lately examined
this very question of a new franchise for England with political

courage as well as speculative acuteness, have all specially dwelt
on the extreme danger of basing that new franchise rudely and
exclusively upon a principle that, once conceded, must expand
—a principle that, by avowedly reducing your borough franchise
so as to admit manual labour without any equipoise, without
any test or condition beyond that of finding a roof to cover it
at 2s. 4d. a-week, must end by giving to manual labour the
political power over the capital that employs and the mind that
should direct it. An hon. member in the course of this debate
referred to the opinions of Mr John Mill, than whom no severer
reasoner adorns our age; but what are Mr Mill's opinions?
Sternly against all the arguments by which the proposed franchise is defended. He would give, it is true, a vote to every
man; but in order to counteract the effect of numbers so created,
he would give to a man of superior education or property, such
as a farmer or a tradesman, four or five votes—to a man of
still higher education and property, five or six votes. More
lately Mr Mill has declared in favour of the scheme propounded
by Mr Hare and explained by Mr Fawcett in a very remarkable
pamphlet; a scheme that is based upon the principle of securing
representation even to the smallest minorities. These ideas are
so against the taste of the House and the inclination of the
public, that their adoption may be impossible; but I mention
them to show that here are consummate reasoners whose doctrines of government belong to the boldest school of Liberal
opinion, and who are yet more anxious than the highest Tory
amongst us to secure to property and intelligence a power that
shall not be overborne by the influence of numbers.

The Member for Birmingham says there is no cause to fear
the influence of numbers or of the working class in the bill that
is now before us. He says, firstly, that the proposed addition as
regards the boroughs is not considerable; secondly, that the total
constituency will still be very small in proportion to the adult
male population. But the Member for Birmingham fails to see
or to grapple with the argument of my right hon. friend the
Member for Buckinghamshire. It is not with my right hon.
friend a question of numbers alone, but rather of fitness. In

fact, though I accept the assurance of the right hon. gentleman
the Home Secretary, that the most conscientious pains were
taken to obtain accurate returns, yet he must pardon me if I say
that, without entering into the dispute between him and the
Member for Marylebone, those returns must seem incredible to
any gentleman who will use his own powers of inquiry and
observation—for a £6 house is a house at 2s. 4d. a-week; but if
any gentleman will inquire in the small rural towns or even the
large villages in his neighbourhood, he will find that there are
scarcely any houses in them that are let to the most ordinary
artisans at less than 2s. 6d. a-week; but if 2s. 6d. a-week be the
lowest rent paid by a journeyman labourer in a small rural town,
what must it be in a populous borough where the average rental
cannot fail to be higher? Just consider. Many gentlemen,
no doubt, have built plain cottages for their own day-labourers;
those cottages cannot cost them less than about £80 each: they
would be contented with a small interest for their money, because, as it is truly said by the Duke of Bedford, who has conferred benefits on the working classes, the more signal, because
so nobly unostentatious, " the country gentleman does not build
cottages for immediate remuneration;" but in a borough town
such houses are built on speculation by small capitalists, who
would not be satisfied with less than 7½ or 8 per cent for their
outlay—that is, more than 2s. 4d. a-week, for a house equal to
the humblest cottage you build for your humblest labourer.
But, granting the returns to be correct as to the present number
of £6 householders, they can afford no criterion of what the
number of £6 voters would be if this bill passed into a law; for
the poor labourer who now pays 2s. a-week for a house (and less
than that he could scarcely pay for any hovel in a borough
town) would gladly pay 2s. 4d. to secure a vote as a good speculation, which will give him a claim on the wealthier tradesmen
of the town who take an interest in elections, should he want a
job of work or a charitable donation at Christmas—those small
gleanings of calculating benevolence which are the perquisites
of poor electors; and on the other hand, a landlord who now
lets houses at 2s. or 2s. 2d. a-week will screw them up to 2s.

4d., in order to increase his political importance by having a numerous tenantry at his command, in constitutional proof of the legitimate influence of property. And you must take with you the fact, which you seem to ignore—namely, that every year, as the prosperity and population of the country increase, the £6 franchise will become wider and wider as to numbers, lower and lower as to the condition of the voter. The £10 occupation is now, in the larger towns, a very much lower franchise than it was thirty years ago. You are legislating for posterity in a direction you can never retrace; and in less than thirty years a £6 franchise must, in the larger towns, be equivalent to household suffrage. We have therefore no fair criterion as to numbers; but in the meanwhile we find, even by your returns, that the addition proposed is quite enough to overbear the existing constituency in a great proportion of the present boroughs; it must materially influence elections in most of the others. We then ask if that addition be composed of a variety of classes; we find it is confined to a single class, and we object to overbear the existing constituency by a single class, without any equipoise or relief.

I shall make our distinction more clear by proceeding at once to the second assertion of the Member for Birmingham. He says that the entire constituency, which he estimates at 1,000,000, will be very small, compared to the adult male population, which he estimates at 7,000,000. But when he would thus make manhood suffrage a standard by which to compose a suffrage that, if more limited, should fairly represent the diversified character and opinions of the whole adult male population, he forgets to omit from his 7,000,000 not only about 700,000 paupers, whom we will put aside, but more than a million and a half composed of soldiers, sailors, mercantile marine, domestic servants, and rural peasants; voters whose tendencies might counteract the opinions of the special class this bill selects for the franchise. And the right way to look at the present suffrage, and at the proposed addition, is evidently this: The present suffrage is a selection, made less than thirty years ago, from those classes of the male population with which popular liberty is most safe;

excluding rural peasants, as too much under the influence of
landed aristocracy—domestic servants, as too much under the
influence of masters—soldiers and sailors, as too much under the
influence of the Crown. But if, while you continue to exclude
from your constituency large masses of the population that represent Conservative elements, you admit a new element, which
our common sense tells us must be exclusively democratic, you
destroy the fair equipoise of representation even by numbers,
and you do not impartially extend the area of a national franchise, but you pervert a national franchise into the monopoly of
a single class. I close, then, this part of my argument with
these plain propositions: First, that it is not consulting the
common sense of the common interest; secondly, that it is not
a fair application of the doctrine of representation by numbers,
to introduce into a constituency already so popular, that in
this vast metropolis, and in many of our great towns, the richer
classes are not represented at all, a new selection from that
special class of artisans, who, crowded together in large towns,
always have been, and always will be, the most democratic and
the most excitable part of the population, without any selection
of an opposite tendency,—so that the more some town has been
rendered populous and flourishing by expenditure of capital
and activity of educated intellect, the less capital and educated
intellect will have a voice in the representation of the place, the
prosperity of which they created and maintain.

And now, Sir, let me observe that it was well said by my
hon. friend the Member for Leominster, in a speech which the
Home Secretary censures for being animated—I cannot retort
the charge on the right hon. gentleman, who spoke as if " he
came to bury Cæsar, not to praise him "—that much of this
argument has been conducted on premises that are not strictly
true. It has been too much assumed that all the working class
are excluded by the present franchise. We are asked to open
the door to them, as if the door had been kept rigidly locked
and barred against them. But is that the case? I apprehend
that in all the metropolitan boroughs artisans must form a considerable part of the constituency. In fact, if your returns are

correct, and if we must prefer them to the calculations of the
Member for Marylebone, it is clear that the main reason why
artisans living in houses below a £10 rental will not add considerably to the metropolitan constituencies, must be because a
large number of artisans in metropolitan constituencies live in
houses that are not below a £10 rental. But, take any borough,
any county,—have not all and each of us several working men
among our constituents? The working classes are therefore
admitted at present. The door is not locked. You say, admit
more, many more; open the door much wider. Very well, do
so; but since you cannot admit them all, let us try and establish some better test than that of a certain amount of poverty.
Do not lower your franchise upon the express principle of admitting the poor solely and wholly because they are poor. The
Member for Halifax, in a speech of much promise, and in the
excellent taste of a gentleman who can unite ardour for a cause
with courtesy to opponents, said, " The best test of fitness for
the franchise is the desire to possess the franchise." Let him
reflect for a moment, and he is too good a logician not to see
that his position is untenable. Desire is no proof of fitness.
We all desire to be rich—is that any proof that we all deserve
riches? We all desire to be strong, healthy, and wise, and how
few of us take the smallest pains to be strong, healthy, or wise?
We must have, then, a better test than desire.

In our bill, we, the late Government, sought to take that
simplest test by which the human being vindicates his claim
to reason—I mean the habit of, frugality and forethought
for the morrow in the man who lives by the labour of the day.
We thus did expand the franchise to the working class, not by
regarding such voters as the mere symbols of four crazy walls,
but in proportion—I do not say as they had a stake in the
country, for every child just born has a stake in his native
country,—but in proportion as they showed they were sensible
of that stake, and had by the mere exercise of a virtue most
useful to themselves—the mere principle of saving for the uncertain morrow—entered into the class of proprietors, and had
become participators in that prudent regard for order which is

the safeguard of property, and the main distinction between
liberty, which is always thoughtful, and licence, which is always
reckless. You dismiss these attempts of ours to modify, refine,
and exalt a mere popular franchise—dismiss them without one
effort of your own to improve them ; and I believe they could
be greatly improved and enlarged by a Government in whom
reformers had confidence, and whom this House honoured with
a majority ; you dismiss not only our notions, but all the re-
monstrances and all the warnings of your own ablest writers,
and you who came into power upon the presumption of superior
capacities for a comprehensive scheme, content yourselves with
what ?—rudely creating an additional constituency upon the
express and sole principle that it is to be poorer and less intelligent than the present, without a single franchise of a higher
nature ; and you make that addition so numerous that in most
of those large towns which are the centres of energy, which the
Member for Rochdale once told us " govern England," it is that
poor and less intelligent class which must take the lion's share
of political power.   And when we are told by the hon. Member
for Birmingham and the hon. Member for Leeds, that a £6
franchise is not so rigidly confined to the working class but
what there are several £6 occupiers who are not actually working men, I say that in no way touches our objection.   They are
equally men subjected to the conditions of poverty and passion ;
and though we are willing to admit poverty and passion into the
franchise, we are not willing to give poverty and passion the
lion's share of political power over capital and knowledge.   And
I say this, not as against the representation of the working or
the poorer classes, but on behalf of their genuine and true representation ; for if you reflect a moment you will own that their
true representation must be more or less perfect in proportion to
the knowledge which may exist in this House of the inseparable
connection between their interests and all our legislative
functions.

  The Chancellor of the Exchequer, in a speech which, whatever
we may think of the Budget it introduced, will remain among
the monuments of English eloquence as long as the language

lasts, told us truly that " the interest of the working man was consulted less by our cheapening the articles he consumes, than by our stimulating the trade which gives him wages and employment." I advance upon that argument, and I say, therefore, that the true representative of the working man is in every wise legislator who stimulates trade, who strengthens credit, who exalts the standard of society, in which the working man rises with every step that raises the common interest of us all. I say that he has a true representative in every profound lawyer who renders justice more accessible; in every enlightened philanthropist who ameliorates the condition of humanity; nay, in every naval or military officer whose professional science suggests sounder defences, not only for the land we inhabit, but for the protection of the commerce which employs the millions, and which rises or falls with the honour of the flag that is only the safeguard of our wealth because it is the symbol of our power. But, are these the kind of representatives the working class would generally prefer if they constituted the great majority of electors? I say boldly, No. For even in America, where education is far more equally diffused than it is with us, it is the common complaint that such are not the kind of representatives they prefer. Just hear what is said on that score by an American addressing his fellow-citizens—not a political malcontent declaiming on a popular hustings, but a man of high education (Mr Doherty) calmly addressing the literary societies of Lafayette College, and the title of his lecture is " Fears for the Future of the Republic." After stating, as a well-known fact, that the more respectable citizens even of the commercial and industrial classes will tell you that they " scorn to mix in politics, their time can be better employed," he goes on to say: " Thus, the vast machinery of this huge republic in all its departments is for the most part left to the control of bands of men who make politics a trade—men who laugh at integrity, are insensible to patriotism, are regardless of intellect—who hate the man who tells the truth and will not cringe to them, and love the one who lowest bends, yet cheats them in the end. . . . Surely it is of vital importance to the wellbeing of a State that its legis-

lature reflect the wishes of the people. . . . Yet there are those
who legislate for the different States of the American Confeder-
acy who are unable to read, much less to frame a statute; who
know nothing of our past history, present wants, or future
prospects; who are ignorant of the constitution, and would not
dare to fill the humblest of clerkships, yet occupy seats in legislative halls. But their ignorance is their least fault. Corruption
swarms around each capitol, daring the gaze and defying the
power of outraged constituencies; legislation is bought and
sold. Within a year it has come to light that in one of the
vigorous States of the west, the majority of the legislature, with
many of the State officers, in violation of their oaths and of
honour, were purchased each for a given price. Better for us
and for our posterity, better for our peace at home, our character
abroad, that the legislature of Pennsylvania should meet but
once in ten years, than that the State should be disgraced by
such representatives and dishonoured by such laws." Yet these
are the representatives whom the majority of the working classes
elect, and these are the laws those representatives pass, uninflu-
enced by that aristocracy to whom the hon. Member for Birmingham ascribes all the evils we endure.

So much for America. Now look to England. Let me ask
who in our time has been the man who has had the largest
share of the especial confidence of the working classes? Not
the hon. Member for Birmingham. No; it was Mr Feargus
O'Connor. And is there any member present who would say
that at this moment the interests of the working classes are not
better represented in this House by such gentlemen as I have
described, and whom we may recognise wherever we direct our
eyes, than they would be if they could turn this House into a
synagogue of Feargus O'Connors? But this bill is to amend the
representation. How will it do that? Will it make the House
of Commons wiser? Will it make our councils more enlightened?
Will it increase the knowledge, the integrity, the pecuniary independence, and the mental discipline, without which we should
have no strength in public opinion if ever we had to protect our
freedom against an able tyrant and a standing army? We read

in that masterly contribution to our history which Mr Forster has just published, that when Charles I. attempted illegally to seize five members of this House, all London rang with cries of "Parliament!" "Privilege!" and why? Because at that moment this House represented property, station, and knowledge, as well as patriotism and valour; and therefore it had strength in public opinion. But a few years later Cromwell expelled all the members, and locked up the House itself; and there were then no cries of "Parliament!" "Privilege!" There was scarcely a murmur heard out of doors. Why was that? Because the House was then only a Rump Parliament. It had ceased to represent property, station, and knowledge; and therefore it had no strength in public opinion, though its majority, even then, were stanch reformers; nay, they were actually discussing a new Reform Bill, not altogether different from that of the hon. Member for Birmingham, at the very moment Cromwell and his pikemen entered. Is there any gentleman here who will tell us he expects to return to Parliament a wiser man—a sadder man, perhaps, he may be—when he knows he has ceased to represent property, station, and knowledge, and has become the delegate of the poorest householders in the borough he represents?

But how will this measure improve the constituent body? When that question was asked in the debates on the great Reform Bill, the answer of the reformers was crushing. You then got rid of the boroughmonger, who sold his borough—of the potwalloper, who sold his vote; and your substitutes were trade, commerce, manufactures—that combination of various interests which is found in the middle ranks of society, which cannot be called a class, because it comprises all classes, from the educated gentleman to the skilled artisan, and which, therefore, does represent a high average of the common sense of the common interest. You then did not merely extend the franchise. The Home Secretary has taken pains to prove that. To use the words, I think, of the late Lord Grey, "you purified, you exalted the constituency." But when you are asked, "How does the little Reform Bill purify and exalt the constituency?" what

will you answer ?   You will say, " It is true we found many
persons of respectable means and excellent education, who complained that they were without a suffrage ; we did not attend to
their complaint, but where we found persons living in lanes and
alleys, at a rent which afforded the fair presumption that they
had little property and less education, we conferred our new
franchise exclusively on them.   And so we purified and exalted
the constituency ! "

Sir, let me venture to give you an illustration of the manner
in which the little Reform Bill will probably work out the
amendment of the representation, and purify and exalt the constituency.   I will first assume that the state of the world
renders it likely that for some years to come our party differences will occur upon questions affecting our foreign relations.
Let me suppose some such question on which Parliament has
been dissolved, some question that shall not trespass on what we
should now call delicate relations ; only perhaps a new quarrel
with China.   Nothing more likely than that !   Suddenly, then,
there appear before your new constituency in one of those
boroughs which the noble Lord reserves as the nursery of rising
genius and the refuge of ill-treated statesmen, two dignified and
imposing persons, whom that new constituency do not know
from Adam : but these are rival candidates ; Thomson is a rising
genius, Browne an ill-treated statesman ; Thomson supports the
Government—genius that rises generally supports a Government;
Browne sides with the Opposition—ill-treated statesmen naturally do.   They both proceed to canvass Mr Smith, one of your
new electors, a journeyman plasterer—the hon. Member for
Leeds thinks that plasterers are entitled to a preferential difference—living in a frail tenement, much in need of plaster, and
struggling hard to pay off a harassing debt of £3.   Thomson,
who supports the Government in a naval and military expedition to Pekin, appeals to Smith's patriotism for the chastisement
of the Chinese barbarians and the prestige of the English name.
Browne condemns that criminal and somewhat costly expedition,
and is eloquent on the rights of humanity and the inoffensive
character of an oriental but industrious population.   The more

the candidates talk, the less interest they excite in the breast of
Smith, one way or the other, for the affairs of China. In fact,
his whole mind is absorbed in the consideration of those £3
which neither of these eloquent strangers helps him to pay.
Now there appears a third person on the stage, and he whispers
to Smith, " Vote for humanity and Browne; vote for the preservation of the Celestial Empire and its countless millions, and
you shall have 30s." Smith indignantly rejects a bribe thus
coarsely offered ; nevertheless it cannot but occur to him that
30s. would pay off half his debt, and for the first time in his
life he begins to conceive an interest in the affairs of China.
Now there appears a fourth person, the real *Deus ex machinâ*—
a solicitor, or a solicitor's confidential agent—a fellow-townsman,
a man whose word is as good as his bond ; and he whispers to
Smith, " You are an honest man, and not to be bribed ; I know
all your affairs ; you are tormented by a paltry debt of £3 ; that
debt shall never trouble you any further if you vote for Thomson
and your country's glory." Well, Smith begins to think of his
wife's anxious face, of his children's scanty supper—thinks
what a blessing it would be to rise the next morning free from
the incubus of those £3 ; and as he so thinks, can you wonder
that he begins to care no more for the Celestial Empire than the
Celestial Empire cares for him ? The man's heart is tempted,
and the elector's vote is bought. That is the origin of corruption; and such corruption soon becomes contagious in proportion
as you multiply voters to whose knowledge China is a phantom,
and to whose wants £3 are the Indies.

These instances occur now ; but will you tell me that they
will not be much more numerous under your new constituency
—ay, and on questions far more vitally important to England
than an expedition to Pekin ? But why more numerous ? Because poverty and debt are not the staple of your present constituency. But reduce your franchise to almost the humblest
tenements in which poverty can face debt, and I leave the
conjecture of the probable result to your own indulgent knowledge of human nature. Are we to be told that the ballot would
cure this ? The ballot ! Why, is there a gentleman old enough

to sit in this House and yet young enough to believe that if our
friend Smith, who is not a bad man, and who will not break the
promise he has given on a consideration, could drop into the
ballot-box a vote, perhaps, against the inclinations of his party,
he would not have a conscience still more placidly resigned to
that chastisement of the Celestial Empire and that vindication
of his country's glory by which thus quietly, unobtrusively, and
without giving offence to any one, he could pay off his debt
of £3, and perhaps by that vote serve to add £3,000,000
more to the debt of England? The hon. Member for Birmingham has a more speedy and decided cure for this evil. He
would get rid altogether of these nurseries of rising genius,
these asylums of ill-treated statesmen; he would have only constituencies so numerous that they are less likely to be bribed in
detail than bribed wholesale, by some system of direct taxation
which shall reduce the duties on the articles £6 householders
consume, or defray all the expenditure necessary to protect the
houses they inhabit and the freedom they enjoy, at the exclusive
cost of persons who are better lodged than themselves. This
kind of corruption I hold to be infinitely more dangerous than
the other; for a nation may continue great and flourishing even
though rich candidates do bribe poor electors, but the greatest
nation in the world must become bankrupt and ruined if the
poor could carry any system of taxation which embodies a principle that confiscates the property of the rich. Therefore, though
I am far from saying that a bolder redistribution of seats may
not be required for the ultimate settlement of this question,
I say that if that redistribution is to be based on a £6 franchise, without any equipoise, in all the larger urban constituencies substituted for smaller boroughs, you will render the
danger of a low franchise immeasurably more formidable, and
though there may be less individual bribery than among small
constituencies, you will incur a much greater risk of that general
political corruption which ends either in the spoliation of property or the loss of freedom. Yet, if you pass this bill, the Member for Birmingham is quite right in thinking that an extensive
redistribution of seats, which shall give the same £6 franchise to

urban multitudes, must follow. "Give him," he says, "this £6 borough suffrage, and he will there fix a lever that shall lift about a hundred gentlemen round him out of their seats, and launch them into the abyss of space." That is the very next of what he mildly calls "successive steps ;" and when I heard him thus inhumanly predict the massacre of the confiding innocents who were then actually grouped around his very knees, I turned towards those unfortunate gentlemen with a thrill of superstitious awe at the despondent resignation with which they seemed to hear the executioner announce their doom. Well, then, I think this change will not make the representative body wiser nor the constituent body purer. But an hon. member said in the former debates that "this was an age of progress ; " and from that fact he argued that, because we had railways and steam therefore we ought to have a £6 constituency. I do not see the *sequitur*. Steam and railways are produced by the science of the learned and the capital of the rich; and I cannot understand by what principle of logic I am to call that a progress which places our legislation at the mercy of men who are the reverse of learned and the opposite of rich. The Home Secretary says he supports the bill "because the time has come to make some further progress in the same direction in which we made so great an advance in 1831." But by this bill you do not advance ; you go back, and in the direction from which that great reform so resolutely departed ; you go back by one long stride towards the old scot-and-lot voters, whom the great Reform Bill was originally designed to get rid of—go back to the very constituency which the experience of centuries had proved to be venal. It seems to me that we thus engender the coarsest vices of democracy without any of its redeeming grandeur. Pure democracy, in the classic sense of the word, has conferred on the civilised world too many benefits as well as warnings not to have its full share of enthusiastic admirers among men of cultivated minds and of generous hearts. But for pure democracy you must have the elements that preserve its honesty and insure its duration. Those elements are not to be found in old societies with vast disparities of wealth, of influence, of education—

they belong to the youth of nations, such as colonies ; and when
any gentleman cites to us the example of a colony for some
democratic change that he would recommend to the ancient
monarchy of England, I can only say that he has not studied
the hornbook of legislation. The acute democrats of that sublime republic by which we are all unconsciously instructed
whenever we discuss the problems of government—the acute
democrats of Athens—were well aware of the truth I endeavour,
before it is yet too late, to impress upon you ; they were well
aware that democracy cannot long coexist with great inequali-
ties of wealth and power ; they therefore began by ostracising
the powerful to end by persecuting the wealthy. And I cannot
forget, since I have referred to that noble commonwealth, which
may almost be called the England of the ancient world, that one
main cause for the decline and fall of Athens has been traced by
those writers, whose authority the scholars I see before me will
agree to accept, to the adoption of the very principle you now
commend to us—I mean the extension of the suffrage to a class
the most eager for political change and the least accustomed to
weigh political consequences. That extension would have been
then justified by much the same arguments you use now. It could
have been truly said that the extension was not very large in
itself ; that it still left the whole suffrage small compared to the
whole of the male adult population ; that it did not admit even
the majority of the working classes, for the working classes
there were chiefly slaves or settlers ; it would have been said,
" Do you fear your own countrymen ? Can you dispute the intelligence of any class of Athenians?" and, indeed, the humblest
Athenian had facilities for education that we cannot give to our
working men. All such arguments would have been very
plausible—they are the arguments we hear to-day. But, nevertheless, the extension did contrive to give to poverty and passion
a preponderating power over capital and knowledge : and the
results were soon visible in a series of " successive steps " ; in
new tamperings with the suffrage in the same direction ; in a
plentiful crop of eloquent demagogues outbidding Liberal statesmen ; in a system of direct taxation, which was unjust to the

rich, and made the rich either indifferent to politics or hostile
to liberty; in unwise expeditions called for by a brave and
eager population, who called for them the more loudly because
the rich paid for them; in the destruction of the fleets which
had secured to the England of the ancient world the empire of
the seas; in her subjugation by her near and formidable rival,
who possessed a genius more military than her own, whom her
free speaking had seriously offended, and who, under the conduct of a chief of whom it was said—pause, and think whether
the same can be said of any foreign chief now living—"that
where the lion's skin fell short, he eked it out with the fox's,"
while her orators still talked about "progress," while her factions still wrangled for power,—sailed into the Piræus itself, and
gave her liberty to the winds.

But why do we all hastily yet languidly agree to shovel this
question away, to accept this or any measure of reform, though
what it is to reform none of us could satisfactorily explain? Is
it not because we all do desire for the next ten or twelve years
to have done with the subject? And I can well understand
that gentlemen on both sides should feel eager this very session
to try and effect a compromise which, though not final, will give
a new constitution a trial for at least half the term of years
which we have given to the constitution of 1832. To attain
that object I should myself be prepared to approve a measure
really comprehensive and substantial, that should unite a larger
representation of numbers with some prudent securities for the
fair representation of property. For it is better, of the two, if
we are to alter our house, to alter it so as to get rid of its chief
inconveniences, than it is to pass the best part of our lives in the
hands of the architects. One may put up with a great deal of
alteration if one can say, "Thank Heaven, one is settled at last;"
but there is no inconvenience equal to that of never being settled
at all. But is there one gentleman who can flatter himself or
us that if we pass this bill we are one jot nearer to settling the
question of Parliamentary Reform? There is not a single inconvenience of which educated men complain that this bill even
attempts to mitigate; no attempt to lessen the expenses of elec-

tions—in counties, I suspect that those expenses will be doubled; no attempt to enfranchise the many enlightened and respectable men who happen not to be householders; no attempt to lessen the chances of bribery—on the contrary, as we have seen, to increase them. Thus the next general election will not inaugurate this Reform Bill, but rather record the dissatisfaction of its own supporters at its crudity and incompleteness, and their solemn pledges that they will continue with increased ardour to struggle—what for? Why, for a new Reform Bill. So that this measure is only the shoeing-horn to some fresh miracle of cobbling, in which, with weary feet and in " successive steps," we shall plod the same dull road, sure to pass our nights again under the same old sign of the Blue Boar. I say, then, as men of business, we do not get our consideration; that when we have paid the bill we do not get that acquittance and receipt which can alone reconcile our doubts as to the justice and propriety of the demand. The Member for Birmingham says persuasively, "Take this, or you will get something worse." But if we take this do we not strengthen his hands to give us the something worse into the bargain? Thus we go into Committee on this bill with the conviction beforehand that it pleases no one and settles nothing,—that, do what we can with it, it will remedy no evil, produce no benefit, satisfy no class—not even the class of the working men; all we shall have done, if we pass the bill, is to place an empire which rests its wealth and greatness upon causes so artificial and delicate that, once destroyed, that wealth and that greatness could no more return to England than they could ever again return to Venice, in the hands of men whose means of existence and facilities for education are—if a household test be any test at all—nearly one-half below the lowest standard of the existing suffrage in our towns.

So much for the bill itself. A word now as to the time in which we are called upon to pass it. The Home Secretary says he hopes there is to be no ignoble resort to the Fabian policy of delay, while at the same time he rejoices that there is to be a Committee of the House of Lords to consider whether that Fabian policy in England may not be entitled to receive the same praise

that it received in Rome, where it was called, in classical expressions that have passed into proverbs, " The salvation of the State
and the shield of the Commonwealth." And it does seem to me
the height of inconsistency to concede a Committee of the other
House of Parliament upon the very points that we are called
upon to take for granted, so that this House may stamp its
approval on the bill simultaneously with the publication of evidence which may show that if we had waited for three months
we should have found that we had been legislating for remote
generations upon data on which the Home Secretary would not
have filled up the humblest office in his public department, nor
accepted a tenant on a seven years' lease for the smallest farm
on his private estate. But even if no such Committee had been
conceded, I would ask if there be not two very evident causes
which render this special time peculiarly unfortunate for dis-
carding a legislative body with which the nation has become
familiar, and choosing another of which it can know nothing.
Those causes are, first, the state of affairs abroad ; secondly, the
state of our finances at home. On the one side, all the signs
and omens that indicate storm; on the other, the gulf of an enormous deficit which this Parliament first sanctions and widens,
and then, like many a private speculator, commits suicide rather
than face the day of reckoning.

But let us first glance at the state of affairs abroad. The
Chancellor of the Duchy said in the debate before Easter,
" Affairs abroad were critical when you (Lord Derby's Government) introduced a Reform Bill. War in Europe was then
imminent; you did your best to prevent it, but that war soon
broke out." Perfectly true ; and, as an *ad captandum* argument
addressed to a £6 constituency, the right hon. Baronet's answer
would be very clever and telling. But addressed to this House,
as at present constituted, it seems to me to be a poor resort to
what schoolboys call the *tu quoque* kind of logic, and not quite
worthy the right hon. Baronet's just reputation for ability and
candour. The difference between the two periods of time is
immense. That difference has become infinitely more marked
since the commencement of the session. The noble Lord who

is at once the introducer of this bill and the responsible Minister for Foreign Affairs, has not only acknowledged but enforced that difference in speeches in the House and despatches to Foreign Ministers, which have been equally worthy of himself and faithful to the sentiment of the country; and I am sure there is not a loyal gentleman on this side of the House who will not pardon and perhaps even sympathise with me when I say that, looking towards the chief under whom I once served as a private soldier, I rejoice to think that here at least I can equally defend my country's honour and his renown. Well, then, will not the noble Secretary tell his colleague the Chancellor of the Duchy that the difference between the two periods of time—between the time when Lord Derby's Government introduced a Reform Bill, and the time in which we now are—is immense? In a war undertaken by France for the independence of Italy, there was nothing that threatened England; in the peace concluded by France, with the enlargement of her boundaries, can we say the same? We see before us now, as we saw then, a neighbour of gigantic power. He said then to us, " This power I will not use for one selfish object." We had no right to disbelieve him. Now we not only see the power but the use that is made of it; and events have shown that our neighbour can say one thing and mean another. You now know the character and conditions of the French empire; you now know that the peace of the world and the security of England hang on the nod of a single man, whose thoughts none of us can penetrate, whose ambition none of us can measure. At the stroke of his pen the existing geography of Europe may be changed as rapidly as in his own country a republic that vied with the American collapsed into a sovereignty as imperial as that of the Roman Cæsars—a sovereignty, like theirs, preserving the forms while it destroys the substance of liberty; more dangerous to its neighbours than the ancient monarchies around it, because it is as little bound by their scruples as it is by their treaties. It has the young blood of the revolution out of which it sprang; it inherits the licence and the force of the multitudes who deem themselves crowned in its coronation. Thus, it combines in a terrible union the arts and necessities of a brilliant demagogue with the armies and the objects of a military chief. Such a combination is rare; it has never hitherto occurred in the history of the world without threatening the landmarks of its neighbours; and woe to the nation that it finds unprepared to cope with its twofold power over the multitudes that it dazzles and the armies that it wields! And the danger is the greater because we deal with no vulgar tyrant, no petty dissimulator. The Emperor of the French has those high attributes of genius which render even his defects popular and majestic with the people that he governs. He has capacities for organisation not inferior to those of his illustrious uncle, and he consolidates both his ambition and his intellect by an inflexible singleness of purpose, by a mixture of secrecy in design and promptitude in action, which give the vigour of Richelieu and the astuteness of Mazarin to the leader of 600,000 soldiers. Such are the character and conditions of the French empire, involving nothing that would justify our taking one step either to court its hostility or forfeit its alliance, nothing that should make us depart from our position as an insular commercial population by seeking to excite a counter-league among the Powers of the Continent before they themselves invoked our assistance, but involving much that requires unrelaxing vigilance as well as disciplined judgment on the part even less of Ministers than of the House of Commons. And therefore it does seem to me a wanton imprudence to discard at this moment a legislative body whose fidelity to English interests and English honour has been proved and tested—which certainly cannot be called worn out and effete which is actually younger than most of the youngest members among us, which has not spent thirty years in acquiring some familiar acquaintance with its arduous duties—for a raw and untried legislative body, chosen by the minimum of political experience to meet times that may require the maximum of political knowledge.

The Home Secretary says this transfer of political power will be a security against invasion, and that if Napoleon I. had not been so unpopular, he might have defied the armies that invaded

his capital.   What is meant by that argument and that historical illustration ?   Is the Queen of England unpopular ?   Has
the nation shown that it requires a £6 constituency to teach it
the virtue of self-defence ?   Or, if it be implied that the House
of Commons needs amendment in one simple respect to render
it more disposed and more resolved to resist an invader, I deny
the ungrateful imputation.   This poor House, as at present constituted, has borne us gallantly through a war which tasked all
our national virtues, and revealed to us all our administrative
defects.   With an energy which had no signs of decrepitude, it
has adapted our armaments to the improved science of the age,
and placed this country in a state of defence which will need
steady patience and self-sacrifice to maintain.   Are we sure that
that patience and self-sacrifice will equally characterise the new
constituency and their new representatives ?   No doubt we shall
have members just as anxious for what is called the honour of
the country, who will make high-sounding speeches against
truckling to absolute sovereigns, and insist on the right of the
House of Commons to become the garrulous confidant of every
secret which Cabinets would keep to themselves.   But will the
new representatives of the new constituency be as provident of
practical defences as they may be lavish of verbal provocations?
Will they as readily submit to the taxation which is necessary
to self-defence, so long as the world shall see wars commenced
for the propagation of ideas, and peace concluded by the acquisition of domains ?   Sir, it is possible that they may possess all
such requisite qualities in a higher degree than ourselves and
our constituents ; but at least there is a doubt the other way,
and seeing that doubt, it would be no such great infelicity if, at
a juncture so critical, we could be contented to let well alone ;
if we could defer putting this great nation into the lottery of
chance until we could see more distinctly the face of the goddess
who presides at the wheel,—until we could judge whether, in
truth, we behold in her that Fortune who smiles upon peace and
commerce, "*dominam æquoris*," or whether she be rather that
more terrible deity—

"Clavos trabales et cuneos manu
Gestans ahenâ "—

whose attributes are calamity and war. But still more do I think it would have become this Parliament to remit to its successor a less formidable balance-sheet of deficit and revenue. I say nothing here against the Budget or the Treaty, on which I have refrained from all other opposition than that of a silent, and, I will add, a reluctant vote; reluctant, partly because of the sincere, and, may I say in his absence, the affectionate admiration in which I hold not more the talents than the character of the Chancellor of the Exchequer—partly because, though I doubt the prudence of both those measures, the Treaty and the Budget, I fully recognise the generous and enlightened hopes upon which, whatever the issue, they may rest their vindication. I say nothing, then, against the financial scheme of the Government; but I do say to this House, which has sanctioned that scheme by so large a majority, that if we, the Parliament of Lord Grey's Reform Bill, have been the trustees for this infant constituency, it would surely be well if we could render accounts to the ward whose year of attaining majority we so impatiently advance, without presenting to its earliest consideration a debt or deficiency of £10,000,000 or £12,000,000, which we leave its inexperience to settle without an effort on our part to lessen its embarrassment or to warn its councils. If we are to assemble this new *tiers état*, it is a sinister coincidence with a very dark page in history that the appeal to numbers should be simultaneous with a deficit which we have not the happiness to supply, and problems in the science of taxation which we have not the courage to solve. But all this is for your consideration, the consideration of the Queen's responsible advisers, and of that majority by whom the late Government were displaced, rather than for any exclusive or obstinate resistance on our part, which, if unavailing, would be obviously unwise.

The Chancellor of the Duchy somewhat scornfully asked us, " Why don't you divide?" and answered his own question in the same breath, " Because you know you would have a majority against you!" In return, I ask him, not scornfully, but in a sober appeal to his love of truth, "Granting the fact of that alleged majority, does it not contain members more than enough to turn the scale in our favour if they voted according to the opinions they express in private ?"

Now, it is because there is at present to be no division, because we would not, if possible, make that strict demarcation of parties which would not faithfully represent a real difference of opinions, that I hope I may, without presumption, solicit the serious reflection of those enlightened reformers who do not desire change for the mere sake of change. I know, indeed, that there are some persons who believe that progress consists in always stopping on the road to alter the springs of the carriage in which we travel. I know that there are some who think that man was made for nothing better than to pass his whole existence in the ecstatic contemplation of interminable Reform Bills. But let us flatter ourselves that such amiable enthusiasts are to be found chiefly out of doors, and not among us, to whom education and knowledge of the world may fairly be supposed to have given the ordinary attributes of common-sense. We cannot disguise from ourselves that, whether we look at home or abroad, this is a somewhat critical moment in the destinies of our country—one in which we would rather summon the highest wisdom, the ripest experience we could obtain for our guidance, than merge such wisdom as we do possess, such experience as we have acquired, in the arbitration of men who have never been hitherto called upon to judge of questions so complicated and grave, and from whom, if you once appoint them, you can never have a court of appeal. I do not say that the reasons I have urged as to the state of Europe or as to our own financial deficit are reasons that the Government could openly put forward for withdrawing this bill; but they are reasons which their own supporters might privately urge upon them, and they are reasons which might satisfy their own good sense and justify them before the public, if, having honourably fulfilled their pledge to introduce a Reform Bill, this bill was withdrawn on the obvious and unanswerable ground that it has failed to give general satisfaction. Nor do I consider that failure a serious reproach to this or to any Government. A Reform Bill, so easy to the theorist, is very difficult to the practical statesman. The hand of the true artist may well tremble when he applies the hammer and the chisel to the palladium of his country's laws. I do not presume to think that anything I can say will have the least influence upon the Government; but they would be wrong indeed, if they did not respect what may be said, or, if not said, what they know is thought, by their own temperate and tried supporters. If, however, you tell us that, be the bill good or bad, you are resolved to persevere in it; that what we think its defects you hold to be its main principles; that you will not wait for the report of the Committee you have conceded to the other House; that you will avail yourselves of the natural reluctance which the members for boroughs may feel openly to declare against those new constituents to whom, next December, you would condemn them to appeal,—if that be the course which, as the Queen's advisers, you deem it your duty to pursue, then I can only express a fervent wish that the result may justify your reversal of all the rules by which the statesmen even of republics would rather seek in similar time and circumstance to strengthen the hands of the executive, than transfer to the wide circle of an unaccustomed multitude the nice and permanent adjustment of national finances, and the cautious preparation against perils which already alarm the boldest statesmen and menace the strongest thrones.

XXX.

A SPEECH

DELIVERED IN

THE SHIRE HALL AT HERTFORD

On Thursday the 9th of October 1862.

On Thursday, the 9th of October 1862, the Hertford Agricultural Society held its annual meeting. In the evening the usual dinner in the Assembly Room of the Shire Hall was presided over by the Marquess of Salisbury. In answer to the toast of the Members for Hertfordshire, with which was specially coupled the name of Sir Edward Bulwer Lytton, the following speech was delivered.

My Lords and Gentlemen,—In rising to return thanks for the honour you have just conferred on me and my colleagues, I am reminded that the first occasion on which I took part in the public affairs of this county was at an agricultural meeting similar to the present, held in this very town and in this very room. When I look round I recognise many of the faces with which I then first became acquainted ; and owing, I presume, to the salubrious habits and the peaceful consciences which belong to agricultural pursuits, I see in those faces so little of the wear and tear of time that I could almost fancy it were yesterday when my health was first drunk by the farmers of Hertfordshire. Yet the years which have elapsed since that day have witnessed so many stirring events that they constitute one of the most important epochs in the history of the world. France has undergone three revolutions—the fall of a constitutional monarchy, the stormy interlude of a democratic republic, the restoration of a military empire. The old rulers of Lombardy, Tuscany, Naples, have disappeared from those lands, and the map of Europe has been altered to admit the kingdom of Italy. Austria, long the haughtiest representative of the principle of absolute monarchy, has commenced the experiment of constitutional government; Russia has laid the foundation of a new political and social existence in recognising the value of free labour and abolishing the institution of serfs; China has opened her ports to our merchants and her capital to our ambassadors. We ourselves have twice gone through the calamities of war, in the siege of Sebastopol and the suppression of the Indian revolt. On the other side of the Atlantic, that great republic which boasted a superb exemption from the evils and perils which beset ancient States and monarchical forms of government has been violently rent in two; and whatever may be the issue of a struggle in which, as yet, we see only the lavish expenditure of blood and treasure, no far-sighted politician can suppose that the curse of slavery will long survive the separation of which it is the most ostensible, though it is neither the only nor perhaps the most powerful cause. So many startling events, tending to vast and permanent effects on the destinies of the human race, have scarcely ever before been crowded into a space of time so short as that which has elapsed since I first addressed you in this town. But, all the while, we have continued to hold our peaceful meetings in honour of that agriculture which, as it is the earliest art men learn when they form themselves into social communities, so it remains to the last the most solid foundation of the prosperity and wealth of nations. Since the first meeting I attended in this town I can see a great and marked improvement, not so much in our exhibitions as in the object which the exhibitions are intended to promote—I mean the better cultivation of the land. Agricultural improvement, so far as the adaptation of science is concerned, must be always slow compared with

those improvements which science effects in the machinery
employed in manufactures ; for in manufactures any new idea
requiring experiment addresses itself only to one wealthy class
—the master manufacturers. They have the capital to try the
experiment, and they are tempted to do so by the expectations
of very large profits. But in agriculture speculative or scientific
improvement must pass through a double process. An experiment that requires outlay and entails risk is, as a general rule,
first made by the proprietor who farms his own land ; but, as
long as it stops there, it is only a scientific experiment—it is
not a practical agricultural improvement. It only becomes a
practical agricultural improvement when the tenant-farmer,
satisfied that the result will pay, takes it up, not as a question of
science, but as a matter of business. And he is naturally more
slow in the adoption of a novelty than the manufacturer, because,
however plausible the novelty may be, still it does not proffer
those vast and immediate gains which a new invention may
bestow on the manufacturer. No farmer makes a great fortune
by one lucky hit. For these reasons speculative improvements
are comparatively slow before they become generally adopted
by practical agriculturists ; but, once adopted, they are permanent. There is no more retrogression in English farming than
there is in English politics. But there is a great distinction
between what is called fancy farming and practical husbandry,
and that distinction will be seen in the balance-sheet. I remember an amusing anecdote of a certain nobleman, who was a
great farmer and also a great epicure. He kept a famous prize
ox ; he kept also a famous French cook. Once on a time he invited some distinguished friends to accompany him to his country
seat, and sent the cook on a few days before to prepare for the
entertainment. As soon as he arrived he was impatient to show
his friends his prize ox, and carried them off to the farmyard.
When he came to the stall in which the ox was kept, lo and
behold, the ox was gone ! He called to the herdsman, " Why,
where is my prize ox ? "   " Please your lordship," said the man,
" the French cook came to look at him two days ago, and
admired him greatly ; since then the ox has disappeared."

Much astonished, my lord hastened to seek an explanation of
the cook, and found him very busy in his private room near the
kitchen. "What is this story about my prize ox,—what have
you done with my Durham ox?" "Ah, my lord," said the
cook, "I have him here, safe and sound;" and so saying, he
opened a cupboard, and, on one of the shelves, showed his lordship a small jar. Pointing to the jar, he said, with great com-
placency, "There! you see, my lord, he was rather too tough for
a roast; but I have stewed him down into a famous sauce!"
Now I am sometimes reminded of that anecdote when some
gentleman fancy farmer carries me over his model farm. One
sees much to admire in expensive nicknacks and clever inventions, but when one delicately inquires into the state of the
balance-sheet the admiration cools. And many a fancy farmer
who wants to look at his net profit, as my lord wanted to look
at his prize ox, may be astonished to find how many pounds of
solid substance may be scientifically stewed down in a very
small jar of sauce. So much for mere fancy farming; but as to
practical husbandry, I have no doubt that if any competent
agricultural judge who had not visited Hertfordshire for the last
fifteen years were to visit it again now, he would be greatly
struck with the progress we have made, whether he looked at
the tillage and the stock, or whether he conversed familiarly
with that great body of tenant-farmers who have contributed to
this day's exhibition so many excellent specimens, not only of
cattle, but of men. For man is the most improvable of all
created beings in this world; because it is through the hand and
the brain of man the Creator effects the improvements on the
earth, which is allotted to man for his dwelling-place, and in the
products of nature, which are bestowed upon man for his uses.
That much of the agricultural progress made in our county
may be ascribed to these annual meetings no one can reasonably
doubt; for the more men are brought together in friendly competition, and in the social interchange of ideas connected with
their own calling and occupations, the more their minds must
be warmed in the desire of improvement, and the more the range
of their own observation will be expanded and enriched by the

hints and suggestions they receive from the experience of others.
To these meetings, also, I think we may ascribe much of that
visible improvement in the comforts and the social position of
the labouring class which forms one of the most pleasing features
of the age in which we live. For the labourer has his share in the
honours of these meetings—he contests for a prize in skill as a
ploughman or a shepherd ; and I am sure all farmers will bear
me out when I say that there is no department of skilled labour
more important in husbandry than that of a thoroughly good
ploughman and a thoroughly careful shepherd. Seeing, then,
that these meetings bring together as exhibitors of skill, the
landlord, the farmer, and the labourer, in their several modes
of competition ; seeing that even those prizes for the labourer
which are not devoted purely to skill, and are therefore liable to
some objections, still in our society encourage the spirit of independence, and the enrolment into benefit societies, and thus
by energy and foresight raise the labourers and their families
above the charity of the parish,—I think it is scarcely possible
these meetings should not produce a good effect on the social
position of the labouring class, or that, after applauding in
public all generous sentiments that do honour to the labourer,
we should return to our own homes without a hearty desire to
treat those who serve us honestly and faithfully, not only with
kindness, but with respect. Gentlemen, I have observed that at
the agricultural meetings held elsewhere this year much stress
has been laid by eminent speakers upon the importance of utilis-
ing the sewage of towns to agricultural purposes. Upon that
head Lord Derby, himself a great agricultural authority, has done
much, in his very remarkable speech at Preston, stating the result of the experiments at Wellington College, according to the
plan of the filter introduced by the Prince Consort, and by the
prize he has offered to any company who shall profitably to
themselves utilise the liquid manure of a district comprising
4000 inhabitants : Mr Gladstone also, with the acuteness of a
mind accustomed to seize the strong points of any question to
which it applies itself, has very eloquently enforced our attention to a means of producing wealth, which, though sufficiently

familiar to other countries, has been hitherto signally neglected by our own. I remember, when I held the colonial seals, the trouble and toil it cost me to secure from some distant islands a scanty supply of guano, while all the time, close at hand, a few of the London sewers were every year casting away into the Thames more than half a million's worth of a manure considerably more valuable for the general purposes of agriculture than the guano which ships were fitted out to bring home, in order that it might be retailed at a price which rather fits it for the phials of an apothecary than the fields of a farmer. I said half a million's worth of money was thus thrown away, but this is a very low estimate of the real waste. In Flanders, for instance, where I have been lately, the value of sewage is calculated according to the numerical population, especially in towns. It is there calculated at £1, 7s. a-head yearly. In Belgium it is calculated at a still higher rate. So that, if the population of London be taken at 2,000,000, a means of increasing the productive wealth of the country which, according to the estimate of Flanders, would be worth about £2,700,000, is exclusively devoted to poison the waters of the Thames, and administer gratuitous disease to her Majesty's metropolitan subjects. If we may condescend to take lessons from barbarians, the Chinese may in this respect be our teachers. The rapidity with which the Chinese bring almost any soil into cultivation, and, when brought into cultivation, the enormous crop they contrive to take from mere handfuls of land, have been the wonder and admiration of travellers. But the great secret of the Chinese is in the utilisation of sewage. The proverbial fertility of Belgium is owing, in much, to the same cause. But it is not only the sewage of London which is wasted, but that of all our own rural towns; although in them there appears a more impatient desire to remedy acknowledged abuses than seems to be the characteristic of city aldermen and metropolitan boards. When I consider how many populous towns there are in this country, I heartily wish we could send among them a few enlightened Chinese engineers to devise the best practical means by which our townsfolk might be enriched by the manure they could sell, and our farmers enriched by the manure they could buy. But in the meanwhile, until some such scheme is devised and agreed to, we must fall back on our old friend the farmyard dunghill, assisted, indeed, by various chemical manufactures, but never to such a degree as to supply its place. Professor Liebig is, no doubt, right in considering the chief art of productive husbandry to consist in the skilful application of manure. David Hume tells us, in one of his essays, that all the vast apparatus of our government has ultimately no other object or purpose than the distribution of justice, or, in other words, the support of the twelve judges. So it may be said that all the apparatus of productive husbandry has ultimately no other object or purpose than the distribution of justice to the soil—in other words, the application of that manure which gives back to the soil the nutriment we take from it, or supplies the nourishing properties which nature had neglected to bestow. Eight hundred years ago there was a very learned dispute whether or not the earth was an animal. We have now discovered that the earth is so far an animal that it requires to be fed, and will not bear to be starved.

A remarkable instance of this truth is mentioned by a celebrated agricultural authority in some of the Southern States of America, such as Maryland and Virginia. In those States there were large districts of some of the most fertile land in the world. The crops they yielded were prodigious, but, unluckily, the cultivators neglected the manure; they took from the land the alkalies and salts which they did not replace, and these districts have now become so hopelessly sterile that they have been altogether abandoned as a desert. Now, if it be true that the fertility of the soil thus depends on the nourishment we give to it, there can be no stronger argument for the perfect confidence which ought to exist between landlord and tenant, so that the enterprise of the former may not be checked by any reasonable fear that he should not have his fair share of the profits in whatever he permanently adds to the fertility of the soil. For, on the one hand, the farmer cannot, on the long-run, enrich himself unless he does justice to the land; and, on the other hand, the landlord cannot, on the long-run, benefit his estate

unless he does justice to the cultivator. The healthiest condition of productive industry, whether in farming or anything
else, must be that which attracts to its cultivation capital and
intelligence by the rational calculation of adequate returns.
Now, when I look forward I can see many causes at work to
give assurance to investments in agriculture, whether for the
owner or the occupier. The increase of population, the certainty that new towns will spring up in the neighbourhood of
railway stations, the tendency to building even in the quietest
old rural towns if sufficiently near to railway communication,
above all, the vast and progressive influx of gold—all must serve
every year more and more to increase the value of the land,
widen the demand for its produce, and maintain the standard of
its remunerative prices. I turn from prospects which may
reasonably give hope and confidence to the agriculturist to express
the deep sorrow with which we must all contemplate the unmerited sufferings of our fellow-countrymen in the manufacturing districts, and our sympathy is rendered still more acute by
our heartfelt admiration of the fortitude and patience they have
shown. I would fain hope that the princely capitalists of
Lancashire, whose fortunes have been made by the hands now
stretched out to them for work or for bread, will seize this
opportunity to prove that their gratitude is in some proportion
to their wealth. It is not benevolence alone—it is·policy, it is
wisdom, to win to themselves the hearts of their mechanics at
the moment when those hearts will most lastingly remember
kindness, and so strengthen that tie between employer and
operative which can never be loosened without danger, and
perhaps with more danger in the crowded population of manufacturing towns than in any other combination of capital and
labour. But supposing, as I will not doubt, that the rich men
of Lancashire nobly discharge their duty to their afflicted poor,
still, I fear that the distress may extend beyond even their
means to deal with it ; and if so, since the profits derived from
the industry of mechanics have been not only local but national, so I think it becomes us to make the aid to their suffering
as national as have been the profits which their industry has

diffused. Whenever such general movement may commence,
I am sure that this county will be among the earliest in the
generous competition of patriotic benevolence. For my own
part, I know that I could not more faithfully represent a warm-
hearted agricultural constituency than by assisting to prove to
our suffering countrymen how completely we merge in one
common sentiment of Christian brotherhood all angry recollec-
tions of the old feud between cotton and corn. This year has,
indeed, from its commencement, been a year of sorrow. To-day,
in the list of toasts which my noble friend proposed from the
chair, we miss one that in former years immediately followed
the toast in honour of our Sovereign. I do not seek to revive
the freshness of that grief which overshadowed every hearth in
these kingdoms when we first heard that the Prince Consort
was no more. For though the virtues of those we lose make
sorrow more poignant at the first shock of bereavement, the after
remembrance of those virtues becomes in itself a consolation ;
and no man can be said to have wholly passed from earth who
leaves behind him one of those rare examples of unassuming
goodness, of serene and disciplined wisdom, which are, perhaps,
less recognised in life than revered and imitated after death.
The chief characteristic of a prince in all respects so truly illustrious appears to me to have been this : He so regulated his
whole life and nature as to bring them both into harmony with
one systematic idea of duty. Thus duty with him was not a
stern constraint, a harsh obligation, but rather a pleasurable
obedience to the habits of his life and his instincts of happiness.
He did not seek to cultivate one faculty alone, but rather to
develop in due proportion all the faculties which served to en-
noble and complete his existence as man ; and the success with
which this was achieved becomes visible at once when we contemplate his life and deplore his loss. Other men, with some
special talent more conspicuously displayed—other men more
strikingly, because, perhaps, more irregularly great—we may
readily discover; but looking around the civilised world among
those whom rank or fame gives to our survey, I think we should
find it difficult to select a life more beautifully consistent with

its allotted duties, or presenting a larger aggregate of those attributes which form the intellectual and moral dignity of man. We must comfort ourselves with the thought so exquisitely expressed by our Poet-Laureate, that the Prince we lament is still—

"The silent father of our kings to be."

My noble friend * has intimated to you that next year we shall be called upon to celebrate the nuptials of the heir-apparent to the throne. May those nuptials be solemnised under the brightest auspices which can connect the happiness of princes with the felicity of nations! May that terrible strife among our American kinsfolk be then decided in the way most propitious to the permanent welfare of a people whom Providence has endowed with so many noble qualities, and placed in regions so vast, and so safe from all ambition except their own! May the industry now so mournfully suspended in our manufacturing districts be again renewed, and rendered more independent of the faults which it does not share, in the States which it cannot control! And thus may our beloved Sovereign find in the happiness of her children, and in the content and prosperity of all classes of her people, those consolations which can best cheer and sustain her heart, whether as the mother or the Queen!

* The Marquess of Salisbury.

XXXI.

A SPEECH

DELIVERED IN

THE HOUSE OF COMMONS

ON THE 7TH OF MARCH 1865.

On Tuesday, the 7th of March 1865, the Member for East Suffolk, Sir Fitzroy Kelly, moved in the House of Commons—" That upon any future remission of indirect taxation, this House should take into consideration the Duty on Malt, with a view to its early reduction and ultimate repeal." After a lengthened debate, the motion was rejected by 251 votes to 171. In seconding the resolution the following speech was delivered.

SIR,—I rise to second the motion of my hon. and learned friend.* In his able and exhaustive speech he did not exaggerate the importance attached to the relief from the malt-tax by the great body of agricultural producers ; and the amount of the tax, which, no doubt, seems to many gentlemen the strong reason for retaining it, seems to the farmers the strongest argument in favour of its repeal. What the farmers say is this : " When you tell us that this tax produces £6,000,000 a-year, you only bring more vividly before our eyes the extent to which we are defrauded in the fair exercise of our industry and skill. Here you call in free trade in order to compel us to vie

* Sir Fitzroy Kelly.

with the corn-growers throughout the world; and when in this struggle we turn to that crop on which we ought most to rely, because in that crop we are most a match for the foreigner, your free trade resolves itself into a tax of £6,000,000 on our raw material; and you make the very amount of the spoliation the reason why we should submit to be despoiled." But it is not only against the free cultivation of barley that the tax militates. Its tendency must be, more or less, to derange the natural process of agriculture in the unfettered selection of crops. Agriculture is a course of tillage spread over a certain series of years in a certain rotation of crops; and in that year in which the farmer would and ought to sow barley, our common-sense must tell us that the presence of this tax at once obtrudes itself on the consideration of his choice, and will often induce him to select another crop more exhausting to the land, less appropriate to a judicious place in the regular course of his husbandry, and less lucrative than barley would be if barley were left free from the exciseman. You cannot, therefore, wonder to find many farmers declaring, at the various meetings which have been held on this subject, that they will not grow a bushel of malt so long as the tax lasts. And if the tax thus deters farmers from selecting a barley crop even in the barley-growing districts, how much more will it tend to prevent the introduction of that crop in other parts of these kingdoms to which it would be invaluable as an article of cattle-food, if it were not frightened away by a duty of 21s. 8d. a quarter? Thus, by the positive discouragement you give to a crop in which England naturally excels every other nation, you exclude it altogether from many soils to which it would be well adapted, and you stint the whole agricultural wealth of the country to a far greater amount than the revenue benefits by so mischievous a tax upon a raw material. The question becomes still more important as to the operation of the tax, not only against the farmer, but against every class of consumer, and against the elementary source of national wealth which consists in the fertility of the soil, when you consider its injurious effect upon the quantity of stock kept. For stock implies two things; first, meat to

the consumer—secondly, manure to the soil. Whatever tends
to restrict the quantity of stock kept, tends to make meat less
plentiful and of higher price, and tends also to rob the land of
the manure necessary for its nourishment. If you have no
stock, you have no farmyard heap. If you have no farmyard
heap, you have no guarantee for the permanent and continuous
fertility of the soil. Artificial manures are like doctor's drugs—
they may do great good for a time, they act as restoratives or
alteratives; but they can no more supersede the necessity for
the natural manure of the farmyard heap than doctor's drugs
can supersede the necessity for food. The farmyard heap is the
food of the soil, and nothing can supply its place. Now, let me
ask any of those distinguished practical agriculturists, of whom
there are so many in this House, if I am not right when I say
that just in proportion as, since the repeal of the Corn-laws,
successful farming has ceased to depend upon the price of corn,
it ought to depend upon the increased cultivation and keep of
stock? And yet, I ask again, can there be a greater discouragement
to the increase of stock than a law which restricts the farmer
in the growth of his own food for it ? And what kind of food ?
Why, precisely that which can be grown upon almost any soil.
Therefore, this tax, which some consider only the grievance of
the farmer, and others ridicule as a mere question of beer,
operates against every constituent you have in towns or boroughs; because, by discouraging stock, it raises the price of
meat, and by defrauding the soil of the manure which is its
most lasting fertiliser, there is nothing that the soil can yield
which it does not render dearer, while it diminishes the taxable
wealth of the whole community. But the Board of Trade has
issued a Report on the eve of this debate, which, in common
fairness to members, who in questions of practical detail naturally desire time to confer with practical authorities, it ought to
have issued some weeks ago, containing an account of a course
of experiments on cattle-food; by which Report it is made to
appear that barley unmalted gives more weight to cattle and
more milk to cows than barley malted; and thus, it is contended
by a powerful daily journal, that one main argument for the

repeal of the tax is destroyed. That those experiments were made fairly, the name of Mr Lawes is to me a sufficient guarantee. As a Hertfordshire man, I am too proud of the fame of that eminent chemist to disparage his authority. But Mr Lawes, were he here, would agree with me when I say that the whole history of physiological science shows how little faith is to be placed in any preliminary course of physiological experiments—or even in a second or third course—however plausible they may be. For instance, a series of experiments was made on the transfusion of new blood into diseased subjects, which appeared at first so triumphantly successful, that it created a profound sensation throughout Europe. Everywhere medical men adopted the practice, but the result so upset the theory founded on these experiments, and caused so many sudden and violent deaths, that the Parliament of Paris actually declared the transfusion of blood to be criminal, where it was not formally authorised by the medical faculty. The inventor, despite the unquestioned success of his early experiments, was sent into banishment, and the whole system fell into discredit till revived in our day and placed on a scientific basis. But how ? Why, by allowing that the first process of experiments, though apparently so successful, was altogether based upon an erroneous principle ; that the subsequent course was equally fallacious, because adhering to the same error of principle, and showing by experiments founded on a principle before unacknowledged, and now generally recognised as sound, where and how the process may be beneficial and where it must be fatal. But in the whole history of experiments nothing has required so many repetitions, and undergone such revisions of scientific opinion, as experiments analogous to those of the Board of Trade which have been made upon the relative merits of articles of nutrition. Here the deductions drawn from the first course of experiments, made by the ablest authorities, have been almost invariably disproved by a second course of experiments, and the second disproved by a third ; and to this day the whole subject is one of the most complicated and mysterious in which rival physiologists can engage. I think that one of the last of these in-

quiries on the merit of comparative articles of nutriment made
by the physiologists of the Continent was whether, according
to scientific experiments conducted on principles of selection
exactly similar to those adopted by the Board of Trade, only
selecting varieties of men instead of varieties in the inferior
animals, more nutrition was contained in the roast beef of Old
England or in the boiled leg of a donkey. I believe the first
experiments were in favour of donkey; but I am now assured
that, on second thoughts, sound philosophers give the preference
to beef. Sure I am, however, that if the raw material of donkey
yielded to the revenue £6,000,000 a-year, a Board of Trade
would never be at a loss to find a preliminary abstract report to
justify its predilection for donkeys. Therefore, Sir, with all
respect to the Board of Trade, I object to take their Report as
in any way settling the question. We are not to suppose that
during all these years farmers themselves had not been testing
the relative merits of barley and malt as cattle-food, with every
inducement to prefer barley because it is untaxed. Numberless
persons have made these experiments. I will single one, because
he is as high an authority as even Mr Lawes on this subject—
Mr Booth of Catterick, Yorkshire—who, as the largest stock-
breeder in England, and perhaps in the world, has tried both
barley and malt in every conceivable combination, and found
that though barley might require to be very slightly steeped, it
must be steeped enough to be chargeable to the tax in order to
be of general advantage, and in that case he would have given
it the most important place in cattle-food, if the tax did not
render it too expensive. Thus I am quite sure that we shall
shortly hear from numbers of persons of unquestionable authority, that the result of their experience is totally at variance with
the Report of the Board of Trade. But we will now assume,
for the sake of argument, that the Report establishes the fact
at which it aims, and even then it will not affect, except to
strengthen, our proposition that the malt-tax operates against
the increase of stock. And for this reason, assuming that unmalted barley is better than malted barley for the food of cattle,
still it will be the inferior barleys devoted to that object. But

the malt-tax, as the leading journal I have before referred to allows, is a fine on the inferior barleys, and a fine which the same authority admits is sufficient to discourage the sowing of inferior barley—that is, to discourage the growth of cattle-food in barley, whether it be malted or unmalted. My right hon. friend the Chancellor of the Exchequer, whose faith in the legitimate laws of competition, and whose vast information on all subjects belonging to philosophical inquiry, must make him at heart somewhat sceptical as to the value of those experiments on which the Board of Trade seem to rely, saw that in the application of malted barley to cattle-food there was an argument with which it was difficult to cope ; and therefore, in his bill of last year, he attempted to encourage the experiment of malting barley exclusively for the purpose of cattle-food. I wish to do the amplest justice to the enlightened consideration for the interests of the meat-consumer—in other words, for the whole population of England—which is evinced by the intention of this bill. But I am sure that his candour will at once allow that the effect of that bill must be extremely partial. I am ready to concede, for the sake of argument, that it has done more good than is generally supposed ; but, on the other hand, it must be quite clear to him—it must be quite clear to every man of sense—that only a very small number of farmers and stock-keepers will attempt the experiment of malting for cattle-food, with all the vexatious restrictions heaped upon the experiment, with all their jealous dislike of the exciseman, with all their natural and excusable desire not to co-operate in assisting a contrivance by which the tax itself is to be retained—a very small number indeed, compared with those who would grow barley for the sake of malting if malt were free from duty, and they could count on the double profit of malting, both for the food of cattle and the drink of man. And out of that great increase in the quantity of malted barley the larger part would necessarily go to the food of cattle, because that is the proper destination of the inferior barleys which at this moment are almost a drug in the market. But, apart from the direct application of malt to cattle-food, and apart from the Report of the

Board of Trade, and regarding only the application of malt to
the popular beverage of malt liquors, the repeal of the malt-tax
would inevitably tend to the increase of the quantity of stock
kept. For malt so applied, if free from duty, would be a new
and large item of profit to the farmer; it would thus increase
the general farming capital, and that increase of capital would
find its natural, because its most profitable, vent in the increase
of stock ; while, if the working class paid less for their beer than
they do now, they would of course have more to spend upon
butchers' meat ; and thus there would be at once created an additional supply of, and demand for, that main article of human
food, meat—all tending to the encouragement of keeping stock,
and by the manure produced from the stock all tending to the
increased fertility of our soil, even for wheat crops, and therefore all tending to the cheapening of bread itself. For it is
clear that the manure which the farmer would obtain by grow-
ing untaxed barley he would devote to the land which is to
grow untaxed wheat. Is it not a strange anomaly that you
should say to the bread-producer, "You must give us the cheapest
bread which unlimited competition with foreign countries can
secure ;" and then inflict on the bread-grower a tax which
directly frustrates your object of cheap bread; because it mulcts
the capital by which the bread-crops are produced at home, and
cheats the land of the nourishment which the bread-crops require? If this tax raises £6,000,000 a-year from the raw material of the agriculturist, what is it but £6,000,000 withdrawn
from one of the most reproductive sources of the wealth of
the nation ?   I ask, then, is not this relief essential to the
consummation of free trade ?   Is it not the fair demand of
skilled labour to be free from a tax upon the raw material ?
And if you wish that raw material to be worked up so as to
contribute a fair benefit to the consumer, do you suppose that
you can effect that object by the partial experiment of a handful
of maltsters with the excisemen at their backs, and all the complicated machinery by which malt may be rendered unfit for
the use of man ?   No ; you can only effect your object in the
common-sense natural way, by the unshackled competition of

the cultivators of the soil, by whose skill, industry, capital, and labour, the raw material of the soil is to be raised and increased. Now there has been a strange attempt to prejudice the true merits of this question by narrowing them to the mere effect of the tax upon malt liquors. But, quite apart from that article of consumption, I think I have shown that the tax affects the price of meat and of bread; that it affects the productive fertility of the soil, and therefore, of course, everything which the soil produces. But its effect on malt liquor is not a thing to be ridiculed. First, as to quality. I bring no charge against respectable brewers. I do not believe that they adulterate beer by any deleterious ingredients. But it is not from the respectable brewers that the workmen get their beer. The beer of the working class is bought retail, and we are told by an eminent chemist that the beer retailed to the working class is agreeably compounded of quassia, wormwood, and *cocculus indicus*, which last has the special advantage of being a poison that insures speedy intoxication. So here I grant that you may say to the working man, " It is true that the tax raises the prices of your beer, but then it gives you these two blessings in return—it accelerates the stupefaction of drunkenness, and shortens the probation of this mortal life." Secondly, as to the effect of the duty on the price of malt liquors. I shall not here attempt to add anything to the calculations of my hon. and learned friend. Whether it only tax a quart of malt liquor at 12½ per cent, as my right hon. friend the President of the Board of Trade assures us—or, as my hon. and learned friend contends, 50 per cent—that is a matter which I leave entirely to those more competent than myself to deal with. I may, indeed, think it strange that malt liquor is only taxed 12½ per cent, when the malt which we in the innocence of our hearts assume to be its principal ingredient is taxed 70 per cent; but I am old enough to know that there is no conjuring trick equal to that of figures in the hands of a clever Minister. I am contented to take my stand on the simple certainty, which the President of the Board of Trade is the last man to dispute—namely, that according to the law of competition, which affects the operations

of trade, the repeal of the malt-tax would give to the consumer
of malt liquor his most probable chance of having the best
quality at the lowest price ; and while the tax lasts he certainly
has neither. But permit me to add that I think it would be
difficult to persuade the working man that you apply your
legislation fairly to him when, in the name of free trade, you so
largely reduce your duties on the beverage of the rich, and
then, in the name of the revenue, refuse all mitigation of a tax
on the beverage of the poor—taking such special pains that the
working man shall not have the best drink at the lowest price,
that your last legislation on the subject exhausts the ingenuity
of mechanicians in order to exclude the man from the advantage
you are willing to give to a cow or a pig. But, Sir, the malt-
tax is entitled to our first consideration, not only for the
reasons I have stated, but because it now stands prominently
foremost among the objects for which the income-tax was first
imposed. What the farmers feel and say is this : " You have
levied an income-tax, of which we pay a share, for the avowed
object of establishing free trade as the mainspring of all fiscal
legislation. Availing yourselves of this mighty instrument, you
have given relief to other classes of the community in the taxes
or duties by which their energies were most crippled, or of ·
which their complaints were most loud ; but, all alone, we agriculturists have been thrust out of the pale of your benignant
consideration. The exciseman stands between us and the free
culture of our soil, just as he stood before free trade was an
experiment tried upon ourselves, or the income-tax drew from
our pockets moneys which have gone to the relief of others. You
have conceded to fellow-sufferers, far less numerous than we
are, all those arguments against the principle of excise duties to
which you turn a deaf ear when they are urged by us. Bricks
and soaps and paper have all had priority over our complaints.
But we now ask—and is it too much to ask ?—that the income-
tax should complete its object, and give us, however tardily,
some share of the relief which our contributions to that income-
tax have so largely assisted to give to all industrial occupations
except our own." " Oh," but it is said, " we do not dispute

the justice of your demand, but then your grievance is so lucrative to the Exchequer. How can you expect us to repeal all at once a duty that yields £6,000,000 a-year? A mere reduction would not satisfy the agitators, and would not get rid of the exciseman." And finally, reasoners of this kind sum up by saying, "Since we cannot give you all, we will give you nothing." But is that the way reformers deal with reforms? or is it in that way we are to "rest and be thankful"? Why, every abuse would last to the end of time if one party did not concede a something and the other party accept a something as an instalment of the whole demand. Do not forget that in this very temperate motion we do not ask you to take off the tax all at once. We only ask you to begin to take it off by any instalment you have to spare, and continue to bear us in mind whenever you can take off old taxes without imposing new ones. I do not deny that I desire and that I argue for the ultimate and total repeal of this tax; but I say this on behalf of our friends the farmers, that they are like other Englishmen— show them that you are in earnest to redress their grievance, and they, in turn, will have confidence in you as to the mode and manner of doing so, without too sudden a derangement of your financial operations; but do not dismiss them by the mockery of saying, "Since we cannot at once give you complete justice, we will give you no justice at all. Instead of justice we give you a Report from the Board of Trade." I earnestly entreat hon. gentlemen on both sides of the House to regard this question with that fairness and freedom from prejudice which I am sure is their natural desire upon all matters that affect the general interests of the community. Do not be biassed against the motion because it emanates from these benches; do not suffer it to become a party question; and do not regard it as a mere farmer's question, on which you have no interest if farmers are not your constituents. It is one of those instances in which the grievance of the producer is the wrong of the consumer. And, indeed, if I have proved to you how the tax raises the price of meat, meat is much more consumed by your constituents in towns than by our labourers in

the counties. And now as to the amount of the tax. Is it
really so great a difficulty if you will but grapple with it ? The
Chancellor of the Exchequer told us last year, on introducing
his Budget, that since 1860-61 the real diminution in our taxation had been £6,668,000. That is, within three years, above
£500,000 more than the proceeds of this malt-tax which, we
are now told, is protected from even an approach by the sanctity
of its colossal injustice ! But you say that approach cannot be
made with safety to the revenue. Yet so safely to the revenue
did you sweep away more than six millions and a half of taxes
on industry in three years, that last year you had two millions
and a half again to give away, and this year I believe you have
much the same. All these great reliefs were effected because
you were in earnest to effect them while you could avail yourselves of the income-tax. Be only as earnest to complete, by
this relief, the objects of that income-tax, and ways and means
will be found in this case, as they have been found in others,
in which a relief to the national industry has proved to be the
readiest means to increase the national income. I have always
said of this House of Commons, in which it is more than
thirty years since I first had the honour of a seat, that there has
never been a popular assembly, on the whole, so alive to the
principles of political honour, nor an aristocratic assembly, on
the whole, more desirous of doing equal justice between man
and man ; and it is from a respectful but profound conviction
that neither according to honour nor to justice you can play
fast and loose with those professions and pledges in free trade
which make the repeal of the malt-tax the logical and inevitable consequence of the Corn-law, that I entreat you not to
reject the motion of my hon. and learned friend.

XXXII.

A SPEECH

DELIVERED IN

THE HOUSE OF COMMONS

ON THE 13TH OF APRIL 1866.

On Thursday, the 12th of April 1866, the Chancellor of the Exchequer, Mr
Gladstone, moved in the House of Commons the second reading of the ·
Electoral Franchise Bill, as the first instalment of the scheme of Parliamentary Reform projected by the Government. The Member for Chester,
Earl Grosvenor, thereupon moved an amendment, which was seconded by
the Member for Lynn Regis, Lord Stanley, affirming the inexpediency of
considering any measure of the kind until such time as the House might
have before it the whole Ministerial plan for amending the representation.
A discussion arose upon this which lasted for eight nights, the original
motion for the second reading being carried at 3 o'clock on the morning of
Saturday, the 28th of April, by 318 votes to 313, giving a narrow majority
of 5 to the Government. During the second night of the debate the following speech was delivered.

[Called to the House of Lords by the title of Baron Lytton of Knebworth.
His elevation to the Peerage gazetted on Friday the 13th of July 1866.]

SIR,—I approach this subject with deep and sincere anxiety. I
cannot bring myself to regard it in a mere party point of view.
It is not to my mind a question whether the Government of to-
day is to be confirmed or displaced; it is not to my mind only a
question how many seats a party called Liberal, or a party called

Conservative, may gain or lose. The consequences of the measure
before us go far beyond these considerations. They affect, for
good or for evil, the permanent character of this House, whether
it be regarded as the fair representation of various classes and
various interests, or as a faithful likeness of the mind and state
of the whole nation, or as a deliberative assembly requiring an
amount of prudence and of cultivated intelligence beyond that of
any other popular chamber in the world ; because no other popular chamber, either in Europe or America, exerts the same control
over the executive, arrogates the same authority in maintaining
peace and provoking war, or, by the temper of its debates and the
grandeur of its renown, commands the same influence over the
ideas and the destinies of mankind. My right hon. friend the
Chancellor of the Exchequer, speaking elsewhere, said that the
magnitude of the proposed change is imperfectly understood in
the country ; yet in his speech here last night it seemed to me
rather his object to conceal its magnitude and parade its insigni-
ficance. A reform is the correction of abuses, a revolution is a
transfer of power. A bill for the redistribution of seats is a correction of abuses ; a bill for a large alteration of the franchise is,
and must be, more or less, a transfer of political power. The
Chancellor of the Exchequer gives no glimpse of that part of the
Government scheme which belongs to reform, and I think I
can show that he greatly understates that part which belongs to
revolution.

Sir, the last time her Majesty's Government proposed a Reform
Bill I ventured to state, that while the admission of a certain proportion of the working class into the franchise was essential to a
well-balanced representation,—first, that that class was not incon-
siderably represented at present ; and, secondly, that a £6 franchise would give to it the lion's share of the representation. Both
of these propositions were strongly contested, but contested by
none with more confident assurance than by my right hon. friend
the Chancellor of the Exchequer. In condescending to answer
my remarks, he asserted that the working class were now, except
in some infinitesimal degree, altogether excluded from the pale of
the constitution ; and that a £6 franchise, according " to the best,

most comprehensive, and most accurate information that could be obtained," would admit them in numbers so moderate that it would be idle to talk of the lion's share—it would admit them to less than one-third of the whole borough constituency. Now it is clear from the statistics furnished by the Government, that in both those propositions I was within the facts. Now we know that by the existing suffrage the working class already command something more than a fourth of the whole borough constituency and that a £6 franchise would give to it that lion's share, that electoral preponderance over all other classes of the borough con-stituencies which the Chancellor of the Exchequer frankly says Parliament never contemplated, and is not prepared to concede. Therefore, as the lowest verge to which the Government can ven-ture to descend, my right hon. friend contents himself with pro-posing a £7 franchise, which gives to the working class not fa short of half the borough constituency, taking it altogether— namely, as 333,000 to 362,000 electors of the other classes. That may be the proportion on this year; but it is not for this year that we legislate. And even granting that a £7 franchise is not lowered by Parliament, a £6 rental is raised to its level by time, and raised so rapidly that within three years from the next regis-tration, owing to permanent causes which necessitate the rise of urban rentals, the man who pays between £6 and £7 a-year for his house will pay £7 and become a voter. And if you pass this bill you give in all Parliamentary boroughs an additional and irresistible impetus to the rise of rent. It will be the interest of landlords and builders, the object of political parties, the natural desire of petty householders who covet a vote, whether for its own sake or as money's worth in some shape or another, to bridge over the narrow space that divides the £7 voter from the man who pays a trifling iota less; for it is not the rental of £6, but rather the rental of £6, 10s., or 2s. 6d. a-week, which forms the general staple of rents between £6 and £7; and the hon. Member for Leeds (Mr Baines), addressing his constituents the other day, truly said that the absence of the ratepaying condition is equivalent to the other 10s. in the pound. So that it must be perfectly clear to every man of sense and candour that, should you pass this bill,

that which is now a £6 rental will be a £7 franchise within three,
or at most four, years—viz., within the natural life of the present
Parliament; and thus that you will create that very preponderance
of the working class which the existent £6 rental would insure,
but which the Chancellor of the Exchequer tells us Parliament
never contemplated, and is not prepared to concede. This does
not rest on assumption; we have ample evidence of the fact in the
case of the £10 franchise. Look down these statistical tables and
see how comparatively few occupiers there are in the £9 column;
and why? because the old £9 occupiers have been absorbed into
the £10 franchise. And the reason why the increase of the £10
voters was more rapid in the early years after the bill of 1832
than it has been lately is, that in those years the process of the
absorption left less for the following years to effect. As a general
rule, at whatever rent you wish to fix a franchise, especially if
freed from ratepaying conditions, you must calculate the real
numbers so admitted to be within three years those that are represented by the rental of £1 below it. But some hon. gentlemen have said, that if the poor householder was induced, by the
gain of the franchise, to pay more for a better house, that would
be a social benefit, and an argument in favour of the bill. Yes;
but the rise of rent does not necessarily mean the improvement of
the house. Many gentlemen present know that they must now
pay £300 a-year for a London house which four years ago would
have been thought dear at £200. Nothing in this age of progress
is so rapidly progressive as the rise of rents in all the large towns.
In Parliamentary boroughs the house that is now worth £6, 10s.,
even £6, will remain just as squalid as it now is; the £7 franchise
raises its rental without bettering its accommodation. But then
it is said, with great plausibility, that the vote itself is a moral
benefit to every man, whatever his education or condition of life;
it raises his sense of dignity and self-respect. Does experience
tell you so? Was the vote a moral benefit to the freeman and
potwalloper? Do you suppose that the freemen were corrupt
merely because they were called freemen? No; they were corrupt
because they belonged to a condition of life in which, no doubt,
there are many upright and earnest politicians, but in which there

are many others who, of two rival candidates, prefer Smith and a
£5-note to Brown and the Rights of Man. You disfranchised
the freemen of Yarmouth. Did you extinguish corruption at
Yarmouth? No; you find this very year that the same class of
men are not less corrupt as petty householders than they were as
freemen. The Chancellor of the Exchequer, on the first reading
of this bill, cited as a notable illustration of the soundness of his
proposal a distinguished instance of "the intelligence and self-
guiding power of the working class." Where does he go for that
instance? To one of those eight boroughs in which the electors
of the working class are most equal in number to those of the
middle class? No; he goes to the borough of Rochdale, where
the electors that belong to the working class are only as one to
twenty of the electoral population. Does he not see how his
illustration tells against his argument? These admirable specimens of the working class required no £7 franchise to develop
their intelligence and self-guiding power. Is there anything in
the air of Rochdale more favourable to virtue than the air of Yarmouth? No; but those voters of Yarmouth had been for a long
series of years exposed to the strongest temptations poverty can
undergo when it is canvassed by wealth—temptations to which
these noble operatives of Rochdale had never been subjected. But
the operatives of Rochdale having been left thus free to mature
uncorrupted their self-guiding power, would now, I grant, be strong
enough to resist such temptation. To artisans of that kind,
whatever the political creed, I am willing to grant the franchise.
Willing, do I say? That word is too cold. I might almost wish
that, like some old commonwealth of Greece, we could admit
them to the franchise by acclamation, too proud of such fellow-
citizens to ask what rent they pay for their houses. But if you
want to make a safe experiment of a working-class suffrage, and
an experiment fair to themselves and true to the dignity of honest
and thoughtful labour, are you sure that it can be made by the
abstract principle of your bill? that is, by a uniform abasement
of the franchise applied equally to all boroughs, whatever their
population and whatever their character? Perhaps for such an
experiment the wiser plan would be to revive that variety of suf-

frage which is agreeable to the ancient custom of the constitution, and which was strongly recommended by the high authority of Sir James Mackintosh, in any further extension of populous constituencies; and having decided how many boroughs should be devoted to majorities of the working class, then select those constituencies in which the prevalence of skilled labour tends to create a superior class of artisans, and in which their numbers alone would be some safeguard against the bribes of a candidate; and giving there such a suffrage as would amply secure your object, decline to apply the same low rate of franchise to those other and numerous middle-sized boroughs in which the skilled artisans are too few to become a fair representation of the intelligence and integrity of their class, and the electoral population not sufficiently large to frustrate the bribery by which the ambition of the rich man tempts the necessities of the poor. For, do consider what are these boroughs in which, take them altogether, we are asked to make this abrupt and wholesale transfer of electoral power. Are they not really the predominant influence on the legislation of this House, and therefore in the choice and control of the imperial Government? Despite the greater wealth, despite the larger numbers, represented by the county members, the boroughs have so decided a majority in the House of Commons, that no Government can last which does not obtain the support of a considerable proportion of the borough members; whereas a Government opposed by the almost unanimity of county members, if it has the general support of the boroughs, carries its measures and secures its existence. Gentlemen have gone into calculations as to the number of boroughs in which the working classes at a £7 franchise will have majorities. The Chancellor of the Exchequer estimates the number at 60 boroughs, or 101 seats; but in a very able pamphlet by Mr Baxter—a namesake of the hon. Member for Montrose—the result given of a very elaborate calculation is, that the effect of a £7 franchise would be absolute majorities in the election of 95 members, nearly majorities in the election of 93, and from one-third to two-fifths in the election of 85. But if I am right in maintaining that the rise of rent in Parliamentary boroughs will rapidly make what is now a £6 rental a £7 franchise, the number will be considerably increased; and in most of the boroughs where the working classes will not actually have the majority, their proportion will be so large that the election will be practically in their hands. It seems to me that this fallacy pervades the argument of the Chancellor of the Exchequer—that it is only in those boroughs where the working classes are to have a clear majority that he considers their influence predominant. But a class may have a minority so large as to be practically predominant. In the county I represent it is said, and perhaps truly, that the tenant-farmers can carry an election; yet the tenant-farmers do not appear by the books to be much more than a third of the constituency. A class that has a third of a constituency has, by combining itself with one party or the other, an election in its power. When, therefore, you hand over the boroughs to the urban working class, it is the urban working class who will ultimately become the arbiters of all that concerns the system of this elaborate monarchy and this commercial commonwealth.

But it is said, " Well, but you have been admitting the urban working class to a fourth share of the suffrage without danger; you have not even been conscious that they were admitted, and therefore it can be no danger to give them a half share upon a principle which must rapidly give them a preponderant majority." Sir, that argument reminds me of the Irishman's bull : " If one quince can give so good a flavour to an apple-pie, how wonderfully good must be an apple-pie that is all quinces." The franchise of the urban working class is a generous stimulant to the action of a free state. But it is a stimulant, and you may carry a stimulant too far. The physician may recommend a certain quantity of alcohol in our daily drink, and the more it does us good the less are we conscious of the amount of the alcohol we have taken. But would the hardy Scotchman, who was all the better for his temperate glass of whisky and water, advance to a finer state of health, as the Chancellor of the Exchequer implied in his speech at Liverpool, in proportion as he swamped the water and increased the whisky ?

So much for the persuasive line of argument adopted by the Chancellor of the Exchequer; but the hon. gentleman the Member for Birmingham (Mr Bright) gives us, instead, what schoolmen call the *argumentum baculinum*. He says, "Wretched Parliament that you are, take this change now before some accident occurs, by which the working class may compel you to take something much worse!" And it is not the fault of the Member for Birmingham if one of those accidents does not now occur in the shape of a fortuitous concourse of tumultuary atoms, extending from Charing Cross to the doors of the House of Commons. Sir, on this subject of accidents, something is said by Montesquieu, which the Emperor of the French thinks sufficiently striking to quote with approval in his preface to the 'History of Cæsar.' "It is not Fortune," says Montesquieu, "which rules the world. There are general causes which act in every monarchy, and all accidents are subject to those causes. If the failure of a battle has ruined a State, there was a general cause which made it necessary that State should perish through a single battle. In a word, the principal cause drags with it the particular accident." If, then, we wish to create a general cause that may make any particular accident of a revolutionary character fatal to the independence and dignity of this grand Assembly, let us accept this argument of the bludgeon, and proclaim to the masses that we yield to intimidation that which we refuse to reason. And, Sir, if we desire to create a general cause that may make any particular accident of a democratic character fatal to the mixed Constitution of this country, let us at once accept this Bill, which, should any accident occur of a nature to accelerate the impetus and widen the circle of democracy, makes the political leaders of the urban working class the masters of the situation. Sir, I am not one of those who have an abstract and absolute horror of democracy, and who can only speak of it in the language we apply to something monstrous and abnormal. I recognise democracy as one of the genuine and legitimate forms of national polity. Like every form of government, it has its defects and faults. But it has also merits of its own—merits identified in the history of the world with marvellous achievements of individual genius, of national energies, of passionate devotion to the public cause. I would even here undertake the defence of our Anglo-Saxon colonies from much that has been said against them. But democracy seems to me essentially the Government that belongs to societies in their youth, and in which the habits of men, even more than their laws, produce a certain equality of manners and education. There is no special form of Government adapted to every varying community in every different epoch of its existence. But if there be a country in the world in which democracy would be a ruinous experiment, it is surely a country like England, with a very limited area of soil compared to the pressure of its population, with a commerce so based upon credit and national prestige, that it would perish for ever if by any neglect of democratic economy, or, what is more probable, any adventure of democratic rashness, our naval power were destroyed; and with differences of religious sects so serious that we should find it impossible to precede democracy by that universal and generous system of education without which it would be madness to make the working class the sovereign constituency of a Legislative Assembly. I may here, indeed, quote the authority of the Member for Birmingham, who, speaking the other day at Manchester on the subject of education, showed that in the States of New England education did not follow, but long preceded, the establishment of democracy. So that even in America, despite the unequalled bounty of nature, the true fathers of the future republic made a period of 150 years of education, brought home to the door of the poorest citizen, precede the establishment of a democracy, the action of which is even now qualified by checks on the Representative Chamber which, as I will show you presently, are unknown to the English House of Commons. But this Bill, you may say, does not create such a democracy. No; but it is the inevitable step to it, and it is received and understood as such by its enthusiastic supporters out of doors, who, laughing at it as a settlement of the question, even of the franchise, hail and applaud it as an instalment of the principle to which absolute democracy is the only goal. This Bill, I say, is the inevitable step to democracy, not so much because of the actual franchise it gives now either in towns or counties, but because of the abstract principle, adorned by the eloquence of members of the Government, which alone wins to their Bill the approval of the National Re-

form League—viz., that every working man has a right to a vote;
and while no political community could exist for a quarter of an
hour if all rights which speculative philosophers say we take from
nature were not merged in an acquiescence to the social compact,
that we have no rights except those that we take by law, this
solitary right of an electoral vote forms an exception, and the
privation of it constitutes a wrong. By this principle you create
and sanction and perpetuate a discontent on the part of every
working man whom the suffrage you bestow on his fellow-work-
men still excludes, and you gather round the doors that your
principle keeps ajar the millions whom your principle invites to
enter. "What, then," says the Chancellor of the Exchequer?
"Do not regard these new applicants as an invading army. Are
they not your own fellow-Christians? Are they not your own
flesh and blood?" I share in the amazement general among his
warmest admirers, how a man like my right hon. friend can
descend to a species of argument so hollow in itself, and so perilous in its logical deductions. So hollow in itself, because suppose, for instance, I introduced a Reform Bill by which I admitted
rural voters to swamp the urban voters, as you propose to admit
the urban voters to swamp the agricultural element; and suppose
I said, "Do not regard these honest farmers as an invading army.
Are they not your own fellow-Christians? Are they not your
own flesh and blood?" Would you not answer then—perhaps
less civilly than we wish to answer now—"All that may be very
fine ; but the mind and opinion of one set of fellow-Christians are
not to be overborne by the flesh and the blood of another set?"
But see how perilous are the deductions to be drawn from an ir-
relevant platitude when it is used as an argument by a man in
authority, and inscribed, as the very few Liberal journals which
favour the Bill say that this platitude shall be inscribed, on the
banner of Democratic Reform. I will assume for the moment—
my right hon. friend will pardon and correct me if I am wrong—
that the Chancellor of the Exchequer is not in favour of universal
suffrage. But how can he oppose it consistently with his own
inscription on his own banner of Reform? What has he to say
to the millions who will ask him one day, "Are we an invading

army? Are we not fellow-Christians? Are we not your own
flesh and blood?" Does he think it will be answer enough to
give that kind of modified opinion which he put forth last night,
and to say, "Well, that is very true. For my own part, in my
individual capacity, I cannot see that there is any danger in admitting you, but still you know it is wise to proceed gradually.
A £7 voter is real flesh and blood, but you are only gradual flesh
and blood. Read Darwin on the origin of species, and learn that
you are fellow-Christians in an imperfect state of development."
That which is an amiable sentiment when applied to the claim of
all mankind to our humanity and compassion, becomes a doctrine
formidable to those who dislike universal suffrage when it is
applied to a principle of political franchise by the most conspicuous Minister of the British Crown. Sir, the most painful
part of this discussion is that which is forced upon us by the
Government statistics, sharply separating the working class from
the rest of the community, and thus rendering it difficult to argue
against the abstract principle of Democracy without wounding the
honourable pride of men with whom every employer of labour, be
he manufacturer, merchant, or country gentleman, is brought into
affectionate and familiar contact. Do you suppose it does not go
to the heart of a gentleman if he utter a word which, either from
his own defect of language, or from an unfair perversion of his
meaning, hurts the manly feelings even of the humble labourer with
whom he has formed an intimacy as cordial as any which exists
among those equals whom he calls his honourable and noble
friends? And what man of letters does not revere those lofty
aspirations of the educated artisan towards a more perfect form of
human society—which may, indeed, be Utopian, but which form
an eternal link between the aims of educated labour and the
dreams of philosophy and genius? But surely, looking to this
present state of this workday world, it is no disrespect to the
urban working class if, in their relation to the State, I object to
cut out of them a rude slice, and, without any test whatever of
intelligence, give to that slice a preponderating influence in the
constituent body and the legislation of this complicated empire.
Why, Sir, I should have the same objection to the preponderating

influence of scholars and men of science, or of great merchants, or
of a territorial aristocracy. Each of such sections, however indisputably honest and intelligent, would fail to represent that common
sense of the common interest which is best expressed by the word
" commonwealth," and which can only be fairly represented where
the middle class is, on the whole, largely preponderant. Not that
the middle class has not as many faults of its own as any other
class above or below, but that, on the whole, it the most faithfully
represents all the interests and opinions which constitute the
mind and welfare of a nation, and the most felicitously reconciles
the securities of order with the demands of freedom. And are
men to be stigmatised as traitors and conspirators because they
desire to preserve from virtual disfranchisement and political
subjugation the middle-class constituents of which they are as yet
the trustees ? The Chancellor of the Exchequer lays much stress
on the fact that all the working class do not pull together—that
they are not all of one mind as respects politics. I do not say
that they are ; but I say this—that where the working class obtain
a marked and general predominance, they cannot fail to colour
and influence legislation, especially where questions in which they
feel a special interest are concerned. All clergymen do not agree
in politics ; but if they returned the majority of Members, I fancy
you would feel their influence in a division on church rates. All
farmers do not agree in politics ; but if they returned the majority
of Members, you would feel their influence in a division on the
malt tax. All working men do not agree in politics ; but as
soon as they return the majority of Members, rely upon it you
will feel their influence in those questions between labour and
capital, between manufacturer and mechanic, between supply and
demand, upon which the very existence of this commercial England depends. Even in foreign affairs as well as domestic, the
very virtues of the working men, in their detestation of what they
consider tyranny and injustice, would be a perpetual source of
danger, did they return a majority of Members. The Member for
Birmingham says, this Bill is wanted to save the country from the
risk of war, provoked by the depravity of Tories. It might be
answer enough to say, that all the wars in which we have been

engaged since 1815 had their origin under Liberal Administrations. But what says the hon. Member for Brighton (Mr Fawcett), who spoke on the first reading of this Bill with so much ability and promise? Why, that the working class would have gone to war with Russia on behalf of Poland. That is quite consistent with their generous tendency to side with the weak against the strong. A House of Commons, had the large majority been chosen by the working class, would then have wished to provoke a war with Russia. But a war more disproportioned to our powers, less sanctioned by our interests, and more vainly exhaustive of blood and treasure, the imagination of man cannot conceive. Why do such dangers never occur in America and France—countries in which universal suffrage is adopted? Because both in America and France the popular Chamber has not the same voice in foreign affairs, in creating Cabinets and determining the choice between peace and war. And the example of both those countries makes the fact clear, that in proportion as you lower the scale of franchise to the preponderance of the working class, the safety of the State compels you to limit the powers and authority of the Representative Chamber. Nay—if law did not, public opinion would. The more you lower the standard of the constituency below the average education of the country, the more you will transfer the intellectual power of this House to some upper Chamber, whether it be an English House of Lords or an American Senate. Take America itself. Every man there looks, not to the House of Representatives, but to the Senate, on questions that affect the general interests of the nation. The Senate there alone discusses foreign affairs, and when it likes can become the executive body, resolve itself into a Secret Committee, and exclude the reporters. The wise safeguard of America against her popular suffrage is in the scantiness of the powers she leaves to her House of Representatives. I daresay you might grant not only the £7 franchise, but even universal suffrage in this country, with safety as to foreign affairs, with safety as to making and unmaking Cabinets, and with safety to everything except genuine freedom, if you then left to the House of Commons as little influence, power, weight, and authority as are left to the Representative Chambers of America and France.

But, Sir, whatever objection there may be in the principle of
this Bill itself is increased to an extent which no man can define by the mode in which the Government propose to deal with
it. We are favoured with a volume of statistics, by which we
are to compute how many boroughs will represent a majority of
the working class, how many will represent a majority of the
middle class, to what degree the balance between rural and urban
constituencies will be disturbed or maintained ; and yet it is perfectly clear that all our calculations may be made utterly worthless by a new distribution of seats and a new definition of the
boundaries of boroughs. It is true that, before we proceed to
Committee, the Government will favour us with their ideas on
these subjects. But how? By Bills with which they do not
intend to proceed till this Bill becomes law. What answer have
you to the masterly argument of my noble friend the Member
for King's Lynn? "Supposing we were satisfied with the
scheme submitted as to re-distribution, what guarantee should
we have that that scheme might not be altogether changed next
Session?" Possibly, during the recess, those "advanced Reformers" who advise her Majesty's advisers may declare that a
scheme much more comprehensive is absolutely essential, and
her Majesty's Ministers may think it necessary to listen to their
advice. Possibly the material and spirit of the Government
may be as much changed next session as by one lamented loss
it has been changed since the last ; and the Cabinet of 1867
may as much vary from the Cabinet of 1866 in its views of Reform as the Cabinet of 1866 has varied from the Cabinet of 1865.
But the Government will, I understand, declare that, as it
stands or falls by this Bill, so it will stand or fall by its other
Bills—that is, next year. Well, but if it carries this Bill and
stands, before it carries the other Bills it may fall, or Parliament
may be dissolved, and the whole question as to seats and boundaries and remedies against corruption may be referred to new
constituencies created by a Bill of which the only ardent advocates are in favour of electoral districts and vote by ballot. But
if, having once passed this Bill and made it law, we were then
to proceed immediately to the other Government measures

necessary for the completion of their scheme of Reform, would this House be as competent as the Chancellor of the Exchequer assures us to the task of making that scheme conclusive and binding? We should be literally Members without constituencies. We should have extinguished our old constituencies, and be without authority to act for the new constituencies, that have never chosen us. Suppose we did deal with some 20 or 30 seats, and in so dealing failed to satisfy the next Parliament, chosen by a more democratic suffrage, would not our successors say, with truth, that when we extinguished our constituencies we had lost the right of representatives to prejudge questions affecting the electoral bodies to which we were without any existent responsibilities? And with what heart should we set about the most ordinary work of legislation! With what uncertainty of temper should we address ourselves, no longer to the men who sent us here, but to that Virgilian threshold of souls not yet launched into the world, whom we must seek to propitiate before they are even born! We should drag out the rest of our doleful existence like those monks of La Trappe who have no other thought but that of *memento mori*, and no other occupation but that of digging their own graves. Sir, my right hon. friend the Chancellor of the Exchequer must forgive me if I venture to doubt, whether there is an educated man in this House or out of it who accepts the validity of his reason—the want of time—for thrusting upon us this measure, isolated and detached from all other portions of a general scheme of Reform, and insisting that we shall affirm its principle without even a guess as to the constituent bodies to which that principle is to be applied. No, Sir; every one must feel that the true reason for this mode of dealing with the question is that which was so frankly announced some months ago by the hon. gentleman the Member for Birmingham, namely, that if the House can be persuaded to pass this Bill in its simple and severe integrity, the Bill itself becomes the leverage for lifting out of the representation, whether in this Parliament or the next, many of the very Members who may thus be entrapped to their own perdition—many Members, indeed, whom a Bill for redistribution of seats

may spare for the moment, but whom a Parliament chosen by
the provisions of this Bill will sacrifice to the *manes* of those
whom they have assisted to destroy. Indeed, I have observed
that in all the public meetings held in favour of this Bill, no
speaker has accepted the reason for not proceeding simultaneously with the question of redistribution, but every speaker has
accepted the reason stated by the Member for Birmingham
(often interrupted by loud cries from the body of his audience),
—" Let us in, let us in, and we'll soon settle the question of
seats." Sir, no one can blame the Member for Birmingham for
the candour with which he avows his share in a conspiracy to
which I will not be so discourteous as to apply the epithet of
" dirty," but a conspiracy in which Members are to be allured to
resign " this pleasing, anxious being," and kept so blindfold that
they have even not the privilege to " cast a lingering look behind." But with all deference to my right hon. friend the
Chancellor of the Exchequer, I think the House has a right to
complain of him that he does not imitate the candour of the
Member for Birmingham. Sir, the leader of this House is more
than the chief of party, more than the organ of a Cabinet—he
owes a duty to the House itself, and in all things that appertain to
our common existence we have a right to expect from him an
ingenuous frankness, incompatible with these masked batteries
and these crafty decoys into the dark. If there be among us
any Members who, in voting for the principle of this Bill, will by
the completion of the scheme it involves destroy their own seats
in Parliament, I think they have a right to be so far warned of
their fate as to have the scheme put plainly before them by the
Minister who, in leading the House of Commons, represents that
good faith and straightforward dealing between man and man,
without which no conceivable suffrage could make us the true
image of the English nation.

Now, Sir, before I conclude, let me, with great respect, address
a few words to those moderate Liberals who do not desire to be
buried alive in that memorable tomb in Westminster Abbey in
which the last of the Whigs is to rest, and his countrymen to be
thankful that he can repose. To them I say, with the Chan-

cellor of the Exchequer, "Be wise, and be wise in time." Be
wise before you cross the Rubicon and burn your vessels. There
is a story of a famous French preacher, who, delivering a sermon
on the duty of wives, said, "I see a woman present who has
been guilty of disobedience to her husband, and, in order to
point her out to universal condemnation, I will fling this breviary
at her head." He lifted the book, and every female head present ducked and dived. "Alas!" said the preacher, "the
multitude of the offenders necessitates a general amnesty."
Now, I see a gentleman opposite who is guilty of detesting this
Bill, and yet intends to vote for it : and if, in order to point him
out to universal condemnation, the courtesies of Parliament
would permit me to fling these statistics at his head, so many
heads opposite would duck and dive that nothing but a general
amnesty could deal with such a multitude of offenders. Sir, I
am the last man to disparage that loyal discipline of party by
which we must all so often suborn our individual opinions to
the decision of those whom we accept as our leaders. I do not,
therefore, presume to impugn the motives of any fellow Member
who, though detesting this Bill, yet intends to vote for it. But
I believe that the respect and gratitude of that large portion of
the Liberal public which is represented by so powerful a majority
of the Liberal press, will be the reward of those who, on a
question so grave, and of which the results are so irrevocable,
prefer the welfare and safety of their native country to a blind
submission to a Government that has not even the courage of
its own opinions ; for it does not dare to invite to its Cabinet
the powerful orator who tells it the way to go ; and thus, at least,
make him responsible to his Sovereign for the counsels he dic-
tates to her Ministers. For my part, I can honestly say that,
looking to the nature of this Bill, the mode in which it is introduced, and the arguments by which it is defended, my vote
against it will be given, not as Conservative against Liberal, not
as employer against workman, not as Englishman against
Englishman, but as Englishman for the sake of our common
England.

XXXIII.

A SPEECH

DELIVERED IN

THE FREEMASON'S HALL

ON THE 2D OF NOVEMBER 1867.

On Saturday evening, the 2d of November 1867, Lord Lytton presided as Chairman at the Farewell Banquet given to Mr Charles Dickens prior to his departure on a Reading Tour in the United States. In giving the toast of the evening, the following Speech was delivered.

MY LORDS AND GENTLEMEN,—I now approach the toast which is special to the occasion that has brought together a meeting so numerous and so singularly distinguished. You have paid the customary honours to our beloved sovereign, due not only to her personal virtues, but to that principle of constitutional monarchy in which the communities of Europe recognise the happiest mode of uniting liberty with order, and giving to the aspirations for the future a definite starting-point in the experience and the habits of the past. You are now invited to do honour to a different kind of royalty, which is seldom peacefully acknowledged until he who wins and adorns it ceases to exist in the body, and is no longer conscious of the empire which his thoughts bequeath to his name. Happy is the man who makes clear his title-deeds to the royalty of genius while he yet lives to enjoy the gratitude

and reverence of those whom he has subjected to his sway.
Though it is by conquest that he achieves his throne, he at least
is a conqueror whom the conquered bless; and the more despoti-
cally he enthralls, the dearer he becomes to the hearts of men.
Seldom, I say, has that kind of royalty been quietly conceded to
any man of genius until his tomb becomes his throne, and yet
there is not one of us now present who thinks it strange that it is
granted without a murmur to the guest whom we receive to-
night. It has been said by a Roman poet that nature, designing
to distinguish the human race from the inferior animals by that
faculty of social progress which makes each combine with each for
the aid and defence of all, gave to men *mollissima corda*,—hearts
the most accessible to sympathy with their fellow kind ; and
hence tears, and permit me to add, and hence laughter, became
the special and the noblest attributes of humanity. Therefore it
is humanity itself which obeys an irresistible instinct when it
renders homage to one who refines it by tears that never enfeeble,
and by a laughter that never degrades. You know that we are
about to intrust our honoured countryman to the hospitality of
those kindred shores in which his writings are as much " household words " as they are in the homes of England. And if I may
presume to speak as a politician, I should say that no time could
be more happily chosen for his visit ; because our American kinsfolk have conceived, rightly or wrongfully, that they have some
cause of complaint against ourselves, and out of all England we
could not have selected an envoy more calculated to allay irritation and to propitiate goodwill. In the matter of goodwill
there is a distinction between us English and the Americans
which may for a time operate to our disadvantage ; for we
English insist upon claiming all Americans as belonging to our
race, and springing from the same ancestry as ourselves, and
hence the idea of any actual hostility between them and us shocks
our sense of relationship; and yet in reality a large and very
active proportion of the American people derives its origin from
other races besides the Anglo-Saxon. German and Dutch and
Celtic forefathers combine to form the giant family of the United
States; but there is one cause for ever at work to cement all

these varieties of origin, and to compel the American people, as
a whole, to be as proud as we are of their affinity with the English
race. What is that cause? What is that agency? Is it not
that of one language in common between the two nations? It
is in the same mother tongue that their poets must sing, that
their philosophers must reason, that their orators must argue
upon truth or contend for power. I see before me a distinguished
guest, distinguished for the manner in which he has brought together all that is most modern in sentiment with all that is most
scholastic in thought and language; permit me to say, Mr
Matthew Arnold. I appeal to him if I am not right when I say
that it is by a language in common that all differences of origin
sooner or later are welded together—that Etruscans, and Sabines,
and Oscans, and Romans, became one family, as Latins once, as
Italians now? Before that agency of one language in common
have not all differences of ancestral origin in England between
Britons, Saxons, Danes, and Normans, melted away; and must
not all similar differences equally melt away in the nurseries of
American mothers, extracting the earliest lessons of their children
from our own English Bible, or in the schools of preceptors who
must resort to the same models of language whenever they bid
their pupils rival the prose of Macaulay and Prescott, or emulate
the verse of Tennyson and Longfellow? Now, it seems to me that
nothing can more quicken the sense of that relationship which a
language in common creates, than the presence and the voice of
a writer equally honoured and beloved in the old world and in the
new; and I cannot but think that wherever our American kinsfolk welcome that presence, or hang spell-bound on that voice,
they will feel irresistibly how much of fellowship and unison there
is between the hearts of America and England. So that when
our countryman quits their shores he will leave behind him many
a new friend to the old fatherland which greets them through him
so cordially in the accents of the mother tongue. And in those
accents what a sense of priceless obligations—obligations personal
to him, and through him to the land he represents—must steal
over his American audience! How many hours in which pain
and sickness have changed into cheerfulness and mirth beneath

the wand of this enchanter! How many a combatant beaten down in the battle of life—and nowhere is the battle of life more sharply waged than in the commonwealth of America—has caught new hope, new courage, new force from the manly lessons of this unobtrusive teacher! Gentlemen, it is no wonder that the rising generation of a people who have learned to think and to feel in our language, should eagerly desire to see face to face the man to whose genius, from their very childhood, they have turned for warmth and for light as instinctively as young plants turn to the sun. But I must not forget that it is not I whom you have come to hear ; and all I might say, if I had to vindicate the fame of our guest from disparagement or cavil, would seem but tedious and commonplace when addressed to those who know that his career has passed beyond the ordeal of contemporaneous criticism, and that in the applause of foreign nations it has found a fore-taste of the judgment of posterity. I feel as if every word that I have already said had too long delayed the toast which I now propose, " A prosperous voyage, health and long life, to our illus-trious guest and countryman, Charles Dickens."

XXXIV.

A SPEECH

DELIVERED IN

THE TOWN HALL AT ST ALBAN'S

On Monday the 2d of August 1869.

On Monday, the 2d of August 1869, the British Archæological Congress was held in the Court House of the Town Hall at St Alban's, under the Presidency of Lord Lytton. The following was the Inaugural Address then delivered.

LADIES AND GENTLEMEN,—Allow me first, in your name, to welcome to the county of Hertford, and to this ancient town of St Alban's, the distinguished members of the British Archæological Association who honour us with their visit. That Association was commenced in 1843 by the zeal and energy of a few earnest students of our national history as elucidated by our national monuments. Among the foremost of those students was our guest, Mr Thomas Wright, whose delightful works have done so much to render us familiar with the manners and customs of our ancestors. It is stated by one of my predecessors in this chair, that at the time the Association was formed, the taste for antiquarian research was very partial, and somewhat languid; that there were no local museums in which objects of national antiquity could be collected, and even the British Museum had no special place for their recep-

tion ; that, with some illustrious exceptions, archæology was rather
the amusement of amateurs than the study of practical thinkers
and profound scholars ; and that it is mainly owing to the labours
of this Association that local museums may now be found in most
of our principal towns, and that archæology has been raised from
a graceful accomplishment to the dignity of a philosophical science.
I should not have ventured to accept the distinguished office I
hold to-day, if I had found that it had been generally occupied on
similar occasions by professed archæologists. But it seems that
when the Archæological Association selects any particular county
for its annual Congress, its more eminent members consent to forego
their own claims to the chair of President in favour of some inhabitant of the district they visit, who does not pretend to rival the
learning of those he represents ; but who reveres the studies which
they adorn, and is familiar with the localities whose monuments
attract their research. These, indeed, are my sole claims to the
distinction conferred upon me by the British Archæological Association. As a writer I should be ungrateful, indeed, if I did not
acknowledge how much I am indebted to the archæologist whenever I have endeavoured to trace upon my canvas some image of
the past ; while, as a Hertfordshire man, I am proud to think that
our county is worthy of the visitation, from which its history and
its monuments will derive fresh illustrations and additional interest. Camden, indeed, has said in his ' Britannia ' that " for the
renown of antiquity Hertfordshire may vie with any of its neighbours, for scarce any other county can show so many remains."
Archæology has been called the handmaid of history ; and, indeed,
without its aid, history would as little represent the particular
time it endeavours to recall as the drawing of a skeleton would
represent the features and the form by which the individual human
being was recognised while in life. It is to the skeleton of a former age that archæology restores the flesh and the sinews and the
lineaments that distinguish it from the countless centuries of which
it is a link, clothes it in the very garments that it wore, and re-
builds the very home in which it dwelt.

But archæology is not only the handmaid of history, it is also
the conservator of art. It disinters from neglected tombs the in-

ventions of departed genius, and bids them serve as studies and
sources of inspiration to the genius of a later day. When the
Baths of Titus were excavated at Rome, the attention of Raphael
was directed by a fellow-artist to their faded arabesques. Those
arabesques roused his own creative imagination, and under his
pencil reappeared on the walls of the Vatican in new and original
combinations of form and colour. Nay, that discovery, and the
train of ideas it aroused, may be said to have suggested the delicate
tracery and elaborate ornament of that new school of architecture
called the *Renaissance*, out of which grew the palaces of Fontaine-
bleau and Heidelberg, and which we have nationalised in England
in those noble manorial residences which adorn the reigns of Elizabeth and James.

But it is not only history and the plastic arts which are indebted
to the science of the archæologist. It is amongst his labours to
guard from oblivion the myths, the traditions, the legends of former days; and critical and severe though his genius and its obligations must be, still it is to his care that we owe the preservation
of many a pure and sacred well-spring of poetry and romance,—
well-springs from which Spenser and Milton, Dryden, Gray, Words-
worth, and Scott, have drawn each his own special stream of inspiration, to refresh the banks that he cultivated, and nourish the
flowers that he reared. Last, and not least, of our obligations to
the spirit of archæology is, that it stimulates and deepens in the
heart of a people sentiments of pride and affection for the native
land. In proportion as we cherish the memories of our ancestors,
and revere the heirlooms they have left us, in monuments reared
by their piety, or bearing witness of their lives and their deeds,
the soil which they trod becomes hallowed ground; and we feel
that patriotism is no idle name, but the mainspring of every policy
which makes statesmen wise, and the borders of a state secure.
Indeed, if we look back to the annals of the world we find that
there is no surer sign of the impending downfall of any nation
than a cynical contempt for the memorials of its old renown.
When Gibbon gives us the mournful picture of Roman corruption
and decrepitude, just before the final extinction of the Western
Empire and the accession of a barbarian king to the throne of the

Cæsars, he tells us "that the monuments of consular or imperial greatness were no longer revered as the glory of the capital; they were only esteemed as an inexhaustible mine of materials, cheaper and more convenient than the distant quarry." And with this miserable desecration of objects that attested the majesty of Rome, the very name of the Roman passed away; and, to borrow the expression of a French writer, "the descendants of Brutus became the vassals of the Goth."

But, ladies and gentlemen, if the national spirit and the love of country be thus generally nourished by that searching but reverential study of the past, which is called archæology, there is an inherent principle in the human mind which makes the affections more intense by limiting their range. A man, for instance, may take but a lukewarm interest in the antiquities of the whole British empire, compared to that which he may readily be induced to take in the antiquities of the county to which he belongs. "Things distant," says an old writer, "affect us feebly; things which are brought under our eyes rouse our emotions, and appeal to our hearts;" and so, when a man of some intelligence and susceptibility of feeling finds that localities with which he is familiar are the sites in which great events took place, or in which great men had their residence or their birthplace, then the whole scene takes a new interest, a new charm; an importance and dignity are given to the places through which he passes daily, perhaps to the very fields which surround his home; he conceives a pride in that portion of the land in which Providence has cast his lot, and insensibly—for all such operations of the mind are insensible—that pride extends its range from his immediate district to the nation and the race of which he is a member. For this reason I think that the British Archæological Association has done most wisely in holding an annual Congress at successive divisions of our common country. They thus sow in one place those seeds of patriotism and of art which are wafted to other places more remote, till that same culture of ideas which had commenced in a county town gradually embraces the surface of the kingdom; and in visiting our county, and selecting St Alban's for their central meeting-place, the Association will find memorials and reminiscences that illustrate the

history of our native island from its earliest date to its halting
point in our own day ; from the ancient Briton whose ancestor, if
Welsh tradition be true, crossed what is called in Welsh language
" the hazy sea," from the land of the Crimea, to the beloved and
lamented statesman who had a home at Brocket, and under whose
auspices was closed that last British war undertaken for the cause
of European civilisation, which has left the tombs of heroes on
those Crimean shores from which came the exiles that have given
to Scotland, Wales, and England, their common name of Britain.
I need not say to you who listen to me in the Town Hall of St
Alban's, that round the spot on which we assemble one of the
bravest and fiercest of the British tribes held dominion.   Far and
near, round this spot, we tread on ground which witnessed their
dauntless if despairing resistance to the Roman invader.   But here
let me pause to make this reflection.

The difference between one race and another appears to be according to the mental organisation by which any given race can
receive ideas from a more civilised race by which it is subdued, or
with which it is brought into contact.   If it cannot receive and incorporate such ideas, it withers and fades away, just as the Red
Indian withers and fades away beside the superior civilisation of
the American settlers.   But England never seems, from the earliest
historical records, to have been inhabited by any race which did
not accept ideas of improved civilisation from its visitors or conquerors.   The ancient Britons were not ignorant barbarians—in
our modern sense of the word barbarian—at the time of the Roman
conquest.   Their skill in agriculture was considerable ; they had
in familiar use implements and machinery, such as carriages, the
watermill, the windmill, which attest their application of science
to the arts of husbandry.   They had formed towns and cities in
which was carried on a trade so flourishing that Gaul is said to
have derived from Britain the supplies with which it resisted Rome.
But there were some ideas they received from the Romans utterly
unknown to them before, and which are incorporated in the civilisation we now boast and enjoy.   They received the idea of facility
of transit and communication.   The Romans were to the ancient
world what the railway companies are to the modern.   They were

the great constructors of roads and highways: the word "street"
is a vestige of the Roman; it is derived from *stratum*, a paved
causeway. The Britons owed next, to Roman ideas, the introduction of civil law; and the moment the principle of secular justice
between man and man was familiarised to their minds, the priestly
domination of the Druids, with all its sanguinary superstitions,
passed away. The Britons owed next, to Rome, that institution
of municipal towns to which the philosophical statesman, Mons.
Guizot, traces the rise of modern freedom in its emancipation from
feudal oppression and feudal serfdom. At the time the Romans
finally withdrew from Britain no less than ninety-two considerable
towns had arisen, of which thirty-three cities possessed superior
privileges; each of them possessing a municipal government distributed amongst annual magistrates, a select senate, and a popular assembly; possessing the management of a common revenue,
and exercising civil and criminal jurisdiction. Amongst the most
famous of these cities, I need not tell you, was the ancient Verulam, which was a *municipium* in the time of Nero, and of which
the remains are now being brought more clearly to light by the
labours of the Association, under the skilful guidance of Mr Edward
Roberts. I understand that the plan of the city has now been distinctly traced, and I am told by Mr Roberts that it bears a close
resemblance to that of Pompeii. Two houses have been already
disinterred; and on Wednesday you will be enabled to see at least
the stage, proscenium, and orchestra of the ancient theatre—the
only Roman theatre, I believe, yet found in this country; and the
whole of which will shortly, by Lord Verulam's liberal permission,
be laid open to inspection, and form one of the most valuable ac-
quisitions to the treasure-house of British antiquities. Lastly, it
was to the Roman conqueror that the Britons owed, if not the first
partial conception, at least the national recognition of that Christian faith whose earliest English martyr has bequeathed his name
to St Alban's.

When we pass to the age of the Anglo-Saxons, their vestiges in
this county surround us on every side. The names of places, familiar to us as household words, mark their residences: the terminals
-by, -bury, -ley, -wick, -worth, -ham, are indicative of Saxon homes,

and there is no county in which they more abound than Hertfordshire. And here I may be permitted to observe that the main
reason why the language of the Anglo-Saxon survived the Norman
invasion, and rapidly supplanted the language of the conqueror,
does not appear to me to have been clearly stated by our historians. I take the reason to be simply this: the language that men
speak in after life is formed in the nursery,—it is learned from the
lips of the mother. Now those adventurers of Scandinavian origin who established themselves in Normandy did not seek their
wives in Scandinavia but in France ; and thus their children learned
in the nursery the French language. In like manner, when they
conquered England, those who were still unmarried sought their
wives among the Saxons ; in the second generation such intermar-
riages were almost universal ; and thus the language of the mothers naturally became that of the children, and being also the
language of the servants employed in the household, the French
language necessarily waned, receded, and at last became merged in
the domestic element of the Anglo-Saxon, retaining only such of
its native liveliness and adaptability to metrical rhyme and cadence
as served to enrich the earliest utterances of our English poetry in
the Muse, at once grave and sportive, at once courtly and popular,
who inspired the lips of Chaucer.

I need not say to my listeners that throughout the Heptarchy,
till the consolidation of the several kingdoms under one imperial
ruler, the town and neighbourhood of St Alban's are part and
parcel of Anglo-Saxon history ; and if I do not dwell on the memorable events connected with this locality during that early epoch,
it is because we are promised some essays on that subject by our
distinguished and learned visitors. In this county, too, are the
scenes of ,fierce and heroic conflicts between the Saxons and the
Danes. Where now stands the town of Ware anchored the light
vessels which constituted the Danish navy, as it sailed from London along the Thames to the entrance of the river Lea. There
they besieged the town of Hertford, which had been a place of
some worth even in the time of the Britons ; and there the remarkable military genius of Alfred the Great, at once acute and patient,
studying the nature of the river, diverted its stream into three

currents, and stranded the vessels of the invader, which were seized as spoil by the Londoners. The site of the fort erected by the Danes, and of the two forts built by King Alfred, has, I understand, been ascertained by a resident of Hertford, who has promised a paper on the subject. Further on, in the little town of Welwyn, the historian of our county tells us that, "according to common fame, the massacre of the Danes began ;" probably at Danesbury, a name which, I believe, signified a fortified Danish camp. Nor are we, in this county, more destitute of memorials of the turbulent ages which followed the Norman conquest. When Prince Louis of France invaded England, no stronghold, with the exception of Dover, resisted his siege with more valour, or with greater loss to the invader, than the Castle of Hertford. Under the soil around those old walls which now enclose the peaceful residence of our legal friend, Mr Longmore, as if to show that in the progress of civilisation the rage of war is transferred from the battle-field to the courts of law,—under that soil many an invading French-man found his homeless grave. That castle at Hertford was, in the Wars of the Roses, possessed by Margaret of Anjou ; and here, in St Peter Street, at St Alban's, on the 22d May 1455, her ill-fated husband, Henry VI., pitched his standard against the armies of the White Rose, led by Richard Duke of York, and the great Earls of Warwick and Salisbury. And here again, on the 17th of February 1461, he was brought from London by Warwick, and made the nominal and reluctant representative of a conflict against his Queen, who, however, delivered him from the custody of the Yorkists, and sullied her victory by such plunder and cruelty as a few days afterwards insured the crown to Edward IV. On the summit of the church tower at Hadley is still seen the lantern which, according to tradition, lighted the forces of Edward IV. through the dense fog which the superstition of the time believed to have been raised by the incantations of Friar Bungay, a famous wizard. Through the veil of that fog was fought the battle of Bar-net—a battle among the most important of English history, whether for its immediate consequences or its ultimate results. On that field of Barnet the power of the great feudal barons expired with Warwick, the kingmaker, and a new era in the records of liberty

and civil progress practically commenced ; for I am convinced, by
a somewhat careful study of that time, that the contest between
the houses of York and Lancaster was not, as many historians
have treated it, a mere dispute of title to the throne, or a mere
rivalry for power between the great feudal chiefs. There was also
a great political and moral principle at stake in the conflict. The
house of Lancaster, with its monkish king, represented the elder
and more intolerant spirit of papal persecutions. It was under
that house that the first religious reformers had been mercilessly
condemned to the gibbet and the flames ; and in the martyrdom
of the Lollards, Henry IV. and Henry V. left a terrible legacy of
wrath and doom to Henry VI. Besides the numerous descendants
of the Lollards, large bodies of the Church itself, including the
clergy, accepted notions of religious reform ; and these necessarily
were alienated from the house of Lancaster, and inclined to the
house of York. With the house of York, too, were the great centres
of energy and intelligence—London and the principal trading cities.
The commercial spirit established a certain familiar sympathy with
Edward IV., who was himself a merchant, venturing commercial
speculations in ships fitted out by himself. Thus the battle of
Barnet, which confirmed the house of York on the throne, was in
fact fought between the new ideas and the old ; and those new
ideas which gave power to the middle class in the reign of Henry
VII., and rendered the religious reformation in the reign of Henry
VIII. popular, despite its violent excesses, shared at Barnet the
victory of the king under whom was established the first printing-
press known in England.

But Hertfordshire is not eminent only for the memorable events
connected with our national history, nor only dear to the archæologist for the material relics of antiquity : the names of great men
consecrate localities, and are often more familiar than the records
of a battle, and more lasting than monuments of stone. Our
county has furnished either the birthplace or the home of no in-
considerable persons. According to tradition, Cashiobury was
the royal seat of Cassivellaunus, the commander-in-chief of the
British kings who stormed the camp of the Romans in their
march upon Verulam ; and passing to the noble family that now

holds its domains, Cashiobury found an owner as brave as its old
British possessor in the first Lord Capel,—faithful in life and in
death to the cause of Charles I. Near to the town of Hitchin, in
which stood the priory of the White Carmelites, now possessed by
our esteemed friend, Mr Delmé Radcliffe (the author, by the by,
of a charming book entitled 'The Noble Science,'—a name that he
applies, not to the science of archæology, as he ought, but to the
science of the chase, of which he is a distinguished professor), near
to that town, in the rural hamlet of Offley, died the magnificent
Offa, founder of St Alban's Abbey. King's Langley was the birthplace of Edmond de Langley, the brave son of Edward III., afterwards created Duke of York. Close beside it, at Abbot's Langley, was born Nicholas Breakspear, afterwards Pope Adrian IV.
Moor Park is identified with the names of Cardinal Wolsey and of
the ill-fated Duke of Monmouth. At Aldenham lived for a time
the father of the great Lord Falkland, who must there have passed
some years of his studious boyhood. Knebworth, before it passed
to the family of which I am the representative, belonged to that
flower of chivalry, Sir Walter Nanny. Baldock owes its origin
to the Knight Templars, who had also a lodge at Temple Dinsley.
Gobions belonged to the illustrious Sir Thomas More. Sir John
Mandeville, the famous traveller (who, if he invented his travels,
beat us all in the art of romance), was a native of St Alban's.
Thomas Stanley, the learned author of the 'Lives of the Philosophers,' lived at Cumberlow. Sir Ralph Sadler, that great ornament of his time as a soldier, negotiator, and statesman, lived at
Standon, and is buried in its church. Welwyn is immortalised as
the home of Edward Young, the author of 'Night Thoughts;' and
in our generation, of one of the greatest scholars England has ever
produced, Mr Fynes Clinton, the author of 'Fasti Hellenici.' Pan-
shanger is associated with the name of Cowper,—a name rendered
illustrious not only by the great lawyer and statesman in whom
the title originated, but also by the poet who has made himself
a name at every hearthstone where the English language is
read or spoken. The delightful essayist, Charles Lamb, boasts
his descent from Hertfordshire, and his genius has raised from
obscurity the little hamlet of Mackery End. Future archæologists

will revere at Brocket the residence of two eminent men who in our
time have swayed the destinies of this country as First Ministers
of the Crown,—Lord Melbourne and Lord Palmerston,—men
akin to each other by family connection, and akin still more by the
English attributes they held in common, an exquisite geniality of
temper united with simple and robust manliness of character. Our
guests will visit, at Hatfield, a place rich indeed with brilliant
memories and associations. There may be seen the tower from
the top of which, according to the story, the Princess Elizabeth
envied the lot of the humble milkmaid ; and there, in the park,
may still be seen at least the trunk of the tree under which she is
said to have received the news of her accession to the throne. A
little beyond the site of the old palace they will inspect the noble
halls which were erected by Robert Cecil, and restored to fresh
splendour by their late lamented owner ; of whom it may truly be
said, that his active mind never neglected a duty, and his loyal
heart never forsook a friend. And what Englishman—nay, what
stranger from those foreign nations to which, conjointly with the
posterity of his native land, Francis Bacon intrusted the verdict
to be pronounced on his labours and his name—would not feel
that he is on haunted ground when he enters the domain of Gor-
hambury, and examines the relics of that abode in which the
Shakespeare of philosophy united the most various knowledge of
mankind with the deepest research into the secrets of nature and
the elements of human thought ?

Such, ladies and gentlemen, are some among the objects of interest to which the notice of our visitors is invited. I should apologise for much that the limits of my space compel me to omit ;
for there is scarcely a town, a village, an old manor-house in
Hertfordshire, which has not some relic, some association, some
tradition, which may commend itself to the true archæologist.
Nor ought I to forget how diligently the records of our county
have been preserved by native historians, whose descendants still
bear the honoured names of Clutterbuck and Chauncy. While
another resident of Hertfordshire, Joseph Strutt, the celebrated
author of ' English Antiquities,' has laid in the neighbourhood of
Welwyn the scene of our earliest English romance, ' Queen Hoo

Hall,' which suggested to the more brilliant genius of Walter Scott the immortal tales of 'Ivanhoe' and 'Kenilworth.'

Ladies and gentlemen, so long as we keep the past before us as a guide, we are not altogether (speaking humanly, and with due submission to the decrees of Providence), we are not altogether without some power to shape the future so as to preserve, through all its changes, that national spirit without which the unity of a race disappears. It has been vouchsafed to England to diffuse her children and her language amidst realms unknown to the ambition of Alexander, and far beyond the boldest flights of the Roman eagle. Ages hence, from the shores of Australasia and America, pilgrims will visit this land as the birthplace of their ancestors, and venerate every relic of our glorious if checkered past, from the day of the Druid to that in which we now are; for while we speak we ourselves are acting history, and becoming in our turn the ancients to posterity. May no future Gibbon trace to the faults of our time the causes which insure the rise and fall of empires. Century after century may our descendants in those vast new worlds, compared to which Europe itself shrinks to the dimensions of a province or a shire,—century after century may they find still flourishing on these ancestral shores, nor ashamed to number the men of our generation among its fathers, a race adorned by the graces of literature, and enriched by the stores of science! May they find still unimpaired, and sacred alike from superstition and unbelief, the altars of Christian faith! may our havens and docks still be animated by vessels fitted for commerce abroad, or armed, in case of need, for defence at home! Still may our institutions and our liberties find the eloquence of freemen and patriots in our legislative halls, and the ermine of Justice be unsullied by a spot in the courts where she adjudicates between man and man! These are the noblest legacies we receive from the past; and while we treasure these at every hazard, and through every change, the soul of England will retain vitality to her form, and no archæologist will seek her grave amidst the nations that have passed away.

XXXV.

OUTLINE OF A SPEECH

INTENDED TO HAVE BEEN DELIVERED IN

THE HOUSE OF COMMONS

ON THE 1ST OF MAY 1839.

[Besides the numerous Speeches delivered by Lord Lytton both within and without the walls of Parliament, and from which the foregoing, to the number of forty-one, have been selected, there were many others prepared by him for the debates both of the Lords and Commons, from the actual delivery of which he was precluded by purely fortuitous circumstances. As manuscript drafts of the outlines of several of these have been found among his papers, it has been thought advisable to include in the present collection those at any rate which are here subjoined.]

ON Wednesday the 27th of February 1839, the Member for Reading, Mr Sergeant (afterwards Justice) Talfourd, moved the second reading of the Bill introduced by him for the better regulation of the Law of Literary Copyright. An amendment was thereupon moved by the Member for Kilkenny, Mr Joseph Hume, that the Bill be read that day six months, in which proposal he was strongly supported by the Member for Bridport, Mr Henry Warburton. Eventually, on Monday the 8th of July, by reason of the opposition it had encountered, the Bill was withdrawn by its originator. Prior to this, on Wednesday the 1st of May 1839, while the projected measure was yet under the consideration of the House in Committee, the following speech was intended to have been delivered.

SIR,—It seems to me that the main objections which have been urged against this Bill by the hon. Member for Bridport—objections which, urged with all his ingenuity, and under popular pretexts, have perhaps induced many to share his opposition—rest

upon one or two misconceptions of the probable practical operation of this Bill as regards the cheapness of publications. Before,
however, I come to this point, let us see fairly what is the question
before us. It is not necessary to enter into an argument to prove
that the works of literature are property. The law has already
decided that they are property for a certain period. For twenty-
eight years a man's book is a man's property. My hon. and
learned friend contends that that period is not sufficient. He
brings in a Bill to prolong the period. That, then, is the simple
question before the House. Not whether a book is or is not property; but is the present term in which the law does consider it
property sufficient? Whether the extension of time should be
sixty years, or more or less, is fairly a question for Committee, and
is, I own, a matter fairly worthy of consideration. But all we
have now to consider is—shall the present term be or be not extended? The hon. Member for Bridport says that he will only
argue this question as a question of expediency—of utility to the
public. Sir, upon that ground I will meet him. The hon. gentleman contends that the extension of copyright will tend to increase
the price of works. Now here comes what I consider the practical
view of the case, which I will endeavour to explain to the House.
The price of a book after the first few years does not depend upon
copyright or not; it depends upon whether it be or be not of a
popular nature. The more popular the nature of a great author's
work, the lower the price at which it sells. There is no copyright
to the 'Vicar of Wakefield;' there is no copyright to Newton's
Principia. You have editions of Goldsmith at less than 1s.; you
have not one cheap edition of Sir Isaac Newton's Works. Why is
this? Because millions read Goldsmith, and only a few read
Newton. If you were to publish the 'Principia' for 6d. you would
probably not increase the sale, and you certainly would not pay
print or paper. Now take two other examples. There is a
copyright in Lord Byron; there is no copyright in Dryden.
Dryden is, as a poet, equal to Lord Byron, but he is not at this
moment equally popular. The only good edition of Dryden sells
for £10, 10s. You get an excellent edition of Lord Byron for £1.
There are no copyrights to Locke, to Hobbes, to Cudworth—three

of our greatest philosophers; there is not one cheap complete edition
of any of these writers. What, then, are the cheap works now
disseminated, and which you justly value? They all belong to the
lighter class of writers—light essays, fictions, novels, elementary
or popular treatises ; and you will find if you examine practically
that you get these cheap in proportion not to their being a copyright or not, but in proportion as they are of a nature to please a
larger or a smaller circle of readers. I contend, then, that strange
as it may appear at first, it is practically true that when the copyright is in the hands of the public, you do not get better or
cheaper or more numerous editions. That this holds especially
good in all, I do not say the higher, but the more solid and scientific branches of literature, because precisely in proportion as they
are solid and scientific, they address themselves to the few ; and
if you deny this, I ask you to make out your case—I ask you to
show me the cheap editions of your great old authors in which
there is no copyright—I ask for your cheap editions of Sir Walter
Raleigh, of Sir Thomas Browne, of Lord Bacon's complete works—I
ask you where are the cheap editions of Swift complete, of Dryden
complete—indeed, of the prose works of Bolingbroke complete? It
is but the other day after the lapse of centuries that you have any
new complete editions of your great Dramatists—of Marlow, of
Peele, of Massinger ; and in comedy, of Farquhar and Congreve.
My hon. friend the Member for Leeds is bringing out an edition
of Hobbes. Does his bookseller allow him to bring it out in a
cheap form? No ; he knows that only a few persons will buy it
whether it be cheap or dear ; and the price must be high accordingly. Nay, sir, I must even contend that books are so far an
exception to the ordinary rules of political economy, that it often
happens that a new edition of a great writer—a writer great, but
not perhaps very popular—is not produced, because the bookseller
has no copyright, and because, therefore, should the speculation
answer, he incurs every risk of being undersold by some others,
who will never, however, hazard the first undertaking. This has
often come under my own knowledge. It was but last year that
a bookseller informed me he had meditated a new and a cheap
edition of one of the greatest writers in our language, now almost

out of print ; but was deterred from it by the very probability of its success—by the probability that just when it began to pay, another edition would appear and prevent the profits. So far, then, as your argument goes, that books must necessarily be cheaper where there is no copyright, most of the facts are against you ; and where they may appear in your favour, it will be not in these works that augment the sum of human knowledge ;—not in works of science, philosophy, or reasoning ; not those works which you mean when you talk of cheap knowledge ; but in works of fancy, of fiction, of popular poetry, which sell cheap not because there is no copyright, but because they are popular by their nature. Now, Sir, what does the learned gentleman propose ? Why, by extending copyright for sixty years, we will say, after the author's death, to give his children a property not only in the pecuniary value of the work but the fame of the writer. Can you conceive no case—cannot you conceive many cases—where this, instead of making the works scarcer and dearer, will make them more numerous and cheaper ? How many writers there are who, though most valuable, may not be so widely popular as to make it worth an indifferent bookseller's while to risk his capital in a new edition of his works. A bookseller naturally looks to everything as a matter of gain. He must have a profit, and a large profit, when he hazards his capital. But let copyright be the property of the son, and the son has an interest more identical with the public than that of the mere trader—the son has an interest in the fame of his father, and will be contented with little or no profit if he can build up, in a popular edition of his father's works, the most durable monument to his memory. Who so likely to benefit the public, who so likely to give you the cheap knowledge or the cheap amusement you desire, as the man who feels that every eye that glances over the page in which his father's soul yet lives, is doing homage to his own birthright of honourable reputation.

Well, Sir, then, having got the ground clear from the most plausible objection, we come at once to the plain, broad question, Is the present term long enough or not ? Sir, for some works I believe it is long enough to afford a fair remuneration, but not for others. Ninety-nine times out of a hundred, the poet, the novelist,

the popular essayist, the author in that literature which belongs
to wit or imagination, rises at once to celebrity and pecuniary
reward.   It is a remark as old as Tacitus, that all which belongs
to fiction is rapid in its effect, all that belongs to science is slow ;
but works that address only the few—works of research, of industry, of less genius, perhaps, than the others—all these are many
years before they bring any remuneration. I know an instance in
the University which the hon. Baronet represents.   A work has
been produced that is among the greatest European scholarship
can boast.   The author, formerly a Member of this House, devoted
the best part of his life to it.   It is a work on the Chronology of
Greek History—a work that has thrown the greatest light upon
the most important period in the ancient world, which has cleared
up a thousand obscurities, refuted a thousand fallacies—a work
without which no scholarship can be accurate, no library complete.
Yet this, from its nature—this could not make its way into sale
for many years.   The University of Oxford, I believe, much to its
honour, contributed to its expenses in the first instance ; but now
at the end of nearly twenty-eight years, it just begins to remunerate the illustrious toils of a laborious life.   By your present
law—if the author die—his son will receive nothing but three or
four volumes in quarto.   If you pass my friend's law, you bequeath
to that son an annuity in the obligations his father has conferred
upon the literature of Europe.   Sir, the hon. gentleman has
argued that this Bill can only benefit one case in a thousand ; but
why does he persist in forgetting that it can only affect the public
where that case occurs ?   It is a law that can only come into
operation precisely to reward genius, or to remunerate toil.   But
I do not allow that this Bill benefits only rare and singular cases.
I say that, upon expediency alone, whatever encourages, whatever
honours, intellectual cultivation, tends to raise the character and to
elevate the notions of an entire people.   The more highly you
show that you estimate what civilises mankind, the more you diffuse
those principles and sentiments in which the grace and polish of
civilisation are to be found.   This is not all.   I agree that men of
great genius when they sit down to compose a work do not think
of pecuniary rewards ; and so far, if you think that genius, which

was meant to be your master, is only fit to be your slave—that you are to seize the toils, but to grudge the hire—so far, I agree with you that this Bill does nothing. But there are other men of excellent talents—not poets, not writers of fancy, not belonging to the first class of intellect, but who very fairly and very honourably pursue literature as a profession—men of industry, statists, compilers, writers of your cheap literature, whose minds have the happy gift to popularise knowledge, who write on the elements of history or science, and who may reasonably expect that their works will become popular class-books. Now I do know that there are many such who would, in the way of professional calculation, devote their time and abilities to works of the most useful nature, and probably of the most permanent use to the public, if they could hope that, by so doing, they might secure an income to their children; so that stimulants of this nature, I do believe, would be most useful to the public itself. Sir, I have sought to argue this question as one of practical expediency, and to fight it upon the ground upon which the hon. gentleman has placed it. But I cannot pass in silence over the distinction he would draw between expediency and justice. The expediency of a great nation is to do justice by redressing every injury, and, where it happily has the power, to evince gratitude for every service. Talk of this as a class Bill—as a Bill which tailors or bakers would suggest for their own class—that, Sir, is not the language which we ought to address to the prayers of men who have given a lustre to their country. Indeed, it should be our boast that the humblest craftsman, if he complains of insufficient or limited protection to what the law has already considered his property, ought to receive at least a respectful hearing of his complaint; and if this were a Bill brought in by the tailors or bakers of Bridport, I very much doubt whether the hon. member would think it right to say that it should not even be brought into that House to which every class complaint even should find its way. But I own that while I would do justice to every man however humble, it seems to me that there is yet more sanctity in the justice we confer if true, and the people are under obligations never to be repaid to the parties that complain. Sir, what is our power in the world? It is our moral power—the homage due not less to our arts than to our arms. A hundred years ago, and the English language was scarcely spoken out of these islands. Go now through the whole north—through Germany, Bohemia, Hungary, Norway, Sweden, even in Russia—and our language is the study even of the humbler classes. In the extension of our language, who does not see the extension of our influence ? Who does not see the new and close connection it forms with other States and our own ? It is one of the great helps to commerce ; it is one of the great cements of peace. To whom and to what do we owe this ? Not to our victories, nor to our laws ; not to your debates in this House. You owe it to the labours and to the men to whose children you would now grudge 6d. a volume upon the heritage of their fathers. And among these, your benefactors, there is no man who has done so much to win you the affection and admiration of the great northern nations,—no man who has contributed to render the English language familiar to the lips, and the English interest dear to the hearts, of your allies,—no man who has done so much as Sir Walter Scott. His children are among your petitioners. Sir, I need not ask my learned friend to persevere. His gallantry and zeal in this question, beset as it is with a vehement and able opposition, foreign as it is to the more popular questions in this House, have been worthy of his talents and his character. And I do hope that the time has now arrived when that fair extension of rights — an extension in the principle given already to the authors of Spain, of Germany, of Russia—will not be denied by the legislators of England to men who have no interest and no fame apart from the civilisation and the glory of their country.

XXXVI.

OUTLINE OF A SPEECH

INTENDED TO HAVE BEEN DELIVERED IN

THE HOUSE OF COMMONS

ON THE 9TH OF MAY 1856.

—

For several years the aboriginal Indians inhabiting the Mosquito coast in Central America were under the protection of the British, who held possession of Belize, together with a group of islands in the Bay of Honduras. This arrangement was for a long while regarded with some disfavour in the United States. At length, in the April of 1850, the two Governments entered into a covenant with each other that neither should assume dominion over any portion of Central America. Scarcely five years had elapsed, however, after their having ratified this treaty, when the United States charged the British Government with a violation of its share in the agreement; whereupon the latter undertook, with certain reservations, to cede the disputed territory to the Republic of Honduras. Eventually, in 1859, the whole matter in dispute was brought to an amicable adjustment. While the negotiations were yet pending—the relations between the two countries being at the time in the most critical position—the Member for Hertfordshire, Sir Edward Lytton, early in the session of 1856, entered upon the papers of the House of Commons notice of a Motion having reference to the dispute, then trembling as it were on the suspension of a hair, between the two Governments. Upon three several occasions—on Monday the 4th of April, again on Monday the 5th of May, and finally on Friday the 6th of June—the Member for Herts asked for the diplomatic correspondence, the production of which was essential before his motion could be submitted to Parliament. Upon each occasion the Prime Minister, Lord Palmerston, deprecated the discussion as inadvisable, because calculated, just possibly, to prejudice the whole question in dispute, and, while so doing, to hamper, and even, it might be, to irritate the negotiations. Deferring upon each occasion to the Premier's appeal for "judicious forbearance," Sir Edward Lytton postponed his motion again and yet again, until the imbroglio that at one time seriously threatened war, and that Lord Palmerston, on the 6th of June, spoke of as "certainly of a very grave character," was of itself dissipated. But for this, on Friday the 9th of May 1856, the only day that was ever really set apart for the discussion, the following speech would have been delivered.

———

SIR,—I rise to submit to the consideration of the House the disputes with regard to Central America which have formed the subject of this correspondence between her Majesty's Government and that of the United States. And however justly diffident I may feel of my own capacities to fulfil the task I have undertaken, I think the House will allow that it is no trivial, no unseasonable topic which I would obtrude upon its notice. Not trivial, for we can have no political object more important than that of cordial relations with the people of America ; not unseasonable, for I thought it my duty to ascertain that her Majesty's Government did not think a discussion here would be injurious to the progress of friendly negotiations ; but that they rather concurred with me in the hope that it might serve to remove some of those misunderstandings, and allay some of that irritation, amongst our American kinsmen, which have occasioned to us on this side the water one prevailing sentiment of anxiety and regret.

Nor do I think that my motives in the introduction of this question are unworthy the gravity of the occasion ; for it is my belief, on which those who are higher authorities in the party with whom I have the honour to act, entirely agree, that in this delicate and critical stage of negotiation no elements of party should be admitted into the resolutions I propose. And, indeed, I shall treat the whole subject not as between party and party, but as between nation and nation.

And first, Sir, in arguing the differences between ourselves and the Government of the United States, I shall put out of sight as far as possible that contingency of an appeal to arms which has been somewhat prominently brought forward in the American

Legislature and journals, and which, perhaps, some newspapers of our own have not sufficiently discouraged. I shall rather assume that here are two nations bound together by every tie of interest and affection, which have nevertheless disputes to settle, but cannot discuss those disputes without making use of the same mother tongue, which ought to suggest softened tones and conciliating expressions.

The House is aware that the controversy between ourselves and the Government of the United States arose out of the interpretation to be given to a treaty made in 1850 for facilitating the construction of a canal and other modes of interoceanic communication across the isthmus of Central America. The disputes relate to subjects with which that treaty was only incidentally connected—viz., the Protectorate which Great Britain affords to the Indian tribe of Mosquitos; secondly, her Majesty's settlements at British Honduras and its dependencies; thirdly, our claim or title to Ruatan and the Bay islands.

I shall deal first with that question most complicated, most immediately important, and which I think in America has been the most misrepresented—I mean the Mosquito Protectorate.

It is absolutely essential to clear this question from every doubt as soon as possible, because if that Protectorate exists still and is binding upon us, it may at any moment become necessary to exercise it against General Walker or any other representative of the Nicaraguan Government; and if the Americans are led to believe that to that Protectorate we have no right, our attempt to defend the Mosquito Indians against the aggressions of General Walker might suddenly bring us into collision with American citizens; blood might be shed by one unlucky shot; and war might thus inevitably break out between the two nations of the world, in whom war would be not only a crime but a blunder.

The House will pardon me, therefore, if I go at length into this subject. We are speaking to-night not only to England but to America; and if I enlarge upon any topic which seems antiquated, trite, or wearisome, you will forgive me when I assure you that I will touch upon nothing which I do not believe to be of importance in dispelling some misapprehension prevalent amongst the American public.

For that reason I do not bind myself to this book. I have examined all the available public documents on the subject; and I think I shall go far towards the peaceful settlement of disputes, if, where I respectfully differ from the American Government, I can make the English honour and the English right incontestably clear to the eyes of the American people. For, as Mr Fox well said, "When a dispute is clearly stated, its settlement is more than half concluded."

You will see by the two statements of Mr Buchanan in this book, that on the part of the American Government he questions, first, the genuine antiquity of the Mosquito Protectorate ; secondly, that he disputes our right to have renewed that Protectorate after a convention with Spain in 1786, by which we bound ourselves to evacuate the Mosquito territory ; thirdly, that he asserts that for the last six years we have been guilty of bad faith, because the treaty of 1850 abolished the Protectorate, which nevertheless, in 1856, we still retain.

To all these points I shall address myself with the respect due to the Minister and Government of a kindred and illustrious people, but also with that plain speaking which becomes a member of the British Parliament anxious to clear from the shadow of a doubt the good faith and honour of his country.

Sir, our first connection with the Mosquito tribe followed close on our conquest of Jamaica under Cromwell in 1655. Within four years after that event we commenced a settlement upon the eastern coast of Yucatan, principally for the purpose of cutting logwood. And Belize—which is a corruption from the name of Wallis, the Scotchman who first established a footing there, with the assent of the natives—became our headquarters. At that time there prevailed along the coast of that isthmus now called Central America—and according to a vast mass of concurrent authorities, which gentlemen will find cited in the "Correspondence on the Mosquito Territory" presented to this House, July 3, 1848, in a district which ranged from Cape Honduras to the mouth of the river San Juan—a powerful and independent tribe, the Moscos, to which we have given the name Mosquitos These Indians had never been conquered by Spain, never ceded to that power any territory or dominion. Naturally enough, we and these Indians, united by common hostility to Spain at that period, came into connection as far back as the reign of Charles II.; and a Mosquito chief came to Jamaica and placed himself and his people under the protection of the British king. And here it is important to observe what both the United States and the Spanish republics at variance with us have totally lost sight of—viz., that in the famous Madrid Treaty which we obtained with Spain a few years afterwards in 1670, Spain ceded to Great Britain "not only full right of dominion and possession in all lands, countries, islands, colonies, and dominions whatever, situated in the West Indies, but in any part of America which Great Britain or her subjects did then hold and possess." And the treaty adds that, "under no colour or pretext whatsoever, should any controversy be moved concerning the same hereafter." But that clause embraced Belize and the Mosquitos who had then passed under the British sceptre. The Governor of Jamaica had already established a settlement on the Mosquito coast, to which were sent, in the first instance, Justices of the Peace from Jamaica, and subsequently, in 1740, a superintendent appointed by the British Crown. We erected a fort at our principal station on that shore, at Black River, mounted cannon there, and hoisted the British flag. The evidence of all this you will find in Macgregor's 'Commercial Tariffs,' Part 17, compiled from the State Papers of the Board of Trade and Plantations, and published before any disputes with the United States had arisen; and all this is extremely important to this part of our case in answer to the arguments of the American Government, in order to show first, the antiquity of that connection with the Mosquitos, which is now held to be a recent usurpation; and, secondly, that the Mosquitos were wholly independent of Spain; and that, therefore, even granting that the Spanish revolutionary republics inherited the rights of old Spain in those parts, they could not inherit what Spain never actually possessed; could not inherit that Mosquito territory in which, to use the strong but not more truthful

words in the ' Commercial Tariffs,' " the Spaniards never had any
footing, claim of occupancy or possession, from the beginning of
the world to this day." And you will find, and so will the
Americans, on referring to the documents I have cited, that the
only civilised power which ever held possessions either at Belize
or in Mosquito, was Great Britain; and that she held such
possessions by the best of all possible titles—viz., the voluntary
assent of the aboriginal natives.

Sir, from the reign of Charles II. to this year of Queen Victoria
in which we now are, there is no instance on record that this
Indian tribe has ever broken a single compact made with us ; and
the question will arise, whether in honour and humanity you can
so violate the compact which I will prove to you, you have made
with them, and which still exists, as to leave those you have
pledged yourselves to protect without any safeguard from exter-
mination by the very enemies they have provoked in your behalf,
and at your instigation.

But in refutation of the antiquity of this Protectorate, Mr
Buchanan was instructed by his Government in Mr Morcy's de-
spatch of instructions, July 2d, 1853—published in the American
edition of the Correspondence—to refer to a debate in the House of
Lords, 26th March 1787 ; and Mr Morcy says that nothing could
be more fatal than that debate to the pretensions now set up by
Great Britain for herself and the Mosquitos. This debate was on
a motion by Lord Roden condemnatory of the convention with
Spain in 1786 ; and Mr Buchanan says that, in that debate, " Lord
Thurlow abundantly justified the Ministry, and proved that the
Mosquitos were not our allies, were not a people we were bound
by treaty to protect." I could not help smiling when I found
that Lord Thurlow was raised into a valuable, and it seems
unimpeachable, Parliamentary authority on a case of proof. An
American statesman even as highly instructed as Mr Morcy or
Mr Buchanan, is not bound to know all the characteristics of our
departed lawyers. But according to the general opinion of his
contemporaries, Lord Thurlow, though a personage of great learning and talent, was the man of all others who as a Parliamentary

speaker made the boldest assertions, and supported them with the slightest testimony ; so much so, that Lord Brougham, in his ' Sketches of Statesmen' says of Lord Thurlow's mode of debating that it was a " vamped-up, delusive, and almost fraudulent oratory." I looked for the debate, curious to see what proof, in the teeth of historical facts, Lord Thurlow could have adduced. The debate is not in Hansard, but it will be found in the ' Annual Register,' and a fuller account in Debrett's ' Parliamentary Register.' Well, it is as I suspected. Lord Thurlow is stated to have gone into the history of the Mosquito settlement from 1650 (which was a mistake to begin with, for no settlement had then begun) to 1777, deducing arguments from the facts he mentioned in order to prove that Mosquito could never be fairly called a British settlement ; and he subsequently alleged that the " Mosquitos were not our allies, not a people we were bound to protect ; " but of the proofs on which Lord Thurlow rested those arguments and assumptions there is not a vestige. But the proof is rather the other way ; for Lord Stormont, who was really an authority on the subject as a former Minister, before whom the subject would have come officially, not only said " that we held Mosquito by as good a claim as we held Jamaica, but quoted different periods to prove that our right was recognised by treaty ; " and Lord Roden produced documents signed by General Dalling, the Governor of Jamaica, to prove that a superintendent had been sent to the settlement on the Mosquito shore, there to form a government, and quoted a State Paper dated 1744 as a proof that there had actually existed there a Council of Trade publicly recognised by this country ; and Lord Hawke corroborated this statement by instancing treaties as far back as 1672-1717. Sir, all those documents are still extant. And I may add that another State Paper, confirming these proofs of our peculiar and ancient connection with Mosquito, was presented to this House in 1822, and will be found in the 16th volume of our ' Parliamentary Accounts and Papers.' So much for the *ipse dixit* of Lord Thurlow in an obscure party debate in one branch of the Legislature, by which it is sought to annihilate all the treaties and documents actually

stored in our archives, proving the existence of the Mosquito
Protectorate for more than a century previous to the convention
with Spain in 1786.

Well, but in that year, Great Britain—in pursuance of the
general peace with Europe and America, which, humbling
though some of its conditions were, the exhaustion of our resources compelled us to accept in 1783—agreed with Spain to
evacuate the Mosquito territory, stipulating that no severities
should be exercised against the Mosquito Indians for the assistance they had loyally rendered to us. And the American Government actually now contend that in consequence of that convention
good faith for ever precluded us from renewing our connection
with that tribe. Why, I should have thought that, of all men in
the world, our gallant children the Americans would least permit
their Government to deny that fresh wars destroy old treaties.
Almost immediately afterwards Spain declared war upon us
again, and the treaty of 1786 expired with the first cannon-shot ;
as the Americans themselves tell us that their first cannon-shot
would shiver into atoms the treaty they signed with us in 1850.
But if we did in the renewal of the Protectorate violate our good
faith to Spain, what power had a right to complain of us ? The
United States ? No ; Spain, and Spain alone. But though, as I
shall now proceed to show you, we renewed the Protectorate very
soon after war broke out again—though I will show you it was
in full force when commercial treaties with Spain were renewed in
1814, and exercised while Spain still retained all her possessions
in Central America—not one word of complaint, reproach, or remonstrance was ever addressed to us by that power. And Mr Buchanan's
arguments, page 262, to the effect that we held ourselves bound
by the convention of 1786, are all based upon his non-acquain-
tance with the time when the Protectorate was renewed. He
demands to know when we did renew it. Lord Clarendon gives
him no answer. But as much stress is laid on this question ; as
Mr Buchanan infers that it could not be in various years rang-
ing from 1801 to a considerable period after 1821 ; and as Mr
Clayton in his speech in the American Senate, January 4th, 1854,
lends the authority of his distinguished name to the assertion,

" that we did not renew our Protectorate till 1848, six days after
the United States had acquired the country in the Pacific "—
thereby creating a most irritating suspicion in the mind of the
American public that we suddenly revived the Mosquito Protectorate as a counterbalance to American progress: so I will give
the answer that Lord Clarendon withholds. Sir, I will presently
show, perhaps to the surprise of this House, certainly to the surprise of America, that our Protectorate was renewed as far back
as the year 1800 ; but the first formal act of our protection involving our good faith and honour to the Mosquito tribe was on
January 18th, 1816, when we formally crowned their chief in
our own settlement at Belize. Now, that the House may see that
this act of coronation was no mocking and childish proceeding—
was not the farce which it has been represented in America, but
a solemnity animated by human, Christian, enlightened motives,
and implying a pledge on our part of the strongest nature—I will
read some extracts from the very interesting letter of Sir George
Arthur, our Superintendent at British Honduras, to the Mosquito
king first crowned by us in 1816. It will be found at page 49,
in the " Correspondence on the Mosquito Territory."

" BELIZE, *January* 14, 1816.

" PRINCE GEORGE,—Your request to be crowned in the settlement, in the presence of your chieftains and such of your people
as are assembled here, I shall most cheerfully comply with ; and
beg to propose that the ceremony shall take place on Thursday,
18th inst., the day in which we commemorate the birth of her
Most Gracious Majesty the Queen of England; and I sincerely
trust that you will not be disappointed in the advantage you
expect to derive by its being understood that you are in a particular manner under the protection of the British Government."
(Observe, and above all, let America observe, how important these
words are as to the obligation on our honour thus formally incurred as far back as 1816.) Sir George then proceeds to congratulate the king on having been brought up in the Christian
religion, enumerates the victories the armies of our Prince Regent
had obtained, and adds: " But dazzling as such glory is, it will not

convey to his Royal Highness more sincere and lasting satisfaction than he will enjoy if, through your means, the Mosquito nation, and the numerous tribes of Indians around you, are brought to partake of the blessings of civilisation. This was the great object which the King of England had in view when, on the death of your father, he held forth his hand to protect you and your brother." Now, this passage answers the American query, When did our Protectorate recommence? It shows that it recommenced in 1800, exactly half a century before the Americans thought fit to complain of it! Sir George Arthur goes on: "And from the same motive has his Royal Highness the Prince Regent continued to you his powerful protection;" and thus touchingly concludes : " If you would convince his Royal Highness, beyond the extent of words, that you are truly grateful and sensible of the blessings you have derived, I will tell you, Prince, how you may do so. Make your people happy ; struggle to wean them from their present habits to a state of civilisation ; introduce amongst them good and wholesome laws ; above all" (says Sir George), "endeavour to introduce the Christian religion, in which you have been educated. This will be the best reward his Royal Highness can feel."

Sir, is this the language of selfish ambition? Are not these words that may find an echo, not only in the hearts of all present, but in every Christian home amongst our angry brethren on the other side the Atlantic. We crowned a second king in 1825, and a third in 1844—a momentous period, when disputes had already broken out as to the Mosquito territory with the Spanish republics, and when this country was under the Government of Sir Robert Peel, pre-eminent for many illustrious attributes, but for none more than a deliberate caution in all our foreign relations, which would have never allowed him so to sanction the Mosquito Protectorate if he had not resolved to defend it. Why have I thus established the antiquity of our connection with the Mosquitos, and shown that, with the exception of 14 years from 1786 to 1800, it continued unbroken for nearly 200 years? Not to deduce therefrom an assumption that we cannot, therefore, abandon this Protectorate, or that we would not strain every point to conciliate the

United States upon that score. No ; but to satisfy the Americans, as one honourable man may satisfy another, that the date of the renewal shows that it was not, as Mr Morey calls it, a convenient pretension on our part either to countercheck the progress of the United States in California, or to molest the Central American republics, which did not then exist ; and secondly, to show that our positive good faith is concerned not to abandon that Protectorate till some reasonable and efficient substitute be provided, and thus to induce the Americans to concur with us, as one friend would concur with another, in devising some mode by which we may reconcile our honour to their interests and wishes.

And now we come to the time when the necessary exercise of this Protectorate against external aggression led to the present unfortunate disputes. The colonies of old Spain in Central America had revolted, and become independent republics. Those little States were formed out of the captain-generalships of the Spanish Crown, and their territorial range had constantly varied in extent, according to the dignity of the respective officers placed over them. Their several boundaries were therefore very obscure and undefined. The territory of the Mosquitos, but more especially an important station at the mouth of the San Juan river, which the Mosquitos claimed as theirs from time immemorial (and for a small settlement, 15 miles from which it appears at least certain that some settlers of old Spain had paid tribute to the Mosquito king), became an object of dispute with these republics. New Granada put forth the first claim to it ; Costa Rica advanced her pretensions; and so did Nicaragua. Aggressions were made on the Mosquito territory. In 1838, while these States were united by confederation, we addressed to them a notification of our views as to the bounds of the Mosquito territory, and our obligations to protect the claim of the natives. In 1840, when that confederation had become virtually extinct, a commission was issued by Colonel Macdonald, Superintendent of British Honduras, for regulating the internal affairs of Mosquito, and in 1844, under the vigorous administration of Sir R. Peel, Mr Patrick Walker was sent there as Agent and Vice-Consul ; and it appears by the despatches of Mr Chatfield, our Consul-General in Central America, that Lord Aberdeen, in 1845, decided that this station at least belonged to the Mosquitos; for Mr Chalfield writes, Sept. 11, 1847, page 56 of Mosquito Correspondence, "that he had not only claimed for the Mosquito king the territory from Cape Honduras to the mouth of the river San Juan, but had inserted the words 'without prejudice to the right of the Mosquito king to any territory south of that river,' partly on the views of the noble Viscount, but partly also on the views confidentially communicated to him in Lord Aberdeen's despatch of the 23d May 1845." Thus, as all our disputes with the United States on this score arose out of our assumption that the station at the mouth of the river San Juan, now called Greytown, belongs to the Mosquitos; so, if we are wrong, we were led into that error by Sir Robert Peel and Lord Aberdeen, two of the most wary and experienced statesmen who ever governed this country. Meanwhile, however, the station at San Juan had been seized unceremoniously by the Nicaraguans; various attempts were made to negotiate the matter to determine the right boundaries of the Mosquito territory, to settle the claims of the rival Spanish republics, and to induce the Nicaraguans peacefully to withdraw till these questions could be decided. Nicaragua refusing, and only answering by insult and threats, a small vessel was at last commissioned by our Government to place itself at the disposal of our Vice-Consul. That small vessel, at his orders, expelled the Nicaraguan Government off the station in January 1848, but with such chivalrous courtesy, that the heroic Nicaraguan commandant and other valiant officials, who had declared they would resist to the last drop of their blood, paid a polite visit to the ship that had expelled them in the course of the same evening, and partook of refreshment provided on the occasion by our English hospitality. The station then assumed that name of Greytown, by which it has since acquired so sinister a celebrity. And here I must observe, in vindication of the alleged harshness of this step, that it was not taken till several years had been wasted in vain upon friendly remonstrance, and that the protection afforded to the Mosquitos would have been a sham pretence, unworthy this monarchy, if we suffered what we had declared to be their possessions—not only by the noble Viscount, but by the cautious lips of Lord Aberdeen in 1845—to be usurped by an ambitious and greedy neighbour; and that even granting the Mosquito title were doubtful, or, what we shall all admit, that that station ought to be occupied by a civilised people, other States besides Nicaragua then claimed the station; and it was just to all parties not to allow one State forcibly to possess itself of a port that might be of great commercial value to the whole of Central America, and to which its title was not satisfactorily proved. What was its title? Nicaragua and the American Government have relied on a royal decree of Spain in 1796, by which they maintain that San Juan was made a port of the second class for Nicaragua. Now, if Spain had never any right to this, or any part of the Mosquito territory, either by the conquest or cession of the natives, her mere decree could not assign away what did not belong to her. But granting that Indians have no territorial right in the eyes of civilised Christians, still, did that decree give an exclusive claim over the station at the mouth of the San Juan to Nicaragua? No. I have looked into that decree myself, and I find that it made San Juan a port of the second class, not for Nicaragua alone, but also for the whole of the ancient viceroyalty or kingdom of Guatemala, within a range of 300 leagues from the capital, including, therefore, Costa Rica and New Granada. So that, even according to this decree, the Nicaraguan Republic had not the smallest right to seize upon that place for its own special and monopolising possession.

The Nicaraguans being thus expelled, appealed to the United States, as indeed they had done before when they anticipated that expulsion. The United States at first took no notice whatever of the appeal. But America about this time had annexed to itself, upon grounds which I do not presume to question, the very substantial acquisition of California, in the previous possession of Mexico; Central America became an object of importance in connection with California; there was a project to unite the Atlantic and Pacific by a canal up the river San Juan, and thus Greytown, situated at the mouth of that river, suddenly arose into a place of great consideration in American eyes. The Democratic party in America were then in administration under President Polk; of that Government Mr Buchanan was Secretary of State, and he sent an agent, Mr Hise, to Nicaragua, to arrange matters respecting this canal. Mr Hise made a treaty with Nicaragua which would have compromised the American Government to a clause that sanctioned the Nicaraguan claims to Greytown, and pledged America to support that claim, even by arms if necessary, against Great Britain. But, fortunately, President Taylor and the Whig party now came into power, and this treaty they refused to sanction ; they sent out another agent, Mr Squiers, who also made a treaty less comprehensive than the former one, but still containing clauses which, in acknowledging the Nicaraguan claim to the river San Juan from sea to sea, and engaging to protect an American company in the secure enjoyment thereof, would have given to us America as a declared enemy if we contested that Nicaraguan claim ; and if we at once acquiesced in it, would have made our surrender to the fear of a powerful State what we had just refused to the remonstrance of a weak one, humiliating and discreditable. This treaty was then before the American Government ; and if accepted by them and ratified by the Senate, such would have been the stern and perilous alternative before us. In this critical juncture my near relation, Sir H. Bulwer, was sent as Minister to Washington. He arrived in America when the whole of that republic, as you will see by these papers, was in a state of angry excitement against us, occasioned partly by the apprehension that the Mosquito claim to Greytown would interfere with the American plan of the canal up the river San Juan, partly because one of our vessels had lately taken a small island— Tiger Island—in the Bay of Fonseca, so that it was said we meant ambitiously to command the proposed interoceanic communication on either side. The first object of Sir Henry Bulwer was to soothe this irritation, by showing the fallacious grounds on which it rested. Explanations were given by him as to the accidental seizure of the island alluded to, which was also immediately abandoned by our Government. That difficulty over, what remained ? Why, the obstacle which the Mosquito possession of Greytown under our protection imposed on the construction of the canal, and on its freedom when constructed. For the purpose of solving this difficulty, the project of a treaty was drawn up by him and Mr Clayton, the American Minister for Foreign Affairs. That treaty being entirely approved of by her Majesty's Government, was also finally accepted by the American Government, though the difficulties which stood in its way may be appreciated when I observe that a treaty of this nature has to be approved of in America, not merely by the President and his Government, but by the Senate and its Committee of Foreign Affairs; and these two bodies were then in opposition to each other, so that our diplomatic Minister had to negotiate as it were with both. Nevertheless, he succeeded in the principal object of his mission with such good fortune and rapidity, that within three months of his arrival at Washington, he had completed that treaty, the purpose of which Mr Clayton had declared just before his arrival he saw little or no hope of effecting at all; and while before that time, such had been the excitement and party spirit in America, that Mr Clayton said, " It would require great caution on both sides to prevent a collision between the two Governments." I am certain that every American will say that from the date of that treaty up to the day Sir Henry left Washington, England never stood more high in the affection and respect of the American people. It is not for me to speak of the abilities of a public servant with whom—since I have never myself served my country in a public capacity—it is naturally the pride and honour of my life to claim so near a relationship; but I scarcely remember any instance of a treaty which promised to be so important in its results, which involved questions so delicate, and in which the assent of two parties in the State was to be conciliated, being settled, to the perfect and unqualified approbation of the home Government, with an equal degree of promptitude and despatch.

Well, now, let us look to the intention of that treaty known by the name of its two negotiators. Every one who has read this book, however hastily, more especially the despatches of Sir H. Bulwer, Numbers 16 and 19, will see that it was not the purpose of the treaty to deal with the Mosquito Protectorate otherwise than was necessary for the purposes of the canal, and other modes of interoceanic negotiation. Why was this? Because the immedi-

ate object of Great Britain was to satisfy America that the canal
should be made, and when made, free from British control; and the
object of America was to obtain that satisfaction as soon as possible.   It was therefore obvious to both the negotiators, as it must
be to our own common-sense, that to effect this, nothing should
be mixed up in it to which neither America nor Great Britain
could agree.   America never has acknowledged the right of protecting Indians as an independent sovereign tribe, and for this
she assigns an adequate reason in one of her State Papers—to wit,
that if she recognised our right to hold Indian chiefs independent,
we might claim equally to protect Indian chiefs on the borders of
her own great lakes and rivers.   But on the other hand, we could
not abandon our peculiar protection to the Mosquitos, to which
the honour of the country had been pledged by every Government
since 1800, without a due care for their safety, the provisions of
which might be necessarily long and complicated; yet, since Mr
Clayton had said, according to Mr Crampton's despatch, Oct. 1,
1849 (p. 4), " That the only part of the Mosquito territory of the
least importance to Nicaragua—and that importance dependent
on its connection with the proposed canal—was the part embrac-
ing the river San Juan, and the territory claimed by Nicaragua
from the Machuca rapids to the sea," might not the Protectorate,
since it could not be admitted expressly into the treaty, be so
arranged that it should be left an abstract question, to be settled
at leisure hereafter, and so defined and so restricted in the meanwhile, that, to use Mr Clayton's own words in his speech in the
American Senate, be an obstacle to the design in question ?   How
could this best be done ?   Fortunately, the American Minister in
London, Mr Lawrence, had decided that point by asking the noble
Viscount, then Minister for Foreign Affairs, in a note, Nov. 8,
1849—" Is it the intention of the British Government to occupy or
colonise Nicaragua, Costa Rica, the Mosquito coast so called, or
any part of Central America ? "   The noble Viscount replies, Nov.
13th, it is not the intention of the British Government to do
any of these things; " but with regard to Mosquito, however, a close
political connection has existed between the Crown of Great
Britain and the State and territory of Mosquito for a period of

about two centuries; but the British Government does not claim dominion in Mosquito." Now, what was the nature of that close political connection with the Mosquitos? It was their protection against external aggression. Well, what do the negotiators do? They take the very question of the American Minister, and the answer it received from the English Government; they form the purport of those words into a clause of the treaty; and they define the political connection with the Mosquitos claimed by our Government by saying that "neither we nor America will make use of any protection either State affords or may afford, any alliance either State has or may have, with any people, to fortify, occupy, colonise, or exercise dominion in Central America." Something has been said about the ambiguity of our diplomatic language; but I fearlessly ask the House what could a diplomatist do more, in order to avoid ambiguity, than embody the very words of the accredited Minister of the opposite contracting party—the very answer those words receive from his own Government—and define and restrict the claims of his Government precisely in the sense in which that Government intended it? But if any one would contend that Sir H. Bulwer should not have negotiated this commercial treaty, unless he had settled without dispute the separate political question of the Protectorate, this Blue-book will show him that that treaty could not have been signed at all. What does Mr Clayton himself say on this score, at the very first hitch, the very first idea of delay, in his letter to Sir Henry, July 4th, 1850?—" It is not to be imagined that it is the object of your Government to delay exchange of ratifications until we shall have fixed the precise bounds of Central America" (but until those bounds were settled, you could not settle the Mosquito question), " for this would not only delay, but defeat, the convention." And if it had been defeated, what then? All America would have believed that we intended to make the Protectorate an excuse for obstructing the canal on which she had set her heart; that treaty with Nicaragua, which would have given us a decided enemy in America, would have been completed; and before the end of 1850, the chances are that there would have been war with the United States. And this, not on the ground of our maintaining the Mosquito Protectorate, but on the much more plausible and popular ground, that we made the Protectorate hostile to the greatest commercial interest which the United States then conceived themselves to possess.

Now, Sir, what is the question raised ? The American Government now does what I will show you generally the former American Government never did at the time of the treaty, nor for two years after it was signed never did, till it was under a President who openly maintains the Monroe doctrine of America for the Americans, which would sweep us not only from Mosquito and Belize, but from Canada itself. The American Government now contends that the first article of the treaty not only restricts but abolishes the Mosquito Protectorate, and accuses us of bad faith because we cannot accept that interpretation. But is there a jurisconsult in all Europe who could so accept it ? Why, the protection is admitted ; its continuance is admitted ; you shall not do so and so, "in right of the protection you afford, or may afford." " May afford " means the future. Exactly parallel instances occur in ordinary life. Most gentlemen present have either let or hired a house or farm. Well, in the terms of such tenure, how often are words put to the effect that you shall not, in right of your holding, carry on some kind of trade or factory in the house, or that you shall not sell the hay or straw grown on the farm ? But is there a lawyer in Europe, in America, in every part of the world where the prolific family of lawyers have ever themselves gained occupancy or possession, who will contend that saying you shall not do such a thing in right of your holding, is not a proof that to the holding itself, with that exception, your right is undisputed by the other contracting party? But the strongest point Mr Buchanan makes in his ingenious statement is on the word " occupy." He says, that " if any individual enter into a solemn and explicit agreement that he will not occupy any given tract of country then actually occupied by him, can any proposition be clearer than that he is bound by his agreement to withdraw from such occupancy ? " The first mistake here is in the construction of the word " occupy " in its diplomatic sense. I have looked through the whole voluminous ' History of Treaties ' by Count de

Garden, and I find that in the language of treaties, occupation in the territory of another power has invariably a military or imperial signification. Thus, when in 1810 the Emperor Napoleon desired to annex Holland to France, he insisted upon occupying Amsterdam—that is, to occupy it for a time by an armed force. But look at the word—according to Johnson's Dictionary, to occupy is to possess, or rather to take possession. In neither sense of the word did we occupy the Mosquito territory at the time of the treaty, nor do we so occupy it now. Do we occupy it as a possession for the English ?—so much the contrary, that the chief use we make of the Protectorate is to prevent the English obtaining possession —prevent their acquiring lands there by private bargains with the Mosquito chief. Do we occupy it by a garrison ?—certainly not. Do we assume dominion over the Indian king ?—so much the contrary, that we compel the few English who are in the territory to acknowledge his sovereignty, of which the Americans complain. But granting that the ordinary interpretations of the word " occupy " will not be accepted by American grammarians, we will drop grammar, and come to mathematics. And it can be mathematically demonstrated that " to occupy " is something very different from to "protect." The clause in question proves that; for its sense is, you shall not occupy, in right of the protection you afford, or may afford ; but if the occupation meant the same thing as protection, then the only sense of the clause would be, you shall not occupy in right of occupation—which, in the language of Euclid, is absurd. But that this distinction between occupation and protection was clearly understood by the Americans, through their representatives—that is, their Governments and Ministers—I will prove from their own official documents. Mr Lawrence, the American Minister, writes to the noble Viscount, Dec. 19, 1853 (p. 102), to complain of an alleged outrage on an American vessel in the port of Greytown, by a British brig, for the purpose of collecting dues in that port, and asks if that outrage was authorised by our Government, and says: " Because, if answered in the affirmative, the President will consider the proceedings as a violation of the treaty of 1850, by which Great Britain has stipulated"—what ? not to protect Greytown or the Mosquito territory ? No;—" not to make use of any protection she may afford Nicaragua, the Mosquito coast, or any part of Central America, for the purpose of assuming or exercising dominion over the same." Can words more decidedly express that the treaty left the protection existing, but forbade it to be used for the purpose of dominion? and can any words show more clearly that by dominion was not meant what is now assumed—viz., the residence of a regular agent at Bluefields, who advises the Mosquito king; but what Mr Lawrence is there condemning—viz., an armed force under British colours, not needed for the purpose of protection, but collecting revenue, which is an act of dominion, and is therefore immediately disavowed and set right by our Government? For if it were then assumed by the treaty that we were to withdraw altogether from the Mosquito coast, abandon this Indian tribe, recall the agent who advised its king, was it not the very occasion in which the American Minister would have said, "But what business have you there at all? You have resigned your protection by the treaty of April 1850; you are still occupying that territory, still exercising dominion, because you advise its king. A year and a half have elapsed—when do you mean to go?" But I have now a much more decisive testimony to adduce. Soon after the treaty was signed, Mr Daniel Webster, one of the greatest statesmen who ever adorned either the New World or the Old, whose fame was a link between two hemispheres, succeeded Mr Clayton as Minister for Foreign Affairs. Sir H. Bulwer knew Mr Webster intimately, and was constantly engaged with him, as this book shows, in various plans for settling all differences about the Mosquito territory. Mr Webster, therefore, thoroughly knew the intentions of the negotiators, the spirit of the treaty, the nature of the Protectorate. And two years after the treaty was signed—March 18, 1852—Mr Webster writes to Mr Graham, the Secretary of the United States Navy, and uses these important words: "It is well understood that Great Britain is fully committed to protect Greytown as belonging to the Mosquito Indians; and it is not probable that she would see Nicaraguan authority, or any other authority, take possession till pending negotiations are closed." And now, Sir, I call into court as a witness on our side no less a person than the American co-negotiator of the treaty, Mr Clayton himself. Is there any real difference of opinion between him and Sir Henry Bulwer as to the retention of the Protectorate ? Not at all. Mr Clayton indignantly vindicates himself from the charge of General Cass, an eminent member of the Democratic party, that he (Mr Clayton) understood by the treaty that our Protectorate was abandoned ; and says emphatically in his speech in the Senate, January 4, 1854: "It never was contended by me that the British Protectorate was abolished by the treaty of 1850. What I contended for is this, that the treaty disarmed the Protectorate. It is stated in Lord Clarendon's letter of the 27th that her Britannic Majesty did not by the treaty intend to renounce the Protectorate. I have not claimed that it did." And he then proceeds to argue what we all agree to, that the treaty was intended to modify and restrict the uses we might make of that Protectorate. One more witness, and I close this part of the case. The then Attorney-General, Mr Reverdy Johnson, who was consulted by Mr Clayton on the very words of the treaty as they now stand, says in a published letter to Mr Clayton, December 1853, "that though the object of the treaty was to disarm, it did not abolish, the Protectorate, nor (mark this) was it thought advisable to do this in *ipsissimes verbis.*"

One word only as to the expression that the treaty disarmed the Protectorate. Sir, for all purposes of ambition and dominion it did disarm it, and effectually. Let America understand that we do not deny that. But when it is said that it disarmed us from actually protecting those we are still pledged to protect, and to such an extent that if the Mosquitos were about to be expelled or slaughtered, or their territory annexed by a freebooter, we could not land a soldier or arm a ship in their defence—if that interpretation be contended for, my only answer is, that such an interpretation is an insult to the honesty of England and the common-sense of mankind. I remember a heartless witticism, ascribed, I think, to an Italian potentate, who had promised his protection to an innocent man involved in a false accusation. The man was condemned to death, he appealed to the prince, who was not stirring in his behalf, " Did you not give me your word to pro-

tect me?" "No, my friend," said the prince, "I did not give
you my word, but words." And when this great nation promises its protection, even to a helpless Indian, and he appeals to
us to save him from the executioner, and cries, "Did you not
give me your word to protect me"? are we to answer, with the
Italian prince, "No, friend; we, the monarch and the people of
England, did not give you our word, but words?" Now I hope I
have made thoroughly clear, both to the House and to the American people, this part of our case; that I have shown—1st, the
antiquity of the Protectorate which has been impugned; 2d, that
by the date of its renewal in 1800, we could have had none of the
sinister designs against American progress which has been assigned
to us; 3d, that the treaty did not abolish the Protectorate, and
that this was fully admitted by the American negotiator of the
treaty and by the American Government for two years after the
treaty was signed. I am now going to show how sincerely desirous we have nevertheless been, through all our Governments,
Liberal or Conservative, to remove all causes of dispute on that score,
by voluntary resignation of the Protectorate on any terms that might
acquit us of dishonour to the Indians we abandoned; for, indeed, as
the noble Lord the Member for London, in a despatch to Mr Crampton in January 1853, very justly remarked, the Protectorate had
now ceased to be any advantage to us—we must desire to get
rid of an unprofitable charge the moment we could do so with
good faith to those Indians who had been so loyal to us. It is
perfectly true, as has been stated, that all which the treaty left
of the Protectorate was indeed a shadow. But what was that
shadow? Sir, it was the shadow of the British flag! That
flag to which the weak have so often crept for refuge—that *stans
columna* which—

> " Urbesque, gentesque, et Mare Bospori
> Regnumque matres barbarorum,
> Et purpurei metuunt tyranni."

And that sublime banner could not be withdrawn from those it
had sheltered for two centuries, until we could be sure that its
departing shadow left behind it the safety which the substance
had bestowed The book shows you that the moment the treaty

was signed, Sir H. Bulwer hastened to propose arrangements for the withdrawal from the Protectorate, and the cession of Greytown to a civilised State. The plan most favoured by him and the Government would have been to transfer Greytown and the Protectorate of the Mosquitos, in such territory as might be allotted to them, to Costa Rica—to which, having been always on friendly terms with those Indians, we might more satisfactorily commit their charge. But, unluckily, the Americans had to a certain degree committed themselves to Nicaragua, and our Minister at Washington ascertained that Nicaragua would not hear, at whatever compensation to herself, of this transfer to Costa Rica. Under these circumstances, to so great a degree did England carry conciliation, so anxious were we to prove our desire to settle this matter in the way most agreeable to the United States, that though it was some mortification to our pride, Sir H. Bulwer was instructed by the noble Viscount to offer to resign Greytown to Nicaragua itself, provided the United States did not, by any clause in its treaty with Nicaragua, sanctioning the claim of that republic, assume the appearance of hostile dictation; provided also that some indemnity were given to the Mosquito king—that he were left undisturbed in the territory assigned to him, and some favourable concessions were made to the claim of Costa Rica to the south bank of the river San Juan, to which, having read all the documents, I think its title is clear and undisputable. And now I begin to point out to the House a fact which ought to have great weight with America—it is not America herself that has been the obstacle to a settlement of this question, it is that unhappy little State of Nicaragua. This proposition was received with favour by America through her Minister, Mr Webster. It was discussed in the presence of the British Minister, Mr Webster, and the agents of Costa Rica and Nicaragua, the 11th July 1851. And while the Minister of Costa Rica fully assented to the English proposition, the Minister for Nicaragua refused, and put in one of his own, which Mr Webster, on the part of America, said, " he could not urge her Majesty's Government to accept of." And pray let America heed this—Mr Webster said, "the Nicaraguan proposal deferred matters to a long protracted and indefinite issue ;"

and the bent of his other arguments was to show that though there might be some little difficulty to be made here and there on the plan our negotiators had suggested, it was upon the whole such a one as it was for the interests of Nicaragua to accept.

Here, then, America will see that our Government did, through Sir H. Bulwer, so far back as 1851, make a positive proposal for the entire settlement of the question of our Protectorate, which her own Minister favoured, and which Nicaragua alone prevented being carried into completion. Then all further question was deferred till the Nicaraguan agent could receive fresh instructions from his Government. But on the 12th of August, Sir H. Bulwer reports that this agent had ceased to be representative of Nicaragua. A revolution broke out in that republic, and it became impossible to renew practical negotiations with it. England for these delays is therefore not to blame. Can she prevent revolutions in Nicaragua? But, however, Sir H. Bulwer had the satisfaction, before leaving the United States, to put everything on a footing that promised a complete arrangement of all debated matters. And all would, according to the natural consequence of matters as he left them, have been long since amicably settled, but for this intractable Nicaragua—ever in hot water, ever unable to govern itself, and ever insisting upon involving in its own wretched dissensions the two great branches of the Anglo-Saxon family. For after sundry propositions, which I pass over as imperative, at length, in Lord Derby's short administration, and under Lord Malmesbury, to whose conduct in these affairs I do not think gentlemen opposite will deny the praise of great vigour and promptitude, and remarkable good sense, we were on the very point of settling the whole dispute. The basis of a treaty was actually signed by Mr Webster and Mr Crampton ; agents were sent to Nicaragua, Costa Rica, and Greytown to carry it out. Costa Rica agrees ; Nicaragua again refuses ; Mr Webster, as you see by Mr Crampton's despatch to Lord Malmesbury, page 198, declares that refusal so unreasonable, that he was ready to settle the matter without further reference to her. Unhappily about this time occurred the death of Mr Webster—that great man, whose lofty intellect commanded the field of politics from an eminence high above the momentary passions of party, and whose fame wove a link between the two nations. Thus again, not by the fault of England nor of America, but of Nicaragua, the peaceful settlement of these matters in 1852 falls to the ground as it fell in 1851. And now the noble Lord the Member for London came into office, and he suggested, by a despatch to Mr Crampton, in January 1853, that Greytown be declared a free and independent port, connected with Mosquito by such terms of friendship and alliance as may be agreed upon. Lord Clarendon succeeding supports that proposition. The American Government declares, and still says, "Hand over Greytown and the Mosquito to Nicaragua, and, thanks to American citizens, Nicaragua has disappeared." The House is aware that a band of originally Filibusters, under a skilful and daring adventurer—I beg him ten thousand pardons —now General Walker, has upset the Spanish Government of Nicaragua, publicly and ceremoniously shot her most popular general in the market-place of her capital, and being reinforced it is said by 2000 American citizens, now holds in contented acquiesence, or in timid subjugation, that martial spirit and that legislative wisdom which had defied all the armaments of England. The American Government says: "We will not help you ; treat with the Government of Nicaragua ;" and Nicaragua, according to America, has at this moment no Government at all to treat with ! The United States have refused to recognise the Government of which General Walker is Dictator, and to receive his diplomatic agents ; nay, it is with the United States that General Walker—that is, the Government of Nicaragua—has come into collision ; it is the property of their commercial company that General Walker—that is, the Nicaraguan Government—has just confiscated ; it is in their Senate that General Walker—that is, the Nicaraguan Government—has just been declared by the negotiator of the treaty, Mr Clayton, "to be a ruffian and a pirate." And therefore, if we were to do what the Government of the United States tells us to do, treat with the Nicaraguan Government—that is, with General Walker—and not consult the United States at all, it would surely be to the dignity of the United States that we should offer insult and outrage. But to add to the embarrassments that be-

set this part of the question, General Walker has lately declared by
an edict that Mosquito is annexed to Nicaragua; and may, for
what we know, be about to enforce that insulting defiance to
Great Britain at the point of the bayonet. And if the American
Government, while declaring by solemn treaty that it will exercise
no dominion in Central America, cannot prevent its adventurous
citizens from obtaining dominion in the very republic whose
independence it asserts, whose claims it espouses against ourselves
—surely, at least, it might respect our position, thus grievously complicated, and give us the weight of its friendly influence against the
difficulties which its own citizens have created. For what is the
difference between us and the American Government on this
score ? They desire us to withdraw from the Protectorate : we
desire to do so. But we say before withdrawing, " We must see
that somehow or other our poor Indian ally is safe from aggression or extirpation." They say, " No ; withdraw first, and leave
what Mr Buchanan calls the miserable remnant of that tribe,"—to
what ? Why, to the hope he expresses that Nicaragua, who cannot
protect herself, will then recognise the qualified right of the tribe to
occupy such portions of the soil as she may vouchsafe to them, and
that Nicaragua alone is to have the right to extinguish that occupancy. And in this difference between us what has America
to gain ? Nothing. What have we to lose ? Everything ; for
we should lose our honour. Do not let them reply by exaggerated pictures of the degradation of these Indians. If the red
men are degraded, is it not by contact with the vices of the white ?
And is that a reason why we should consign them either to a
ruffian or a pirate, or, reduced in number and tamed from their
old warlike habits, to those petty Spanish tyrants who boast that they
are the successors of Cortes and Pizarro, and profess the same scornful political creed by which these ruthless destroyers justified
every crime and every treason upon a race which they excluded
from the pale of civilised humanity? Is it not an American historian who has taught us to shudder at those crimes and those
treasons, and warned us against admitting their repetition ? And
is it not the indignant pathos with which he has described Spanish
outrage and Indian wrong, that has made us place the volumes of

Prescott by the side of our Gibbon and Macaulay? Gentlemen
will all remember that old line of our schoolboy days—

" Homo sum, humani nihil a me alienum puto."

Sir, it is said that that line was suggested to Terence by the
great Scipio, and that when it was first uttered in a Roman
theatre, all that heathen audience rose as if in electric recognition
of its sublime and touching fellowship with mankind. Sir, I send
that line across the ocean in answer to those who say that these
poor Indians are aliens from our civilised faith and honour; and
I speak it in this nobler theatre, and before this Christian audience. Here, then, apologising for the time it has taken me, I
close the case of the Mosquito Protectorate. I have shown the genuine antiquity of the connection; the obligations it has imposed
on our honour. I have shown that the treaty of 1850 did not
abolish it by the admissions of the American negotiators, and by
all American Governments before the present one. I have shown
that we have made new propositions to withdraw from it, two of
which were received with favour by the American Government itself;
and that the sole difficulty in the way of meeting the wish of the
United States to transfer the Protectorate to Nicaragua was occasioned first by the obstinacy of Nicaragua herself, and now by the
fact that Nicaragua has passed to the dominion of American citizens,
whom the American Government can neither control nor acknowledge. This is our case: let Americans say if it be not a just
one; if it be not one that entitles us to the most conciliatory
sympathy and co-operation on their part; and whether they can
accept so hollow a pretext to increase their naval armaments, and
threaten war upon the land that was the cradle of their infant
greatness, and is still the sacred burial-ground of their Saxon
fathers.

I now come to the two other questions of British Honduras
and the Bay islands. I shall take them in connection with the
more recent correspondence between our Government and the
United States. Sir, the statement of Lord Clarendon (in reply to
Mr Buchanan's statement) of May 2, 1824, seems to me unex-
ceptionable, and, indeed, admirable in argument and temper; but

in Lord Clarendon's previous despatch of May 27, 1853, there occurs a mistake which occasioned the greatest irritation in America, the consequences of which we still feel. In that despatch Lord Clarendon says Great Britain has nowhere in the treaty of 1850 renounced, nor even had any intention to renounce, the full and absolute right which she possesses over her own lawful territories in Central America, such as that designation was understood and declared by the negotiators of the treaty. Now, Sir, this mistake is doubly unfortunate. For the negotiators of the treaty understood, the Government understood, the noble Viscount, as appears in his own despatch, September 10, 1851 (p. 541), understood, by the designation " Central America," only the territories comprehended in the five Central American republics in which we have no lawful territories at all. If Lord Clarendon means by these words to refer to British Honduras or the Bay islands, then he gives up the very point for which our adversaries contend—viz., that those places are in Central America which we dispute. Or if he means them to apply to what alone we do hold in Central America, as that designation was understood by the negotiators of the treaty—viz., the Mosquito Protectorate, he cannot call it our lawful territory, and say we had no intention to renounce it without a flagrant violation of the treaty of 1850, and a direct contradiction of all that he himself and previous Governments since 1850 have declared. This sentence fell like a bomb upon the American public ; and as, unluckily, it reached America a few weeks after the President's inaugural address had reached ourselves, so it was said in the Senate that " it was necessarily supposed to be a note of defiance to that address." Mr Clayton saying courteously, and thinking justly, that it must be a verbal inadvertence—that it could not apply to the Mosquitos, but by a mistake to British Honduras—and that a statesman so distinguished as Lord Clarendon could not persevere in such an error,—addressed a letter to Mr Crampton, comprising questions to which he asked a prompt and full reply. That reply he received and read in the Senate. Mr Crampton says in it : "I regret that I am at present unable to supply you with an explicit explanation of the passage in the dispatch, from which it seems to be inferred that Belize is stated by the Brit-

ish Government to be in Central America, as I am not in possession
of any official communication from my Government in which that
question is distinctly treated. A fair inference, however, from the
text of treaties and other documents to which I have access with regard to the title of Great Britain and its dependencies, would lead
me to conclude that British Honduras is situated in Mexico, and
not in Central America, properly so called. In this opinion I have
good reason to think that the Government of the United States
concur." In comment on this note Mr Clayton emphatically says :
"The only map upon which American statesmen can rely is that
which presents Central America as defined by our own Government, and it is designated by a treaty with Central America,
December 1825, with the five Central American States—Costa
Rica, Nicaragua, San Salvador, Honduras, Guatemala ; these are
all that constitute Central America in any legal, political, or commercial meaning of that term. The subject is so understood by
Great Britain as well as by us." Now, while this shows a mistake
upon the part of Lord Clarendon, and a mistake which was so far
unfortunate that it has been subjected to a misunderstanding
which has pervaded the spirit of all subsequent negotiation, yet,
apart from a verbal error in our Government, it substantiates our
case as a nation, and proves that by the treaty of 1850, every
article of which is rigidly confined to Central America, we did
not, as our adversaries contend, in the slightest degree compromise
our claims to Belize and its dependencies, which are not included
in that designation by the American Government itself. And
when Mr Buchanan has raised a question thereon by a reference
to old maps, perilous indeed would it be to the United States to
allow any question to be raised as to the designation which limits
Central America to the five said States; for if, on the one hand,
Mr Buchanan would find any part of British Honduras or the
island of Ruatan placed by such maps in Central America, so, in
the very same maps, down even to the map published by the
Society for the Diffusion of Useful Knowledge, which has been
quoted against us, he will find, as Mr Clayton himself says in his
speech, the southern sides of Mexico, including Texas and California, placed within Central America ; and therefore it would be

from California and Texas that, according to such maps, by the
treaty of 1850, the Americans would have to withdraw all occupation and dominion. Thus Belize and its dependencies are
exempted from the engagements of the treaty of 1850, and the
American Government has not a leg to stand on, in raising
thereon any dispute as to our possessions. But to place the
matter beyond a doubt, the noble Viscount, foreseeing that some
cavil might be raised on the authority of old maps or geographical
traditions, instructed Sir Henry Bulwer to obtain that declaration
which I have before referred to, and by which Mr Clayton ex-
empts from the treaty British Honduras, though with a slight
variation from Sir Henry Bulwer's diction ; for he says, not
British Honduras and its dependencies, but British Honduras and
the small islands known to be dependent on it. It has been said
that that variation was intended to affect Britain : if so, it would
have been very disingenuous to do so by a side wind ; but in
point of fact I will presently show that it does not affect whatever
may be our title to Ruatan at all.

Yet I think it sound as well as conciliatory policy to volunteer a
promise never to extend the territory we there held at the time of
the treaty. For, to go back to the territory we held in 1786 by
virtue of the convention with Spain in that year, is a demand
which, made upon such a principle, this House could never permit
a British Government to accede to ; for if we once established a
precedent that we are to go back to obsolete conventions for the
limit of domains, without regard to the subsequent wars that an-
nulled them, it is more than Belize which would be affected ; we
should unsettle the title-deeds of our empire in every part of the
world. Nay, such a precedent would shake the foundations of
every throne in Europe. Before quitting this part of the case, I
must respectfully point out to the Government what appears to
me another mistake in the mode in which they have conducted
their argument and created difficulties for themselves : this mistake evidently grew out of Lord Clarendon's first verbal error on
the proper designation of Central America, and it has pervaded
and embittered all our subsequent negotiations. When I have
seen it stated that Mr Clayton disputes our construction of the

treaty, I have been amazed; because, as we have seen, he does not dispute it as to the retention of the Protectorate, or the exemption of British Honduras. I have asked Americans to explain, then, what is the construction Mr Clayton can dispute; and I am told that it is that distinction which our Government has made between the past and prospective sense of the treaty. Neither, Sir, can I understand that distinction. It must, I think, have been suggested by some legal adviser, adopting Lord Clarendon's early mistake, that Belize might be included in the engagements of the treaty; for in point of fact, as far as I can see, no such distinction exists. As to Mosquito, you had no dominion there at the time of the treaty, and you are bound to have none hereafter. But if you had a dominion there apart and distinct from the Protectorate at the time of the treaty, I think your distinction would be wrong, and you would be bound to withdraw from it; and this you yourselves acknowledge, since, when Mr Lawrence complained of what would have been an act of dominion by the collection of revenue by armed force, you at once disavowed it. As to British Honduras, since it was not referred to by the treaty in the past, it cannot be affected by the treaty in the future. I submit, therefore, to her Majesty's Government, to drop a distinction which has embroiled the whole question into a vexatious quibble, which has led the American public to suspect that you have those ulterior ambitious designs of which, as a nation, we are innocent; and if you have raised that distinction for the purpose of covering the colonisation of Ruatan, you have committed the mistake of involving all the strong points of your case in the questionable argument you have set up for the weakest.

I come hastily to the question of Ruatan and the Bay islands; as to the smaller islands annexed to Ruatan, I am not ashamed to say that I know little about them; for I suspect there are few in this House who are much wiser. I shall leave it to the Government to enlighten us on that score with statistical information which will have all the charm of novelty, and the vantage-ground of a recondite learning which none of us will be able to dispute. But it is upon your claim to Ruatan that the other islands of the Bay colony, I presume, depends; and about Ruatan I do know some-

thing. The question here, as to title, lies in a nut-shell. Does
Ruatan belong to Central America? if so, you are bound to withdraw from it, unless you can show it to be *bona fide* a dependency
of Belize. There is no reference to Ruatan in the treaty. But
Mr Clayton admits in his speech, January 16, 1854 (and the admission is important), that we, the American Government, knew
that the British Government had, before the time of the treaty,
laid claim to Ruatan, an island on the Atlantic side of the States
of Honduras and Guatemala. But whether that island was or was
not a part of the British West Indies or a Central American State,
was a question which the American Government determined to
leave to be settled hereafter." It is clearly, therefore, out of the
treaty. Nay, more—the American Government being cognisant of
our claim to it in 1850, yet resolved to leave it to be settled hereafter ; and Mr Clayton's declaration made simultaneously with the
treaty, notwithstanding its reserved phraseology as to " small
islands," could not affect one way or the other what he thus expressly declares his own Government left to be settled hereafter ;
nor could he indeed have had it in his eye, since you see by Mr
Crompton's last despatch that he says "we had as good a claim to
it as we had to Jamaica." It has now, therefore, to be regarded
solely on its own merits. Now there are two points of view in
which to look at this question ; first, as geographers and mere
lawyers—secondly, as politicians and statesmen. Were I a geo-
grapher or a mere lawyer desirous to assist our Government in retaining this island, I think I could show strong reasons for believing that our title to it is good ; but not on the ground in which
our Government are disposed to place it. I do not think you can
fairly call it a dependency of Belize. And if ever it were so,
surely it has ceased to be the dependency of a settlement when you
have raised it into a colony under the Crown. As to the policy
of that colonisation, though it is signed by the name of my right
hon. friend the Member for Droitwich, the responsibility of it, I
believe, rests with the previous Whig Government, by whom the
Act had been framed and completed ; and my right hon. friend only
did what any one just coming into office, and whose attention had
not been previously directed to the bearings of the question, might

naturally have done, when he affixed his name to a deed already completed by statesmen of great experience and distinction. As I am without the slightest data to conceive the motives or excuses for that act, I leave it to the Government to state their own case here—contenting myself with saying, meanwhile, that to me it seems to have been a very questionable and ill-advised proceeding. But Mr Clayton intimates what may be a better title to it than that of a *bona fide* dependency of Belize—viz., is it not a part of the British West Indies? For who is the highest authority of all modern geographers? the one whom all scholars are in the habit of accepting? Undoubtedly it is Malte Brun. And he enumerates Ruatan categorically among the British West Indian Islands. Moreover, I think, though I will not presume to say that I am certain, that I could show not only by logical inference but documentary evidence, Spanish as well as English, that it was actually in our possession at the date of the Madrid Treaty in 1670, and formed a part of the West India possessions then ceded to us by Spain. But even if this be not so, still, seeing that it has been off and on in our possession for generations before the Spanish republics existed, or the term of Central America was heard of, it is for our adversaries to prove that it belongs to a State in Central America. But so difficult would they find that proof, that their utmost researches have hitherto failed to do more than show, that when at one time Great Britain suspended her hold on it, the republic of Honduras took possession of it, and was expelled by Great Britain as an illegitimate intruder. But that would give Honduras no better claim to Ruatan than a man would have to my hat if I left it on the hall table, on the plea that I had resigned my pretensions to it because it was not actually on my head. But it is one question whether the title be good, and another question whether the possession be desirable. And since I am not addressing geographers and lawyers, but statesmen and politicians, I think I can show you that we have no interest in the retention of Ruatan and the islands you have annexed to it, which can make them an obstacle to a general arrangement of all disputes. Lord Clarendon himself, according to a despatch of Mr Buchanan in the American edition of the Correspondence, allows that Ruatan is of little value to us. To us, indeed, it can never be of the smallest use, except as a naval and military station—for what purpose?—to overawe Central America—the very part of the world in which we are bound never to attempt dominion! If we are to do our duty to it as a colony, it must involve us in great expense, and constant anxiety and trouble. It is an island assailable on all sides, and, considering the jealous neighbours by whom it is surrounded, it should be fortified and garrisoned ; it abounds in creeks and coves favourable to filibusters and buccaneers. Your flag may protect you from the invasion of any regular State, but not from the perpetual harassment of lawless adventurers. You will have these General Walkers by the dozen! And since Ruatan really is the key to a great part of Central America, your retention of it is a standing grievance and menace to the whole of that isthmus. It will involve you in undignified and everlasting disputes with the petty Spanish republics ; and above all, since Mr Buchanan is right in saying that the geographical position of Ruatan is such as would allow Great Britain, if she pleased, completely to arrest the trade of the United States to and from the isthmus,—so, as long as you keep that island, war with the United States is a thing probable—friendship with the United States is a thing impossible. And therefore, although there must be many preliminary considerations before resigning these islands,—first, as to whether they should be given to Honduras or raised into free ports—secondly, as to the cautions against their becoming the nest for pirates and buccaneers, much more threatening to the peace and commerce of Central America than Great Britain can be,—yet still I ask you to concur in the guarded proposition that they are not of such importance to us as to present an insuperable obstacle to some general and amicable arrangement for the solution of all disputes.

But all disputes our Government has now, though somewhat tardily, offered to submit to arbitration. Mr Buchanan objects —but on what ground? He says that his interpretation of the treaty is supported by the almost unanimous opinion in America. This, begging his pardon, cannot be ; for while he says the treaty necessitates our abandonment of the Mosquito Protectorate, Mr Clayton, its negotiator, and a chief of the great Whig party, says, as we have seen, precisely the contrary. And while he would bring British Honduras into the terms of the treaty, General Cass, the organ of the great Democratic party, says, in his speech in the Senate, that "Sir Henry Bulwer obtained its exemption from the treaty so clearly by word and deed as to preclude all controversy on that topic." And thirdly, while Mr Buchanan says that Ruatan is clearly an island in Central America, Mr Clayton implies as clearly that it is in the British West Indies. But I have seen it stated in American journals, and in the American Legislature, that the affair has gone beyond arbitration. Beyond ! Why, in 1813, a year after America had declared war on us, and while war was actually going on, it was the President of the United States who proposed to us the arbitration of the Emperor of Russia ; true, that Great Britain then, not very wisely, rejected the offer ; but in 1822 the Russian mediator was called in to determine the construction of the 1st article of the Treaty of Gand. But I find it is said, " Yes, we might accept Russia as an arbiter, but that is the only power sufficiently independent for us freeborn Americans." Is it so ? Why, in 1831 America accepted the King of Holland as an arbiter in the interpretation of the 5th article of the Treaty of Gand ; for somehow or other—I say it good-humouredly—our American children, though uncommon acute on most matters, are apt to be rather dull as to the interpretation of treaties in any way disagreeable to themselves. Thus, so far as arbitration is concerned, there is ample precedent for it, and precisely in parallel cases—viz., in the interpretation of treaties. But shall I say why I think the present American Government might be disinclined to arbitration ? The reason may be found in a pithy sentence in the Russian arbitrament of 1822, signed Nesselrode. Russia then said, " The question can only be decided according to the literal and grammatical sense of the article in dispute." But as to the treaty of 1850, who can say that in the literal and grammatical sense of the words " the protection you may afford," means the protection you must not afford ? or that our other possessions not mentioned in the treaty, and reserved from its engagements by a special declaration, have dropped out of her Majesty's empire through the gap of a grammatical ellipsis ?

And now that I have referred to the war of 1812, I must say

that if anything could warn the Americans from hostilities with us for a dispute of this kind, it is the fact that when they went to war with us in 1812 upon certain alleged complaints, that war ended leaving the complaints so much what they were before, that Count de Garden observes, in his 'History of Treaties,' " The conclusion of the war decided nothing upon which the Americans had taken up arms, and only adjourned the solution of many grave difficulties." Nor was it till 1842 that those differences which had lasted nearly half a century were settled. And how settled then ? By arms, by threats, by insisting upon quarrel? No ; by what I now press upon the American Government and people, I hope not in vain—by friendly arrangements which, to use the words of the convention of 1842, " contained nothing to compromise the honour and dignity of the two nations."

Sir, if the United States Government refuse arbitration, I urge it upon her Majesty's Ministers not to consider that the means of conciliation are exhausted ; but then to propose what I think would have been far better, in the first instance, than the arbitrament of a foreign power—viz., commissioners similar to those who in 1842 produced such happy results. And I do this the most sanguinely, because this is what Mr Lawrence himself suggested in 1849.

This treaty of 1850 is worth preservation. True, that nature, more powerful than diplomatists, has raised unforeseen obstacles to the construction of that canal which it was intended to open and secure to the universal commerce of mankind. But it operates equally for all other international communication upon that favoured isthmus ; under its provisions the magnificent railway of Panama unites the shores of two oceans and the enterprise of two worlds. Other communications will no doubt be effected. But grander than those communications themselves is the principle which that treaty first established, a principle designed to disarm the ambition of nations in order to promote the civilisation of the globe. And the document which records that sublime idea ought not to be ravished from the archives of the Anglo-Saxon family by the miserable squabbles of Nicaragua, and the lawless audacity of desultory freebooters.

Here I would fain conclude, but I am so anxious that the Americans should not be misled, that, not for the purpose of threatening, but for the purpose of inducing calm reflection amongst that highly educated people, I will add some truths that may not misbecome the lips of a member of this House. In a very influential American journal supporting the Democratic Government, and representing the opinions of what may be called the war party in the United States, there occurs an article commencing with remarks upon the bad faith of John Bull, &c., which I shall omit, lest they might excite angry feelings amongst ourselves, and proceeds thus: "All that is necessary to bring Palmerston and Clarendon to a definite understanding and reparation, is a bold and uncompromising demand for a yea or no, peace or war; a firm stand will secure the rights without the hazards of war, and, this being done, all further trouble for the future will be saved," (how? by keeping faith with us as to the treaty No. 1 ?) "by knocking the Bulwer and Clayton treaty on the head, and by falling back on the Monroe doctrine of British non-intervention in the affairs of our independent neighbours." Now this is calculated to instil a very dangerous error into the mind of the American public; and I would guard them, and, if I may say so without offence, I would caution certain of the most eminent members of this House, from anything that may encourage the belief, which more than all else involved us in the war with Russia—viz., that conciliatory expressions are the proof of cowardly dispositions. And do not let the Americans be induced by those agitators who abound in all free States to suppose that by making what they call a firm stand, yea or no, peace or war—in other words, by leaving to Great Britain no option to armed resistance except humiliation, and dishonouring any combination of powers on the face of the globe—can obtain from us the rights of war, which here mean the rights of conquest, without also incurring its hazards.

Sir, it has been well said in the American Senate that the government of individuals is temporary and ephemeral; but the government of principles which maintain the good faith and majesty of England will, I believe, last as long as there is a throne

to her sovereign and a free voice to her people. It is true
that we are divided by parties, but I think that there is no
party in the State that would condescend to make political capital out of national dishonour. Where England is concerned in
her bearing to foreign nations, or the maintenance of solemn
obligations, whether to monarchs or to savages—I turn fearlessly
to the high-minded gentlemen beside, around, and before me, and
ask them if I may not tell the world that there we can forget that
we are partisans and only remember that we are Englishmen.

In these American journals, and in the American Legislature, I
have seen a vehement repetition of that cry which some amongst
ourselves, from perhaps the noble error of too sensitive a national
pride, have unreflectingly appeared to sanction—viz., that in the
late war with Russia we have lost military caste and prestige which
we must be longing to redeem. I am not here to defend the
whole conduct of that war. I have felt as painfully as any man
every disaster we have incurred, every blunder we have committed.
But I have seen as proudly as any man that with every disaster
our spirit has increased—with every error our intelligence has
quickened ; and whether in the opinion of unjust and superficial
critics we have lost for a moment military prestige or not, a calm
belief pervades this country that at the close of the war we are in
reality a far more formidable power than we were at its commencement. I do not think, therefore, on the one hand, that we
have really any wounded national vanity which would tempt us to
pick a quarrel with our neighbours for the purpose of recovering
military prestige ; and if we could cherish so puerile and paltry a
desire, I am certain that the last people with which we would
court hostilities are our own flourishing and giant children. But,
on the other hand, it is not presumption to say—and I say it not
to America, but to the whole world—that if any foreign State,
relying on these chimerical notions of loss of prestige, should
force us to war on behalf of our rights or those of the humanity
we have undertaken to guard, it would find to its cost that it was
no mutilated shield that it touched, no paralysed arm that it provoked, but that England had only cleared the rust from her aegis
and added weight to the thunders of her bolt. And do not let our

noble kinsmen be led by their party zealots to expect that war will give them better terms than we would amicably offer now. Now, we will all go to the utmost verge of conciliation ; but let one drop of British blood, nay, one drop of Indian blood under British protection, be unjustly shed by those whom we now earnestly solicit to be our friends, and will conciliation then be the thought uppermost in our minds ?

Oh, Sir, let us all hope that America, being thus both propitiated and warned in time, will meet the frank cordial hand we extend to her, not with a clenched fist, but with as cordial and frank a clasp. I have loved that American people from my earliest youth. In my connection with literature, if I may be pardoned for alluding to what, after all, next to the earnestness of my convictions, is my best title to the kind indulgence the House has shown me, I have felt proud and grateful at the thought that I am perhaps better known in America than I am here ; and if I had not my own reasons to respect that people, I have learned enough of their high qualities from my nearest relations during a residence amongst them, to place them in my affectionate esteem, next only to my own countrymen. Well, then, let them judge of the general temper of the people of these realms, if I, with all these predispositions in their favour—I, no supporter of the Government except where that Government becomes the abstract representative of the royal dignity and the national renown—if even I say, " anything to conciliate America but the honour and dignity of England;" and if she asks those—No, ten times no ! whatever be the hazard ! "

But it is not thus I would conclude. I have referred to the arguments of Mr Buchanan with the frankness of discussion to which the citizens of free nations are accustomed, but I hope, also, without deviating from that respect due alike to his high personal repute and his late dignity as the Minister of an illustrious and mighty Commonwealth. It is said that he has left us as a candidate for the highest office the American Republic can confer, and we may therefore presume that the conciliatory words he so gracefully uttered on the occasion of the farewell dinner given to him in this metropolis were addressed not only to ourselves but to his

own countrymen; that he knew when he deprecated hostilities
between them and us, he was speaking in conformity with the
genuine sentiments and substantial interests of the people over
whom he is going to preside.   And, Sir, it is in order to support
him in the gracious task of conciliation, and to invite the Americans to hasten the settlement of disputes we are anxious to close
for ever, that I ask you to accept the resolutions I am about to submit to the House.   I ask you, while temperately upholding the
honour of your country, still unequivocally to attest your desire
to reunite yourselves to your American kinsmen, and prove that
you cherish no ambition on the other side of the Atlantic so much
as that which may retain the reciprocal influence and sympathy
which ought to last as long as the two nations utter in the same
language the thoughts by which they civilise the earth, and the
prayers which they address to Heaven.

XXXVII.

OUTLINE OF A SPEECH

INTENDED TO HAVE BEEN DELIVERED IN

THE HOUSE OF COMMONS

ON THE 10TH OF JUNE 1859.

ON Tuesday, the 7th of June 1859, the Address in answer to the Speech from the Throne was moved in the House of Commons by the Member for South Lancashire, the Hon. Algernon Fulke Egerton, and was seconded by the Member for Portsmouth, Sir James Elphinstone. Thereupon the Marquess of Hartington, the Member for North Lancashire, moved, by way of amendment, that the following words be added to the Address :—
"But we beg humbly to submit to her Majesty that it is essential for securing satisfactory results to our deliberations, and for facilitating the discharge of her Majesty's high functions, that her Majesty's Government should possess the confidence of this House and of the country ; and we deem it our duty respectfully to represent to her Majesty that such confidence is not reposed in the present advisers of her Majesty."
A discussion arose upon this which lasted for three nights ; at the close of the last sitting a, vote of Want of Confidence in the Ministry being carried upon a division by 323 to 310, giving a majority of 13 against the Government. But for the severe illness which alone prevented the then Colonial Secretary, Sir Edward Lytton, from taking part in the debate, the following speech would have been delivered by him in vindication of his ministerial colleagues.

SIR,—I have often had cause to thank this House for the indulgence with which it has honoured me ; but I have never so much needed that indulgence as now, when, to all other defects, I must add those which are inseparable from bodily suffering and weakness.

Sir, my interest in the result of this motion is less personal than that of my colleagues, though I do not think it is less keen. For I only hold office because I cannot quit it while a motion, aimed at a Government whose responsibilities I have shared, is still undetermined.   If the motion be carried I shall share the defeat of my colleagues; if it be lost, my successor will benefit by the triumph.   In neither case, therefore, does the desire of office influence the views with which I regard the bearings of the questions which the House is invited to decide.

Sir, I fully recognise the principle so strongly urged by gentlemen who have preceded me—that whatever be the Government her Majesty may appoint, it should enjoy the confidence of this House.   But I hold that there is a wide difference between the recognition of that principle and the adoption of a rule that the House is to have no confidence in any Government that does not find a clear majority in the party it more specially represents.   If this rule is to be imperatively enforced, I do not foresee the possible duration of any Ministry formed from the ranks of the gentlemen opposite.   For no man will tell us that because gentlemen sit yonder on the same side of the House, they are therefore all of the same party—all professing the same opinions, all advocating the same objects.   Nay, I will venture to say that there are at least one-third of the members I see before me who agree much more with gentlemen on this side the House than they agree with the other two-thirds with whom they are topographically connected. It may be as convenient in political records as it is in natural history to make general classifications comprehending the most copious varieties.   But one specimen of the grand mammiferous division does not more differ from another in the length and breadth of its proportions, than one member in the general classification of Liberals differs from another in the length and breadth of his opinions.   Indeed the varieties embodied in the verbal classification of Liberals are now so openly acknowledged, that we are given to understand that the next Liberal Cabinet is to be a Cabinet of selected specimens.   The noble Lord the Member for London is reported to have said at the meeting which witnessed the affecting reconciliation between himself and the noble Viscount, that the next Cabinet should no longer represent one party; no, it should represent three—the old Whigs, the advanced Liberals, and the distinguished individuals on whom the honourable appellation of Peelites is bestowed. Thus, then, in order to obtain a Government which is to have a following superior in numbers to the single party of the Conservatives, no less than three parties—all classified, it is true, under the term of Liberal, but all having till lately expressed opinions utterly antagonistic with each other—are to be caged up in a Cabinet, and are henceforth to be brought into harmony and concord. On a former occasion, the hon. gentleman the Member for Birmingham urged upon the two noble Lords, who are now profiting by his peaceful exhortation, the example of the old Scandinavian heroes, who spent their nights in Valhalla over the loving cup, poured out of the skulls of their enemies. But if they are now to resemble those mythological warriors, they are not only to drink the loving cup to-night, but with the morrow they are to start up in arms and renew the encounter. And however differences and quarrels may be appeased for a special occasion, I do the distinguished men who are to compose the next Cabinet too much justice not to imagine that the loving cup will be exhausted by the heartiness with which they gulp down the reluctant draught; and that when they meet in the Cabinet it will be with the true Scandinavian spirit—with flashing eyes, and arms outstretched to destroy each other. For surely it cannot have been merely personal dissensions that so long kept apart men of so lofty a public spirit. If it be so great an outrage on the Constitution that the Government should be in a minority when it only counts its own party supporters, how could the noble Lord the Member for the City, to whom the Constitution is as it were put out to nurse—that Constitution which, with more than motherly fondness, he is always dandling, and rocking, and petting, and physicking—how could the noble Lord have allowed this grievous offence on that beloved Constitution for more than a whole year, without a struggle to defend it from the arms of this sacrilegious minority? Certainly, if the principle be so sacred, last year was the time to enforce it. The Government then were in an acknowledged minority, so far as their supporters were concerned; war had not then burst forth in Europe—no dangers to our own country appeared in the distance. In a sudden change of administration there would have been but the average degree of public inconvenience. But now, when men of all parties demand that our fleets should be strengthened, our armies increased; now when, on the silent instinct of self-preservation, rifle-clubs are forming in every town, every village, and England, like Sparta, supplies the want of stone battlements by the living ramparts of armed men—now you find it the exact moment to displace one Government without a single element of concord, and doubting in that which is to succeed it—I say, without a single element of concord, either in foreign affairs or domestic. In foreign affairs—who does not remember the character which the noble Viscount has received from the gentlemen below the gangway, who are now to be his colleagues for adjusting the balance of Europe? Is it domestic affairs? is it reform and vote by ballot? is it church rates? is it economy, or the disposition of patronage, who have been the great disputants? Is it not the one half of the future Cabinet with the other half? And do you mean to tell us, when you speak of the necessity of a strong Government to command the deference of foreign powers, that it is a Government thus formed that is to impress Europe with submissive awe—that is, to preach the wisdom of moderation to Germany, and the virtue of sincerity to France?

Sir, I think that the Liberal party, using that term in its widest and noblest sense, never made a greater mistake than in thus asserting the doctrine that the House of Commons must withhold its confidence from a Government, not on account of specific charges, not on account of overt acts plainly set forth in a substantive motion and supplied by documentary evidence, but simply because all other parties patch up their differences and unite against the Government. They may outnumber its habitual supporters. I say it is a mistake, because sooner or later the precedent must be brought fatally against yourselves. It is the inherent necessity of a Liberal party to be subdivided into many sections. The more free Parliament becomes, the more popular our representation; the more that imperative condition of Liberal politicians will increase, the more numerous will become its sections, and the more distinct and vital will be the differences between them. It is with politics as with religion—in proportion as you allow liberty of opinion, sects will multiply. In religion you may class them all under the name of Dissenters, in politics you may class them all under the name of Liberals. You may unite the one or the other for the purpose of putting down here an Establishment, or there a Government. But there is this difference between religious and political sects. Religious sects only combine to remove what they regard as a common grievance ; they do not afterwards combine to amalgamate doctrines and settle differences. But political sects must reconstruct as well as destroy. As soon as they have triumphed over the Government they would pull down, they must settle the articles of faith for the Government they set up. This will be always hereafter the great difficulty of Liberal politicians ; but if they desire to make it insuperable, they will adhere to the principle put forth to-day—viz., that a Government, without reference to its merit or its faults, must never count on the general protection of the House, but exclusively on the support of its own partisans. For thus, in proportion as each section of the Liberals is thrown into power, preponderating more or less over the other sections, the Government it forms will in reality have but a minority of its own supporters, and be invariably at the mercy of any division in which the ambition of those on one side the House can join with the variegated discontent of those upon the other.

I cannot help considering, then, that the House should be very wary of exercising its undoubted right to a want of confidence in the Government. Whenever an opposition party conceives that by uniting for the moment all the various sections within its scope, it may succeed so to scrape the ground as to glean a majority ; but if that be prudence on ordinary occasions, it does seem to me a duty upon the present ; because, put it as we may, the first requisite for England at this moment is to strengthen the Executive in its attitude towards foreign powers. But how can that object be achieved by this motion ? Grant it to be successful, and the gentlemen opposite transfer themselves to these benches, it can only be, I apprehend, by a most narrow and hair-breadth majority,

comprising all those who a few months ago were at daggers-drawn
with each other, and confronted by one of the largest and most
united bodies that ever sat in opposition.   And the only intelligible principle upon which, in the eyes of foreign nations, this new
Government could have come into power, would be one of decided
sympathy, not with Italian liberty, (for what Englishman would
not sympathise with that?) but with the armed ambition which
makes liberty its pretence and dominion its object.   For what is
the ground on which you insinuate attack on the policy of the
present Government in this war?   You say it has Austrian leanings ; but if you would wait for the papers that will be shortly
before you, you will find that that charge is wholly untrue ; that
we have made no scruple in expressing our disapproval whether of
the mode in which Austria governs the Italian territories that are
hers by treaty, or of her interference in the affairs of Central Italy.
But we have deprecated, and we do deprecate, the war, in which
nothing seems certain but the sacrifice of human life.   In Italy, I
grant, among those who now share in that war, this dislike to the
war itself is considered to be Austrian leanings.   They say the
power that is not with us is against us, and they anticipate with
joy the downfall of Lord Derby's Government, because they consider its successor will pronounce its sympathy with the allied
belligerents sufficiently loudly to necessitate in a short time our own
appearance on the field.   Read any Italian newspaper, and you
will find that calculation plainly expressed.   If you disappoint it
by preserving in act that strict neutrality which we hold to be the
duty and the interest of England, you will find all your difficulties,
as a negotiator, multiplied a thousand-fold; for while Austria
will regard you as an enemy, Italy will suspect you as a deceiver.
If you do not disappoint that calculation—if you are led on to
take any part in this struggle, you will hasten the rush of all
Germany into the field, and will be lending yourselves to those
objects for which France desires the destruction of treaties that
now bind her boundaries, for which Russia has obtained at
Villafranca her entrance into the Mediterranean, and sees in the
depression of Austria her march towards the bed of the sick man.
I put out of sight as reasons for this motion two excuses that can

deceive no candid understanding: 1st, it is said that the Government should be displaced because, with the best intentions, it was unable to preserve peace; 2d, because, with larger concessions than a Conservative party ever made before, it was unable to frame a successful Reform Bill.

Sir, I say no man believes in the substance of these excuses. With regard to the first—if you were sincere, you would wait at least for the evidences to be brought before you, and not judge the Government unheard. With regard to the second—if producing an unsuccessful Reform Bill disqualifies members from producing another, the last man to aspire to office should be the noble Lord the Member for London. And if there be amongst gentlemen opposite any large party particularly anxious, not that the question of Parliamentary Reform should be kept, as Mr Fox regarded it, as a convenient party flag to be taken out and paraded at general elections, and then to be carefully furled up and put by with the general lumber of drums and ribbons, or whatever else may in popular elections be the most noisy or the most flaunting —but as a measure which ought to be settled with as little delay and as little turbulence as possible,—I defy those gentlemen to say that a Reform Act proposed by the party now in power would not sooner be passed through the Legislature and become the law of the land, than any bill which may have to be filtered through all the degrees of purification from democracy in the Cabinet which is to unite Manchester and Tiverton.

The real question is plain to us in this country—it is but a party trial of strength upon any pretences that can be found. Abroad, I fear it will not be so considered; abroad, I fear it will be regarded as a direct expression of sympathy with a war that may not be limited to its first avowed object, but which may not rest till all Germany interposes to save Austria from being hurled out of the balance of power, and France and Russia united as the arbiters of Europe.

Sir, be that as it may, one thing that alone has occurred in this debate gives me hope amidst the dangers which I foresee. It is the declaration made here and elsewhere on the part of the Government, and, so far as I can judge, responded to by the leading statesmen in opposition, that, however this division may terminate, it will be for the strengthening of the Queen's Government, in upholding the dignity of England with foreign powers. Should the decision be in favour of gentlemen opposite, and they should succeed in forming an Administration, it would be my sincere desire not severely to criticise its materials, not ungenerously to obstruct its policy, and to forget the triumph of an adverse party in remembering the immense difficulties which at this time beset every monarchy, and the grave responsibilities which every Englishman owes to our common country. On the other hand, should the present Government be victorious, I trust that a similar spirit will be shown by gentlemen opposite ; and that we may all remember that, whatever our desire to remain neutral, neutrality depends upon others as well as ourselves ; and the more England manifests her power, the more her neutrality will be respected. But the power of England is not alone in her fleets and armies. We could not afford, like Austria, to leave 20,000 lives on a single battle-field. France alone may equal our fleet—France and Russia together would greatly surpass it. Our power is not in those demonstrations of physical force in which we should destroy ourselves if we sought to vie with despots ; our power is in that ascendancy of mind over matter which belongs to the normal exercise of intellect and freedom, and which ought to find its utterance here. Foreign powers wishing to molest us, will ask less what number of soldiers can England spare, or what number of ships has she in the docks, than—what is the temper of the House of Commons ? Are its actions so evenly balanced that nothing has there such interest as the strife for power ? If so, we need not fear England. Whatever we do to its prejudice, if condemned by the one faction, will find its advocate in the other.

But if diplomatists report to their royal masters, " Deceive yourselves not ; the House of Commons, with its array of sturdy patriots and matchless statesmen, will forego all their quarrels and rally as one man round their country if you conspire against its interests or sully the whiteness of its honour." Oh, then England will be safe ! No spies will be sent to calculate what may be our fleets or what may be our armies.

NO CONFIDENCE MOTION, 1859.

Meanwhile, if there be some gentlemen amongst the opposite ranks whose votes are not yet pledged, and who hold in equal affection the welfare of their country and the permanent interests of the Liberal party, with which they are accustomed to identify that welfare, I respectfully entreat them to pause, and weigh well the consequences of the vote they may give to-night.

For the country it is a serious thing to dislodge a Government that stands before Europe as having steadily, earnestly, consistently sought to preserve the peace of the world, and having declared firmly to all the powers already engaged in, or now upon the verge of war, that England will be impartially neutral—it is a serious thing to dislodge a Government which has unequivocally put forth this policy, upon pretexts and cavils which will lead the belligerents to suppose you do not condemn the war, and your neutrality will not be impartial.

For Liberal measures, taking first the mere question of Parliamentary Reform, it is a great responsibility you assume when you say, We will reject all compromise with a party so rooted in this old land of ours as the Conservative party ever must be; we will disdain to enlarge the popular representation with their aid; we invite their opposition, and we will not effect a popular boon unless as a party victory which must divide all England at every hustings at the very moment you desire to unite all England against every foe.

But for the party itself—you are told that a motion of this sort is necessary to unite and keep you together. Permit me to remind you of a precedent in which exactly the same language was held, and I will leave you to consult history for the effects that precedent produced upon the Liberal party.

Towards the close of the last century there were two divisions in the Liberal camp, each headed by eminent men calling each other noble and right hon. friend. I mean the Rockingham Whigs headed by Mr Fox, and the Chathamite Whigs headed by Lord Shelburne.

These two great men—and both possessed the most admirable qualities—had secret grudges against each other, the causes of which have never been made perfectly clear in the memoirs of the time. But it was judged by the Liberal party, as a whole,

essential that these two statesmen should patch up their differences and form a Cabinet in common.   It was even then as now
—that is the only way the Liberal party can be united well.   Lord
Shelburne was a man of large ambition, of enlightened views, and
profound though subtle policy.   Mr Fox it would be superfluous
to praise.   He was the most forgiving of men, and ever ready
to coalesce to-day with the politician he had devoted yesterday
to the scaffold.   These two great men therefore came together;
they formed a Cabinet, as two noble Lords, who will pardon the
comparison, may form one next week.   What was the result?
Human nature was human nature in the last century as it is in
this; secret animosities could not be appeased by open concord.
Rancour found its way into the Cabinet.   Lord Shelburne and
Mr Fox might have quarrelled with comparative impunity to the
Liberals if they had continued to sit apart, but they quarrelled in
the Cabinet.   One took refuge with Lord North—one struggled
for a short time, to lose power for ever; and both together prepared the way for the rise of Mr Pitt, and the longest exile from
power which the Liberal party has ever known.

Do you think there is nothing apposite in this precedent?
Pause before you commit the hopes and strength of your party to
the chance of an alliance between two noble statesmen, in whom
friendship cannot be sincere unless they have outlived memory,
and filled the loving cup in the stream of Lethe.

Remember that the Latin poet puts into the same sentence—
a sentence so hackneyed that at least we are all familiar with it
—the " graves principum amicitias, and " ignes suppositos cineri
doloso."

XXXVIII.

OUTLINE OF A SPEECH

INTENDED TO HAVE BEEN DELIVERED IN

THE HOUSE OF COMMONS

On the 14th of July 1859.

Lord Derby and his colleagues having, in consequence of the adverse vote of the House of Commons on the 10th of June 1859, given in their resignation on the following day, the Member for Haddingtonshire, Lord Elcho, gave notice on Thursday, the 30th of June, that upon the following Tuesday week he would, with especial reference to the Italian Question and the policy of the late Government, move the subjoined resolution :—

"That, in the opinion of this House, the correspondence respecting the affairs of Italy which has been lately laid before Parliament, shows that the late Government have perseveringly directed their efforts towards the maintenance of peace, and an amicable settlement of the differences between the contending powers ; and that, while they have preserved the strictest impartiality, they have at the same time upheld the honour and dignity of this country ; and that it is further the opinion of this House, that the policy of strict neutrality and mediation between the contending powers which has been pursued by the late Government, should be adhered to by her Majesty's present advisers."

On Tuesday, the 12th of July, the Secretary of State for Foreign Affairs, Lord John Russell, in announcing to the House the interview which had taken place the previous day between the Emperor Napoleon and the Emperor of Austria at Villafranca, when the preliminaries of peace had been signed between the two sovereigns, appealed to the Member for Haddingtonshire to withdraw his motion, then down for Thursday, the 14th of July, as inadvisable, if not actually obsolete, under the circumstances. Lord Elcho therefore readily assented to withdraw it, though, in asking for leave

to do so upon the date last mentioned, he spoke at some length in explanation of his motives in bringing forward his resolution. Had the discussion
come on, which its proposal on this occasion must have necessitated, the
following speech would have been delivered.

Sir,—I think the course which this country has hitherto adopted
with regard to the war in Italy has been the right one. To my
mind, the policy which it becomes a nation to observe in the dissensions which agitate its neighbours, has been very clearly laid
down by Lord Bolingbroke in one of the best, though least known,
of his political writings. He says that every nation belonging to
the European system has an interest more or less in the preservation of the balance of power; but that its interference for that preservation must be in proportion to the individual interest in the
particular quarrel by which it is threatened or disturbed. To do
otherwise, he says, would be to lose sight of our own particular
interest in the pursuit of a common interest : it would be nothing
better than to set up for the Don Quixotes of the world, and engage to fight the battles of all mankind. The state which keeps
its own particular interest constantly in view has one invariable
rule to go by; and this rule will direct and limit all its proceedings in foreign affairs, so that such a state will frequently take no
share, and frequently a small share, in the disputes of its neighbours, and will never exert its whole strength except where its
whole interest is at stake.

Sir, Lord Bolingbroke makes these remarks as applicable to an
old quarrel between France and Austria, in which he ridicules
what he calls the absurd alternative to which England, by neglect-
ing the rule he lays down, was compelled; the alternative either
to conquer for France—which he says was equally impolitic and
unjust—or against France, in order to conquer for the Austrian
Emperor under the greatest disadvantages possible. And I think
that Lord Bolingbroke's advice became doubly cogent by the apt-
ness of the illustration by which the advice was enforced. We
limited ourselves to that degree of interference which was propor-

tioned to our interest in the quarrel—an interference of remonstrance, of attempts to prevent bloodshed—and to substitute friendly mediation for the certain evils and uncertain benefits of war.

But peace having been now hastily arranged in a private conference between the two Emperors, the resolution of my noble friend would bind us to be as apathetic for the security of peace as we were neutral in the calamities of war. I must decline thus to fetter the hands of the Government. I must decline thus to separate England from the side of every ally, and to proclaim her indifference to the security of the Christian world. It seems to me that we may be now called upon to take exactly that part in the dissensions of our neighbours which corresponds with our particular interest. And precisely because it was not for our interest to enter into the evils of a war, it is for our interest to form one of a congress which may correct, amend, and consolidate the conditions of a hasty and imperfect peace.

All that is said by my noble friend and others against the articles of that peace, as roughly sketched out at Villafranca, seems to be an argument against his motion. It is a peace, says my noble friend, in which England has not been consulted, in which the avowed objects of the war have not been fulfilled, in which Austria still holds her grip on the independence of Italy, in which there will be found all the seeds of revolutionary discontent and of future war. And the peace so characterised he would leave to its operations, without one generous effort on the part of England to improve the conditions that he blames, and prevent the consequences he foretells.

Sir, I do not think that is the becoming position for a nation which not only occupies so high a rank, but which has always volunteered its voice on behalf of all that can advance or civilise mankind, even where its interests would not permit it to promise the succour of its arms. Some things in themselves are blessings, though their natural effects may be warped or frustrated. Freedom is in itself a blessing, though it sometimes suspends the security of order. And surely peace in itself is a blessing, even though its conditions may be crude, and its contingent benefits may seem doubtful. We have often interfered on behalf of freedom, and with a view to reconcile its action to the legal order it displaced. We may interfere on behalf of peace, and with a view to reconcile its conditions to the objects for which blood has been shed and dominions transferred. I cannot doubt what those objects will be in the eyes of an English Government responsible to the House of Commons. If England take any part in the councils of a Congress, that part must be on the side of all proposals which appear the best calculated to confirm the independence of Italy under such institutions as Italians may deem the best suited to themselves and the necessities of the age. No matter who may be our Ministers, chosen from this side the House or the other, I can understand that they would widely differ if they had to negotiate in the conduct of a war; but I am persuaded that they would abide by the same large and grand principle if they had only to advise on the conditions of a peace in which they spoke the voice of those English doctrines by which populations have prospered and order has been inviolably preserved. And therefore I would not deprive Italy of a safe and rational adviser in a council in which her permanent interests are at stake.

But suppose it is said, that the peace, after all, be concluded on principles as crude and as maimed as those on which it commenced,—Would not England, if she took a part in the Congress, have a share in the discredit to which the peace might be exposed?

Sir, I think not. As we had no share in the war, so we cannot be responsible for the fact accomplished in a sudden cessation of arms. No discredit can attach to us, even if we fail wholly to improve the conditions of a peace to which we were originally no party, which we neither made nor could prevent; but credit and honour attach to us, as they do to all men who, whether they succeed or not, cast their influence on the side of human interests; for success ebbs and flows with the tide of human affairs, but the consistent advocacy of good stands forth clearer and bolder in every ebb and in every flow, as the landmark of future ages. And it is

on that advocacy, often failing for the moment, but never discouraged, that England founds her repute, and identifies her solitary power with the common interests of the world. And therefore I say, succeed or not, England would be untrue to her own
fame if she neglected any peaceful chance of rectifying the errors
and improving the condition of her neighbours. But take the
other alternative. Suppose you rigidly abstain from a share in
the Congress, however honourably invited—do you mean to tell
me that we shall be in a station of greater dignity if the affairs of
Europe be settled without us, or in a position of greater safety,
when we have shown our supreme indifference to the triumph of
every principle and the interests of every ally?

Sir, even neutrality in war has great hazards for a nation so
powerful and so courted as England. It may not be able, however rigid its intentions, to preserve that neutrality free from the
insult or aggression of the belligerents when the war is over;
deep discontent at the power which has taken no share in the
strife of its neighbours is pretty sure to be bequeathed. No
party owes it gratitude; all parties regard it as egotistical and
selfish. If Austria had not been neutral in the Russian war,
I doubt much whether France and Russia could have agreed so
cordially in her recent humiliation. But when a nation like
England is not only neutral in war, but declines all interest in
the peace that follows—when it withdraws its weight from both
scales in the balance, and has neither arms for the war nor
counsels for the peace—I cannot imagine a position more inevitably
exposed to the resentment of human nature. And here there
would be no pretext for this absolute segregation from the other
civilised communities of Europe. A nation may have no interest
in war—that is readily conceded. But every nation has an interest in peace—that no one can deny. And England in this
instance has an interest clear and prominent, because all the belligerents are her allies—France, Sardinia, Austria. Alliance with
each and all of them will be hollow and delusive if you say to
those whom you call your friends, Fight or make up—you can
have only reproach from us. We blamed your war too much to

have part in it, and now we condemn your peace so totally that we will not even consult with you as to its provisions.

Sir, by this course it seems to me that we abdicate our place in Europe, and draw down upon ourselves the hoarded indignation of those with whom by skill and by wisdom we might now cement the ties of respect and friendship.

XXXIX.

OUTLINE OF A SPEECH

INTENDED TO HAVE BEEN DELIVERED IN

THE HOUSE OF COMMONS

ON THE 12TH OF MARCH 1860.

On Monday, the 12th of March 1860, the Chancellor of the Exchequer, the right hon. W. E. Gladstone, moved in the House of Commons the second reading of the Paper Duty Repeal Bill. After some discussion a division was taken, when the motion was carried by 245 votes to 192. On Wednesday, the 13th of June 1832—nearly thirty years previously—Sir Edward Lytton, then Mr Bulwer, as Member for the city of Lincoln, was the first to submit to Parliament the advisability of abolishing what afterwards came to be generally reprobated as the taxes upon knowledge. Upon the later occasion just now referred to, the Member for Hertfordshire contented himself with giving a silent vote among the majority. Had he taken part in the debate, something like the following speech would have been delivered.

Sir,—I should have much preferred giving a silent vote on this occasion ; but considering the importance which my hon. friends around me attach to their view of the question, it seems to me more respectful to them, and a duty I owe to myself, to state the reasons why I am compelled to differ from those with whom on so many other subjects I hold it an honour to agree.

It is nearly thirty years since I first submitted to the House certain arguments against that class of taxes of which this paper duty is the last survivor. My opinions against such taxes, and this excise duty in particular, have never altered ; on the contrary, they are strengthened. And if I were now, at the very moment it most needs my support, to desert a principle to which publicly and privately I have expressed my undeviating attachment, I should only prove that there was something in politics which I valued more than honesty and truth. The last persons to excuse me for that would be the frank and high-spirited gentlemen amongst whom I sit. And, indeed, I am consoled for the thought that my vote and opinions on this subject may displease though it cannot surprise them, by the persuasion that on other subjects, vital to the permanent interests of their party, I may serve them less feebly in proportion as my defects as a debater are covered over by the belief that I am sincere.

Here I am contented to leave, so far as I am personally con-cerned, the vindication of my vote. But as I have a warm inter-est in the success of the measure, which was not a party one when we sate on the opposite benches, so I will ask the indulgence of the House when I state why I think, as a legislator, that the repeal of the paper duty is wise and good in itself—and why, as a Conservative, I hold that there are collateral reasons of policy which make it desirable that it should be settled at once.

And first, before considering whether the paper duty be or be not a tax upon knowledge, I take the simple fact which no one can deny, that paper itself is a manufacture. Upon that manu-facture an excise duty falls in the most unequal and unintelligible degree of severity. One description of material is taxed at 150 per cent, another at 3 per cent, and a third description is exempted altogether. It checks the fair play of competition by penalties equally inquisitorial and capricious ; and for every million that it may yield to the Exchequer, it locks up another million of the money of the country which would otherwise flow through repro-ductive channels. Well, but is it not a general rule on which political economists are agreed, that an excise duty, even where it falls less harshly on a domestic manufacture, cannot be repealed without giving to that manufacture greater stimulus and develop-ment? Nay, is it not a grand financial truth, which on former occasions has been so firmly maintained on our side the House that I have thought it an article of our hereditary political creed, that no mere relaxation of a custom duty ever gives to a domestic trade the same rapid and inevitable stimulus which it receives from the total abolition of an excise ? What on earth is there in this manufacture of paper which should make it an exception to all other manufactures, or justify that strange confusion of ideas by which gentlemen say, The repeal of this duty only benefits a few,—forgetful of that solid fact on which financial reforms rest their foundation—namely, that to widen a trade by relief from the fetters that cramp it, is to give new employment to many ? Take all analogous experiments. In 1841, before the duty on glass was taken off, the number of glassmakers was 7407. In ten years after the duty was repealed, the number was 12,095. In 1841 the number of bricklayers and brickmakers was 3957. You took off the duty on bricks, and in ten years the number was 99,145. Can the application of the same principle fail us here in the paper duty ?—here, where you deal with a manufacture infinitely more crippled and opposed than were either bricks or glass, and employing a material adaptable to an infinitely larger variety of industrial occupations ? For the great mistake which seems to have run through all the argument of the opponents to this repeal is, to assume that paper is only a something on which letters are written and newspapers printed. Now, it may be a matter of very fair speculation whether water‑pipings or carriage‑panels made of paper will answer— very fair speculation if we were engineers and coachmakers. But no one acquainted with the principles of mechanics can deny that the material we call paper possesses to a superior, almost to an unrivalled degree, properties adaptable to the general purposes of ornament and use. And I fearlessly ask the many gentlemen present, whose knowledge of that science of mechanics is far deeper than mine, whether they can tell me any other material which equally combines these qualities, so invaluable to the practical workman—elasticity, resistance to pressure, the minimum of weight with the maximum of durability ? Even in its thinnest and frailest form, a sheet of paper, nay, even of papyrus—this magnificent benefactor that we call paper—resists for countless ages the wear and tear of time.

And to the tenacity of its plastic fibre we owe our knowledge of all in law, or in freedom, or in science, which enriches the age we live in with the stores of all the ages that have gone before us ; while, thanks to its quality of adhesion, you can render this seemingly flimsy substance not only more durable than oak, but as pliant as wax and as solid as marble. I remember last year that I observed in the office of Mr Philip's auction-room an ornamental temple, which I admired extremely as one of the best specimens I had ever seen of oriental art. All its details were exquisitely sharp and clear, and the whole had that brilliancy of polish which can never be given except to a very hard substance. But it seemed so delicate that I was almost afraid to touch it. "Oh, sir, you need not fear," said the office clerk ; "you would find it very difficult to break the slightest bit of it. It has come a long way without the least injury." "Indeed !" said I ; "is it not some rare kind of alabaster, which is a bad material for works of art, because it is so brittle ?" "No, sir ; it comes from Japan, and it is made of paper." I mention this to corroborate the argument so powerfully urged by the Member for the Tower Hamlets, and to show that in this material of paper we have a substance which, when freed from this pestilent excise duty, will offer a variety of uses not now contemplated, and increase through numberless channels of art and trade those national resources which, after all, have no other fountains than English industry and English skill ; and whoever will clear those wellsprings of national wealth from such obstructions as this excise duty, does much more than repeal an oppressive tax,—he feeds the channels that supply our Exchequer, maintain our armies, and employ our labour. I say labour, because, pass now from the manufacture itself to the labour which the manufacture creates and feeds, amongst the humbler classes of those rural tradesmen whose interests as a county member I am forbidden to forget. Hear on this what Mr M'Culloch says in his Commercial Dictionary : "The apparatus and machinery of the manufacture itself are of a nature that requires constant renovation and repair ; thus it effects a considerable demand for the labour of a great variety of trades—the carpenter, the wheelwright, the woollen manufacturer, the iron and brass-founder, the wire-worker, &c.; and hence," says Mr M'Culloch, emphatically, "this paper manufacture is of much greater importance as a source of employment than might at first be supposed, or than it was formerly considered by governments." But if a source of employment now, when the manufacture is so fettered and crippled, how much more when the repeal of this excise duty will allow free play to inventions useful to almost every trade, applicable to almost every employment? And when my hon. friend the Member for Tamworth says, "This is the remission of a tax affecting the interests of a limited industry at the expense of the general public,"—I say, that I can conceive no tax so injurious to the general public as that which limits an industry that may be extended wherever the arts of men require a plastic material unequalled for its combination of suppleness and durability.

My hon. friend the Member for Dorsetshire will forgive me if I do not admit his proposition that the excise duty on paper differs from that on glass or bricks because certain paper-makers say that they cannot get a sufficient supply of the raw material of rags. I thought that argument, if argument it be, had been sufficiently disposed of in former debates. But first, it is only a very small part of the manufacture which requires rags at all; and secondly, that portion of the manufacture which does at present depend upon rags is deprived of that free scope for invention by which a substitute for rags may be devised. And when it is said that a substitute is impossible, because a prize has been offered to find a substitute and no one has won the prize—my answer is this,—Did you ever know a man worthy to win a prize who, after he left college, ever condescended to try for one? Do you believe Lord Macaulay and Mr Hallam would have tried for a prize? Do you believe Mr Dickens or Mr Tennyson would try for one? And do you believe that what they would think below the dignity of literature, a Faraday and a Liebig would not hold to be below the still austerer dignity of science? Of course no substitute for rags is yet discovered; and why? Because your excise duty paralyses invention. It is scarcely fair to expect a man to discover new material for paper when the law leaves it uncertain what is paper and what is not. And again, your excise duty excludes competition; and it is competition alone that perpetually quickens and perpetually improves upon invention.

I could say much more upon this head; but it forms no part of our business as legislators. Our vocation is to free the national industry from that which our common-sense tells us must be an impediment and a clog, and then leave the national industry and the national intelligence to do the best they can to help each other. And when the paper-maker—who, when the interest of the land was concerned, was the most vehement of all free-traders—now cries out about his dependence on a foreign market for a raw material, I will first ask the representatives of manufacture and commerce whether they will accept for the paper trade a necessity not conceded to that great cotton manufacture, whose magnitude is so vast that its distress would be felt throughout the empire, but which cannot by any possibility get its raw material at home—and next, I ask my hon. friends the country gentlemen whether it would not indeed be an insult to the land, if Parliament conceded to the paper-makers the very arguments it would not hear on behalf of the farmer?

I pass now from the consideration of the benefits which the repeal of this duty would bestow on the inventions of manufacture and the employment of trade, and let us fairly see its operation as a tax upon knowledge.

Here let me ask, not men of letters and scholars, but all gentlemen engaged in the practical affairs of life—what is that which is most essential to a commercial and civilised community like ours? Is it not the freest and the cheapest channels for the communication of ideas? How are ideas communicated so as to reach the widest audience and leave the most lasting impressions? Is it not by the medium of that material on which ideas are stamped and made the durable property of all men? Paper is thus the raw material of the most liberal of all manufactures—the manufacture of knowledge recorded and diffused. How, then, can we admit that the free circulation of ideas is essential to all that constitutes not only the local eminence or intellectual renown, but the positive hard money-making wealth of the nation, and yet contend that a tax upon the material which all ideas are compelled to employ is no tax upon knowledge ?—and, said some hon. gentlemen, " the very last tax that you ought to repeal."

But it is said—when you have removed this duty, neither books nor newspapers will be any the cheaper. Sir, let me here place before the House what I believe to be the truth.

There are three distinct classifications of literature. I will take first that with which the wealthier class of the public is most familiar—new works, affording interest or amusement to a wide circle of persons of good means and average education. I mean that which is generally called light literature, or the literature of the day. Here I own fairly that the item of the paper duty is very little felt either by the publisher or the nation. The wealthier public will have books of amusement ; they are accustomed to them in a certain form and type. And as the reader very seldom buys them, he cares very little at what price they are bought by the circulating library to which he subscribes.

This class of literature the repeal of the paper duty will very little affect ; and authors who obtain such success in it as to command their own prices, may defy the power of the Legislature to harm as to help them.

But there are two other kinds of literature without which the intermediate literature I speak of would be very frivolous or very fugitive :—

First, the literature of scholars ; secondly, the literature of the people. On both these classes of literature the operation of the paper duty is most burthensome and grievous. But especially burthensome and grievous to that higher kind of work which conveys to the public the learning of universities and professions, of art and of science. That kind of work, which, though it may ultimately confer a lasting renown on the author and his country, can only, at the first, have a very small number of readers, and may be many years before it becomes a standard addition to our libraries.

Mr M'Culloch, in his Commercial Dictionary, calculates very accurately the cost of a book which sells at 12s. retail, and of which 500 copies shall be printed. Now 500 copies are a tolerably large edition of works of the graver kind ; but I suppose these 500 copies were all sold. What is the sum at which Mr M‘Culloch estimates the net profit left to author, publisher, commission, and the interest of capital? Why, the net profit of the entire sale costing £176, 18s., is only estimated by Mr M‘Culloch at £16, 8s. It is true, however, that Mr M‘Culloch then deducted from the profits 10 per cent for advertisement duty, since repealed ; and the net profit, therefore, would be now £26, 8s. But what is the amount of the paper duty on this small profit? Why, £4, 15s., or more than a sixth part of the entire profit to be divided between author and publisher. But the publisher, as a man of business, naturally takes care of himself. He either declines to publish a work on which the returns are so small, or he takes care to secure himself from risk ; so that, in point of fact, the whole loss from the paper duty falls upon the fund set apart for the author's remuneration. It either stops him from publishing at all ; or, as it falls exclusively on his share of the profits—and that share we may compute at the half—it robs him not of a sixth but of a third part of his profit ; more than 30 per cent of his very scanty remuneration. Well, then, I think it is clear that this duty must be very prejudicial to the higher and graver class of literature, from which all other classes of literature take their noblest nourishment, and by which the knowledge that spreads throughout the many is constantly recruited and deepened by the severer thought and scholarship which are at first only addressed to the few. Ask the professional man, the surgeon, the divine—ask the philosopher, ask the scholar, who cannot expect to sell more than 500 copies of his work in the first instance, whether a duty that takes away a third or even a sixth part of all the profits he could gain if he sold all his copies, while it increases in an equal proportion all the risks of loss,—ask him if this paper duty is no tax upon knowledge ; ask him whether it may not often serve to deter him, if his pecuniary means be small, from giving to the world what the world might find of lasting value ;—and I should be perfectly contented to rest your vote upon his answer. Well, the tax next falls with immense weight upon the literature of the people—that is, upon works sold at the lowest possible price, in the hope of obtaining the widest possible audience. The paper consumed here is a principal item of cost, and the duty falls upon that paper so heavily that the first thought of a people's publisher is so much more what should be paid to the exciseman, than what should be paid to the author, that he very seldom includes that magnificent standard literature of ours in which the copyright is expired, and nothing to be paid to an author at all. Why is this? Because the paper duty necessitates the choice of books adapted to the widest class of readers—that is, books by living or very recent authors; and these books are chiefly books of fiction. I am the last person to disparage that class of literature, which often conveys a good deal of instruction as well as amusement. It is, and always will be, the class of literature which has the largest sale. But I do desire that every class of my countrymen who read at all, should have full access to those other books which time has sanctioned as the grandest heirlooms of the English mind. And those books will be introduced into a people's library, whenever the repeal of the paper duty allows a people's publisher to count on a fair profit by a comparatively limited sale. No paper duty could exclude any very popular author from a people's library, or lessen by a shilling the profits he might command. But I will tell you the writers whom the paper duty does exclude from their fair place in a people's library : it excludes not only Robertson and Locke, but Dryden, Addison, and Johnson.

Well, then, I think I have made it clear that this tax does fall with impolitic severity upon the very classes of literature which we are most bound as Conservatives scarcely less than as statesmen, to keep clear from all obstruction : first, those books which, though adapted to the time, are, if I may quote the noble illustration of a great writer, "the aqueducts which convey to the plains and valleys below, the pure springs that first rise on the hill-tops of learning ; " and secondly, the works which are intended to supply to the humblest readers channels not only of innocent recreation, but of disciplined and manly instruction. And yet we have been told that the repeal of this tax is only a boon to the member for Birmingham and the penny newspapers. I say, on the contrary, that if there be anything dangerous in the politics of the member for Birmingham, anything ignored or prejudiced in the doctrines favoured by penny newspapers, the best antidote must be in that free communication between science and lofty knowledge, and the literature read by the masses, which this tax, as far as a tax can do in the nineteenth century, tends to obstruct and cut off.

With respect to the penny newspapers, I neither know nor much care whether they would be sold at a lower price or not. Cheapness does not depend only on the price; it depends also on the quality of an article. And I know that the repeal of the paper duty must tend to improve the quality of the low-priced papers, for these reasons : first, because the duty falls on the fund set apart for the writers, and must therefore narrow the market from which writers of high education and social position are obtained ; secondly, because though the penny newspaper may not lower its price, the fourpenny paper, such as the 'Times' and others, certainly will. And the nearer in point of price a paper of the vast resources and intellectual vigour displayed by the 'Times' approaches to a penny paper, the more the penny paper must exert itself to improve the character of its contributions, or else that approach of the 'Times' would destroy it.

Well then, Sir, this duty is an obstruction to a manufacture, an extinguisher on invention, a hindrance to trade, a tax upon knowledge, from the highest to the most popular; and lastly, it is a monstrous, and now perhaps the only exception, to that spirit of legislation which the public are determined to exact from any party that may hold the reins of Government.

But I am now willing to throw aside all these arguments—to suppose the tax does no particular harm to manufactures, trade, or knowledge. And then I ask you to look, as general politicians, at the present condition in which the tax stands, and tell me whether, on all grounds of policy, the time has not come when it must be relinquished.

When it is said that the tax is a permanent source of revenue, I close on that assertion with amazement, and I say that precisely because it is not permanent, because it is loosened to its foundations, and has received so mortal a blow that it cannot possibly recover, you ought to welcome its happy release from a lingering but inevitable death.

Just consider. Can imagination conceive anything more the reverse of permanent? Take first the resolution of the House in 1858, which declared that the duty was not to be considered a permanent source of revenue—a resolution taken when we were in office, with the assent of the leader of our own party, then Chancellor of the Exchequer, and who in reality scouted the fall of the tax in one of those withering denunciations by which it is the glorious privilege of genius to blight and destroy injustice. After that resolution and that speech, are we to get up on this side of the House and exclaim, " Don't touch that tax—it is a permanent source of revenue "? Next comes the report of the Commissioners of Inland Revenue. What do they say? "The tax is no longer tenable. We cannot conceive a more undesirable position for the heads of a department than that in which we are placed, when, in answer to complaints from persons whose trade is annihilated by the exaction of a duty from which other competitors are exempt, we can only say that such is the necessary consequence of the existence of the tax." I don't pause to reply to those who have insinuated that this report was cooked up in subservient compliance with the desire of a Minister of the Crown. My own experience of office was certainly very short, but quite long enough to convince me that the supposition that the heads of an English public department should, at the wish of an English Minister, commit their names and sanction to a deliberate falsehood, could only have proceeded from the gloomy imagination of some misanthropical Chartist. But whether or not the Commissioners of Inland Revenue did conspire with the Chancellor of the Exchequer to deceive the country by a fraudulent report, I ask you whether, after that report was made public, any one could believe that the tax could be a permanent source of revenue.

Then comes the vote of the House last session—the House of Lords rejects that bill on the ground that there was a deficit, and the country could not spare the money. This year the Government say there is a surplus; that surplus gentlemen on this side have admitted, because they have asked the Government to give it away in something else. The Government again bring forward the repeal of the duty in a still more earnest and urgent form than they did last year, by making it a part of their whole financial system. And do you believe, after all this, that a single man out of doors can suppose that this tax, stricken, reeling, dying faster and faster at every attempt to delay its passage to the grave—is a permanent source of revenue? Permanent, No! Suppose my hon. friends succeed: that the tax is not abolished this session; that early next session my right hon. friends around me come into office, and find a surplus not larger, not less uncertain, than you have now. Do you believe that the abolition of this tax would not be a necessity on which their Cabinet must resolve? Either I know nothing of the House of Commons, after nearly thirty years' experience of it, or the House of Commons would exact this measure from a Conservative Government much more passionately than they ask it from the noble Viscount's. But if there be a thing in the world which, as a Conservative, I deprecate, it is that the party I belong to and desire from my heart to serve and honour, should violently oppose on this side of the House the measure they meekly concede when they pass to the other side.

Well, but if you feel what, as men of sense, you must feel, that this tax is not a permanent source of revenue, then all the argu-ments by which you would retain it solely and wholly on the ground that it is permanent, are cut away from you.

And indeed the whole argument which has induced so many of my friends to prefer a reduction of the tea duty to a repeal of an excise appears to me extremely fallacious. It is said, " Affairs abroad look uncertain. We may want in a year or two what we take off now, and let us take the tea duty. We can raise that again next year, if we reduce it this; but part with the paper duty, and we cannot reimpose it."

Why is this argument fallacious? Because if you really believe that affairs abroad look so threatening that you ought not to part with your surplus, then you ought not to have proposed the reduction of the tea duty. If you believed you might have to raise it again in a year or two, you gave no benefit to the English consumer, for the full benefit would be to the Chinaman; and

I cannot conceive anything more embarrassing to a trade than to reduce a duty, avowedly not for permanence, but because you thought it likely you could raise it again next year. Surely no man of business would like to rest British commerce upon a system of finance like that.

And again, when you say that whatever the exigencies of the country, you could not reimpose the excise duty on paper, you say much more in favour of its repeal than I would venture to say. For why could you not reimpose it? Finance is not like civil legislation, such as a Reform Bill, on which you can never go back; finance goes backwards and forwards with perfect indifference, seeking only where it can find the most money at the least injury to the consumer. And if you were right, and the repeal of the paper duty should do no good, but be only the wanton loss of a million and more, the Chancellor of the Exchequer when he wanted money would put on that duty again without the slightest remorse. If he doesn't put it on again, it is because, on the whole, the country would be richer without it than with it. And when you say it cannot be reimposed, it is only because the repeal would be found too beneficent to allow the re-enactment. I must take shortly the argument on which this motion rests. It is said, "There is an artificial, uncertain surplus; don't throw it away."

I say you cannot take that ground now. You might at the first have said, "We dispute your surplus—we will have a motion upon that;" and then if beaten you might have said—not even then with much dignity or effect, but still with sufficient plausibility for a party question—"Well, since the House chooses to say there is an available surplus, devote it to tea instead of paper."

But when you first allow the surplus and ask to appropriate a quarter of a million more than the Government does to a relief which seems to you preferable to any other, you cannot, on being beaten, fall back and say, "Since we cannot dispose of the surplus according to our hobby, then we declare that there is no available surplus at all!" Of course you may find subtle and ingenious reasons for this proceeding; but I am sure that you will find none to satisfy the plain ample sense of the people of England. Finally, I come to the collateral reasons why this repeal of the paper duty is resisted. Gentlemen say, " It is put forward in an unconstitutional form, so as to insult the House of Lords."

I dismiss the constitutional argument: in that I agree with my right hon. friends the Members for Cambridge and Oxford Universities.

There is nothing against the spirit and practice of the constitution in the mode in which the Queen's Government have incorporated their measure as part of one financial scheme. And all that it really means is,—They think it so desirable that the question should be settled, that upon it they rest all their financial operations, and their existence as a responsible Government.

But then, nevertheless, it conceals some design to insult the · House of Lords.

Well, on that I agree with the hon. and learned gentleman who spoke for the first time with so much promise and effect— that to judge of an insult you must look to the probable animus, the probable intention. Intention is revealed first by language ; next, by the probable inclination and tendency of the party by whom the supposed insult is offered.

First, as to language. In bringing forward this question, not a word about the House of Lords has been said by the Chancellor of the Exchequer, nor by any other member of the Government, that could have wounded the ears of the most sensitive admirer of that august assembly.

Next, as to the probable intention and animus of the party by whom the supposed insult is offered. What is that party? The Cabinet by whom, not indeed any merely financial proposition, but any mode of framing it which could affect the rights and dignity of the two Houses of Parliament, and endure a sharp Parliamentary contest, must have been thoroughly discussed and examined. How is that Cabinet composed ? Of men likely to go against the House of Lords ? No ; of all Cabinets within the memory of man, this is the Cabinet in which the House of Lords is the most largely and most conspicuously represented. Suppose there were a general election, and I said to every intelligent tradesman or farmer whom I canvassed : " There has been a terrible democratic conspiracy on the parts of the Dukes of Argyll, Newcastle, and Somerset, aided by noble persons of the names of Herbert, and Villiers, and Gower, and Stanley, and Russell, and Temple, to insult the House of Lords in order to please the Member for Birmingham." Do you think that one plain man in the kingdom would be goose enough to believe me? Is it not more likely that he would say : " Sir, I don't think that those great lords and fine gentlemen, whom any history of England tells me are amongst the first names in the peerage, meant to insult the House of Lords even to please the Member for Birmingham ! It is more probable, that as no men can possibly have a greater interest in the welfare and dignity of the peers, and as they had no doubt a great affection for the House of Commons, in which they are proud to have received their political education,—more probable that they thought this mode of settling the question was, upon the whole, best for the interest and dignity of both Houses. And I hope, Sir, that you, as a representative not of the Lords but the people, will not be less careful of the rights of the House of Commons over the taxation of the country, than a Cabinet that contains so rare a proportion of the loftiest names in the peerage is disposed to be"?

No, then, I see no ground for suspecting the Government of an intention to insult the House of Lords. But what I do see, and do feel, is this, that any difference with the House of Lords on a question so delicate as that of the taxation of the country, no matter which is right or which is wrong, is in itself a very great evil. That evil must clearly continue until this duty is repealed. Succeed in your motion, delay the repeal, and you not only prolong, you exasperate and embitter, the evil. The evil is felt in the embarrassment and hesitation which I, in common with all who cherish equal pride and reverence for our two legislative Chambers, cannot fail to feel in touching upon all the solemn considerations which a difference on such a matter as taxation suggests,—perhaps the most vividly to those who say the least upon it. I know not myself how to hint at those considerations without a nervous fear lest, on the one hand, I should say something that might be misconstrued into disparagement of the true functions of that upper Chamber, which I believe to be as wise and patriotic a senate as human ingenuity can devise ; or lest, on the other hand, I may meanly compliment away that right which I am specially sent here to guard—the right of the House of Commons over the public purse. That right we are bound to maintain to the extremest point of its abstract principle, for without that right we have no constitutional powers whatsoever. And if this House were to accept certain doctrines, which I never thought I should live to hear from English lips—doctrines that would make the House of Lords the habitual and regular partner with us in the taxation of our constituents,—if this House could so betray the memory of our ancestors, and the heritage of our children, I know not how one well-born gentleman of spirit and honour would condescend to accept a seat in it.

This embarrassment, or this irritation, in considering a question that relates to the taxation of the people, ought not to be felt an hour longer than we can possibly help it. You can only end it by repealing this tax ; and, the House has sufficiently shown, by repealing it in the mode and manner which the Queen's Government, responsible to her for the dignity of both her Houses of Parliament, recommend to our adoption.

The more, then, I look at all the bearings of the question, the more I feel justified on the vote that I give. And I believe that my hon. friends could sustain no defeat on any other question that would cause them the same embarrassment, involve them in the same practical inconsistencies, accumulate the same difficulties round their return to office, as would follow their success upon this motion. Believe me, there is a something in the nature of this question as it now stands, which makes it desirable for us and good for the country to settle and dismiss the question itself as quickly and quietly as we can.

XL.

OUTLINE OF A SPEECH

INTENDED TO HAVE BEEN DELIVERED IN

THE HOUSE OF COMMONS

On the 2d of August 1860.

On Monday the 23d of July 1860, the Prime Minister, Lord Palmerston, explained to the House of Commons in Committee the Government plan in regard to the fortifications, with a view to the improvement of the National Defences. The scheme, which involved within it an immediate outlay upon the year of £2,000,000, necessitated in the event of its adoption an aggregate expenditure on fortifications of £9,500,000 sterling. A discussion arose which lasted two nights. On the second night of the debate, the Member for Sunderland, Mr William Shaw Lindsay, moved by way of amendment, "That as the main defence of Great Britain against aggression depends on an efficient navy, it is not now expedient to enter into a large expenditure on permanent land fortifications."

At the close of the debate a division was taken, when the Ministerial proposal was carried by 268 votes to 39. Had the opportunity offered during that second night's discussion, the following speech was intended to have been delivered.

SIR,—I think the House is much indebted to the noble Lord the First Minister for the perspicuity with which he placed before us last week the general scheme of the Government, and for the manly tone—neither arrogant on the one hand, nor timid on the other—in which he seemed to me to represent less even to us than to our august ally, that all Europe must arm for defence so long

as France accompanies professions of peace with preparations for
war. But the more I recognise the courage and the wisdom of the
noble Lord's admirable speech, the more I am astonished that he
could ever have been induced to sanction the publication of this
report. I should have thought, considering time and circumstance
in Europe, that an Englishman would rather have bit out his
tongue than blabbed the contents of this document to any listener
not as English as himself.

And it seems to me that the Secretary at War, in his excuses
for that publication, greatly undervalues the good sense of the
country and the patriotism of this House. The right hon. gentleman says that in a constitutional government we must risk a good
deal—that a Government cannot use reserve towards the popular
Chamber ; and, in short, that we cannot have military caution
because we have a free constitution. Permit me to remind the
right hon. gentleman that Belgium enjoys a constitutional government. But when, some years ago, Belgium feared invasion, and it
was thought necessary to strengthen the defences of that country,
she contrived to reconcile constitutional government with military
caution. A secret committee was appointed. Their report has
never to this day been made known to the Belgian public. The
Belgian Minister of War, in presenting to the Chamber the
general plans for the national defence, only quoted a few discreet
extracts from the report, and the sum required was voted without
any revelation of details. The Belgian constitution is as free as
our own—the Belgian representatives are quite as thrifty of public
money as we are ; but the Belgian Ministers did not deem it
necessary to publish for the instruction of French Cabinets and
the excitement of French colonels, the exact places in which
fortresses could be best assaulted, nor the exact amount of force to
be placed on every garrison, nor the exact number of years or
months that must elapse before the improvements could be effected,
so that it might not be the fault of an enemy if he did not fall
upon the country in good time. I think the English House of
Commons would not have been less patriotic than the Belgian
Chamber if the English Government had been as prudent as the
Belgian.

Whatever the differences of party between any of us and the noble Viscount at the head of the Government, his vast experience, his long public services, his great European reputation, the popular and not unmerited belief in his diplomatic sagacity, and his high spirit, would have given him the right to address us and his countrymen on such a subject as the national defences with an authority that few amongst us would have ventured to resist. And I think if the noble Lord had made such a speech as he made the other night—stating that his general scheme was based upon the report of eminent professional persons, which it was obviously inexpedient to publish for the benefit of the very parties from whom attack might be anticipated, and promising that on all the details of that report the highest and most experienced naval and military officers would be consulted—he would have found it just as easy to obtain the sum required as I trust he may find it now ; but with this precious advantage, that you would not have told inflammable and angry populations, whose jealousies you have provoked, whose ambition you have opposed, all the precise places in which you are accessible, all the means you propose for defence, all the disasters you apprehend, all the months and years that must elapse before you can complete your preparations against the danger you increase, when you so openly own that you are afraid of it.

But, Sir, I have heard it said, "After all, we publish nothing which was not perfectly well known before to such of our Continental allies as take a friendly or a philosophical interest in ascertaining the easiest mode by which the conquest of England can conduce to the propagation of ideas." Sir, it seems to me that this apology is so lame that it has not a leg to stand upon. If one of your neighbours, whose honesty you suspect, does happen to know where your butler keeps his plate-chest, and where the rails of your area were loose and broken, I conclude that you would shift the plate-chest and mend the area as quietly as possible ; but if, meanwhile, your butler were to send to this suspected neighbour an exact plan of the interior of your house, with the precise specifications of the proposed alterations, accompanied with a hint that the blunderbuss was out of repair, and the information of the date

at which the new arrangements would be completed and the
blunderbuss in order, your butler would not find a police magistrate
ready to accept his excuse that really he only told the suspected
burglar what the burglar might have known before.

Now, Sir, I can grant that the French Emperor and his War
Department possess already some of the information contained in
this document, though certainly not all the information. But it is
one thing for the Emperor privately to know such matters, and
another thing to make those matters as plain as A, B, C to our old
friends the French colonels. The Emperor is an acute and saga-
cious calculator; he has lived in England, and knows the loyal
enthusiasm which gathers round our throne if threatened by one
breath of danger. He therefore may be quite aware that if it be
easy to throw an army into this country, it would be very difficult
to get that army out again. But the prudent considerations that
would occur to the Emperor are not those which would present
themselves to haughty and impetuous soldiers flushed with recent
victories, longing for fresh employment, and suddenly told by our
own best authorities not only that we are altogether unprepared to
resist an invasion, but that it will be more than three years before
we can be prepared. The Secretary for War says : " I don't care
about showing up our weak places, because the Parliament will '
assist the Government in making them strong." But he forgets
that before we can make them strong time elapses ; and he shows
up to the enemy the weak places three years before he can complete the operations that are to make them strong. Sir, the
publication of this document will be the talk of all the regiments
of France; and it will not only add to the knowledge which the
few might already have possessed as to our weak points, but it
will furnish to the ignorant many a feverish excitement, an eager
intoxicating stimulus, which the Emperor himself may find it
difficult to restrain. It holds out to all the powerful interests
which the commercial treaty has provoked and banded against us,
an excuse for a quarrel before the more benignant effects of the
treaty can take root ; and it may madden the hot blood of the
French armies to come upon us before our preparations are completed, and while we ourselves acknowledge we might fall an easy
prey to a prompt and vigorous invader.

The gallant officer, the Member for Liskeard, said very truly the other night that he had always understood that in warlike operations the thing essential was secrecy. That rule applies with special force to defensive warfare. All history teems with instances how weak garrisons that have kept the secret of their weakness have defied a siege, and how the strongest garrisons have fallen when a spy has betrayed to the enemy a hundredth part of the information by which this unhappy document is made the French Spy of every dockyard, arsenal, port, and basin in the three kingdoms.

What, the other day, enabled even the barbarian Chinese to defeat the English? Was it not that the barbarian Chinese knew how to keep the secret of their own defensive preparations? But if the Chinese had favoured you with a document like this, do you think the English would have been defeated? The First Minister alluded the other night to the memorable paper in which, when the chance of invasion was apparently remote, the Duke of Wellington confidentially suggested his apprehensions of danger and his schemes of defence. But who does not remember how angry the Duke was when those schemes and those apprehensions became accidentally public? And now schemes and apprehensions infinitely more detailed, at a moment infinitely more critical, are thrown before the hungry gaze of wary and hostile critics; as if war was a game in which the first requisite was not only to show all your cards to an adversary, but also to tell him beforehand the cards you intended to play. But the Secretary at War has done equal injustice to constitutional government and the character of his countrymen in the stress that he lays on our habits of publicity.

It is true that our people demand publicity in matters that ought to be made public; but no people on the face of the earth more jealously respect the wisdom of privacy in things that should not be blabbed abroad. When an Englishman says that his house is his castle, he means that he guards his hearth equally from tyrannical laws and malevolent curiosity. But the house which has a common sanctity to all Englishmen is the castle of their native land. And the same Englishman who, when speaking to a fellow-citizen, will indulge the utmost freedom of criticism as to our laws, institutions, government, public men, or national writers, will discreetly guard his conversation when he speaks to foreigners, and would as soon tell to a stranger the faults of his mother, as expose to an exulting Frenchman the defects and infirmities of his country.

There is something which shocks the dignity of that self-respect which a nation owes to itself—something which weakens our position and humiliates our character—in thus sending abroad to all our proud and scornful neighbours a confession of secrets similar to those which every individual gentleman amongst us would keep to himself. For what gentleman would whimper forth a confession of the errors of his household—of the helpless condition of his family—of the fear with which he anticipates the challenge of an enemy—of all the precautions for personal safety which it may be discreet to take, but ignominious to acknowledge? And such a confession in a private gentleman would be still more debasing to a sense of honour, if accompanied with the very excuse made for this publication—namely, that without such a confession a man's own children would not assist him. Is it for England to plead to the House of Commons for defence against foreign powers in the character of a beggar, who must show his sores before he can ask for alms?

I think, in thus doing, that England loses already one of her strongest securities against danger in that moral awe which has been hitherto inspired by the honest pride of her character, the dignified quiet of her self-reliance, and the practical sagacity with which she has been accustomed to repair her defects before her neighbours had time to discover them.

And it is not true that we, the House of Commons, have been so habituated to perfect candour on the part of our Governments, that we should have compelled her Majesty's Ministers to tell France when, where, and how England was to be defended before we would vote any money for that defence. Scarcely a week passes but what some gentleman asks her Majesty's Government for information on foreign affairs, or the publication of some stale correspondence, which the Government declines to grant as inexpedient for the public service. And does not the good sense of the House always submit to that answer? And of all matters in which one might suppose this House would concede to a Government the discretion of reserve, surely there would be no matters so entitled to secrecy as those which apprise the parties from whom you would guard against attack exactly where to find and how to hit you. Here, in this book, you employ the minutest calculations of professional science, in order to proclaim to any watchful enemy the precise number of troops he would have to encounter at any given spot—the precise depth of water in all your basins and harbours—the precise length of shore on which he may land with safety—the precise length of time in which he may find you unprotected—and the precise nature of your engineering operations, so that his own engineers may have ample leisure to frustrate and counteract your precautions. You thus give to a hostile power not only all means of confirming and correcting information he may possess already, but all information that he could not have even guessed before, as to what you intend to do. And the Secretary for War excuses these strange violations of common prudence and ordinary practice, by saying that the English Parliament will have publicity in all things, however imprudent, when he knows that not a member of Parliament denies, or a popular newspaper disputes, the absolute right of the Government to refuse publicity to some comparatively powerless paper about—not the hearths and liberties of our native land, but—some petty dispute at the antipodes.

But if the publicity of this document was so imperatively necessary, why has it been so strangely delayed from the 7th of February to the 9th of June? Surely, if publicity was due to us in the question of this report, as involving finance and affecting taxpayers—surely, surely our Government should have told us what should be our first duty, and what our most necessary expense, before they produced their Budget and vaunted the peaceful effects of their commercial treaty. Is it possible that this document, demanding eleven millions for the defence of the country, could have been kept back on purpose that the House might be misled blindfold into sacrificing revenue by the Budget, and flattered by fallacious promises of amity and peace, and reduced expenditure as the consequence of commercial interchange, into penitent appro-

bation of the treaty ? Could the House have endorsed the Budget,
or approved the treaty, if we had known what the Government
knew when this report came into their hands ? What a satire
on their own measures the Government kept concealed in their
desks ! The treaty says, "A million a-year, and you insure a
customer for life :" the report says, " Eleven millions down, or
your customer will cut your throats." The treaty says, "Send
your iron and coal to assist the harmless industry of France :"
the report says, "Against the armaments that the iron and coal
supply, fortify the Thames and the Medway." And when the
Secretary for War declared there can be no reserve with the House
of Commons—a Government must take the House of Commons
into its confidence—I ask, Where was that candour in the month
of March ? Never was Budget so inflated with promises of peace
—never was a Budget followed by a substitute so heavy with the
charges of war. But the Government had the supplement in their
hands before they laid the Budget on the table, and in order to
secure the Budget they suppressed the supplement. And now the
Secretary at War says : " Our Government can have no reserve
with the House of Commons : we take the House of Commons
into the confidence of brothers :" I say, then, that if the publicity
of this report was due to us, it was due to us four months ago,
and that the moment you choose for its publication is that in
which it can do the most mischief and the least good. For we
cannot now recall the revenue we have squandered away ; we can
no longer consider whether it is discreet, with shores so defenceless, to enlist against us all those formidable commercial interests
of France, which our treaty has alarmed, just when we would
desire other powers to court our alliance. This document meets
them with the piteous cry, " How can we help you ? See, we
shall be more than three years before our own shores are fit to
resist an enemy !" And if it be said by her Majesty's Government, as a reason for their delay in producing this report, that
there is now more cause to fear the ambition of France than there
appeared to be in the month of February, that excuse for delay
would only double the offence of publication ; because the more
you cherish the attack of an enemy as probable, the less you should

publish for his information the mode in which you would defend yourselves, and the date at which your defence will be completed. But if, as I think, there is cause for complaint against her Majesty's Government for the manner in which they have dealt with the House and the country in regard to this publication, sure I am that their faults would be trivial compared to our own, if we refused to place at the disposal of the Queen's responsible Ministers whatever money they declare to be essentially necessary for the defence of our Sovereign and our country. I will not discuss the question whether the sum asked be sufficient. That is a matter in which the responsibility of the Government is so serious that I can scarcely venture to interfere with it. For to ask six millions merely to throw away on imperfect and flimsy defences, rather than ask eleven millions for a complete and comprehensive scheme, would be a sin worse than misplaced economy—it would be a treason to the trust and generosity of the people who commit their safety to your care. I therefore take it for granted that you think six millions as much as you require for the present.

As to the mode in which the money is to be raised, I share the objections of my right hon. friend the Member for Bucks to the plan of terminable annuities. However specious the argument may be in favour of a process which liquidates a debt in paying the interest on it, still the abstract principle of terminable annuities sins equally against the first maxim of thrifty borrowing, and against one of the wisest doctrines of political economy. Against the first maxim of borrowing—because that maxim is this, " Offer the most negotiable securities you possess, in order to obtain the lowest rate of interest;" and against one of the wisest doctrines of political economy, because—but upon that head I will here quote the admirable exposition of Mr M'Culloch : " Though it were true that terminable annuities were as readily negotiable as unterminable ones, we should not therefore be disposed to recommend their adoption. No Government should ever countenance any scheme of public finance that has any tendency to weaken the providence and forethought of its subjects ; and such, we apprehend, would be the effect of the adoption of any scheme of funding on terminable annuities, whether for a specified number of years or for lives. The purchaser of an annuity terminating with his life is in almost every instance desirous, not only of consuming the interest of his capital, but also the capital itself. The same principle most commonly influences, though not perhaps to the same extent, the greater number of the purchasers of annuities at specified and not very distant periods." Mr M'Culloch proceeds to argue these views with great earnestness, and finally sums up his opinion in these uncompromising terms: "As the system obviously strikes at the very foundation of the principle of accumulation, and of all those habits which are most conducive to the interests of society, it should certainly not receive any countenance, whether direct or indirect, from Government."

There, Sir, I leave the financial part of this question, with a respectful expression of surprise that a Cabinet which comprises such champions of progress, and such shining lights of political economy, should in one session go back, first, to the doctrine of commercial reciprocity, and secondly, to the reign of Queen Anne for the exploded arguments in favour of terminable annuities.

With respect to the details in the scheme for national defence, it is only with great humility and deference that I can presume to offer any conclusion not based upon professional science. But while I admit the preliminary importance of securing our dockyards and arsenals from any sudden assault, I think the Secretary for War dismisses much too hastily the opinions of military authorities, whose names carry great weight with them, as to the various modes by which the metropolis may be protected. The right honourable gentleman, indeed, has only noticed one of these modes— that of detached forts a few miles apart ; and he then gets rid of the whole question as to the defence of London by saying its circumference is too vast, and the land in its neighbourhood too dear. But there are military men of the highest reputation who do not assert that London should be defended by suburban fortifications, but that no city in Europe can be more easily and more cheaply secured from a rapid march by intrenched encampments on well-chosen situations—such, for instance, as Reading and Croydon. But these matters, and many other doubts that occur to me in detail, I leave to the criticism of the many eminent professional men whom this House includes amongst its members, only earn-

estly and respectfully urging this upon the Government, that they
will give us a distinct promise that before they adopt the scheme
of the report, they will consult upon its various details with those
illustrious officers whose professional knowledge has been expanded
by the largest practical experience of actual warfare. If the Government will give us that promise, I think our wisest plan will
be to leave to their responsibility the re-examination of all those
doubts which the report may suggest to ourselves.

For my own part, judging from the past history of this country,
in those instances in which a warlike force has effected a landing
—not always for invasion, but sometimes in the vicissitudes of
civil war—all that I would ask for internal defence is, that between
the sea-coast and London there should be some stronghold, even
if it be only an intrenched camp, which might detain an enemy
till the country could recover the effect of a momentary panic or
a first surprise. That is all that would be required, even if we
were attacked next week, to make the whole land bristle with a
force as compact and determined as those unpractised troops who
scaled the heights of Alma, with an army so knit together that an
old veteran said to me, " Sir, they were like one red man ! "

And this brings me to the consolation that I derive from the
publicity given to this report, and, indeed, to the principal cause
which has induced me to rise. Professional men are the best
advisers to their country as to what should be done. But every
member of Parliament has that knowledge of his countrymen
which will not be without utility and weight when uttered to
foreign powers from the floor of the House of Commons. I think
the publicity of the report greatly increases the danger of invasion ;
but I think nothing can diminish the firmness with which we
should meet the danger.

Let not any foreign nation suppose that because we admit that
an invading army might land in spite of our fleets—because we
admit that our ports and arsenals are not adequately fortified—let
not any foreign nation suppose that therefore the invasion of England would not be the wildest and most perilous enterprise to which
a sovereign ever committed the honour of his flag and the existence of his armies.

I grant all that Lord Overstone says with such force on this

Report, as to the disaster to our commerce and to our monetary arrangements if an enemy were to effect a landing for a single hour, no matter what his ultimate fate might be. But it is well, since this report will be read throughout Europe,—well that we should say where Lord Overstone, in his laudable zeal for self-defence, has omitted to show the whole state of the case. To us there would be distress, disaster. Granted. But to the enemy there would be annihilation.

Lord Overstone speaks of the limited extent of our country. True. But that small country is intersected by railways, and the more limited the soil the more quickly the first moment of danger would collect and unite its inhabitants. That limited soil has thirty millions of population—five or six millions, at least, of men in the flower of their age—five or six million adults of that race which has achieved an empire wider than was ever compassed by the eagles either of France or of ancient Rome. Even apart from the mere population, and looking only to the military force we could at once command—including depots, militia, and volunteers—we could bring into the field an army less, indeed, by one-half than France can levy, but four times as large as (after cluding or defeating our navies) France could land upon our coasts. We are not, like Italy, a divided people, hating our own institutions, and loathing our own kings : we should be Englishmen, nerved to tenfold energies, if fighting on our own soil of England ; every old man loving his Queen as if she were his daughter—every schoolboy burning to defend her as if she were his mother. I grant, then, that this document proves how easily a French army could be thrown upon our coasts ; but no military statistics can make me believe that that army would ever return to France except as a wreck, shattered by our force, and spared by our mercy.

Our commercial disaster and distress might be great, but it would be short-lived. The vigour of this country is not less elastic than its resources. In a few years the nation would right itself, as one of its own ships rights itself, with all its sails and all its guns, after a noisy gust or a passing squall. But where would be the Emperor, and where the empire, of France ? It would be swept from the face of the earth. Continental nations would feel

that if the sea could not save England from French ambition, no
pen-and-ink boundaries on their paper maps would be secure ; and
England, once stung by the insult, and roused by the horrors of
invasion, would never rest till she had disarmed and paralysed the
invader. The energies she has shown for the preservation of India
would be puerile compared to those with which she would strain
for the reduction of France to the limits of a power that should
never again dictate terms to the civilised world. If for this purpose it were necessary to unite all Europe, she would subsidise all
the kings of Europe as readily as Lord Chatham subsidised Frederick of Prussia.

Heaven forbid that this should be the melancholy reversal of
all those noble dreams which coloured the eloquence of the Chancellor of the Exchequer when he brought before us the picture of
France and England joined in lasting peace by the bond of commercial interests. Heaven rather grant that these dreams, conceived by his humanity and brightened by his genius, may be
finally realised ; and that each great people, respecting the other,
may convert the armed and menacing friendship of a broken alliance into the benignant strife of commercial rivals, seeking which
shall most civilise and adorn the world. But equality is the
condition of all magnanimous rivalship ; and equality is impossible unless each State feels equally secure against the aggression
of the other.

Sir, why do I insist on the precaution of self-defence when I
think that if we are attacked we could destroy the enemy ? I say,
first, because we have no desire to destroy an enemy, no desire to
destroy the army, by whose side we fought for what we believed
the safety of Europe before the walls of Sebastopol. But soldiers
are soldiers ; and we have no right to tempt human cupidity and
military enterprise by the display of wealth ill guarded. I say it
next, because this mode of self-defence is so very much cheaper
than the other mode which the Member for Birmingham commends
to our preference. Take the utmost the commissioners ask—take
eleven millions—and the interest of the sum raised in the manner the
Government propose would not amount to half the sum that we
have lavished away this year ostensibly for the boon of cheap wines,

but in reality as an experiment of that mode of self-defence by which the Member for Birmingham would raise up the commercial interests of France as the best fortification against her military ambition. As far as the experiment has gone, it seems equally expensive and ineffectual.

Lastly, I advocate the policy of self-defence, because, though I concede to the Member for Birmingham that it is not the interest of France to invade us, yet we all know that though alliances are founded on interest, wars are excited by passion.

And of all reigning sovereigns the Emperor of France is the one on whose conduct you can least reckon, according to the ordinary rules of policy and self-interest. His whole career has been one portentous prodigy. It may be a mad scheme to invade England, with all her armies and all her fleets ; but it would not be so mad as his invasion of France, when he landed at Boulogne with a steamboat and an eagle. In the temperament and the genius of this modern Augustus—more daring, more restless, than his Roman prototype—imagination holds a sway that baffles the calculations of sober reason. He has those strange mysteries of character which we plain men call superstitious ; but they are superstitions of that nature which makes men's motives inscrutable, and their actions marvellous—superstitions as to his mission, as to his destiny, which the startling incidents of his fate have served to deepen and confirm, and which perplex the sagacity of statesmen, as the eccentricities of a comet may perplex the science of astronomers. Deal with the conventional policy of orthodox potentates, and the red-tape routine of methodical cabinets, we, sober Englishmen, very readily may ; but deal with the splendid fantasies of a child of fortune and genius we never can do, except by a double stock of those vigilant precautions by which common-sense defeats the chimeras of genius and commands the caprice of fortune. Therefore, I say, defend your shores. But I say more— defend them not against the Emperor alone. Do not credulously believe that if he were dead to-morrow Europe would be at peace, and England could return at once to the boast of her wooden walls.

The noble lord, the First Minister, says—the atmosphere is

charged with clouds which betoken the possibility of a tempest.
I fear that he might have made his illustration still more forcibly.
I fear that he might have said—those clouds, in their gathering,
have collected so much inflammable matter, that the tempest must
fall before the atmosphere can be cleared. If you look to the
history of the world, I doubt if you can find an instance in which
armies such as those with which France now casts over Europe
so dark and so ominous a shadow, have ever been dispersed except in the shock of battle. And whatever the Emperor's personal ambition, it is in vain to deny that his power over the
French consists in this—that he is the representative of a thoroughly French idea. What is that idea? The aggrandisement
of France—the aggrandisement of France, not by the patient development of her own resources, but by the diminution and humiliation of every other power in Europe whose equal rivalry provokes her jealousies or offends her pride. That idea is not new—
it does not date from the French Empire; it was the mainspring
of Richelieu's policy. It was for this that Richelieu struck at Austria; for this he intrigued in Spain; for this that, while he founded a despotism at home, he encouraged republics abroad; for this
that he fomented our civil factions in England, cajoled our popular
chiefs, and could equally flatter a British Puritan or stir up an
Irish Papist—anything, everything, for the aggrandisement of
France by the affliction of her rivals. Richelieu left that policy
as an heirloom to Louis XIV.; and that heirloom the first Napoleon
seized with the same hand that snatched from Italy the iron crown
of the Lombards—the same unscrupulous but superstitious hand
that, at Aix-la-Chapelle, robbed from the tomb of Charlemagne
the talisman which that great founder of the warlike French race
had worn, as a token that he had received from Heaven a mission
to alter the boundaries of the earth. That talisman Napoleon habitually wore, as if Charlemagne's talisman were a title-deed to
Charlemagne's universal dominion. I have seen that talisman in
the hand of a man who had as few scruples and as much superstition—I have seen it in the hand of Napoleon III.

Well, then, to this French idea of aggrandisement for France
at the expense of her neighbours—this French idea which, in the

midst of her first terrible Revolution, Burke so well described when
he said, "The main object of France is not to be free, but to be
formidable"—to this idea, cherished by the French in all phases
of their history, in all forms of their government, the present Emperor has given new vitality and force ; but if he died to-morrow,
that idea would not perish with him. Just as the talisman of
Charlemagne came fresh from his tomb as if it were made but
yesterday, so the idea to which any man who achieves a high
place in history may consecrate his life, cannot moulder with his
dust. To every Frenchman the idea of the aggrandisement of
France is the real talisman of Charlemagne.

The next candidate to supreme power in France—whether it be
the Emperor's son, or a prince of the House of Orleans, or a legitimate Bourbon, or the President of a Republic—would perhaps
largely outbid the present Emperor in the flattery to the national
egotism, that in seeking to make France formidable renders the
world unsafe.

Therefore, again and again I repeat—let us defend our shores.
We say to other nations, "Make yourselves free with your own
strong hands, and preserve that freedom by your own wise brains."
Let not other nations reply, " But your strong hands withhold the
money, and your own wise brains neglect the means to insure for
yourself that safety from foreign aggression which you preach to us
as the first care of intelligence and the first lesson of duty." Sir,
let us not suppose that this appeal to our forethought is the cry of
a momentary panic. Every year that improves the inventions of
science diminishes your safety as the inhabitants of an island, and
compels you more and more to find in the precautions of art
the securities that nature has ceased to give.

This necessity has been made evident by recent circumstances.
Let us rejoice that it has been so. But that necessity, thus forced
upon us, ought henceforth to enter into all our estimates, and be
the paramount care of every Minister who accepts the responsibilities of guarding from shame and danger the land and liberties
of this English realm.

XLI.

OUTLINE OF A SPEECH

INTENDED TO HAVE BEEN DELIVERED IN

THE HOUSE OF COMMONS

ON THE 19TH OF JUNE 1861.

ON Thursday the 7th of February 1861, the Member for Tavistock, Sir John Trelawney, introduced into the House of Commons a Bill for the Abolition of Church Rates; and on Wednesday the 27th of February, moved its second reading. Upon the latter occasion the Member for the University of Oxford, Sir William Heathcote, proposed by way of amendment, that the second reading should be assented to on that day six months. Upon a division, this amendment was negatived by 281 votes to 260. Having passed through Committee on Wednesday the 6th of March, the third reading of the Bill was moved by Sir John Trelawney, on Wednesday the 19th of June. Thereupon the Member for North Wiltshire, Mr Sotheron Estcourt, moved by way of amendment that the Bill be read a third time that day three months. Upon a division being taken, the House proved to be equally for and against the original proposition—Ayes 274, Noes 274. The Speaker upon this giving his casting vote with the Noes, the Bill was thrown out. It was during this critical night's discussion that the following speech was intended to have been delivered.

SIR,—The arguments in favour of this Bill appear to me to have been placed, upon the occasion of its second reading, on the broadest and most intelligible ground by the hon. gentleman the Member for Birmingham on the part of political Nonconformists, and by the noble Lord the Member for London on the part of conforming politicians.

The Member for Birmingham says : " Gentlemen on our side of the House not connected with Nonconformist Churches, are not aware of the exact state of feeling of those members on this subject. I will tell you," says the hon. gentleman, " what the Dissenters feel, and what they object to."

Here, then, we have an explanation long desired, often asked for, often evaded, not disguised in those ambiguous voices in which subtile politicians seek to gratify Dissenters, yet not to alarm the Church ;—we have the explanation from a Nonconformist, whose worst enemy cannot say that he ever wants the boldness to state a grievance, or the eloquence to make the most of it. " I will tell you," says the hon. member, " what the Dissenters object to. It is not a pecuniary hardship—not a paltry matter of 2d. in the pound : it is a struggle for supremacy—of supremacy, too, on the part of a great Establishment, which is as much political as it is religious; against which their ancestors, the Puritans, fought, and against which they are still inevitably obliged to contend." What! This, then, is what they object to! Not a Church rate, but the Church at any rate. And in order to make unequivo- cally clear what the hon. member means by the obnoxious word supremacy, he immediately proceeds to tell us " what it is that Dissenters in conversing with him find intolerable, and are determined to destroy." Not this one isolated claim of the Church establishment, but the whole structure and organisation of that establishment as an English institution. Not alone its supremacy, but all the checks and safeguards against a purely ecclesiastical supremacy in the appointments it must receive from the Crown, in the patronage it must accept from the laity. All that renders the Church of England so peculiarly English, are the special objects of detestation and attack. " You," says the hon. gentleman, " are the only Church in which the loftiest dignitaries are not appointed by ecclesiastical authority ; " and he proceeds to commend to our preference not only the organisa- tion of American Episcopacy, in which bishops are chosen by devout men of the congregation, but even the hierarchy of Rome, in which bishops are appointed by the Pope.

I will not pause to defend what is here assailed, or it would

ABOLITION OF CHURCH RATES.

be easy to show that the powers of appointment vested in the Crown, and even the lay patronage of livings—though in the last there are abuses which I should be glad to see corrected—were regarded by our ancestors as checks upon a purely ecclesiastical supremacy, and safeguards against that segregation from the general interest of the community, which is supposed to be the bias of corporate bodies that are altogether self-elected.

But be our system good or bad, it is enough to know from a witness who comes into court for the express purpose of enlightening our ignorance, that the total abolition of Church rates is the first blow for the total abolition of all against which the Puritans fought—against all that distinguished the Church of England from a Papal hierarchy or an American sect.

But before I here address myself to Churchmen, I would wish to argue the question fairly with the hon. member, on the very ground on which he says that Dissenters would place it. I thank the hon. gentleman for his historical reference. I thank him for reminding us of those stormy days in which the Puritans fought against the Church. I am not about knowingly to utter a single word against those earnest and resolute men ; not a word, I hope, that may justly wound the ear of their descendants. I am disposed to grant much of what the hon. gentleman has said as to the obligations our freedom owes to the Puritans. Not indeed to the extent to which he goes in the pardonable heat of oratorical hyperbole ; not to the extent that we owe all our liberties to the Puritans. All our liberties result from a great variety of causes, but from no cause so potent and so acknowledged as the habit of self-government and the right of a local majority to levy a rate for application to a local purpose. But still, up to a certain date, in the contest between Charles I. and his Parliament, the Puritans not only rendered great services to freedom, but secured for themselves all that their descendants enjoy at the present day. Up to what date ? Up to the moment before they fought against the Church. Before a sword was drawn they had obtained perfect equality with the Episcopal Churchmen. They were the most powerful party in the House of Commons ; they had even members of their body amongst the

Peers. All this did not content them; and they resolved to fight against the Church. They had every advantage for that contest in the time they chose. Never had our Church so many enemies; never—thanks to Laud and the Star Chamber—had it alienated so many friends. The word chosen by the hon. member is historically correct. The Puritans fought against the Church. For a time they triumphed. Bishops were expelled from the House of Lords; twelve of that body were impeached for treason. Laud's head fell upon the scaffold. The Episcopal Church was voted away by the House of Commons; a Presbyterian Church was proclaimed instead—but that was never acknowledged by the nation, nor by the bulk of the Puritans themselves. In point of fact, the result of the fight was that complete severance of Church and State, that unfettered competition of all varieties in religious faith to which the hon. gentleman would invite us to retrograde. But who were the ultimate sufferers? was it the Churchmen? No,—it was the Puritans. The most intelligent and gifted of those foes to the Church—the men who, by mental culture and generous humanity, most resembled the divines and teachers of modern Dissent —were overborne, silenced, swamped by the wild fanatics who followed fast on the abolition of one standard discipline of worship. The nation woke terrified, shocked by that reviling of ignorant zealots, outbidding each other in perversion of Scripture; and the main cause that gave Charles II. his throne without even a battle, without even one prudent check on his arbitrary power, was the yearning impatient desire of the people to have back a Church of standard doctrine and decorous ritual, which might guard the sanctity of the Gospel and the dignity of human reason from the visions of a Harrison and the burlesque of a Barebones. The Church against which the Puritans had fought was restored; but how fared it then with the Puritans? Where, then, were the power and prevalence of that once mighty party?

Sir, they had sown the wind and they reaped the whirlwind. All they had gained for England and themselves before they had fought against the Church, fell from their hands; and instead of being the haughty arbiters of conflicting fates, so sternly did public opinion visit upon them the issues of that fight, that two centuries elapsed before they rose again to the ranks of equal citizens, by the repeal of the Test and Corporation Acts. And that was the result of the fight against the Church!

Therefore, I say, addressing myself solely to Dissenters, regarding the question from the very ground on which the Member for Birmingham tells us the descendants of the Puritans place it,—I say, that if history contains any warning by which politicians may profit, it is a warning not to renew against the Church, where it is infinitely more free from salient points of attack, that strife in which a triumph so brief and so dearly purchased was followed by a reaction so signal and so complete, even amongst the very generation that had shouted for the expulsion of the bishops, and gathered round the scaffold of Laud.

I have no sentiment of rancour against the Puritan ancestor of the Dissenter. I myself had an ancestor whose memory I venerate, whose name I bear, and who represented in the Long Parliament the same county I now represent—a man not indeed a Puritan, but voting with the Puritans in the same divisions as Hampden or Pym. And as his descendant I would say to the descendants of those with whom he was in that great war of the giants, continue to share with us in all things the blessings of that freedom for which our common ancestors strove—continue to give to us Churchmen, competitors on these floors for all the high prizes of ambition and renown; but beware, for your own sakes, how you refuse to be the tolerators of a tolerant Church, which supplies to all your preachers the standard of a rational doctrine, and the example of a culture which stimulates a correspondent bearing on the part of Nonconformist divines. That Church you must summon to your aid whenever you have to meet a common foe. Against the wit and intellect, the philosophy or research, of infidel and sceptic writers, that Church —skilled in all the arguments, versed in all the learning, which the disciplined culture of endowments seems to bestow—stands by the Dissenter's side, to guard with him, guard for the poor and the ignorant, guard as the common inheritance of all the sects and all the nations embraced by Christendom, one great manual of human duties, one grand brotherhood of human hopes.

So much for the argument against the Church through the Church rate, on the very ground taken for the political Dissenter. I don't apologise for the length at which I have discussed it; because, unless you believe that the Member for Birmingham here fails in that plain speaking for which it is his rare distinction to be honestly and inconveniently conspicuous, much more of the real gist of the question now before us is to be found in his speech than in the speeches of those who separate themselves from his candour, but unite themselves to his purpose. For those sincere Churchmen who had advised us to adopt this measure for the sake of peace, are thus disarmed of their only cogent argument; because the articles of peace are precisely what the hostile belligerents refuse to sign. The passing of this Bill is no step towards peace ; it is only the capitulation of a fortress to besiegers who do not make war for the sake of the fortress, but who want the fortress for the sake of continuing the war. This brings me at once to the arguments of the noble Lord the Member for London.

The noble Lord says with truth, "that it would be a great advantage to the Church if we could place it in respect to Church rates in the same position it holds in respect to tithes." But tithes were not abolished till a substitute was found. Give us a substitute on equally good security, and you may abolish Church rates as you abolished tithes. But in the same breath the noble Lord quotes the instance of Church cess in Ireland. He owns that in Ireland there was a fund existing on other property, but that here there does not exist the same means of supplying the place of a Church rate. And while, in one sentence, he suggests a substitute in a legal charge upon the land, in the very next sentence he bids us distrust the chance of that legal security, and share his unlimited confidence in the resource of voluntary contributions. Sir, voluntary contributions are an excellent aid but a bad security ; and I don't think there is a lawyer in England who would advise a transfer of capital to that high-sounding investment. The noble Lord then proceeds to what I may call

the main plot of an argument, conceived and conducted on the
tragic principle of gradually preparing the mind to submit its
reason to the influence of terror. "This agitation," says the noble
Lord, "is bad for the Church. I know well what a Dissenting
agitation is. I know how Dissenters combined to put an end to
the slave trade and slavery. They will use the same machinery
in this instance." The very same machinery perhaps. But have
they the same stuff for the fabric, have they the same force for
the steam. Long before Dissenters were heard of, long before the
word Protestant was known, long before the Papacy was armed
with its temporal power and spiritual thunders, the genius of the
gospel itself brought to bear against slavery in Europe the same
machinery which was already fast reconverting the gods of the
Pantheon into the inventions of Homer. And when that machine
which had centuries before destroyed the slavery of the white
men was employed against the slavery of the negro, the noble
efforts of Dissenters were as nobly assisted by the eloquence and
zeal of Churchmen. The slave trade, indeed, was condemned
in Parliament before a single Dissenter had a seat in the House
of Commons; and when at last slavery received its final death-
blow throughout that empire by the emancipation of the West
Indian slaves, to whom was entrusted that crowning triumph of
Christian humanity? To an enemy of the supremacy of the
Church? No, to the very man who now, as Earl of Derby, gives
all the authority of a name eternally connected with the abolition
of slavery, against your proposal for the abolition of Church rates.
How then can the noble Lord quote the success of an agitation,
popular with Churchmen, headed by Churchmen, based on the
broadest principles of our common Christianity, and so carefully
anxious to conciliate the claims of property with the rights of
men, that it sanctioned the vote of twenty millions for the vindication of its unselfish object? How can he quote the instance
of that success as an argument for the probable success of an
agitation which is to array the Church against the agitators,
which is not to unite but to separate the believers in Christianity; which has for its ostensible object the exoneration of
property from one of its most ancient burthens, and for its

latent purpose the assertion of a principle by which all the property of the Church may hereafter be called in question? For see what is asked from us in this Bill; and what must be the logical consequences if we give up what is asked! You would make it illegal for Churchmen to raise a rate among themselves for the repair of their own churches. You are provided with no substitute, and you say, that for such repairs they may depend exclusively on the chance of voluntary contributions. What can be a more direct blow at the very root of a National establishment? For is it not the most absolute condition of any National establishment whatsoever, that it cannot depend exclusively on voluntary contributions for the maintenance of what is necessary for its uses as a National institution? And can anything be more necessary to the uses of a National Church than the maintenance of places at which its members may worship? This is not all. Once make it illegal to support the fabric of the church otherwise than by voluntary contributions, and you cannot fail to facilitate and encourage the effort to make it also illegal to support otherwise than by voluntary contributions, the ritual in doctrine, the hierarchy, which constitute the only reasons why the Dissenter objects to maintain the fabric itself. The very argument you now found on the smallness of the sum raised by Church rates, that it is only £25,000—and if Dissenters were exempted from payment, it is only £150,000—is to me an argument against a surrender which offers to the ordinary elements of human nature stronger temptations to larger demands. This small sum does not much tempt the passions of cupidity and envy; it offers no aid to secular purposes. But once bring the law to cover the usual distinctions of *meum* and *tuum*, by taking from the Church, without any compensation, that which the Church had before possessed, and you licence those passions which covet our neighbours goods, you fix the eyes not only of all the enemies of the Church, but even of large numbers amongst the less educated classes who now peaceably recognise its benefits, upon all the wealth of its endowments, which an application of the same principle might confiscate to the supply of some popular want, or the relief from some unpopular burthen. If agitation can be so successful in the first pitiful nibble at Church property, the success will whet the appetite; appetite comes with eating, and that proverb is never so true as when the eating is at the expense of others.

For this reason I might dismiss, at once, that cry which in every discussion on the subject is raised with as much pretence as if it were an argument. It is said, "What do you fear that your parish churches will fall to ruin unless supported by rates? What an accusation against the apathy and indifference of your own wealthy persuasion, to suppose that you could not subscribe among yourselves to support your own places of worship!" The answer to this is sufficiently obvious. It is not a question whether churches would or would not fall out of repair if left wholly to voluntary contributions. As long as the Church itself is acknowledged to be a National institution, so long it is not desirable to apply to the maintenance of the fabric a principle that would very soon after be applied to the maintenance of the preacher. If the parish churches did fall out of repair, there would instantly be this new cry, " How can you longer call your-selves the Church of the Nation ? You fail in the very uses for which you defend an establishment. There, in those rural parishes, where Dissenters the least interfere with you, there, where you ought most triumphantly to point to the civilising influences of your Christian mission, your venerable churches are dilapidated ruins. Down with an established Church which has ceased to fulfil the most simple and least disputed of all its objects !"

On the other hand, if the parish churches did not fall into decay, if they were kept up by voluntary contributions as well as they are now, then the cry would be, " See the good effect of the voluntary principle ! You have applied it safely to the fabric of the church, even in the poorest and remotest rural districts— apply it now to the support of the clergy."

Sir, it seems to me an axiom in government as clear and as positive as any axiom in Euclid, that where an institution is avowedly maintained for national purposes, it can never be left exclusively, no matter how popular, no matter how generally acknowledged its uses may be—never be left exclusively to the

itinerant benevolence of the begging hat. Take an analogous
case—take the Poor Law. If there be a virtue in the world
which distinguishes our age and our land, it is charity to the
poor. Let any call on extra benevolence be made, and voluntary
contributions pour in from all parts of the country. But suppose
one of those political economists, who are opposed to the principle
of a poor law, were to employ against a poor rate the same cry
that is raised against a Church rate. Suppose he were to say,
" Do you think the poor would be left to starve if dependent
solely on voluntary contributions ? See how largely you rely on
voluntary contributions now—see how the poor rate, economical
though it be in amount, fails to do all which it professes to
do. Abolish this poor-rate, which no one has any great pleasure
in paying, and rely alone on the well-known charity of your
countrymen." I know not how any reasoner could accept that
argument so long as he believes it is the duty of a State, no
matter how charitable its subjects may be, to secure some place
where a man may find food for the body, if he will take the
trouble to come to it; and I know not how any reasoner can
accept your analogous argument so long as he believes it is the
duty of a State, no matter how pious its members, to maintain
some place where a man may find food for his soul, if he will
take the trouble to come to it. And surely our Christian brethren,
the Dissenters, ought to forgive us if we cling to this doctrine as
a positive duty. For it only embodies the truth which all our
joint preachers enforce, that if man has an interest in his life,
which is short, he has an interest much greater in the soul,
which lives on for ever.

Sir, if there be any gentlemen who are as yet undecided as
to the vote they are called upon to give to-day, I respectfully
entreat them to extend their view beyond the narrow point to
which it is sought to confine their judgment. They should consider that this is almost the first question on which they have
been asked to reverse that great characteristic of English policy,
which declines to destroy till you are clear as to what you
would reconstruct. It is this which has hitherto distinguished
our reforms from those of other countries, and has made them

durable and safe. I gather from the speeches of her Majesty's Government, that when they ask us to destroy the Church rate, they think it will be desirable, some day or other, to find a substitute for what they take away. What that substitute shall be they cannot determine. They invite us to pull down and take the chance of a squabble as to what we may afterwards build up. In private life a man scarcely allows his bailiff to pull down a barn or a cowshed, if the bailiff cannot clearly explain with what he intends to replace them. In public life the Trustees of the Nation are at once to pull down what has hitherto been a part of the Church of the Nation, and when we ask the Government what they would put up instead, the only answer we can get is, "Something or nothing, as the case may be."

But do those gentlemen who sincerely think that a National Church is a National benefit, believe that they sufficiently discharge the debt of reason and conscience when they say, "We regret the language of the Member for Birmingham, we differ from his ulterior objects." Do you regret his language? You ought rather to rejoice that a man so eloquent scorns to deceive you—that he has told you as plainly as tongue can speak, that if you vote for this motion, you do—whether you like it or not—you do swell the march of the Puritan against the Church. It is no reason because you voted for the second reading of the Bill that you should vote for the third. Many gentlemen may have voted for the second reading, in the belief that some substitute for Church rate would be proposed in Committee. At the third reading nothing is before us but the naked question, "Ay, or No, shall Churchmen be forbidden, after a certain day, to tax themselves according to ancient custom, for the maintenance of their places of worship?" Ay or No, will you put the repairs of your national temples on that exclusive footing of voluntary contribution to which not a single parish in the vast metropolis would leave the reparation of its sewers?

Sir, the noble Lord says, "we shall have this debate on every hustings!"—Well, if it must be so, have we any reason to fear it? It has already been before every hustings in recent elections. I do not find that recent elections need fill us with gloomy despair.

No, the more the question has been discussed, the better it has been for the Church; the more public opinion has recoiled from the unqualified abolition of Church rates, in proportion as Churchmen have evinced a desire to conciliate, and the enemies of the Church have avowed their unappeasable desire to destroy. Where is your old majority of 70 on a second reading ? Last year it fell to 29,—this year to 15. These divisions are the watermarks of opinion, they show where the agitation, which the noble Lord fears may overwhelm us, recedes from the barrier that checked it. Slowly, perhaps, but surely, as a tide when it once begins to ebb.

But though I fear no battles on this question, I agree thus much with the noble Lord—the Member for London—I deplore them, and I should hold that statesman a benefactor to his country-men, and a true servant of that religion which teaches good will to all men, who shall devise [for Church rate a substitute which both parties may accept with honour. But if these feuds con-tinue, the fault does not rest with us who have repeatedly sought to effect a settlement; it rests with those who forbid us even to redress the grievances of which they complain, unless we ac-knowledge that the worst grievance of all is the Church we are brought up to revere. If I decline now to discuss the compromise which has been suggested by my honourable friend beside me, it is because I think this first step to compromise must be the withdrawal of this Bill. When the Dissenter complains of a payment to the repair of a church which his conscience forbids him to enter, though much might be said to argue his complaint away, yet I own for my part that there is a something in my con-science that makes me sincerely anxious to conciliate that scruple in his. But when he says " No, I reject an exemption from my-self, I demand a humiliating triumph over you. No change in the law will content me that does not make it illegal for Church-men to supply what they are taught to believe the holiest of local wants by that system of local self-taxation which is the most ancient custom of English freemen." Then, Sir, the Dis-senter seems to me to unite liberty and the Church in the same cause, and we declare for or against both in the vote that we give to-day.

XLII.

OUTLINE OF A SPEECH

INTENDED TO HAVE BEEN DELIVERED IN

THE HOUSE OF COMMONS

ON THE 4TH OF MARCH 1862.

ON Tuesday the 5th of March 1861, the Member for Taunton, Mr Arthur
Mills, moved in the House of Commons for a select Committee on
Colonial Military Expenditure, and in regard to the general defence of
the British Dependencies. The Committee was nominated on the 13th
of March, and sat during the spring and summer of that year, its report
being published by order of the House of Commons on the 11th of July.
On Tuesday the 4th of March 1862, the Member for Taunton, who had
presided over that Committee throughout, as its Chairman, moved in the
House of Commons a resolution to the effect, "'That this House, while it
fully recognises the claim of all portions of the British Empire on Imperial
aid against perils arising from the consequences of Imperial policy, is of
opinion that colonies exercising the rights of self-government ought to
undertake the main responsibility of providing for their own internal
order and security." Seconded by the Member for Maidstone, Mr Charles
Buxton, this resolution upon the suggestion of the Member for Montrose,
Mr William Edward Baxter, was supplemented with the words, " and
ought to assist in their own external defence." So amended, the resolution
was approved of by the Government, and agreed to by the House.
During the discussion which arose upon this occasion, the following
speech was intended to have been delivered.

SIR,—This question appears to me to lie in a nutshell. If
you want to keep your colonies, you will support the prudent
suggestions by which Mr Elliot modifies the extreme doctrine

recommended by Mr Hamilton and Mr Godley,—if you want to get rid of your colonies, you have nothing to do but adhere to that extreme doctrine in all its well argued severity.

In fact the difference between these two conflicting authorities is to be traced to their fundamental disagreement as to the advantage of keeping colonies at all. Mr Godley, by whom I presume the report signed by him and Mr Hamilton was drawn up, considers that our political connection with our colonies is not that benefit to our commerce which is vulgarly supposed— he has said elsewhere, "that it is desirable to reduce to the minimum their dependence upon us"—in short, he regards them as burthens which we should gradually slip off from our shoulders and he bases his whole report on the assumption that we have no interest in our colonies sufficient to justify the trouble of defending them. Mr Elliot, on the contrary, regards our colonies as sources of wealth, as the stimulants and feeders of commerce, as burthens, if you please, but burthens that strengthen the muscles which are trained to support them, and contribute to the health of the body politic by that habitual exercise and demand on energy which preserve youth and vitality whether to men or to nations. I believe, in this view, Mr Elliot to be right; that may be a matter for philosophical controversy, but one thing is clear, the Queen's dominions would not be safe in the hands of any Government that shall pronounce him to be wrong.

There are three principles laid down in this report. On one of these principles Mr Elliot is agreed with Messrs Hamilton and Godley, namely, that you cannot defend all your colonies in detail. You cannot provide each colony with garrisons and regiments for its separate defence. That is a principle on which every statesman and every military authority will arrive at the same conclusion. It amounts to this, that you must concentre force, and not subdivide it. The fate of our Colonial Empire may be fought in the Channel by all the might of England; it could never be fought at Jamaica with two or three ships and two or three regiments.

The second principle is that colonies should be divided into two classes. One class to consist of military posts, or those in which garrisons are maintained for imperial purposes as distinct from the defence of the special colonies themselves, such as Malta, Gibraltar, Corfu, Bermuda. Messrs Godley and Hamilton think these places should be dealt with exceptionally, and not included in any general scheme of colonial contribution.

The distinction made here is in language both inaccurate and obscure. It is inaccurate, because, for instance, Corfu is not a colony at all, but a free and independent State, placed under British protection for European purposes, and bound by convention to contribute a yearly sum to its own defence;—while there are colonies not glanced at in this definition, which are maintained as stations for the general strength of the Empire apart from consideration for those colonies themselves. Such as Mauritius, Ceylon, the Cape, and others. Now, it is said that such places, held for imperial purposes, should be exempted from the general scheme of contribution. I should observe that they at present contribute more than £153,000 a year. Is it intended that they should cease to do so? No colonies can afford the contribution better. But if that is not meant, it is impolitic to raise the question by placing them, by a distinction clear as to words but obscure as to sense and meaning, in a different category from the other colonies.

The third principle is that in all the other colonies—that is where troops are stationed primarily if not exclusively for the defence of the lives, liberty, or property of the colonists—the entire management and responsibility of the troops shall pass away from the Crown and be vested in the colonies themselves, while a share of the expense (it is suggested a moiety) shall be borne by those colonies, say a joint contribution at an uniform rate, no matter how differently circumstanced each of the colonies, thus uniformly rated, may be. I am convinced, with Mr Elliot, that this is a dangerous principle; and if you attempt rigidly to enforce it, you will lose your colonies.

Take first those colonies in which there is a small white population of planters amidst a numerous black population that your laws have made free. If our laws made the black men free, the white have a right to expect that your force will keep the white men safe. Now, the whites are not numerous enough to protect themselves, nor rich enough to raise the money to pay the troops that may become necessary to protect them. Even now there have been recently two instances of riot in the West Indian Colonies, in which the whites, not having English troops at hand, applied for military force, once to Denmark, another time to France. But if foreign nations are to protect your colonies, it would better become the honour of England and the majesty of her Crown, to abandon them.

For if in one of these West Indian Colonies, the whites, having the predominant power in the legislature, succeeded in organising a military force for which England paid half, but which is as entirely under the responsible control of the colony itself, I am convinced that in any case where a chance riot broke out it would be ascribed to some terrible design on the part of the blacks, the military force would be ordered to act with that imprudent severity which is characteristic of a timorous severity, and that severity might be sooner or later followed by a retaliation on the part of the blacks, with that sanguinary violence which characterises the outbreak of an angry population, and the revenge of an antagonistic race.

Again, take some still smaller and poorer settlement, in which, perhaps, not very wisely, you encouraged your countrymen to settle many years ago among fierce barbarian tribes. Are you to tell these men, struggling for life on the coasts of Africa, that because they are poor, they must dispense with the luxury given to the humble pauper who calls himself a British subject, I mean the security to life and property. To say that, whatever their danger and whatever their poverty, they are to contribute to their defence at the same uniform rate as Victoria and Canada, is to say, that when you invited them to colonise you entrapped them into a shamble. Take next a superior African colony, such as Natal. At Natal there is a tendency to an aggressive policy against the Kaffirs, which requires the constant vigilance and stern discouragement of the Colonial Office. But suppose Natal got up a military force entirely at its own responsible control, as is here proposed, I fear the result would be an armed attack on the most cherished habits and prejudices of the Kaffir tribes, which might be followed in six months by the massacre of every white man in the colony. Lastly, take your greatest and richest colonies—those in Australia and North America. These are colonies in which party spirit prevails even more than it does with us, and accordingly it is the wise maxim of the Colonial Office to have as few debatable points of correspondence with their Government as we possibly can. At present, slight as is the thread by which we hold those possessions, it is as strong as steel, simply because there is no friction on it. But I can conceive nothing that would so wound the loyalty of those haughty provinces, as to start from the principle here laid down, that the mother country has no interest in their preservation, and that we can only send them troops on the same principle of payment with which the grand conferences of the middle ages let out their mercenaries to the Italian republics, or the Swiss indifferently lend themselves to the King of Naples or the Pope of Rome; and I can fancy no correspondence that would so rouse the spirit of party against us, and be so irritating and so feeble, as long public despatches backwards and forwards, all based upon that principle, and all seeking to carry it out in detail, every time a ship was demanded and a regiment changed. The thing in itself would be impossible. There is no place where a garrison is so required as Halifax, for the safety of all North America. Well, but Halifax is in Nova Scotia, which is by no means rich; and is Nova Scotia to contribute to that garrison, while all the rest of British North America escapes contribution to the force that protects it. Take again Newfoundland. We all know the dangerous disagreements that exist between home and that colony with regard to the Fishing grounds. I do not think the high spirit of this country would be reconciled to the tame surrender of the Newfoundland fishermen to the navies of France. But if it were desirable to send ships and men to protect Newfoundland, do you imagine we could wring from Newfoundland a contribution to their payment at an uniform rate with the gold bearing city of Melbourne? A danger that might be prevented at once by

the timely appearance of a frigate or a detachment, may spring
up at any moment in dimensions as vast as ever; but if before dealing with the danger you wait to haggle about the payment the colony is to make, either the colony may be gone or
it may need an army to recover it. Now, the whole of this recommendation by Messrs Hamilton and Godley rests upon one
abstract principle. But does not our experience of life tell us,
that if there be an art beyond the power of statesmen, it is the
principle. An old proverb says, "Beware of the men of one
attempt to govern the varieties of flesh and blood upon one abstract
book;" and I say, "Beware of the politician with one abstract
principle." This is true even if the one abstract principle be
sound. But is the principle here laid down a sound one? It
is this, that England is not bound to contribute towards the defence of her colonies merely because she is interested in their
defence; for in such case the obligation should be reciprocal, and
the colonies, in their turn, ought to contribute systematically and
habitually to the defence of London and Portsmouth, and that,
therefore, the only reason why England is bound to contribute
to the defence of her colonies is, that the Imperial Government
has the control of peace and war, and is, therefore, bound in
honour and duty to protect them against the consequences of its
policy. This argument narrows our obligation simply to defend
colonies when they are threatened with invasion. But I think
this is an unsound view of the nature of our obligation. For
why does England keep any colonies at all? Why accept the
control of peace or war as regards them? It can be for no other
reason than that she thinks that she has an interest in a colonial
empire; nay, an interest so great that she accepts the terrible
responsibilities of war for its defence. If that be the case, the
interest of England enters into the whole consideration of the
question, and cannot be got rid of by saying that the interest
must be so identically reciprocal, that if England defends Newfoundland, Newfoundland should defend Portsmouth. Because
an interest may be reciprocal without its being shown in exactly
similar reciprocity of service. If a policeman defends my house
in London, I am not therefore bound to defend a policeman's

house at Dover. I repay the State in another way, by a general contribution to the wealth that finds a general police. And that is the way in which the colonies repay England, many of them in hard money, by the vast profit they yield to trade or commerce. Mr Elliot cites Australia. She imports into the United Kingdom more than fourteen millions; she takes from the United Kingdom more than eleven millions of home produce. Australia receives from us at the rate of £12 a-head, while the United States of America, our best independent customer, receives from us about 15s. a-head. I am aware that the answer of Mr Godley, seeking to depreciate the value of colonies generally, would be that the United States are a manufacturing population, and Australia has not yet arrived at that point of industrial progress; but the fact remains the same for the present, however it may be modified hereafter. Australia takes from you twelve times the amount in proportion to population that is taken from you by your best independent customer, and four times the amount of your expenditure, civil and military, upon all your colonies put together. Indeed, as a general principle, all colonies, from the greatest to the least, prefer commercial dealings with the mother country. The best proof of this is in French Caledonia, which has much the same wants as Australia. French Caledonia deals with France as Australia deals with England. It would be said by Mr Godley that Australia would continue to do so if she ceased to have any political connection with us. That might or might not be, but I hope the Queen's Government do not mean to gratify the curiosity of political science by trying the experiment. Meanwhile I take the question on a wider ground than that of trade. I say that our colonies repay England not in hard money alone, not, if you please to say so, in hard money at all, but by the rank and the dignity, by the moral power, by the weight in Europe, which are due to a sceptre that casts over earth a shadow so vast and so tranquil. There is an awe which belongs to these attributes of imperial grandeur; that awe strengthens the voice that comes forth from this island on behalf of humanity and justice; that awe may keep from invasion the island itself as the centre of that marvellous combination

of energy and intellect which seems to have found the secret of
controlling the widest extent of empire by the smallest amount
of force. But if you lost your colonies either because you said
with this Report that you could not afford to protect them, or
because they left you when you placed their protection upon a
principle ungracious in itself and impracticable in its applica-·
tion, your authority would forfeit an influence, and your very
shores a security. I will take an illustration of that truth from
the instance of Canada. Mr Godley would select Canada as an
instance of the small commercial profit a great colony, as it grows
up, affords to the mother country. He would say, if Australia
in its infancy deals with you more than the United States do,
Canada, in its maturer growth, deals with you less than the.
United States do. Quite true. Canada imports from us at about
the rate of 12s. a-head, Republican America at 16s. a-head.
True, Canada meets our goods by a duty of twenty per cent.;
true, if Canada were independent to-morrow she might not take
from us a single shilling the less. But will the House of Commons say that there would not be a thrill of alarm throughout
all England, a cry of exultation from our enemies abroad, a more
formidable bustle in the arsenals of Cherbourg and Toulon, if
our First Minister came down to either House to inform us that
Canada had ceased to belong to the Queen of England. But if
that be so, then we have a direct interest in the political connection with our colonies, and something in our plain robust
English understanding bids us reject this Report, which founds all
its recommendations on the dogma, that we have no such interest
whatsoever.

Yet, if you accept the advantages of a great empire, you must
accept its responsibilities. Foremost amongst these responsibilities is a humane care for life and property even where not
threatened by invasion. England would hear with shame and
horror that in any part of the world you called men British
subjects, you placed them nominally under the British flag,
gave them British laws, called them countrymen, and then left
them to be butchered by savages, or to be the prey of civil
war with each other, because you said you had no interest in

their welfare, for they were too poor to pay the same price as the rich did.

When I first entered the Colonial Office I found the saying of an illustrious predecessor, the noble Lord the Member for London, established there as a proverb. He is reported to have said, "the best police is very often the sight of a red coat." I believe this to be a true and a wise saying. The soldier should never be a policeman; but the knowledge that behind the policeman there is a soldier in case of need, is often the cheapest and best guarantee for the peace of the civil community, and the safety of human life. Therefore I dissent from the doctrines of Messrs Hamilton and Godley. I think their abstract principle itself unsound; and with the fall of the principle, fall the reasonings which are based upon it. But I do not the less consider that many of their remarks, and the general spirit of their Report are eminently useful. I think they lead to these two safe conclusions,— First, that the best general way to protect our colonies as against the enemy, is to take care of our navy, and subdivide our forces as little as possible. Secondly, that the Secretary of State for the Colonies should use every exertion in his power to create in each colony, from the poorest and humblest to the richest and most powerful, a disciplined force for ordinary occasions of defence against internal disturbance, whether as police or militia, according to their respective services, and that this should be as much as possible a condition for any extra help that necessity may call for. This was my strenuous object during the time I held the Colonial Seals; and I believe in many places where there appeared no great probability of success, the object has been greatly advanced. To take a few instances—I hear from private quarters, that in Bermuda, Barbadoes, and Prince Edward Island, the recommendations I was enabled personally to give to certain officers whom I sent there, have been actively carried out, and that a laudable spirit of self-protection has recently sprung up. I do not doubt that our own example of volunteers and rifle corps will have a great effect on all our colonies. By steadily pursuing this determined inculcation of self-defence, we shall at last attain our end of rearing up brave and manly

communities, intent on their own internal protection, and by
regular and quick degrees lightening the burthen of the mother
country without loosening the ties that bind the Colonies to the
Crown. But do not attempt to wind up all your clocks with a
single key, nor set those at the antipodes by the minute-hand
of the Horse Guards. I cannot better conclude than with these
judicious and weighty remarks of Mr Elliot:—

   " What has to be solved is not one problem but many. I
despair of discovering among them any self-acting rule which
shall be a substitute for the judgment and firmness of the Ministers of the Crown for the time being. They will, doubtless,
always be guided by a policy, but they can hardly be expected
to despatch such complicated and arduous questions by a single
maxim."

   Is not this plain good common sense ? By that common
sense we now maintain our colonial empire, and it is surely
better not to desert that sober guide for the ingenious speculations of an adviser who tells us that the best way to manage our
colonies is to start from the principle that we have no interest
in keeping them.

XLIII.

OUTLINE OF A SPEECH

INTENDED TO HAVE BEEN DELIVERED IN

THE HOUSE OF COMMONS

ON THE 1ST OF JUNE 1866.

ON Thursday the 12th of April 1866, the Chancellor of the Exchequer, Mr Gladstone, moved in the House of Commons the second reading of the Bill then before Parliament, for the Extension of the Suffrage. A discussion arose upon the amendment moved by the member for Chester, Earl Grosvenor. At the close of the debate the Leader of the House again spoke at great length on Friday the 27th of April, when the original motion was carried upon a division by 318 votes to 313, giving a narrow majority of five to the Government. On Monday the 7th of May, the Chancellor of the Exchequer moved for leave to bring in a Bill for the Redistribution of Seats, which was, after some discussion, read a second time on Monday the 14th of May. While this measure was yet under the consideration of the House in Committee, the Member for Wells, Captain Arthur Divett Hayter, moved—by way of an amendment to the customary proposition for going into Committee, that Mr Speaker do now leave the chair—"That this House, while ready to consider the general subject of a Redistribution of Seats, is of opinion that the system of grouping proposed by Her Majesty's Government is neither convenient nor equitable, and that the scheme is otherwise not sufficiently matured to form the basis of a satisfactory measure." A discussion arose upon this which lasted four nights, the amendment being carried at the close of it without a division, on Monday the 4th of June, the Speaker deciding that the Ayes had it. Upon the third night of the debate the following speech was intended to have been delivered.

SIR,—I came down to the House, not without some expectation that Her Majesty's Government would save us and some of their own habitual supporters from a division on this question. But after what has fallen from the Chancellor of the Exchequer, it appears that they adhere to their former declaration, and that at every hazard they will stand or fall by this Bill, and in this session. Among the geographical conveniences which may be renewed with a certain latitude, the boundary of the Rubicon is not to be included. Well then, we on this have been asked so often in the course of this debate, why we do not hail the golden opportunity of settling, on better terms, it is said, than we shall ever get again, the question of Reform, that I will endeavour, in the remarks with which I shall trespass on the House, to state frankly and plainly the reasons why.

Both the Law Officers of the Crown are positively pathetic in appealing to us to pass this conciliatory measure. The Solicitor-General admits its anomalies, but insists on its moderation, and assures us that it will be accepted with gratitude by the people. That touched me. To earn the gratitude of the people is the laudable ambition of every public man. But in what part of the people am I to look for the gratitude? We are told that the large body of the Liberals will accept this settlement with the greatest reluctance. The reluctance is no less great on the Conservative side. And if those eminent legal authorities were not the advisers of the Crown, they might tell us to doubt the permanent felicity of any settlement which satisfies neither party, unless, indeed, they think that Reform is like matrimony, in which we are told on high authority, it is safest to begin with a little aversion. Well then, granting the aversion, which is indisputable, now as to the gratitude. Gratitude has been defined to be a lively sense of prospective benefits,—and I do not deny that that sort of gratitude may be found among that infinitesmal proportion of the people which occupies the front row of the Government benches. Because, while our acceptance of this Bill would save those gentlemen from a present embarrassment, they take especial care not to bind themselves from again reopening the whole subject, if by so doing they may embarrass any Government that succeeds to them. But that reserve upon their part constitutes the first, though not the strongest, reason why we demur to the acceptance of their Bill. I am old enough to remember the Reform Bill of 1832. And one main reason which secured to that measure, of which I and those who favoured it, were not reluctant but ardent supporters, the warm approval not only of the masses of the population, which this scheme does not obtain, but of the large proportion of the educated classes, which this scheme, I fear, fails to do, not only of historical Reformers, but of Liberals so moderate as the late Duke of Richmond, Lord Goderich, and other eminent disciples of Pitt, Mr Robert Grant, and Lord Palmerston—one reason for that warm approval was this—that Lord Grey's Cabinet, in proposing their measure, stated that in their opinion it was conclusive and binding, and that neither in office nor out of office would they sanction a disturbance of the settlement for which they made themselves responsible. And this was so well understood, that I remember hearing Sir James Graham, seven years afterwards, in 1839, when the collateral question of Vote by Ballot was raised by Mr Hume, say these words, which are to be found in Hansard, "While finality with regard to a great nation does not exist, the pledge of finality was binding on the Members of Lord Grey's Cabinet one and all," and he proceeded to quote this from a speech of Lord Althrop's on the first Reformed Parliament,—"He, Lord Althrop, appealed to every gentleman who was in the last Parliament while the question of Reform was going on, whether the promoters of that measure did not contend that so far as representation was concerned it was to be considered and was proposed as a final measure." I do not attach to these words too severe an obligation. No doubt, many years afterwards, Sir James Graham thought that time had absolved him from the pledge by which he had been so long bound; all I contend for is this—That the statesmen of Lord Grey's Cabinet held and abided by the doctrine that a considerable interval of years must elapse before a Government, which obtained the consent of various parties to a new representative system, in which there must be many sacrifices of individual opinions and local interests, are honourably and morally at liberty to regard that settlement for which they are responsible otherwise than as final.

But we search in vain through speeches of Her Majesty's Government for any satisfactory assurance that in going thus far while in office, they are not perfectly free to go much farther whenever they are in opposition. Take a Member of the Government, whom we had reason to believe the most moderate,—a man of talents so commanding, that he is to your side as splendid an ornament, and as high an authority as the Member for Belfast is to ours. Take the Attorney-General, what does he say ? " The measure cannot be considered more final than any thing else which rests upon an uncertain bases ;" and he has no doubt in his mind that the time will come when all rated householders may be entrusted with the franchise. But he is clear and definite as to the finality of this settlement compared with the chief spokesman of the Government, the Chancellor of the Exchequer—for the only logical arguments and the only impassioned pleas which have been addressed to us by the Chancellor of the Exchequer on behalf of this measure, have been much more in favour of the millions whom it excludes, than of the thousands whom it admits to the franchise. And begging his pardon, if, as he said, " I misrepresented his meaning in the flesh and blood argument," for I would never consciously misrepresent the argument of my most bitter opponent, still less the argument of a man, whom apart from politics, I consider it a great distinction to myself to call my Right Hon. Friend—putting aside the flesh and blood argument, still, if ever it be the destiny of the Chancellor of the Exchequer to enchant the National Reform League by an oration in favour of Universal Suffrage, he would only have to repeat the most brilliant passages in these speeches, by which he sought to reconcile Conservatives to the amount of intellect, property and public virtue, which a £7 borough franchise would do—What ?—Admit ? No, still exclude from the pale of the constitution. Now, when we are invited to recognise the moderation of a settlement between contending parties, which one party proposes for the adoption of the other,—let me ask the Law Officers of the Crown, whether the first question that occurs to our common sense is not this, " Is it a settlement at all ? Do you mean it to be a *bonâ fide* settlement of your claims, or rather an unsettlement of all the grounds upon which the opposite party can resist the peril of further demands ?"

But, have I not said enough to show that Her Majesty's Government leave us in no doubt that it is not a settlement of their claims on behalf of what is called the Liberal party, but a Bill framed to pass—Why ? In order to unsettle our legal powers to withhold assent from any claims which at any time may be required in favour of those very numerous litigants called fathers of families, or deserving but unenfranchised millions. When, therefore, you ask us to co-operate in what you pleasantly call a settlement, you invite us to risk our all in a lottery which does not offer to us a single prize. It is a hazard in which we think we have everything to lose, and in which there is not an honest man opposite who will venture to tell us that we have anything to gain.

It is true that some kindly advisers on the opposite side say to us, " Till this question is settled you cannot hope for your fair share in the government of the country. You may come into power by accident, but it will be only upon sufferance. You cannot settle the question of Reform; and if you attempt it, we come in at any time by an abstract resolution." Sir, that may or may not be true. But as to our incapacity to deal with the question of Reform, I doubt if it be in the power of that united stupidity which the Member for Westminster flatteringly ascribes to us, to frame a measure more characterised by the absence of the intellect which distinguishes himself. But if we cannot have the dignities of office, we as yet are not without some weight, some numbers, and some dignity, as an Opposition. And if, instead of opposing, we take this measure, with such trifling amendments as you may permit, will any practical politician tell us that we should meet the next Parliament in anything like the same numbers, with anything like the same degree of power against further organic innovation which we possess at present? No man will so tell us. The utmost any man can say is this, In the course of time,—say within three

Parliaments, or at the end of nine years,—such great blunders may be incurred by Liberal Governments that a Conservative administration very possibly may have fair play. Heaven only knows if anything which we now value may then be left to conserve; or whether, instead of seeking to save this mixed Constitution from Democracy—we should have been left without power to do that—we may not then rather be called in to save Democracy from that dictatorship which, in ancient states, is its natural successor and relentless destroyer. Danton lived to say that the Revolution, like Saturn, devoured its own children. Had he lived a very little longer, he might have learned that one child was saved from the jaws of Saturn, and was the Jove who dethroned his parent. Whenever democratic action is released from the check of legitimate conservatism, the necessity for order soon replaces the passion for freedom, and the populace hastens to substitute for those constitutional securities against itself which it had blindly destroyed, the force and the will of the single despot whom it creates and crowns, whether he be a Cæsar, a Napoleon, or that advanced Reformer of Huntingdon, whose pikemen expelled the Parliament that had beheaded Charles.

Are we then to be blamed for stupidity and blindness, if we see nothing very alluring in the prospect of ultimately recovering the strength and the numbers we are now invited to throw away; and being called in at some time or other as a Conservative Government, to do—What? Why perhaps to save the gentlemen opposite from a repeal of their own Reform Bills.

But, if we do not consent to a settlement, which, if it settle nothing else, will at least be sufficient to settle ourselves, What then? Oh then the hobgoblin argument, which Bentham places among his fallacies! The hobgoblin of something worse. What is that something worse? Will it begin by a dissolution of Parliament? Do you dare to dissolve on this question? I agree with my hon. Friend, the Member for Malden, that Government ought to do so. The innovation proposed is so great—it affects so largely the existent representative body—that, seeing this Parliament, by the admission of the Attorney-General, was not summoned to deal with Reform, and the mere hustings-talk

on the subject was of the vaguest kind, it seems almost the duty
of Her Majesty's Ministers to ask the constituencies how far they
like the proposed transfer of power—a question to which Her
Majesty's Government and their advisers might possibly get a
very different answer than they obtain from those audiences of
selected agitators, at which, in their individual capacities they
are such distinguished performers. But if the consequence of
repealing this Bill be not a dissolution of Parliament, what
then ? A resignation of Government ? and, let us take the worst,
so great a difficulty to form another, that Her Majesty's Ministers
come back again and propose another Bill ? A Bill more violent,
say the Law Officers, and those who bid us be wise in time. I wish
you would give us a Bill more violent—1st, Because a Bill more
violent would sufficiently alarm the country to range its educated
classes still more largely on our side—2dly, Because though you
could easily make a Bill more flagrantly violent, I defy you to
make a Bill more insidiously unfair. You misconceive the feeling
on our side if you think we dislike a Reform Bill in proportion as
it is comprehensive. We only dislike a Reform Bill in proportion
as it is unfair. No thoughtful man on our side cares how large,
how comprehensive any scheme is, by which you give a due and
legitimate share of representation to the working classes or to
the Liberal party, provided only you give the same due and legitimate share to the numbers, the property, and the educated culture, which statistics, furnished by the Government, may prove
to be arrayed in favour of our side of the House. What we say
is this, that the more your scheme pretends to be moderate, the
more, when sifted by practical politicians, it is found to be
craftily dishonest and elaborately unjust. No one can deny
that Conservative opinion, however imperfectly we may represent it in Parliament, is a mighty element in the social system
of these three kingdoms—a mighty element that deserves to be
fairly represented, whether you regard property, numbers, or
educated intelligence. And yet we all know that it is quite possible to devise a representative system, in which that Conservative element is disfranchised altogether. It is disfranchised altogether in the metropolis. Hear what is said on that subject

by a man who has the just reputation of a great thinker, and whose notions were, I believe, at one time honoured by the authority of the distinguished Member for Westminster. Hear what is said by Mr Hare, in his remarkable treatise on the Election of Representatives. "If we go through many of the streets and squares of the metropolitan boroughs, and form our conclusions of the intellectual rank of the inhabitants from their probable education and means of acquiring knowledge, and when we know that, of these, thousands would in vain approach the hustings to give expression to their views and opinions, it is impossible to look at the nominal representation of the metropolis as other than a mockery of the name." I do not go so far as that—the advanced Liberalism, which forms a powerful party in all free countries, is worthily, and at this time most honourably, represented by the members of the metropolis. But the immense amount of Conservative opinion, intellect and property, which the metropolis includes, is as much disfranchised as if it did not exist. But that Conservative element finds its natural counterpoise elsewhere. It finds it in counties, and in those mixed borough populations where the suffrage is not so purely urban, nor so exclusively given to large numbers, as to overpower all the influences of property, of education, and of local predilections. That is our strength, that is the counterpoise. But the object of this scheme is to strike that counterpoise out of the scale—to destroy it, as far as possible, wherever it can be found. Let the House bear with me for a few moments, and follow my argument. It is a general political truth, not only in this country, but in all communities, that the predisposition of large urban populations is in favour of experimental novelties, and that the predisposition of rural districts is in favour of established institutions. And the experience of all history tells us, that urban populations are anti-conservative in proportion as the franchise is lower, so as to give a preponderate influence to those voters who live by weekly wages, and who, whatever you may tell us of the value of their precarious income, have none of those capitalized savings which give them a sensible interest in the solidity of an existent order of things. Now, where a State that extends a very popular

franchise to great towns, has a large agricultural population, there
is one direct mode,—it seems a very bold one,—but I know of no
other to correct that urban tendency of restless movement, which,
if altogether unchecked, allows no hope of durability to any existent form of Government. And that direct mode consists in
framing those electoral districts, of which we hear so much, on
such principles as fairly represent the proportions both of urban
and rural populations, and then admitting the working classes in
both by a similar low rate of franchise. This is the system
adopted, not only in America but in France. And Universal
Suffrage in France is, no doubt, a Conservative safeguard against
the democratic ascendancy of towns, because it calls on the rural
class to counterbalance those of the urban. And in order to
awaken the prudent reflection of the poorer classes, in the consequences of rash political change, and in order to enlist the
material interest of the working men thus enfranchised on the
side of property and established institutions, the profound sagacity
of the French Emperor devised a system of public loan or finance,
in which the working classes were tempted to invest their savings, and to save in order to invest, so that they have the direct
interest of the fund-holder in the safety of the Empire, and the
maintenance of public credit. But though that system of franchise works well in France for the interests of the Imperial throne
and its system of Government, surely the indirect modes by
which at present we in England endeavour to attain something
of the same counterpoise between rural and urban populations,
works better for English notions of freedom, and for the genuine
interest of that opinion which large towns represent. But it is
this indirect system in England which you are about to destroy;
and I cannot conceive any mode of representation more fatal to
the Conservative interest, more unfair to the proportions of property, intelligence, and even of population, which belong to it
and its natural ally, the rural class, than the mode which the
Government propose and commend for its moderation. In the
first place, according to this scheme the ultra liberal element in
the State is immensely strengthened by a borough franchise so
low and so elastic, that in a very few years it will not only

augment the preponderance of the operative class over the middle class, but the preponderance of the order of the poorer working men over those artisans who are better educated and better paid. For, do let us consider what manner of thing in a very few years will be a £7 house in towns. This is easily ascertained, if you will ask yourselves the very simple question, which I ventured to put to you when this subject was debated some years ago. What does a £7 house cost to build? A builder requires at least 7 per cent. for the capital he invests on building. A £7 house is therefore a house which is built for £100. But even in the provinces, where labour is comparatively cheap, a country gentleman cannot build a decent cottage for his rudest labourer for a £100. A cottage for a married man and his family cannot at present be built under from £120 to £130. Therefore the houses in the great towns, the occupiers of which will, in a few years, be the governing power of the country, must be greatly superior in point of the decent accommodation which morality and health require, to the rudest cottage a small country squire now-a-days builds for his rudest labourer. In proportion, therefore, as population and building extend, we may fairly presume that a £7 house in towns will be the very lowest tenement in which a working man above the grade of a pauper can possibly reside. Nay, even now in the metropolis a £7 rental so much implies, not merely poverty, but actual destitution, that in a list of instances of positive starvation, published under the head of "London Pauperism," in the newspapers a few weeks ago, in cases in which families were found without a blanket to cover them, the rent paid for the houses of these objects of charity varied from 2s. 6d. to 3s. 9d. a week, or from £6, 10s. to even £9 a year. It is impossible to look forward a few years, and not see that such an abasement of the borough franchise universally applied, must swamp not only the middle class but the higher order of educated artisans.

Sir, in the classical mythology there are two symbolical representatives of manual labour, the one is Vulcan, the skilled artificer, the child of Jove, the enemy of Mars, the benefactor of man. That is the archetype of the Educated Artisan, taking his high rank among the agencies, by the side of majestic Order. "Hinc avidus stetit Vulcanus—hinc Matrona Juno." But the other is that king of the Cyclops, "informe, ingens cui lumen ademptum." He is the archetype of an Uneducated Democracy, when it is made drunk and blind by any artful Ulysses, whose cunning can subjugate or delude its strength. I decline to enthrone this Cyclop.

While you thus intensify and augment the democratic element of the State, you do all you can to enfeeble and annul the only Conservative counterpoise. You begin by a county franchise just high enough to exclude those of the humbler classes whose interests and whose feelings are bound up with the land, and you lower to let in upon the agricultural electors a deluge of urban voters, not only without any sympathy with owners and occupiers of the soil, but who regard those owners and occupiers with the jealousy of an antagonistic class. It is a mere mockery, as the Member for Calne has so admirably said, to talk of your generosity in giving more members to counties, when all the counties themselves are thus to be converted into the electoral appendages of towns. As the franchise even now stands, in the Scotch system, we are told that the urban population of Glasgow is sufficient to carry four Scotch counties, and the spirit and object of your scheme is to plant a Glasgow in every county of England.

So much for the destruction of the Conservative counterpoise in counties. Now for the distribution of boroughs. Every one knows that as my right hon. Friend, the Member for Bucks, showed in a speech not less remarkable for its profound reasoning than its accurate knowledge of the subject, the representation of Conservative opinions is not confined to counties. Her Majesty's Government, therefore, duly considering how to manipulate the boroughs they deal with, so as to oust the Conservatives from that relative share in them which they at present possess, begin by an arbitrary line of population of 8000 inhabitants instead of 10,000—as to which, so far as regards fairness to the Conservative party, I leave the whole question to the unanswered speech of the Member for Belfast—next they naturally turn their eyes to

Scotland, and there they find a system of grouping boroughs by
which not a single Conservative member is returned to Parliament. "How does this system work in Scotland!" exclaims the
Chancellor of the Duchy, in a transport of enthusiasm. "Are
you dissatisfied with the result there; the result will be the
same in England." I don't doubt it. Accordingly, by way of
conciliating the Conservatives this is the system they trans-
plant into England, only with this increase of the severity of the
weapon they use against us, that instead of grouping round the
present parliamentary boroughs the unrepresented towns, the
rural districts and villages that lie nearest to it, and in which
there would be that congeniality of interests and sympathies
which is some check upon the undiscriminating passion for restless movement in urban democracies—they club together represented boroughs lying far apart, even in different counties, and
with no conceivable interest and sympathy in common. You
travel miles out of your way in order to swamp an agricultural
borough, sometimes by a seaport, sometimes by a manufacturing
town. Why sir, cohesion is necessary to identity, and the
chemist tells us that identity is destroyed by the separation of
its atoms. You do not destroy the identity of the water as
water, in this glass, if you add to it more water, with which
it naturally coheres. But if you separate its atoms, and turn it
into gas, its identity is destroyed though its atoms still exist—
they are presented by gas and not by water, and so an agricultural
borough would preserve its identity if added to a contiguous
homogeneous neighbourhood with which it naturally coheres, but
loses its identity when its atoms are separated, and appear twenty
miles apart in combination with a distant seaport or some remote manufacturing town. I need scarcely point out how injurious to the interest both of Conservatives and of moderate Liberals
—in fact to all candidates who belong to what we call the class
of independent private gentlemen—this mode of grouping is.
The increased expense alone would be injurious. The Lord
Advocate admits the expense, but then he says, "though the
expense may be greater the bribery will be less." But if you
club together two or three discordant boroughs already repre-

sented, and perhaps already partially corrupt, each with a separate staff of agents, each subjected to a severe contest, I cannot for the life and soul of me conceive how you can diminish corruption by creating a poorer and more needy class of electors, who will learn by a telegram every hour of the polling the rising value of the price of votes. No, these are the seats you withdraw from the ambition of private gentlemen of moderate means and opinions, and put up for sale to monied speculators who covet a seat in Parliament, as proffering to them a substantial advantage in the career of directors to companies, and contractors and speculative adventurers in that strange sort of commerce which pretends to unite limited liabilities with incalculable profits, and which is now a-days called " finance." Our ancestors gave it a ruder name. And as these strangers to the place having nothing to recommend them in local predilections or in distinguished names, will find their success more easy in proportion as they unite democratic sentiment with aristocratic expenditure, so most of these constituencies will be as much transferred to the anti-conservative interest as if they were additions made to the metropolitan boroughs. The members for Calne and Belfast are at a loss to discover the principle of this scheme. To me it seems founded on a twofold object. The first, and no doubt, the most important is, the preservation of Tavistock. Tavistock is sacred. What the consecrated territory of Elis was to Greece, Tavistock is to England. All the rest of the land may be at war, but no invading footstep must profane that little nook of ground " in remoto gramine." Amidst the general disorder and the general havoc, Tavistock, crowned with its double representation, smiles down upon us calm and sublime. The second object is to eliminate as far as possible that comparatively small national trifle, the Conservative principle from the representative system. That principle appears to be the most thoroughly eliminated in the metropolis and in the kingdom of Scotland. Accordingly, the Government significantly begin by an addition of four members to the metropolis and seven to Scotland, and then proceed to apply to the other constituencies a kind of franchise, a kind of grouping, and a kind of boundary

334 THE REFORM BILL OF 1866.

which may most surely realise the process of Conservative disfranchisement which is so successful in the metropolis and in
· the sister kingdom. And this is what Her Majesty's Government call a conciliatory compromise.

Now, I daresay in the eyes of many ultra Reformers out of
doors—it may appear that nothing can be better for the country,
nothing better for the Liberal interest, than the political extinction of the Conservative party. But no Liberal member of Parliament who has had as long an experience of the House as I
have, and who adds to that experience, as most Liberal members
at present do, the culture of an accomplished reasoner, will not
agree with the Member for Calne, that it would be a great evil
for the Liberal party if the Conservative were materially dimi-
nished, and this not only for the reason he states, that if you had
not an aristocratic party to deal with, you would be left free to
face with one purely Democratic, but because even the Democratic party would fall in pieces if it were not in some degree
united by the presence of a strong Conservative opposition.

It is the natural tendency of every movement party to subdivide itself into hostile sections wherever the presence of a
Conservative antagonist, they have in common, is withdrawn—
and it is in those subdivisions that liberty itself incurs its most
customary risk of destruction. It was so in the First Revolution of France when Liberals alone found their way into the
Convention, and wasted their destroying eloquence of hate upon
each other. It was so again in France during that last discordant Republic, which perished by the *coup d'état*. It was so in
our civil wars, when the Royalists were banished from the House,
and the feuds and squabbles of the conflicting Liberals had
their result, first, in the absolute usurpation of Cromwell ; and,
secondly, in the yet more degrading despotism which followed the
restoration of Charles II. Why, even now, one has only to look
at the other side of the House to see how many subdivisions
there now are, only kept from fighting with each other because
as yet there is a Conservative array strong enough to attract on
itself their stout English pugnacity. It was said by an illustrious
statesman, that political parties are like serpents, and are moved

by their tails. But if the parties opposite had not us to encounter, I fear they would be less like serpents than the famous
cats of Kilkenny, and nothing but their tails would be left.
There is, however, a fatal danger to the stability and the freedom
of any State, in which—through some party juggle in the legislative system—any very large portion, even though it be a
minority of the rank and intellect and property of the nation,
is despoiled of its legitimate share of participation in public
affairs. Now the chief, and indeed almost the only reason assigned for your £7 franchise, is the danger of excluding a certain
per centage of the poorer classes from the mere privilege of voting.
And upon that ground we are so willing to meet you that we are
ready to admit to the suffrage quite as many of the working class
as you tell us your Bill would admit. And the difference between
us is, that we think we could make that selection on principles
more just to the other orders of society and more benefical to the
working class itself. But if it be dangerous to exclude a mere
per centage of men of humbler means and education than belong
to any voters now enjoying the franchise, permit me to ask,
whether the danger to the State would not be infinitely greater, if,
seeing how large and substantial a thing the Conservative party
really is—its immense social proportion of culture and energy,
of wealth and rank—you devise a system of representation by
which you are to extend, throughout these kingdoms, the same
kind of virtual disfranchisement which awaits that Conservative
proportion of our people in the metropolis of England, and the
grouped boroughs of Scotland? Here you really would engender
a most serious and rankling, a wide spread and perilous spirit of
discontent among rich and powerful citizens, who could not be
long favourable to any form of Government which ignored their
claims and defrauded them of their just representation.

There is no political lesson more striking in Machiavelli's
great history of Florence, than the clearness with which he traces
those disorders which made the social misery of that commonwealth, even in the most brilliant period of its stormy existence,
to the original mistake of excluding from the Government of the
State a certain section of the nobler classes, who were regarded

and described by the advanced Liberals of Florence very much as the Member for Birmingham regards and describes the Conservatives of England. But that mistake of vilifying and seeking to ostracize fellow countrymen for the crime of being well born and well educated, which might be pardonable in a Florentine shopkeeper 700 years ago, is not pardonable in the 19th century, in an English gentleman, who adds to his many other distinctions that of an ardent admiration for the old times of the British Constitution.

Sir, to sum up what I have said—although I am sincerely anxious to settle this question of Reform in a fair and conciliatory spirit, I object to this scheme, first, because it is not a settlement at all even in the eyes of its advocates ; and even if it were so, it is not a settlement with which we, the Conservatives, could " rest and be thankful." It is so full, not only of those anomalies which must belong to every representative system, but anomalies more intolerable than those which already exist— some of them so evidently created by party spite and by party favour, that this measure could scarcely pass into law before the opinion of the country would demand a new Reform Bill, and Conservatives themselves might be the first to raise that demand. Secondly, Because though I have chiefly confined my argument to a plea on behalf of the intelligence, the property, the numbers which belong to the party called Conservative, yet the plea is equally on behalf of the genuine interests of the Liberal party, and of the freedom and safety of that country which we have in common. For I hope I have shown it is against the interest of both to reduce to the minimum, as you now propose, the principle and party to which the word Conservative applies. Even if you unjustly regard us merely as the drag-chain on the wheel of progress, the more you will miss the drag-chain the faster you go downward and always downward.

The Chancellor of the Exchequer has told us, that if by the rejection of this Bill the Government should fall, an avenger will arise out of their ashes. I venture to think that there is at least equal evidence in history for the prediction, that if the Bill is passed, and if a party in the nation immeasurably more insidious attain its object in the partial destruction of the Conservative party—out of our ashes an avenger will yet most certainly arise—an avenger more lastingly fatal to you, the Liberal party, than it is in the power of the most unscrupulous fanatic of reform to increase the injury by which this legerdemain trick of legislation seeks to conjure us out of sight. I would not give you nine years from the date in which you put an end to that kind of temperate Conservatism which now exists, before the force of circumstance would create an avenger, who, uniting popular attributes with an anti-liberal philosophy, would seeks to destroy all that is now understood by the enlightened name of Liberal,—by that appeal to the genuine democracy of numbers, rural as well as urban, which the daring genius of Count Bismarck at this moment desires to make, when he would crush down the Liberals of Prussia, not by bayonets and military force—the time has passed for that—but by the flesh and blood of Universal Suffrage.

"Time," said the Chancellor of the Exchequer, in that peroration which thrilled us all by the exquisite beauty of its diction and delivery—"Time," said the Chancellor of the Exchequer, "is on our side." It is so. Time is on the side of all destroyers. Time is on the side of every agency which resolves into their ancient conflict that union of every element which informs States and Nations with individual vitality and soul. Time, while we speak, is no doubt at his silent work upon this old Commonwealth of ours. Even at the moment when it will seem to posterity an act of madness on our part to hazard by experiments fatal to every ancient State in which they have hitherto been tried, the doctrines of a race which unites a freedom that seemed hopeless to the philosophers of Athens, a commerce that would have seemed a fable to the merchants of Tyre, with an empire unknown to the Roman Cæsars, and unconceived by the wildest dreams of Alexander. Yes, no doubt, time is upon your side. But time is the enemy and not the friend of genuine patriots and careful statesmen. For it is their task not to hasten, but delay to the longest period permitted to human hope and to human genius, the ultimate victory of Time in the decline and downfall of their native land.

To my humble reason it seems the duty of Ministers of the Crown, and Councillors to the people of England, to preserve a State not old enough for passive submission to decay, not young enough for violent innovation on its routine of habit, from those kill or cure experiments, which are only justified where the disease is terrible or where the life is worthless.

I decline to submit to such experiments this mature, but this healthful and noble Monarchy of England. I decline to range myself on the side of Time. Because on the side of Time as against States and Nations, are the agencies of corruption and the instruments of ruin.

XLIV.

OUTLINE OF A SPEECH

INTENDED TO HAVE BEEN DELIVERED IN

THE HOUSE OF LORDS

ON THE 23D OF JULY 1867.

On Monday the 22d of July 1867, the Prime Minister, the Earl of Derby, moved in the House of Lords the second reading of the Bill for the Representation of the People. A long amendment was thereupon moved by the Earl Grey, expressing reluctant assent to the second reading, in the hope, that in the future stages of the Bill it might be found capable of improvement. The debate was adjourned to the following day, Tuesday the 23d of July, when, after a good deal of discussion, the original motion was carried without a division. Upon the second night of the debate, the following speech was intended to have been delivered.

MY LORDS,—I feel that I have need of all the indulgence of the House in rising to address your Lordships for the first time. If I cannot hope to merit that indulgence, I will endeavour at least not to abuse it, by delaying your Lordships for more than a few minutes.

Whatever force we may give to the arguments so ably stated by the noble Viscount in his opening speech, he has made it clear that one result would attend the adoption of his amendment —that result is delay. Such a delay in passing any measure of Parliamentary Reform as would necessarily arise from re-opening the whole subject in the House of Commons. For the question of the franchise is connected with that of the redistribution of seats, as the noble Viscount allows, but connected in a manner which he does not appear to me to have clearly perceived. It is notorious to all—though the noble Viscount does not deign to observe it—that there are many members on both sides in the House of Commons who only gave their assent to the extension of the franchise proposed, upon the understanding that the disturbance of the existent seats would be moderate and limited, and that understanding made a part of the compromise by which the measure has passed through that branch of the Legislature.

If the Bill is to be sent back to the House of Commons, with the unexpected demand upon a much larger number of its members to sacrifice themselves and their constituencies, we take the best course to rekindle that kind of opposition which has for so many years obstructed the passage of a Reform Bill. Naturally enough all the members whose seats may be threatened by this indefinite proposition, will unite with all those whose fears of the proposed franchise are yet more excited by the awful prophecies uttered in your Lordships' House. And it is not exactly in the month of August that members of Parliament will be in the best humour for re-debating all the abstract principles and all the complicated details involved in this very vague, but very important amendment.

Those who belong to what is called the country party, will not unreasonably consider, that if you are to go into the question of redistribution on a large and bold scale, they are justly entitled, according to relative property or population, to demand a much larger number of county representatives than they at present possess, or than the scheme sanctioned by the Government awards to them.

They have been, hitherto, very reluctantly reconciled to their own defective share of representation by the argument, that their interests or opinions obtain some indirect and partial representation in the smaller boroughs. But there is no anomaly you can desire to correct, so great as the anomaly you would seek to perpetuate, if, upon the very ground of permanence and finality, you annihilate these smaller boroughs, remodel the constituency according to the principles of property and population, and then leave to the counties less than half the number of members which, according to those principles, statistics prove to be their due. Nor can this anomaly be met, nor the equilibrium of rival interests and opinions be adjusted by any device which the noble Viscount can suggest, unless carried to such an extent as would require another year for the construction of another scheme. But that would be a year of angry agitation—agitation carried on by masses of the populace in the heat and ferment of great towns—another year of such agitation would do more evil than the wisdom of centuries could retrieve.

And do not let us forget, as the noble Viscount seems to do, that the only popular agitation as to Reform has been with regard to the franchise, and not with regard to the redistribution of seats; and these agitators will take this amendment in connection with the speeches that have been made against the franchise proposed. They will not fail to observe that the noble Earl, the leader of the Whig party, has spoken with much dislike of a franchise so popular, and declared it to be a change very much for the worse. And the amendment now proposed with his approval, will, I fear, seem to the great mass of the working class a pretext that may serve to defer and to jeopardize the measure which accords to them a franchise that the supporters of the amendment do not cordially approve. No doubt that will be an unjust suspicion which only the less enlightened part of the community will entertain. Practised politicians will perhaps more charitably believe that the amendment is formed in consistent adherence to principle,—the principle of tactics which Mr Fox bequeathed to his successors, namely, that they would find it convenient to retain in the pigeon-holes of their bureaux a something or other about Parliamentary Reform, to be produced or supplied, like a something or other about Irish Church Reform—according as those successors might "rest and be thankful," that is in office— or be restless and dissatisfied, that is in opposition.

My Lords, I will not follow the noble Viscount through the articles of his dissent from the scheme of the House of Commons,

much as I might be tempted to show the objections to which I
think they are exposed, because no man of ordinary experience
and discretion would like to discuss off-hand the principles or
details of a plan affecting future generations which is so loosely
outlined in the programme of an opening speech. But let us
look to the main argument in favour of this amendment. The
argument is, that if we do not effect a larger and bolder scheme
of redistribution now, that subject will be immediately re-opened
by a new Parliament, upon a scale much more extensive and
much more hazardous. My Lords, I think that this apprehension is not well founded. I believe, with Lord Macaulay, that
the law of re-action proceeds in the political world as it does in
the natural, and that after a vast organic change just completed,
you will find that the public of a commercial, manufacturing, and
intellectual commonwealth, will be very much inclined to enjoy
a little repose, and very averse to favour any attempts to disturb
the normal course of legislation, disquiet the operations of industry, capital, and trade, and convulse the peace of the country
by a new agitation for a new Reform Bill. In fact, the true reason
why this measure has been suffered to reach your Lordships is
not from any general desire of organic innovation, but rather from
a fact which many of us seek to disguise from ourselves, the fact '.
that the public is heartily sick of the whole question, and that
having once satisfied the claims of the artisans to the franchise, it
is firmly resolved that Parliamentary Reform shall not again be
lightly made the shuttlecock of rival competition for power.

I daresay much may be said about redistribution of seats at the
hustings, and candidates may as well talk about that as about anything else. But I cannot believe that members returned after the
next general election, will meet on the floor of the House of Commons with a heroic resolve to pass any measure which must crimi-
nate the Parliament to which they have just been elected, and
prematurely restore them to the pure but expensive embrace of a
populous constituency; and such is the infirmity of human nature,
that a desire to retain their own seats for the natural lifetime of the
Parliament to which they are returned, will probably correct the
impatience of the ardent Liberals to redispose of the seat of others.

But if I am mistaken in these suppositions, and the next Parliament should be as much bent upon Democratic innovations as some of your Lordships apprehend, would its appetite for change be gorged and sated with the twelve boroughs by which the noble Earl flatters himself that he propitiates the Cerberus to whom he administers that dose? No, rely upon it, that any scheme of redistribution which your Lordships would favour and the present House of Commons would pass, will be as unsatisfactory to the next Parliament, if that Parliament be such as the noble Viscount anticipates and fears, and therefore as little likely to be permanent as the measure which, in the opinion of the present House of Commons, meets the practical requirements of the time. I will add further, that against any very extensive scheme of redistribution, there is always this safeguard, that it cannot, as I have said, be justly effected without giving a much larger proportion to those agricultural constituencies which are considered to be the least democratic. I believe that the wisest men among the leaders of the movement are thoroughly aware of this fact; and, indeed, I have heard more than one of them express an opinion which is probably well founded, that even the scheme of electoral districts, with which we have been threatened as the ultimate goal of Democracy, would act in this country as it acts in France, so as to diminish the influence of the great towns, and increase that kind of influence which is called territorial.

For all these reasons I think we may vote against the noble Viscount's amendment, without any misgivings as to a reasonable element of durability in the scheme of redistribution approved by the House of Commons and sanctioned by the government. Certainly, without any belief that a scheme upon the details of which it is clear that the noble Viscount has not made up his own mind, would be one whit more permanent than that which his amendment condemns.

And I am strengthened in my distaste for the noble Viscount's amendment, by my persuasion that though your Lordships have the most perfect right to deal with any question that affects the mixed constitution of these realms, yet that the noble Viscount and the noble Earl select in their amendments, that special point of Parliamentary Reform on which it would be wise and gracious in your Lordships not to push your constitutional right to a dictatorial extreme.

It is well known to us all, that the great difficulty in dealing with Parliamentary Reform has been that of inducing members to immolate their constituencies and destroy their own seats. And considering that, at least, the House of Commons does send us up a measure by which forty-five of their members have been sacrificed on the altar of their country, it does seem rather a stern proceeding on the part of noble Lords, safe in the hereditary possession of their own Parliamentary seats, to insist upon a more general slaughter, on the floor of the House of Commons, and ask unsuspecting Members, just escaping to the moors, to become themselves the victims of that more inhuman sport to which they are so insiduously invited.

I really think that the precise number of Heads to be rendered up as a poll-tax to Proserpine may be prudently left to that branch of the Legislature from which the Heads are exacted. And that if we adopt the amendment of the noble Viscount or of the noble Earl, we should establish a precedent which might be dangerously brought to bear against ourselves should the House of Commons, in its turn, ever volunteer its dictation, as to the precise amount of sacrifice which its views of reform might demand from the members of this august assembly.

My Lords, I think that this Reform Bill, taken as a whole,— franchise and redistribution altogether—is quite as large an innovation as any reasonable man can desire. I confess, for my part, that I consent, or rather submit to it with great reluctance, and I am only reconciled to it by the conviction at which I believe most of your Lordships have also arrived, that the time has come when the question of Reform must be settled, and that the scheme to which both parties have agreed in the House of Commons has become the only mode by which that settlement can be practically effected. Still, though I regard the probable results of the measure with deep anxiety, I have not hitherto shared in those fears which have been expressed here and elsewhere, with that eloquence which is never more imposing than when it assumes the attributes of superstition, and peoples the dark with spectres. But if by amendments like this, we are, under the pretext of aiming at an impossible finality, to unsettle that which the House of Commons had unanimously settled, and reversing the natural functions of the two Houses of Parliament, make this branch of the Legislature rebuke the other for being too temperate and covetous in its distribution of the existent constitution, then I shall begin to dread lest the gloomy predictions we have heard should be accompanied by that want of prudence by which fate has sometimes allowed to mortals the fulfilment of their own prophecies of evil. But I do not believe that prudence is a virtue which will ever desert the acknowledged sagacity and moderation which characterize your Lordships' councils, and I think that that virtue will never be more usefully exercised than in declining to incur the difficulties, the embarrassments, the hazards to which we are so needlessly invited.

Here, my Lords, I should close my remarks with a grateful sense of the indulgence your Lordships have shown me, were it not for that kind of attack which the noble Viscount has made upon my noble friend at the head of the Government. I have implied or said, and I should be disingenuous or insincere if I had not done so, that I have no great admiration for the new Reform Bill. But that which I do cordially admire is the courage and frankness with which my noble Friend has exposed himself to the eloquence of sarcasm from an honest conviction that, under all the circumstances, he has done his best for the interests of the country, believing that with the interests of the country must be identified the interests of any party which claims him as its leader. My Lords, let us hope, not for his sake, but for the sake of that country which he adorns and advises, that a measure which so largely extends the foundations of the representative system, may only give additional stability to the fabric it supports, and thus ensure his lasting claims to the national gratitude which animates the ambition of patriots and consecrates the renown of statesmen.

XLV.

OUTLINE OF A SPEECH

INTENDED TO HAVE BEEN DELIVERED IN

THE HOUSE OF LORDS

ON THE 3D OF JUNE 1869.

On Friday the 9th of April 1869, the Earl Russell moved in the House of Lords the first reading of the Life Peerages' Bill, when it was read accordingly after some discussion. The second reading was carried in like-manner after a single night's debate, on Tuesday the 27th of April. Eventually, however, after having passed with several modifications through committee, the Bill was thrown out at its last stage, the Earl of Malmesbury, having on Thursday the 8th of July, when it came on for a third reading, moved by way of amendment, that it should be read that day three months. Upon a division the original motion was lost by 106 to 76. On the first night's discussion of the measure, clause by clause, in committee, the following speech was intended to have been delivered.

My Lords,—It is with great diffidence that I venture to trespass upon your Lordships' attention for a very few minutes upon a question on which there are so many far better qualified to express an opinion. But I think it is generally allowed that one great cause of strength and durability to the institution of the House of Lords is to be found in the theoretical principle, that its honours are accessible to every subject who has rendered adequate services to the country, or exhibited talents of a nature to which a seat in the Upper House of Parliament is an appropriate recognition and reward. And the more completely that theoretical principle can be carried out in practice, the wider, of course, will be the range of persons who feel an interest in the maintenance of the institution. At present, however, the theoretical principle has, no doubt, this obstacle or drawback in practice—that the possession of landed estates, as that kind of property most readily transmitted from father to son, is an essential condition in bestowing hereditary distinctions and privileges. And hence arises the difficulty, that if the conditions be too rigidly observed, the theoretical principle, that the honours of your Lordships' House are open to merit, would be practically too much confined to merit accompanied with property; and if, on the other hand, the condition be too frequently neglected, the order of the Peerage would necessarily become impaired, not only in dignity but in strength. For it is indispensable to an hereditary Upper Chamber, that it should be regarded on the whole as a body of councillors with so great a stake in the permanent interests of the country, as to render them careful to preserve a just equilibrium between too timid a concession and too obstinate a resistance to that spirit of change, which, whether for good or for evil, is the characteristic of a popular assembly. And I need scarcely say, that a nobility impoverished as a body, could not ensure that influence and command that respect which are necessary to the existence of an hereditary aristocracy. For these reasons I venture to think that the power of the Crown would be wisely exercised in a limited creation of Life Peerages, such as is now proposed,—thus on the one hand extending the range of ambition to all public services and intellectual distinction; and on the other hand, securing the Peerage as a hereditary institution from the dangers which result from a separation between rank and property.

It has been said that no one will care for a Peerage that he cannot transmit to his descendants. I believe, on the contrary, that whoever may hold the office of first Minister, will find candidates for that honour so numerous, that I do not envy him the painful task of selection. I do not doubt for a moment that public men of high eminence and great capacities for business, but with small comparative fortune, will feel sensibly alive to a distinction exclusively achieved by merit, and freed from the necessity of inflicting upon their sons the burthen of a title without adequate means of supporting it. I put aside altogether the notion that men so elected to this House will not receive from your Lordships a degree of consideration equal to that with which you listen to the representatives of the largest estates and the most illustrious titles. I have not been long in this House, but I have seen enough of it to feel convinced that there is no assembly in the world, no, not even the House of Commons, in which a man is more valued for that which he is himself, and in which character, eloquence, and knowledge, have less need of superior felicity in the accidents of birth and fortune in order to ensure influence and authority. And this conviction brings me to the consideration of another advantage which I think the creation of a limited number of Life Peers will bestow upon the general institution of the hereditary Peerage. We have seen it stated in some of the public journals that the selection of Life Peers on the ground of special merit or distinction, will cause a comparison between Life Peers so selected and the hereditary members of your Lordships' House. I rejoice to think that comparison will be provoked; for I am persuaded that the result will be to show that the hereditary members of your Lordships' House need not fear competition with any Life Peers, however carefully selected; and the comparison, therefore, will tend to elevate the character of the hereditary Peerage in public estimation, and this not on account of any temporary circumstance by which at this moment so large an amount of intellectual capacity is found on both sides of this House, but because of the very nature of the hereditary Peerage in this country, as distinguished from the mere titular nobility of the continent—because of the care with which the representatives of great names in this country are usually educated and trained towards a participation in public affairs—because of those habits of business which the supervision of great estates, or the cultivation of the active duties which are essential to the maintenance of territorial influence tend to create; and because of that previous discipline in the House of Commons through which

so large a number of those who are afterwards hereditary legislators are brought into close connection with all classes of their
countrymen, and habituated to consider and decide between the
conflicting varieties of political opinion.

Now, I think that the more obviously these attributes of the
hereditary members as at present constituted in England be
forced upon public acknowledgment by the test of competition
with the best men whom a Government can select for the dignity
of the Life Peerage, the more the advantages resulting from the
general constitution of this House will be made apparent, and
the more discouraged will become all speculative theories for the
substitution of a senile or Upper Chamber constructed upon adverse principles.

While thus agreeing with the general prospect and object of
the Bill before your Lordships, I venture to think it would be
expedient somewhat to diminish the number proposed, whether
as a definite total or as the number chosen for each year. Certainly the number proposed is not too large for all the eminent
commoners in England, but it seems to me too large for the
eminent men to whom a seat in a legislative assembly would be
an appropriate distinction. And I need scarcely say that the
fewer the number the more the honour will be coveted and the
principle of the Bill will be attained. This, however, is a mere
matter of detail. I shall cordially vote for the second reading
of the Bill, believing, for the reasons I have stated, that it will
tend to strengthen your Lordships' House in the confidence and
affection of the people, enlist in its support the ambition of a
wider range of intellect and energy, and prove by the competition it accepts and courts, the value and amount of those quali-
fications for the functions assigned to an Upper Chamber, which
the hereditary principle secures to your Lordships' House.

XLVI.

OUTLINE OF A SPEECH

INTENDED TO HAVE BEEN DELIVERED IN

THE HOUSE OF LORDS

ON THE 15TH OF JUNE 1869.

On Monday the 14th of June 1869, the Leader of the House of Lords, Earl Granville, moved in that chamber the second reading of the Irish Church Bill. At the close of that night's discussion the debate was adjourned upon the motion of Lord Lytton, until the following day, Tuesday the 15th of June. The House met in that expectation. Upon the order of the day being read, however, for resuming the debate, the Earl Grey rising, opened his speech in the following words—"My Lords, before addressing myself to the remarks which I have to make on the question before the House, I may perhaps be permitted to apologise to the noble Lord behind me (Lord Lytton), for standing, as I am about to do, for a short time, between him and the House. I am quite aware of how much more worth his observations will be than mine; but by way of explanation I beg to say, that I rose to move the adjournment last night, not knowing that he was about to do the same, and that being, as I believe, in possession of the House, I gave way because I understood that he was going to speak on that occasion. As this was not his intention, I hope there is no want of courtesy in my now availing myself of my claim to priority from having risen first to move the adjournment last night. I trust the noble Lord will accept this explanation." But for the contretemps thus accounted for upon that occasion, the following speech would then have been delivered.

MY LORDS,—It seems to me that the great difficulty of dealing with this question is one which demands a clear and definite understanding of the relations between England and Ireland. These relations are not merely political—they are not merely religious. But the political and the religious relations have become so complicated and so interwoven, that it requires the finest statesmanship to extricate and divide them. On the one hand, a very large numerical population is Roman Catholic, and in the midst of that population is planted a Protestant Church, with endowments, perhaps greatly exaggerated, but still large when we consider that it is the Church of the few imposed upon the religion of the many, and that the religion of the many is absolutely without any ecclesiastical endowment at all. Nor can any defence for an anomaly so great in the elements of free government be advanced upon the plea that this Church of the few has so brilliantly succeeded in making converts and proselytes, that we may hope it will ultimately become the Church of the many. If we could here, as educated men willing to do justice without prejudice and favour, close the question at issue, there is but one conclusion at which we could arrive. But, my Lords, having thus stated fairly, I hope, that side of the question opposed to the Protestant endowments, it is essential to state no less impartially the other side.

It is true that this Protestant Church is the Church of the comparative few in point of numbers, but then the payment of it falls upon property, and is favoured and cherished by the majority of the holders of property. Here you at once encounter a difficulty in itself amongst the greatest which a statesman can deal with. Property on the one side and Numbers on the other. The difficulty becomes excessively aggravated when you have also to consider that England and Ireland form an United Empire, and that the Protestants, though a minority in Ireland, form the vast majority in the three kingdoms of which that empire is composed. Still more is it complicated when there is no denying the fact that the Protestants in Ireland constitute the only portion of the Irish population firmly attached to the Union—the only men you can rely upon in case of civil rebellion and foreign invasion, and that if you inflict upon them any substantial and permanent cause of discontent, you lose every friend you have in the sister island. Nor can any experienced politician for a moment believe that if by a vote of the legislature you annihilated the Protestant Church to-morrow you would propitiate the Roman Catholic population. They would only consider that they had conquered your strongest garrison, and were a step nearer to the realization of their dream—the dream of a sovereign commonwealth independent of all connection with England. I do not pause to ask why this should be. No doubt plenty of causes may be found in old historical grievances, an ample reply to those allegations might be given if the Irish majority were the same race as ourselves. The English people have had plenty of grievances under their own rulers—under Normans, Plantagenets, Tudors, and Stuarts. But these grievances are things of the past with England—they would be things of the past with Ireland, if the past was not always present to a people who only look to the future with a wish to get rid not of their grievances but of their rulers. It is not with the majority of the indigenous Irish population a question whether they shall be well or ill governed. Ask any one of them, and he will give you the same answer as the people of the Ionian Islands gave to all attempts to prove how much better off they were under an English than under a Greek monarchy, that answer was—" Granted : but we prefer being ill governed by men of our own race, whom we choose ourselves, than well governed by the constraint of a race with which we have no relationship and no sympathy." That is what the genuine Irishman will tell you. And do you suppose that he will be a whit more reconciled to your domination because you alienate your supporters and abandon your stronghold ?

These are questions, my Lords, which, on both sides, I humbly think, are not unworthy of your deliberate consideration, and these indeed are the questions which, secretly entertained but not openly avowed by the leaders of party on both sides, have retarded any earnest attempt to deal with the Irish Church.

But are we for that reason to fold our arms and do nothing. My Lords, I think that is no longer possible. I believe it would not be desirable, it would not become a nation at the head of the world— not in military power, not in the influences which are exercised by arms and arts, but in the opinion which prevails throughout civilized communities—that England, though sufficiently careful of the treasure and the blood of her people, tenacious of her rank as the parent of free states, and anxious to do what is right and just, not for the sake of future gain, but for the sake of right and justice. And it is right and just that we should manfully face the difficulties of the question, and endeavour, so far as we can, considering the unhappy nature of the circumstances, to decide impartially between two parties in the sister kingdom—a minority in point of numbers, but preponderant in point of property—and invariably faithful to England, and a vast numerical majority, whom no measure respecting the Church is likely to conciliate to our rule. What, under these circumstances, should we do? That which every judge on the bench does, that which most men in private life are compelled to do every day.

My Lords, I feel how much I need all your indulgence in addressing your Lordships for the first time, and on a question on which so many have a far better claim to be heard. But I am unwilling to give a vote on the principle of this Bill, without explaining the views I have of it, and offering some remarks upon the policy of which it has been made part and parcel.

Lord Melbourne said in supporting the first Reform Bill of 1831—that up to that time, wherever the flag of Parliamentary Reform had been hoisted, he had ranged himself under the opposite banner, and gone beyond others in repelling every approach to Reform—and he then proceeded to enforce the distinction between an abstract dislike to incur the hazards of a great change, so long as the people were undecided on its merits, and the practical wisdom of declining to incur the far greater hazards of resistance wherever the will of the people was unequivocally pronounced. My Lords, this must often be the case with the statesmen of an Upper Chamber, of which the highest attribute is that prudence which consults the safety of the nation ; firstly, by ensuring ample opportunities to ascertain its opinion ; and secondly, by avoiding its angry collision between all the elements of government, which an obstinate resistance to that opinion would create. For though it may often be the duty of the House

of Lords to differ from the House of Commons, it is not in the
nature of things that such an assembly should insist pertina-
ciously in differing from the nation in whose interests it has so
vast a stake. The excellence of its judgment consists in the
Upper Chamber in determining where the House of Commons is
or is not on any question in general accordance with the policy
of the nation it theoretically represents.

What are the circumstances under which this Bill is submitted to your Lordships? The main principle of the Bill, on
the Disestablishment and Disendowment of the Irish Church was
distinctly set forth last year by the powerful party which have
now embodied it in this measure. It was opposed with great
ability by the late Government, and referred by them to the new
constituency which their Reform Bill had created, referred to
with all the advantages which are possessed by an administration that has the dissolution of Parliament in its hands. The
principle at stake was made clear at every hustings, and the result is, that that principle has been affirmed, and the Bill passed,
not only by a singularly large majority of the House of Commons, but a majority elected by the very constituency which the
Conservative Government opposing it had called into existence
in order to ensure a fuller and more perfect representation of
public opinion.

Under such circumstances I venture to submit that any legislative assembly which serves the purpose of an Upper Chamber,
even were it framed, like the Senate of the American Republic,
for the express purpose of acting as a check upon the democratic
tendencies of a popular chamber, and armed with all the special
powers for that purpose which are invested in the American
Senate, would be indisposed to reject the second reading of a Bill,
on which the will of the electoral population was so unmistakably
expressed—and would rather reserve the exercise of its independent judgment for the consideration of such amendments proposed
in Committee, as accepting the principle, might more equitably
adjust its details. For assuming that the measure is not without some evils in itself, those evils might only be aggravated, and
fresh evils created, by a rejection which could not be continued

for more than another year without bringing legislation to a dead lock. The agitation that would attend that delay would not be confined to this question alone—it would extend to other questions connected with its substance, or rising out of its rejection. It is a delay that would thus strengthen the hands of the ultra democratic party in England, while in Ireland it would afford new excuses for denouncing the proprietors of land, to whose influence the rejection of the Bill would be largely ascribed. And to judge by speeches made during the late general election, this agitation would be the more dangerous to the State, inasmuch as it would find its most eloquent leaders in Members of the Government, which, according to the theory of the constitution ought to repress it. Your Lordships may remember that in the course of our war with the American provinces, Lord North said pathetically, " I don't know if our Generals frighten the enemy, but I know that they frighten me." My Lords, I don't know if the speeches of our minister frighten the disaffected, but I know that they are enough to frighten the loyal. And what those speeches may be between this year and the next, if your Lordships should reject this Bill—our experience of the past may enable us to imagine. Seeing then that it can be but a question of time, whether the principle contained in this Bill should be suspended or approved, I come to this conclusion, that this delay is not worth the evils that would attend it, and that the sooner the question is settled the better for the peace of England and the welfare of Ireland. Such being the case, I own that I would fain do in this matter as we do in private life, whenever circumstances compel us to make a choice which we do not altogether approve, and look on the brighter side of the question. But it is not our fault if the brighter side of the question be exceedingly obscured. For my part I have never been a partisan of the Irish Church as at present constituted, I am willing to grant that there is much force in the abstract arguments by which that Church has been assailed. To establish and endow a Church, the religious creed of the great majority in one of the United Kingdoms, is opposed, and to refuse all aid to the Church to which that majority belong, is a policy we find it difficult to defend before foreign nations, and at variance with the spirit of the age. But still, it is a grave thing for any Christian monarchy to refuse all sanction and all aid to any form of religion whatever. It is indeed a thing which no Christian monarchy has yet done. And when the statesmen of foreign nations have blamed our policy with regard to the Protestant Church in Ireland, they have invariably recommended the adoption of their own practice. For instance, in Prussia and other German States, where, in some parts of their dominions there was a majority of one creed opposed to the creed of the Imperial State as a State, they have not disestablished both Churches, but have sanctioned and aided both, and you will find in the same district the Protestant clergy and the Catholic priests equally aided by the State, and living together in the most perfect amity and concord. It is said that a sentiment peculiar to a Protestant population forbade the solution of the difficulty which was recommended by Mr Pitt and Mr Burke, and favoured by many eminent statesmen of the Liberal party, and which was urged in vain upon the Liberal Government in 1866, in a very remarkable speech by the noble Earl on the cross benches. And thus no option was left between a very large reform of the Irish Church and its complete disestablishment. I should infinitely have preferred the former course—the country has decided on the latter. Well, but in carrying out that decision, which effects so vast a revolution in the sister kingdom, it seems to me that there were these two requisites for safe and honest legislation— First, that the most careful distinction should be made between private endowments and the national property, and that you should not pass by a hair's-breadth the boundary that divides what the State gave for State purposes, and that which individuals granted and bequeathed in trust for specific objects of their own. Secondly, that in dealing so largely and so sternly with a subject which must more or less alarm Protestants on behalf of their religion and proprietors on behalf of their property, the Government of the country should do their utmost to mitigate that alarm, and to dispel all notions that they seek the humiliation and downfall of the Protestant faith, nor will abet any wild schemes for the dispossessing men of the property they lawfully hold. I find neither of those requisites in the course adopted by Her Majesty's Government. I take one instance of their disregard for the first. You date the acknowledgment of private endowments from the restoration of Charles II.—1660—and confiscate as State property all the private endowments between that date and the Reformation. And upon what plea? Why, according to the Right Hon. Gentleman at the head of the Government, the ecclesiastical constitution of the Protestant Episcopal Church was not identical with the Church of England before 1660. My Lords, I maintain that this assertion is wholly without foundation. Go back a century, go back to 1560. In that year, as your Lordships well know, the Earl of Sussex, sent to Ireland by Queen Elizabeth, convenes a General Assembly of the Prelates and Clergy, for the establishing an identity between the Church of England and the Church of Ireland, in acknowledging the legal power in ecclesiastical affairs, and the adoption of the English Ritual instead of the Roman Catholic—nineteen prelates were present, and out of that number only two opposed these regulations. The clergy, as a body, offered no opposition to them; and from that date, in all the essential points which constitute a Church, the Churches became identical. In proof of this you will find the ecclesiastical dignitaries were exchanged from one kingdom to another, as they might have been exchanged from one English diocese to another. In 1582 a Bishop of Waterford is translated to St David's; in 1593 a Dean of York is made Bishop of Limerick, and again re-translated to England as Bishop of Bristol, and afterwards of Worcester. Would this interchange have been possible if the two Churches had not been considered identical. But all private endowments bestowed on the Irish Church during this sixteenth century are to be disallowed, and why? Because certain Calvinistic doctrines as to predestination and grace—originating not in the Irish Church, but in the English Church, which had borrowed them from Geneva, favoured by English archbishops, by other prelates, and by large numbers of the English clergy, and especially favoured by the English University of Cambridge, as set forth in the famous Articles of Lambeth—naturally travelled to Ireland, and were, in

the year 1615, received into the Irish Church. But so little did
they take root there, that nineteen years afterwards a canon was
passed by the whole body of the Irish Church, with only one
vote against it, approving and receiving the Thirty-Nine Articles
of the Church of England, and proclaiming the agreement of the
Church of England and Ireland in the profession of the same
faith, according to the Convention held in London in 1562, and
that agreement has continued in force up to the present day.
Is it not then, a monstrous act of spoliation to sieze upon all private endowments granted between 1560 and 1660, upon the pretext that for nineteen years out of a space of three centuries, the
Irish Church had accepted certain speculative doctrines that had
been previously favoured by English prelates and an English
university. Why, my Lords, in our civil wars the English Parliament abolished the English Episcopal Church, and proclaimed
the Presbyterian. But, if you were now legislating for the English Church instead of the Irish, would you deny the sanctity of
private endowments from the date of the Reformation or that of
Elizabeth, upon the plea that for a certain number of years the
English Episcopal Church was held, as it were, in suspense ?
No, my Lords, surely we cannot accept a quibble of this kind
as a substantial reason for robbing the Protestant faith of endowments conferred by men who did not distinguish the exact
points of theological difference between Calvinists and Luther-
ans, but who regarded the Protestant Episcopal Church, both in
Ireland and in England, as constituting one and the same fortress and defence of the Reformed religion against the doctrines
and ritual of the Church of Rome. But when another pretext
for this spoliation is found in the assertion, that some portion of
the private endowments before 1660, might be claimed by the
Presbyterians, and all such endowments are therefore to be denied to the Episcopal Protestants, the iniquity becomes still
more glaring. Because, it is making the claims of one party the
excuse for defrauding both parties; or, in other words, it is robbing Peter in order not to pay Paul. I content myself with
this one instance for that disregard for justice and the sanctity of
private rights and bequests, without enlarging on others which

will be better discussed in committee, and by noble Lords better qualified to treat them. But I must observe in passing, that there appears throughout this Bill a general spirit of animosity against that form of religion which our Protestant Church represents, in comparison with the Roman Catholic—a desire to eradicate the one and to nourish the roots of the other. For instance, capitalization of funds implies permanence. That element of permanence granted to Maynooth is denied to the Protestant preachers of the gospel; and whereas, by the Charitable Bequests Act, an unlimited grant of land is allowed to the Roman Catholic priesthood, the Bill limits the acquisition of land, even by purchase, for the Protestant clergy, to ten acres at the utmost, and thirty acres for the houses attached to sees. The apparent animus of these and similar provisions, is not that of ensuring equality between the two religions, but of initiating a policy that favours the restriction and decay of the Protestant Church, and the permanence and spread of the Roman Catholics; and I think this animus or condemnation will be more apparent when we come to consider the manner in which Her Majesty's Government have regarded that which I have ventured to call the second requisite for safe and honest legislation.

Now, it seems to me that in proposing a measure for the abolition of the Irish Church, a statesman so eminent as the present first Minister might naturally remember, that this Church, whatever its defects, is endeared to the large majority of proprietors in the country, those proprietors of a race akin to our own, settled in that country for many centuries, and encouraged to settle by a continuous series of British statesmen down to the time of Sir Robert Peel, who placed among the most prominent benefits of the encumbered Estates Bill, the probability that British agriculturists would invest their capital in the purchase of Irish lands. And I should have supposed that the chief advisers of the Crown would have deemed it politic and certainly just to convince these Protestant proprietors that in abolishing an ecclesiastical establishment at variance with the creed of the population, he was animated by no hostility to their influence as Protestants or their rights as proprietors. But what says the Right Hon. Gentleman to these Protestants and these proprietors? Virtually he say, "Do not flatter yourselves that the destruction of your Church is the only evil I have in store for you. That is but one of a group of questions. There is the land of Ireland, there is the education of Ireland, many questions, all of which depend upon one greater than them all; they are all so many branches of one trunk, and that trunk is the tree of what is called Protestant ascendency. It is upon that system that we are banded together to make war." My Lords, I do not ask whether this is the kind of language which the chief Minister of the Crown should address to men who had hitherto been the most stedfast friends of the Union; but I do ask whether the policy embodied in this language is one which the people of England intended to support when they gave their assent to the disestablishment of the Irish Church? What is this Protestant ascendency against which you are banded together to make war? What are its constituent elements apart from the ecclesiastical establishment which we are told has rather impeded than extended its growth? Is it not an ascendency derived from causes which give legitimate ascendency to any class of men in any civilised community, causes which every enlightened commonwealth rejoices to find the sources of influence and power, superior property, superior habits of intellectual discipline and conduct, superior immunities from crime, superior veneration for law? Is it against an ascendency derived from these causes that a Protestant Cabinet is banded together to make war? Is this the ascendency that you liken to the Upas tree, under which culture must wither and life must perish? Enter those parts of Ireland in which that ascendency most prevails, enter the great province of Ulster: there indeed you find strong and flourishing this tree that you pledge yourselves to destroy, root and branch, and under its shadow agriculture flourishes, trade prospers, property is sacred, life is safe. Is it this which is really the Upas tree? Or is the tree under which culture withers and life perishes most found in districts where the Protestant ascendency vanishes, and a Romish

ascendency prevails. My Lords, I had hitherto supposed that it
was the boast and pride of England that she represented in
Europe that Protestant ascendency which your Protestant kindred represent in Ireland—the ascendency of a Protestant few in
the midst of a Roman Catholic many, and derived exactly from
the same causes, causes which have their root in that training
of the human mind untrammelled by priestly domination, which
it seems the nature of the Protestant form of worship to discipline
and direct in every land where it offers its sacred counterpoise
between ignorant superstition and cynical unbelief. In the war
that is thus threatened I am not prepared to enlist as a soldier,
nor can I believe that the people of England will rally round its
standard. I do not know whether in consenting to this measure
they are prepared to regard it only as one of a group of questions
that form a general crusade against whatever ascendency, property, education, or attachment to law or order may have given
to Protestant settlers of the English race. It is declarations of
this kind which compel us to enlarge the scope of our survey
from the abolition of the Church Establishment to the threatened
attacks against Protestantism and property, of which it is thus
avowedly the precursor, and I therefore make no excuse if I do
so though in very few words. My Lords, it is idle for men to
say that they do not give encouragement to the spoliation or the
murder of landlords, so long as they proclaim the doctrine, that
if Ireland were separated from England, the conduct of the landlords is such that they would be at once exterminated by the
vengeance of the people. Your Lordships may remember the
story of the Quaker, who said to the dog that displeased him,
" Friend, my principles forbid me to shed thy blood, but I will
give thee a bad name," he shouted, " Mad dog," and the dog was
exterminated by the vengeance that bad name had provoked.
But, my Lords, I do not wish to attach undue importance to
any mere indiscretions of language into a man of impulsive
genius, little accustomed to the restraints of office, like the President of the Board of Trade, may have been hurried away by the
rush of his own eloquence. But, coupling his reported belief
and emphatic declaration that justice cannot be done to Ireland

but by the process of such a change as may take the soil from
those who possess, and transfer it to those who covet it, with the
vague threats against the property of Protestants volunteered by
the head of the Government, and his intimation that it would be
desirable to institute the experiment of dividing land among
small proprietors, I would ask your Lordships, I would ask the
country, while it is yet time, to consider if this be a policy in
the right direction—whether for the prosperity or for the peace
of Ireland? As for the prosperity—is not the interest of the
community proportional to the produce obtained from the land,
and is not that produce proportioned to the capital judiciously
expended upon it? And how can you expect prosperity from
any scheme that would transfer the land to owners with no
capital at all, and starting with that load which breaks the back
of any small farmer in England—the incubus of a debt which he
incurs for his purchase, and which has the first claim upon
savings that should be expended on improvements. And now
as to the peace of the country, if you tell the people of Ireland
that justice requires that a landlord, not tracing his descent to
Celtic ancestors, should sell his property for the benefit of those
whose pedigree is lost in the night of ages, and form legislative enactments to effect that kind of justice—reflect on the encouragement you give to agrarian violence! Suppose the landlord refuses to sell, suppose that in this he resembles the owner
of land in England, and indeed pretty generally throughout
Europe, and would not take 10 or 20 per cent. above the market value for property endeared to him by all his associations
and habits—what an inducement you give to his Celtic neighbour to exterminate a landlord so insensible to Celtic justice! I
firmly believe that by any scheme of this sort the murder of
landlords and their agents would no longer be the monopoly of
a few privileged districts, but would extend to every part of
Ireland in which a Saxon landlord and a Celtic population can
be found. Nay, I even doubt whether a Roman Catholic landlord, though he might be descended from Brian Boru, would
not soon find his tenantry and peasants dissatisfied with an
exclusion from the benefits bestowed upon the tenants and

peasants of the Saxon intruder. My Lords, I warn Her Majesty's
Ministers that so long as they identify justice to Ireland with
schemes for a transfer of land calculated to inflame the poor with
the hopes of dividing the land of the rich, so long may they
despair of establishing respect for the normal laws of property,
or reverence for the sanctity of human life.

No, my Lords, in assenting to the principle of a Bill by which
the Irish Church is disestablished and disendowed, I would
rather console myself by the convictions of an opposite nature,
which I believe are shared by the majority of those who register-
ed their votes in favour of that principle at the last election. I
would fain believe that the Protestant faith, relieved from whatever invidious character a Protestant Church Establishment
amidst a Papal population entailed in its doctrines, will gain
more and more in that influence over the mind of man which is
the loftiest kind of ascendency. Instead of selecting the Upas
tree for its illustration, I would rather compare it to that Ilex of
which it has been so nobly said—

"Per damna, per cædes, ab ipso,
Ducit opes animumque ferro."

I would fain, too, believe that the English people, having thus
amply redressed that which their votes at the hustings have
declared they believe to be a wrong, they will demand from the
Government that strict vindication of the laws instituted for the
protection of property and life which their own experience has
taught them is equally essential to social happiness and political
progress. So that we may approach all that groupe of questions
connected with the ownership and tenure of land, armed with
the power to exact from property all its duties, by evincing our
determination to maintain all its rights. For my own part, I
would a thousand times rather sever Ireland altogether from the
British dominions than retain her at the price of admitting into
our Legislature principles that shake the groundwork of the
wealth of nations, by bungling imitations of an agrarian law.
Bereft of Ireland, England might still be strong, strong in the

causes of that Protestant ascendency which she represents in the Parliament of nations. But let her once be false to that integrity which refuses to frighten, to juggle, or to bribe a man out of that which he possesses as his own, in order to divide it among others, on the plea of preventing revolt or disarming assassins, and she will perish amidst the scorn of that civilisation whose interests her cowardice has betrayed.

XLVII.

OUTLINE OF A SPEECH

INTENDED TO HAVE BEEN DELIVERED IN

THE HOUSE OF LORDS

ON THE 7TH OF MARCH 1870.

On Monday the 14th of February 1870, the Earl of Carnarvon, according to notice previously given, called the attention of the House of Lords to the present relation of the Colonies with this country. In doing so he took occasion to comment upon the somewhat startling circumstance of our having then a grave and dangerous crisis in New Zealand, and of our hearing of a rebellion in the Red River Settlement, at the very moment when a petition was lying before Parliament from certain agitators in British Columbia. Again, within less than a month afterwards, on Monday the 7th of March, the Earl of Carnarvon having, in compliance with Parliamentary routine, duly notified his intention beforehand, inquired from the Secretary of State for the Colonies, Earl Granville, whether Her Majesty's Government would consent, under any conditions, to delay the departure of the 18th Regiment, still in New Zealand, but under orders to sail. Lord Carnarvon moved at the same time for correspondence. It was upon this latter occasion that the following speech was intended to have been delivered.

My LORDS,—It is a matter of comparatively little moment whether Her Majesty's Government are right or wrong in the dispute with a single Colony like New Zealand. But it is of immense importance not only to England, but to the whole scope and future destinies of the civilized world, whether in the antagonistic

circumstances arising out of that dispute should be found hereafter the cause of the dissolution of the British Empire. Whether
it be or be not expedient to arrange certain easy terms with
New Zealand, by which it may obtain the aid of the Queen's
soldiers against a barbarous enemy, is a matter on which the
warmest advocates for maintaining our Colonial Dominion may be
divided. But if in discussing this point, principles are announced
or a tone adopted by the Government which serve to offend or
alarm the Australian and American Colonies in general, and
create among these a belief that England has grown desirous to
part with them, and only disguises that desire by a polite expression of indifference whether they stay or go—that she declines
to respect them as children, and only wishes to keep them as
customers—then the question is enlarged into one so vast, that I
scarcely know the limits to which the consideration it involves can
be confined. It is not only a national, it is a cosmopolitan question.
It is a national question of the utmost importance—Whether
England is really contented to abrogate her magnificent position,
as the head and centre of a colonial system unrivalled for the
extent of the territory it covers, for the intellect and energy of its
citizens, for its unity of race, language, and religion, and still
more for the loyalty of so many scattered populations, to the
sceptre of a single Queen. It is a cosmopolitan question still larger
in its consequences to the human race—Whether we should thus
acknowledge that a colonial system, without parallel in history,
for its success in planting the cities, the commerce, the religion,
the laws of a civilized race, in the midst of barbarous regions,
and bestowing on those communities the freest exercise of self-
government, has been another mistake and failure so far as the
ultimate interest of the parent State is concerned—that we dread
it as a danger, casting it off as a burden, and abandon these
splendid communities, not when they have come to full growth
and maturity, are able to protect themselves, and of their own
accord desire and ask for independence, but while they are yet in
the infant stage of their development, and more likely to unite
themselves to some other savage power able to protect them, and
enlarge the scope for their intellect and ambition, than assume

for themselves a sovereignty, for the secure maintenance of which they have as yet neither wealth nor population sufficient for self-defence. To part from such communities, when consciousness of their own strength to stand alone, makes them demand the completion of National Sovereignty—to part from them thus may be wise and safe, for we then only relinquish unwilling subjects for attached allies. But to part with them now—and with cynical indifference to their security and welfare—is to leave behind the seeds of a rancour that will descend from generation to generation, and to replace loyal subjects by indignant foes.

These new worlds have become so important an element of consideration to the old world of Europe, that there is not a European nation which has not a deep interest in considering what may be the future destinies of Canada and Australia, if England cuts the tie that binds them to herself and to Europe, and leaves them to develop their gigantic resources with no other sentiment for Europe than that of hereditary grudge to the nation from which they sprung. I think that for the sake of England, for the sake of the civilization of which England is still an illustrious representative, we are bound to seek from Her Majesty's Government a plain and clear statement of their views on colonial policy, and know in time for the people of this country to pronounce its opinion, whether the Ministers of the Crown are converts to the philosophy of Mr Goldwin Smith, or whether they can cordially assure their descendants and fellow countrymen now, that they are not indifferent to the advantages and the glory of maintaining the noblest and the freest empire which Providence ever assigned to the sceptre of a single king.

No doubt, my Lords, the terms on which that connection can be maintained so as not to overtask our powers, should be frankly stated. We should best avoid future misunderstandings by saying what we can do, and what we cannot do. And first, with regard to military assistance. It seems to me that wherever a nation plants its flag, it is bound to support its honour. In every war made against a colony for the sake of attacking England, that colony may rely on the utmost aid, military or naval, it is in our power to bestow. But, as we do not profess to have an unlimited military force, we have a right to expect from every such colony a skilled and organised volunteer force in case of need. And in this exaction we confer much greater benefit than we receive. For the condition of the world must be greatly altered before any community can educate itself for sovereign independence that does not early acquiesce in the preparations for self-defence. In vain may you communicate to a colony your industry, your arts, your literature, and your laws, if you do not also communicate that spirit of courage and manhood by which the inhabitants will submit to hardship and privations in fitting themselves to defend from aggression their hearths and altars. I think this rule especially applies to communities like New Zealand, surrounded by savage tribes, and threatened by wars not incurred by the Imperial Government. And where in such wars it is expedient to send forth British troops,—as very generally it may be expedient,—I think that the Imperial Government has a right to demand that the whole polity of the war, the mode of waging it, and the terms of peace on which the war is concluded, should exclusively belong to itself. There is no part of Her Majesty's dominions, whether it be in a colony or at home, whether it be in New Zealand or the province of Yorkshire, in which the Queen's soldiers should be employed in any mode of action that may seem to her responsible ministers idly to imperil or discredit the national flag. And the Sovereign, through her responsible advisers, should alone determine the best modes of employing the imperial forces, and the right terms of restoring tranquillity and peace. With this proviso, I think, that any hostilities from barbarous enemies threatening the lives and properties of British subjects in a colony, are more likely to be terminated with humanity and despatch by a disciplined and dispassionate military force, and thereby brought to a lasting peace, than by the unassisted efforts of the colonists themselves, with all the difficulty they must experience in getting scattered agriculturists to quit their homes and pursuits, and form themselves into an united body, and with all the revengeful passions which the nature of the contest must engender.

And when we hear so much of the cost of providing such

military force as an argument for abandoning any colony that requires it, we must not forget that even in that evil consequent upon extended empire, there is a compensatory benefit to our safety at home. For no political observer of ordinary sagacity can look at the present state of Europe, or indeed consider those stormy elements which enter into the present composition of human nature—and believe that it would be safe for England, however much she may seek to withdraw herself from the councils and interests of Europe, to be without the nucleus and framework of a military force. That framework cannot be adequately formed and maintained within the precincts of these islands. A sufficient standing army at home would not be acceptable to the free spirit of our institutions. Our colonies serve for their safest quarters, and our officers and soldiers may acquire more knowledge of the real art and practice of war in the contests with an actual enemy—even though he be a barbarian than in a lifetime spent on reviews at Aldershot.

And, my Lords, this consideration of the value of Colonies in the military point of view, brings me to the consideration of their infinitely more precious value in their bearings upon that social energy and that commercial enterprise, out of which have grown the wealth and the grandeur of the English nation. I would scarcely pause to examine the comparatively petty and isolated question, whether or not trade follows the flag. On this score it is said by the distinguished historian, Mr Froude, that even customers so good as the Americans import only 10s. worth of our manufactures per head in proportion to the population—while our imports to the Australian Colonies are at the rate of 10d. a head. And even Canada, in spite of her unfavourable tariff, takes four times per head the amount of our products taken by the people of the United States. If Australia left us, or if Canada were united to the American Republic, who shall say that there would be no loss of custom. But this has always seemed to me a small item in the question of gain to a country that has become the centre of a colonial system, just as by a continuous strain upon his muscular force, a man gradually increases his physical strength. And thus in the old classical story Milo began

by carrying a calf just weaned, and carrying it every day, at
length imperceptibly acquired the strength that could with ease
carry the weight of the full grown ox. So a nation that has begun to extend its dominions to the range of infant colonies, finds
itself unconsciously augmenting the fund of all its energies in like
extent—maritime—commercial. The greater the strain upon its
powers the more the powers increase and the more easy becomes
the pressure. Suddenly remove that strain, suddenly bid these
powers relax in their enterprise and their endurance—and the
loss of strength follows the collapse of exertion.

It is not in the diminution of custom with the colonies themselves, that—if you renounce your colonial system—you will
suffer. But you will lose in the general energy by which you now
maintain England in the front of commercial nations. My Lords,
is it necessary that we should abnegate the high rank in which
Providence has placed our country ? Shall we be content to imitate the example of Holland, without the excuse which alone
justified Holland in withdrawing from the magnificent part she
played on the great stage of European interests, and sinking into
the silence and inertia of a fifth-rate power. The excuse of
Holland was poverty and debt—was a national bankruptcy, which
left her unable to support fleets and protect colonies. Have we
come to this ? And are we to hear this melancholy news from a
cabinet composed of all the talents ? Certainly it would be a
miserable confession. But there is a confession infinitely more
disgraceful, which much in the anti-colonial philosophy that I
fear has infected our enlightened government, appears to imply.
No, we are not grown too poor to support our colonial empire,
but it is implied that we have grown too cowardly,—we fear the
enemies to which it may expose us,—we dread to leave any point
at which their cupidity and ambition may assail us,—we spend
vast sums in improving our fleets and artillery, but only for holi-
day display, just as the Chinese place numerous images in front
of their ranks, not to fight, but to frighten the enemy. We are
told—we, the men of a generation only younger than that which
fought with Wellington and Nelson—we are told that Canada
is a free-born possession, that it exposes us to attack from

America, and the statesmanship of panic bids us get rid in time of a possession which we are afraid to defend. My Lords, no man is more for the policy of peace than I am, but I am prepared for any danger which honour compels us to risk—for without honour life is as worthless to a nation as it is to a man. But I am not prepared to encounter all the dangers that must befall England if she once, without a blush, makes that confession of cowardice to the new world and the old. Do it, and prepare for every insult and every aggression. Let Canada indeed say, I wish to be a member of the American Republic; or, I am strong enough to hold my own as an independent State, and I would not utter a word to restrain her choice. But as long as Canada says—I am part and parcel of the British Empire, and am proud to be so, and I desire no change—I maintain that the honour and the safety of England are as much bound to protect Canada from invasion as they are to protect Yorkshire. My Lords, I do not wish to accuse the Government unjustly. I do not doubt that much which has been said by the Noble Earl has been misinterpreted, and excited unnecessary alarm. But there is no doubt that from the accession of the present government to power, we must date the rise of an irritation, a disturbance, an unsettlement in the principal portions of our Colonial Empire, which it will task their statesmanship to allay and remove. They succeeded to the administration of that vast empire when it was singularly tranquil and loyal,—they have contrived in the space of a year to destroy that tranquillity and to endanger that loyalty. You have delegates assembling in London, with loud complaints that the interests and welfare of the colonies are not consulted under your present system of rule, and with schemes and theories for remodelling that system which have as yet no theoretical shape, which it may be impossible to harmonize into any better system than prevails now, if it were administered with conciliatory wisdom. And you find the youngest and the most rising and important of the colonies you have founded—a colony with harbours that could contain all the navies of Europe—with agricultural and mineral wealth that should court the enterprise of countless emigrants, and blest by a climate more temperate than that of England

—you find that colony despatching a Memorial to the United
States, begging their President to negotiate for the transfer of its
allegiance.   Nor can I sufficiently express my surprise and
regret at the instructions which the Noble Earl, the Colonial
Secretary of State, has sent out to the new Governor of that
colony.   I say surprise, for I cannot help thinking that the Noble
Earl must have learned from the late lamented Governor, Mr
Seymour, than whom no abler or more statesmanlike mind could
be found in the whole Colonial Administration, that any proposal
to force a premature union of British Columbia with Canada would
be extremely distasteful to the general population of that colony.
While it was clear from the mixed character of the population
and its geographical situation, that any attempt to dictate its
fusion with Canada, would turn its affections to the American
Republic.   I cannot, of course, say whether Mr Seymour conveyed
these opinions to the Noble Earl, but I have reason to believe
that he entertained them, and that such is the opinion of the
ablest of the British Columbian colonists.   I say this, without any
hesitation, that colony having been founded by Her Majesty upon
my advice as Colonial Secretary, and that advice having been
justified by the rapid growth of the settlement, by the fact that
none of our colonies ever cost so little to found or so quickly
repaid the mother country, by demand for its manufactures and
as a field for its emigrants.   I have naturally a deep interest in its
welfare, and maintain such acquaintance with its progress and
opinions as I can obtain through private correspondence.   Well, if
there be one feeling stronger than another in that colony, it is a
desire to retain connection directly with Great Britain, confident
of the resources that will one day enable it to be an independent
State, with far greater advantages for maritime and commercial
development than are bestowed upon Canada, or indeed upon any
State of its size in the new world.   If there be any feeling of
repulsion it has stronger than another, it is to become the colony
of a colony, and merge itself and its prospects in the government of a province to which it has no convenient access of communication either by sea or by land.   Between these two feelings of attraction and repulsion intervenes the consideration of

junction with the United States. And this consideration cannot fail to obtrude itself, partly because a very large proportion of the colonists are Americans by birth, partly because its nearest and most accessible relations are with the citizens of the United States. In a word, the colonists would prefer to remain English subjects rather than American, but would assuredly prefer being American citizens to being colonists subject to the government of Canada. And I say boldly, that these facts are so clear to any one who will inquire and examine, that I cannot sufficiently express my surprise, that on the 28th of last October, the Governor of that colony should be authorised to publish a despatch from the Noble Earl, dated the 14th of August, going in the very teeth of the popular feeling, and converting this splendid field for English enterprise and emigration, into a petitioner for union with the American Republic. Consider for a moment the present population of this colony; a large proportion of the prevailing population is American, a large proportion German and other foreigners, and the rest is British, but not Canadian. It has no more connection with Canada than it has with Hong Kong. It is just as unwilling to be transferred to the government of such remote dominions as an inhabitant of Westminster would be. And with still better reason—for a man could get from London to Ottawa much more easily than he can get to London from British Columbia. Around this colony lie American dominions—to its haven come American ships: and can you wonder that when the British Government treat with contempt that splendid key to the Pacific, which the American Republic so ardently covets, and would merge it into an inaccessible dominion from which it can derive no earthly advantage, the offended pride and the national interest of the English settlers makes them lend a ready and willing ear to the solicitations of the American emigrants to become part and parcel of a republic which is able to enrich, to people, and to protect the land on which they have built their homes. Is it possible that a statesman could not have foreseen that this Memorial would have been certain to follow the pressure of our Government to incorporate the colony with the Canadian Dominion. And now what an additional element of difficulty

this has created in dealing not only with the colony but with the
United States. I presume that you will decline to negotiate with
America for the transfer, that you will not purchase indemnity
for the "Alabama" claims by the gold mines, the forests, the fisheries, and the harbours of a country as large as England itself,
and still more bountifully endowed by Providence. But your
refusal, unless you reverse your policy, will only add to the
irritation you have roused in the colony, and furnish new excuse
and fresh strength to the ambitious claims of America. It is
the first instance in our time in which a British colony has
desired to place itself under the American flag. If that desire
strengthen and become universal in that colony, it is only
by force that you can maintain your hold, and you give an in-
centive to the States to make war on you, because, at the first
outbreak of that war, the whole of that country from Vancouver to the Red River Settlement will prove your enemy.
If you assent to the transfer, do not believe that the Canadian
Dominion you have lately united would hold together. Nova
Scotia would revolt, and Newfoundland would follow the example. Desertion from one flag to another, once begun, is as contagious as an epidemic. Augustus asked his defeated General,
" What have you done with my legions ? " Shall we live to ask
our exulting Ministers " What have you done with our Empire ? "
Just consider how our home population now presses on our
limited area, and how rapidly population doubles itself. The
genius of our ancestors, supplying the niggard boon of nature,
secured to us magnificent fields for our surplus population, and
amidst them planted colonies speaking the same language,
governed by the same laws, kneeling at the same altar. Of all
these possessions there was not one in which an Englishman
ought to have felt more at home than in the richer soil and
milder climate of British Columbia. To these fields for enterprise men might transport themselves, retaining all the rights of
subjects, entertaining, if they so pleased, the hope to return some
day and take no mean place in their native land. You have
a noble instance of this in your present Cabinet. Two of its most
distinguished members began their career in life as colonists,

they returned to give to their native land the benefit of their intellect and experience. And it is just when so signal a proof is afforded of the field for ambition which a colonial adventurer may obtain as a subject of England, and when in that proof we might lighten the bond between the mother country and its dependencies, that our policy suddenly induces the colonies to believe that we are indifferent to their possession, and afraid to protect them. Can you suppose, with some pretended philosophers, that so long as we can shuffle off our surplus population anywhere, anyhow, it is all one to English interests, that it matters nothing whether Englishmen settle themselves on British or foreign soil, whether they and their posterity remain friends and kinsmen, or become enemies and aliens to us and to our children? Whether or not trade follows the flag, national sentiment does.· And if ever the United States should be at war with England, all the English natives who settle in these States as American citizens, must pay the taxes and obey the councils and contribute to the forces by which the war against England is maintained. But if men discontented with our institutions here, settle in British colonies, imperceptibly, but rapidly, their discontent vanishes, and they become loyal subjects in the new quarters of our dominions. Canadians will tell you of numerous instances of Irishmen who left these shores with the hostile sentiment of Fenians, and becoming prosperously settled in Canada, have forgotten their hereditary grievances, and have become the warmest advocates of connection between Canada and England. Whether as customers for our manufactures and merchandise, whether as outlets for our surplus population, or whether as healthful stimulants to enterprise and energy, I maintain that our colonies are of vital importance to the mother country, and immeasurably overpay the cost and the perils which are the noble conditions of a great empire.

My Lords, I can sincerely say that in the remarks I have thus obtruded on your attention, my feelings towards the noble Earl who holds the office of Colonial Secretary, are the reverse of hostile. There are few men who unite so many valuable qualities for the successful administration of an office which demands knowledge of mankind, the study of complicated affairs and interests, and a love of justice united with generous views and conciliatory temperament. In such qualities I know no one whom I should prefer to see at the head of the Colonial Office, not only in ordinary times, but in times of difficulty and transition, provided only that he has a firm belief in the value of our Colonial Empire, and shapes his policy so as to retain and not to relinquish it. If such be his belief, and such the inclination of his policy, I think he will have no difficulty in explaining away any misunderstanding which have unfortunately occurred, and that it is yet time to reconcile British Columbia to a preference for English dominion, by a frank retraction of all attempt on the part of his government to induce that colony into corporation with the remote and inaccessible dominion of Canada. Do not let him seek to forestall the work of time, and sink the obstacles interposed by Nature, or dream of uniting Vancouver to Ottawa, till at least the highways between them become accessible, and a direct communication links the Pacific to the Atlantic. If he persevere in these premature efforts, he may rely upon it that he will involve himself in immeasurably greater difficulties than are now apparent and will commence a revolution in which all hopes of founding an integral and independent dominion of British America will disappear. It was the boast of a famous hero of antiquity, that he had not indeed certain elegant accomplishments, admired by his country, but that he knew how to make a small State great. May no Minister of England in our time reverse that claim to the homage of posterity, and leave it to history to say, that with many brilliant accomplishments he knew how to make a great State small.

XLVIII.

OUTLINE OF A SPEECH

INTENDED TO HAVE BEEN DELIVERED IN

THE HOUSE OF LORDS

ON THE 18TH OF JULY 1870.

On Monday the 30th of May 1870, the Earl Granville, as Leader of the House of Lords, moved that the British Columbia Bill be read'a first time, and it was so read accordingly. Previously, an order in Council had been issued by the Queen's Most Excellent Majesty, in accordance with the stipulation made by section 146 of the British North America Act, passed in the Session of 1867, empowering Her Majesty to admit the Colony of British Columbia to the Union of the Dominion of Canada. The British Columbia Bill was read a second time on Monday the 18th of July, after a very brief discussion, passed through committee on Thursday the 21st of July, and was read a third time on the following evening. The speech here given was intended to have been delivered upon the occasion of the second reading.

MY LORDS,—I will endeavour as briefly as possible to explain the reasons that induce me to invite you Lordships' attention to the motion of which I have given notice. In itself it refers to a single colony alone, but indirectly it touches upon our whole colonial policy and system. It was at my recommendation, when I had the honour to hold the Colonial Seals, that Her Majesty was graciously pleased to add to her colonial possessions the territory now called British Columbia. The necessity for that

step was pressed upon me by the fact of the discovery of gold
and the excitement which this discovery occasioned on the one
hand among the native Indians and the white settlers belonging
to the Hudson's Bay Company with whom those Indians had
established friendly relations, and on the other hand, among the
citizens of the United States in the adjacent American territory.
I need not say that nothing more provokes the angry passions,
which lead to bloodshed, than the discovery of gold in a territory
unprotected by any legitimate sovereign authority. And that earnest desire to prevent hostile collision with our American kindred,
which has always, in my time, actuated the policy of Great
Britain, necessitated placing soil which belonged to the Crown
under the sanction of the British flag, and the authority of a
government more recognised than that of the Hudson's Bay
Company, and formally appointed by the Queen. The creation
of the colony was thus a political necessity. But by all the reports
which subsequent experience has verified, it was also a political
acquisition of considerable value to the people of this country.
The Colony not only abounds in gold, but in other minerals,
such as the most useful kind of lead, and inexhaustive supplies
of the most valuable kind of coal. Large portions of the land
are exceedingly fertile, and the forests contain perhaps the finest
timber in the world for the purpose of shipping. To these advantages you must add a climate especially suited to English emigrants, it being like that of England, but more genial and equable
—its winters much milder than those of Canada, its summers
more temperate than those of California. Above all, this colony
so rich in its internal resources, enjoys a maritime situation of
which it is scarcely possible to over-estimate its importance.
British Columbia, in which I include, of course, the island of
Vancouver, is the key of the Pacific. I will here quote what is
said by that distinguished American officer, Admiral Wilkes, in
his official report to the Senate, on the commerce of the United
States :—" Except Australia, British Columbia would be the only
important colonial occupation of the Pacific coast by Great
Britain. That station of England will prove of great value in
the future struggle for commercial, if not political, ascendency in

the orient. The harbour of Esquemault is a magnificent haven, fit to shelter a whole navy in safety." Admiral Wilkes then proceeds to show the advantage of Vancouver as the naval station of England on the Pacific, and for the construction, repair, and coaling of vessels, and he then refers to the other advantages of the coast for fisheries, and a coasting trade, saying the salmon, herring, and other fisheries of this region, will equal those of Norway.

It has been supposed that the colony is too remote from ourselves for the purpose of emigration. But since the construction of the Pacific railway, we have, I believe, no British possession requiring emigrants, except the maritime provinces of Canada, etc., nearer to us in point of time. The journey to Vancouver was, I am informed, done by the last batch of emigrants at the charge of the colony, in twenty-five days, and at cost of £25 each, and the price for fertile land is a dollar an acre.

Assuming, then, that the maintenance of a colonial system still forms a part of the policy of Great Britain, and that, while we should firmly reject all overtures to plant, for the barren sake of possession, new colonies in unhealthy situations, and promising no prospective gain to our commerce, we should still hold it our interest and our glory to redeem from the wilderness those places which furnish healthful outlets to emigration, and in proportion as we people them, will give new scope to our trade, and new markets for our manufactures. Assuming this, I do not know a spot in the world in which colonisation offers fairer results to the parent State than the territory which comprises British Columbia and Vancouver.

The colony has only been planted ten years; and in that short time—in spite of serious drawbacks to its natural development, all of which could be easily removed in its present connection with the Imperial Government, but which, as I will afterwards attempt to show, any premature incorporation with the Canadian Dominion would only tend to aggravate—it has amply fulfilled its promise of future importance.

It is of no charge or cost to the mother country. It has secured a yearly and rapidly increasing revenue, which not only

covers its ordinary expenditure, but provides a sinking fund for
the debt it was obliged to contract for the construction of roads
and harbours. It has even furnished a sum for the cost of emigrants. It has laid the foundations of towns. It has established
throughout its territory telegraphic communication. It has constructed roads to its principal settlements, and though, owing to
faults of administration which I shall mention presently, its
trade with this country has been greatly crippled of late, we
have only to look to the returns of its imports from Great Britain
to see how largely it has overpaid to our commerce all that it
has cost us since its commencement.

Its imports from the United Kingdom in nine years to
the year 1868, are estimated at about a million and a half.
Now, while on this million and a half Great Britain received
profits both on the goods and freight in British ships, out of
nearly £1,300,000 exports from the colony, nearly £1,200,000
has been paid to Great Britain in bullion on which the colony
has received no profit, only £116,000 of colonial produce being
received. The profit to our trade which our colony confers may
be estimated at 20 per cent. on the million and a half, showing
a tribute paid by the colony of £300,000, while, in the same
proportion, Great Britain pays a tribute to the colony of only
£23,000 on the £116,000 she takes of colonial produce.

Among the drawbacks to the natural development of the
colony, the first I will name is one which has given great trouble
to those of the colonists who desire annexation to the United
States. Will it be believed that nearly the whole of the land
between the harbour of Esquemault and the town of Victoria
(the capital of Vancouver), a distance of two miles—being
exactly the district for which new settlers would most eagerly
compete—is locked up by the Hudson's Bay Company, or individuals belonging to it, who will not sell or lease an acre, and the
road passes through a primitive forest on either side, without a
tree felled or a shanty built. Every man in the colony knows
the ready manner in which, if the colony belonged to the United
States, the Hudson Bay Company would be required, on pain of
forfeiture, either to improve or to dispose of this land, as they

were required to do with their land in the neighbouring territory of Oregon, where they attempted in vain to pursue the same obstructive policy. Every man in the colony knows in how short a time, did but the island belong to the United States, one uninterrupted street, alive with trade and enterprise, would join the harbour of Esquemault to the town of Victoria.

But I believe it would demand no coercive measures to bring this land into the market, if our Government would only do its duty, I will not say to the colony, but to the trade of Great Britain. By a singular error of policy, Vancouver, which was originally a free port, ceased to be so when Vancouver was united to British Columbia—that is, as soon as the unrivalled advantages for free trade possessed by the harbour of Esquemault became apparent. And the consequence has been, that the imports of British produce and manufactures have been reduced to about one-half what they were in 1864. In 1864 the imports from the United Kingdom were £291,584, in 1868 they were only £152,280.

Make the whole island of Vancouver a free port, placing a custom-house for the mainland at the mouth of the Frazer, and at once you assure the prosperity of the island, and re-open to much greater advantage than before, the markets for our produce. The new harbour of Esquemault would attract ships from China, South Mexico, and the Sandwich Islands, while the great demand for English goods in the United States would create a steady and rapidly increasing trade with the Washington and Oregon territories and San Francisco. And the land now locked up by the Hudson Bay Company would so increase in value, that self-interest would compel them to parcel it out in allotments, and thus realise the dormant capital which now brings them no return.

Of course, if Great Britain would only condescend to take advantage of the unequalled harbour which Providence has added to her possessions, a dock would be necessarily constructed. This would be the first step taken by the United States if the colony belonged to them. American naval officers have expressed their astonishment that the English Government—if

even for the mere sake of economy—did not either construct a
dock or offer inducements to a company to do so. Should any
accident happen to one of the Imperial vessels in the Pacific, it
must now be compelled to dock in a foreign port. The advantage of a dock in the colonial harbour has been pressed upon the
home authorities both by the late able and lamented Governor,
Mr Seymour, and the Admiral who was then on the station, but
hitherto pressed in vain. The Colonial Office, I believe, fully recognise that advantage, but the Admiralty refuse it. And why?
because—and here is another just complaint of the colonists,—
because, forsooth, the Admiralty chooses to transfer its naval
station in the Pacific to the foreign port of Valparaiso, though
no one can deny that our own port at Esquemault has, beyond
all comparison, the finest harbours, beyond all comparison the
healthiest climate, has all the advantages for docking which coal
and ship timber, close at hand, can bestow. And since the Pacific
Railway has been completed, communication with England is
safer, quicker, and more regular, than it can be with Valparaiso.

While the colonists were flattering themselves that by the
energy and intelligence of the Home Government obstacles to
emigration and to commerce which were obviously against the
interests of England as well as of the colony, would be effectually
removed, they are met by the despatch of the noble Earl, dated
14th August 1869, ignoring alike their present difficulties and
their prospective value to the mother country, and strongly
urging the new Governor, Musgrave, to exert his influence, not
for the improvement of the colony, but for its incorporation with
the Canadian Dominion, which is infinitely more isolated and
remote from it than Great Britain is, and which is, at present,
utterly powerless to administer its government or develope its
resources.

I know not of course, upon what despatches the noble Earl
founds his conjecture—" But though on such a question the
colony was not unanimous, yet the prevailing opinion was in
favour of union." The new governor, Musgrave, appointed in June,
could but have just arrived at his destination in August, and I
should like much to see his latest despatches—now that he has

had time to mature his judgment. But now permit me to state a few facts in the teeth of the conjecture, into which those despatches insidiously betrayed the strong sense the noble Lord so eminently possesses. In the year 1867 a very distinguished Canadian settler in the colony, Mr de Cosmas, and who may be considered the head of the confederation party, certainly carried a resolution through the Legislative Council, recommending confederation. But in 1868, when he reverted to that resolution, and named the terms on which a union should be based—not I presume without authority from Canada—terms, in some respects tempting, for Canada was to take upon herself the debt and to effect a waggon communication to Ottawa in three years, provided the Imperial Government would guarantee the loan required for its cost—the legislative council rejected the motion by a majority of three-fourths, upon the ground that even discussion was premature. Premature, not because the Red River Settlement was not then ceded to Canada, but because the Council had not sufficient information and experience of the practical working of confederation in the North American provinces to admit of their defining the terms on which such an union would be advantageous to the local interests of British Columbia. To make that decision still more practically convincing, Mr de Cosmas himself was rejected by his constituents of Victoria, the capital town of Vancouver, exclusively upon the ground of his advocacy of confederation, while candidates who opposed confederation were everywhere returned. And strong as these facts are, constitutionally obtained, they become still more strong if taken in connection with the attitude recently assumed by the Red River Settlement.

That Settlement is incalculably less remote from Ottawa than British Columbia is. The prospective advantages of confederation are to it much more obvious and more accessible than can at present be offered to the wildest imagination of the British Columbians. And if the first impulse of the Settlement has been a revolt which in its very hopelessness of success, shows the heat and strength of the popular sentiment, judge what will be the opposition of British Columbia—which is still proud to consider itself a direct dependency of the English Crown. But if it is not to be that, it is at present more separated from Canada by intervening obstacles of nature, than almost any other British possession. You could far more easily join it to Hong Kong or to the Australian continent.

The noble Earl, in his despatch, talked of British Columbia being made conterminous to Canada by the cession to Canada of the desert territory that lies between. New Westminster or Victoria is not brought nearer to Ottawa—because the wilderness between them may take another name on the map. And across this immense interval of inhospitable space, no communication is even commenced. The noble Earl allows the want of communication, but he flatters himself that if by a stroke of the pen, New Westminster is declared to be subject to Ottawa, Canada would effect the communication. But before we can estimate the probabilities of such an enterprise, we ought particularly to know whether Her Majesty's Government are prepared to endorse the conditions for which Canada appears to have stipulated in the proposals made by Mr. de Cosmas, and guarantee the loan required for the purpose. If they are so prepared, I do not say that I should object—I think that the United States are right in considering that the construction of roads available for military purposes is sufficiently an imperial object to justify State assistance. And my objection to immediate confederation would be greatly removed. But if Her Majesty's Government will not assist even a waggon road by guarantee or contribution, then, I doubt, if Canada can find or raise the millions required for so colossal an undertaking as a railway, or whether any speculative company could be found in Europe for constructing a line of railway where no traffic is likely for generations to pay the shareholders a farthing dividend.

At all events, the British Columbians would be imprudent indeed if they did not say, " Let us see Canada begin this work— let us see what she does to join with Ottawa, the Fertile Belt and the Red River Settlement, before we trust to the chance of her affording us railways and markets on the other side of the Rocky Mountains. We will not willingly consent to relinquish

our separate existence, and sacrifice the magnificent future
which belongs to our maritime situation, backed by a mainland
so richly gifted by nature, and comprising, with Vancouver, an
area of two hundred and thirteen thousand square miles—that
is, double the size of Great Britain,—more than three times the
size of the average States of the American Republic,—eight
times the size of New Brunswick,—ten times the size of Nova
Scotia,—in order to be what ? Why, the province of a province, to
which we have not even an access, except across the territory of a
foreign power, which, in case of war, would be closed against us !"

And the moment that this odious submission is pressed upon
them by the Imperial Government, can you wonder that some
of the colonists now—could you wonder if most of the colonists
a little later—turn longing eyes to their next neighbour, the
United States ? They know how eagerly the United States
covet that destined queen of the Pacific, which the parent state
treats with such contempt, to which you grudge even a dock,
to which you prefer the sickly and foreign station of Valparaiso !
They compare the contempt they receive from you—they compare the terms on which confederation is offered to them by
Canada, to the generosity which the United States has shown to
California—a far less valuable possession for maritime purposes,
and even for mineral wealth, but to which the Republic has
given nine million dollars for the development of its internal
resources. And I ask the noble Earl fairly to consider whether,
by this premature proposal of confederation, he cannot readily
account for that Memorial despatched to Washington, soliciting
annexation to the United States ; and whether, if he continues
to press his scheme, the desire for annexation may not so increase as to become a formidable source of difficulty with the
American Republic, and lose for ever to Canada that outlet to
the Pacific which the progress of time and civilization may
otherwise secure to her. To that Memorial to Washington very
few names are attached—I do not believe they amount to fifty.
It is so improperly addressed, that the comity between nations
ought not to allow the American Government to attend to it—
of itself, we need attach to it no importance. But still it is one

of those straws thrown forth which serve to show how the wind
blows—when you remember the mixed population of the colony,
Australians, Germans, French, Americans, as well as British,
and consider how many settlers there are not connected with us
by blood, who, though easily reconciled to confederation when
communication through Canadian territory shall be effected,
would look upon a premature union, that robs them of their revenue, and gives them a very inadequate share of representation,
as the ruin of their industrial prospects, and a vital blow to the
growth of the colony, from which the sole chance of recovery
would be annexation to the American Republic.

And now, see how injurious to Canada herself may be at
present, the acquisition of a territory which, one day or other, it
must be her ambition to unite to her own.

Suppose British Columbia to revolt—how is Canada to put
down the revolt—how can she even get to the place, except
through the territory of the United States? Suppose that Parliament consent that Great Britain shall assist her, and we send
out a naval force. Of course we stamp out the rebellion, and in
so doing stamp out the last sentiment of loyalty; and whether
the revolt be quelled by the Canadian force or by the Imperial,
the seeds of undying bitterness will be sown, to spring up, some
day or other, not only against ourselves but against the Canadian Dominion. The moment the colony could safely count on
the sanction and help of the American Republic, might she not
throw off the yoke of a province more remote from her than
England is from Siberia, and become part and parcel of a Republic certain to enrich and able to defend her? Might not the
key of the Pacific be lost for ever to the Dominion of Canada
and the empire of Great Britain? There is another forcible
reason why Canada ought not yet to accept of this territory,
and why it is unfair in us to transfer it to her. The Boundary
dispute between us and the United States is still unsettled;
and the Island of St Juan, which commands the mouth of the
Frazer River—that is, the gate into the mainland—is still half
occupied by an American force. And here let me say, that my
last act on quitting office as Colonial Secretary, was to warn my

successor, the Duke of Newcastle, which I did by letter, of the necessity of enforcing the directions I had given to the Admiralty, to have a ship of war constantly at Vancouver until the Boundary question was settled, in order to guard the Island of St Juan from that raid of American individuals to which I foresaw that it would be otherwise exposed. For some reason or another—I know not with what department rests the fault or the misfortune—I know not whether a ship was stationed at the mouth of the Frazer, or whether, if so, its watch was sufficiently vigilant—but that which I foretold took place, the island was seized, and nothing but the prudence and moderation of the then Governor, Mr Douglas, prevented an armed conflict, which might have led to very serious results.

But there still remains the Boundary Question as far from a settlement as ever. And there still remains the Island of St Juan, which dominates the capital of Vancouver, and the entrance into British Columbia, in the joint occupation of an English and American force.

Can you suppose that all the difficulties and perils connected with that unsettled dispute, and the alleged claims of the United States to the Island of St Juan, will not be immeasurably encreased if the colony is transferred to a dominion comparatively feeble, and when every advantage is given to the United States, in the sympathy of all the colonists, who dislike to be incorporated, and will then yearn to be annexed ? You will only confer upon Canada the heritage of a dispute, in which you will have secured every advantage to the rival disputant.

My Lords,—I should not have made these remarks if I did not believe they were made in season. I think it is not too late now, I fear it might be too late some months hence, to reconcile British Columbia to her present relation to the Crown, and to her future chance, when Canada has developed her resources, and constructed the necessary communications, of becoming the most important seaport, and not the least flourishing and powerful State of that immense dominion. It is with the greatest regret that I oppose any desire of the Canadian Government, or people, for immediate confederation of this important colony. In the destines of Canada, I take the warmest interest, and I do not forego the sanguine hope that one day or other a direct line of communication through her territory may realise the noble dream of uniting the Atlantic with the Pacific.

It is in the interest of Canada that I would adjure her statesmen not to jeopardize her security and hazard her prospects, by attempting prematurely to clutch at a possession which is so difficult to reach, and might be no less difficult to hold. Were I myself a Canadian, I would not in common prudence desire the incorporation of the colony until diplomatists have settled whether the Island of St Juan, which commands its harbour and the entrance into its mainland, is legally to be occupied by an American force—and unless the Imperial Government would assist Canada in the construction of those communications, by which alone she could defend the possessions transfered to her. And I should regard the hasty gift of the colony with great suspicion, as indicative of the desire of the Imperial Government to get rid of all North American possessions, and fasten upon Canada all the difficulties and perils connected with the Boundary Disputes. Meanwhile, surely Canada has more than enough on her hands at present, to stretch to the utmost the experiment of incorporating divided regions under one rule, an experiment of which the results must depend upon that law of nature, by which in the political world, as well as in the physical, vast masses are accumulated or dissevered according as their component particles are mutually attracted or repelled. We have in the Australian colonies an example that, at least for a time, kindred colonies may flourish more by severance than confederation. I take one case in point. I obtained Her Majesty's permission to create the colony of Queensland by separating its territories from that of Sidney. And while Sidney has been thus freed from a constant source of trouble and irritation, the encrease of Queensland in prosperity and in population, has been sufficiently marked and rapid to approve the policy of taking into consideration other circumstances than the fact of being on the same continent, in deciding whether one British settlement should be severed from, or incorporation with, another.

Now, in this case I do not hesitate to say what course I should respectfully but earnestly commend to the enlightened and candid mind of the noble Earl. I should urge him to withdraw for the present all schemes of confederating British Columbia with the Canadian Dominion. I know that the noble Earl will say that he would not force the consent of the colonists; but that is scarcely enough. So long as he implies that immediate confederation is the wish of the home government, he keeps alive a dangerous rivalry between the party for confederation, which is chiefly on the mainland, and the party for annexation, which is chiefly on the island, and the energies of the colony for separate self development become paralised. I would urge him, therefore, to direct the Governor to the inquiry, not what may be the eventual destinies of the colony, but what can be done to improve its present condition under the imperial rule. Inquire whether I am right in the suggestions I have presumed to volunteer as to the harbour, the dock, the naval station, the seaport, and the emancipation of the lands between Victoria and Esquemault. Let Great Britain but show her desire to retain and to assist the colony in its own efforts of self-development, and you will hear no more of Memorials for annexation to the United States. The colonists are still loyal to England; do not seem indifferent to that loyalty, and you will win all their hearts.

My Lords, my natural interest in the fate of a colony which I advised Her Majesty to found, and my desire to retain to the Crown and people of this country, an acquisition of which I have endeavoured to show the importance, must be my excuse for this long and tedious encroachment on the indulgence your Lordships have vouchsafed to me. I trust it is needless to say that in the remarks I have made I am actuated by no spirit of hostility to the noble Earl the Secretary of the Colonies. I say sincerely, and not in the mere language of compliment, that few statesmen appear to me so eminently to possess certain qualities invaluable for the office that he holds,—long experience of affairs, great knowledge of mankind, a liberal generosity of sentiment, and a felicitous grace of conciliation,—qualities which

especially fit him to deal, not only with the questions I submit
to his attention, but with those larger and more difficult questions affecting our whole colonial system, which are now agitating the public mind,—provided only that he sincerely feels, and
will unmistakably express an Englishman's desire to retain to
England her colonial dominions, so long as its subdivisions are
willing to recognise her sceptre. On this head, and in answer
to much that has been urged in favour of shrinking from the
responsibilities which superior rank and position devolve upon
nations, even more than they do upon individuals, I might have
something to say, but it will be said by others, and on more
fitting occasions. To my mind, not even the remarkable gifts
of the right hon. Gentleman at the head of Her Majesty's
Government, not even the splendid assemblage of united talents
and contrasted opinions which he has secured to his Cabinet,
could bestow on the people of this country any benefits which
could compensate for the injury inflicted, if to their policy
should be traced the loss of the Colonial Empire.

XLIX.

OUTLINE OF A SPEECH

INTENDED TO HAVE BEEN DELIVERED IN

THE HOUSE OF LORDS

On the 28th of July 1870.

———————

Within three weeks from the death of Lord Clarendon, on the 27th of June 1870, his successor as Her Majesty's Secretary of State for Foreign Affairs, the Earl of Granville, was asked on Friday the 15th of July, in the House of Lords, by the Earl of Malmesbury, for particulars in regard to the negotiations then pending in relation to the threatened war between France and Germany. Similar interpellations were addressed to the Foreign Secretary on Monday the 18th of July by Earl Russell, on Monday the 25th of July by Viscount Stratford de Redcliffe, and on Tuesday the 26th of July by Lord Cairns.

It was not until Thursday the 28th of July that Lord Granville felt himself empowered to enter into anything like a ministerial statement, as to the course pursued in the midst of these critical negotiations by Her Majesty's Government. Later on, another ministerial explanation was given by Earl Granville, on Monday the 8th day August, throwing additional light upon the efforts made by our diplomacy to ward off the necessity of abandoning the exquisitely delicate matter in dispute between France and Prussia, to the supreme arbitrement of war. Upon the occasion of each of these statements a brief discussion took place, the earlier of the two being the one upon which the following speech was intended to have been delivered.

———————

My Lords,—I think that whatever our differences of party, we may all join in cordial sympathy with the noble Earl, the

Foreign Secretary, in the sudden difficulties which attended his accession to the office he now holds, and in approval no less cordial, of his efforts to preserve the peace of Europe.

The noble Earl, on the part of Her Majesty's Government, has very ably and accurately expressed the wish of the English people to maintain a strict neutrality in the war between France and Prussia. And if France can realize the desire she has intimated, to make the war between herself and Prussia a duel between two nations, in which no other nation is required to interfere, and if that war can be concluded as a duel between two individuals generally is by a single conflict in a single field, it is idle to say that England will remain neutral. She could not be otherwise while the independence of Holland and Belgium were respected, and Russia, Italy, Austria, Spain, and Denmark, preserved the tranquil attitude of lookers-on. But, my Lords, suppose the war between two such nations as Prussia and France has no analogy at all with a duel between two individuals. Suppose that it cannot be decided by a single conflict in a single field. Suppose that it threatens such an unsettlement of the great landmarks of Europe as to involve in the dispute the other powers of the continent, will England long be permitted to retain the immunities of a moral lecturer on the calamities of war and the blessings of peace ? My own belief is, that though of late years England has sought to maintain her ancient influence over the civilized world by coupling the most absolute right to intermeddle with the sternest determination not to fight, England is too important to the organization of Europe, and the organization of Europe is still too important to England, to allow her to escape from the necessity of taking part with one side or the other, should the war last long enough to compel both France and Prussia to provoke fresh enmities and court fresh alliances.

We see at this moment on how slight a pretext one civilized State can declare war on another that has given it cause for jealousy and resentment. But there comes a crisis in any European war, where the State which most provoked jealousy and resentment is the State which shrinks out of all participation in the common danger. The example of Austria, in the Crimean war, may suffice to show the eventual evils incurred by a State which absolutely preserves a neutrality that seemed prudent at the moment. If Austria had taken part either with the Western powers or with Russia, can any one believe that she would have encountered the disasters resulting from a neutrality which left both parties indignant at what they considered her selfish inaction? If she had sided with the Western powers, does any one believe that France would have despoiled her of her Italian dominions? if she had sided with Russia, does any one believe she would have been deserted by her old ally in the struggle, to preserve from Prussia so fair a portion of her Germanic Dominions? My Lords, there is one territory, the independence of which we are bound by the most solemn obligations to see respected. I need not say that territory is Belgium. Each of the belligerents has promised to respect the independence of Belgium, provided the other does—not a satisfactory condition!

But history tells us that the promises made by two powers at the commencement of a war, rapidly disappear on the continuation of its progress, and that it is never difficult to find an excuse for saying, that a State whose neutrality ought to be respected, has done something or other to forfeit its privilege. And the power readiest to find that excuse is not necessarily the power which is least honourable, but the power to which the necessities or the conveniences of war best reconcile the sense of honour to the pain of evading a disagreeable obligation.

My Lords, I do not think that the explanations we have yet received as to the draft of treaty between France and Prussia have much tended to allay the anxiety and alarm with which its publication has filled this country. To judge of it fairly, more detailed explanations are required. But even as the matter now stands, one reflection it must awaken. If the seizure of Belgium ever was considered and discussed as probable between France and Prussia, as one would think it must have been before the heads of a treaty could be drawn up, nothing could have been more unfortunate than a policy on our part which has allowed other nations to suppose that England

may be safely left out of all consideration on a question so
vitally concerning her honour—that her navies are maintained
only for show—that however she will bark she never will bite
—and that Belgium might be disposed of without regard to her
obligations, because without dread of her resentment. But if,
my Lords, we cannot yet discuss the question of a treaty upon
which one party says one thing and one another, neither can we
discuss the pros and cons of the mere pretext for this terrible
war. We hear too much about the mere pretext; since about
the mere pretext we can learn nothing. Scarcely do we hear one
statement but it is flatly contradicted by another, and the wisest
judge could not determine a case in which the evidence is contradictory, and the witnesses cannot be cross-examined. Thus
much only we do know, that we could not fairly examine the
pretext any more than we can the treaty, without impugning
the veracity and wounding the honour of one or the other of
these contending parties. And why study these papers, why
discuss the treaty at all ? My Lords, I address statesmen too
practical not to know that it is a mere pedantry to discuss the
abstract rights and wrongs of a nominal pretext for doing that
which the parties concerned had pre-resolved to do.

I am not disposed to attach personal blame to either of the
two Sovereigns, or the two Governments, for what appear in
these papers to have been the irresistible impulse of their several
nations. It is a war of the people on either side, the war of two
antagonistic races, the one to maintain the hereditary position it
has had for centuries, the other to keep, to confirm, and to extend
the position it has recently acquired. The truth is, that we
English are too much accustomed to consider that all other
nations should see with our eyes and judge with our minds.
We have thought fit to regard the doctrine of the Balance of
Power as an obsolete chimera, and in so doing are in some
degree answerable for the armed state of Europe during the last
fifteen years—and indirectly for the war consequent upon the
military spirit engendered by the maintenance of vast armaments
in the time of peace. According to the received theory of the
Balance of Power in Europe, France and England could not be

in the same scale—they might maintain the most cordial terms
of friendship—but the armed alliance of the greatest military
power with the greatest naval power of Europe, could not but
have filled with alarm the other European States, who saw the
navies of England withdrawn from their side in case of need,
leaving them exposed at any time to the armies of a power
covetous of glory, and liable to frequent internal changes, in any
of which a vent from domestic strife might be sought in foreign
fields, in which an additional glory might conduce to the contented re-establishment of civil order.

Thus, from the day on which the force of circumstances compelled us to an armed alliance with France in the Crimean war;
and when certain political philosophers loudly asserted that such
an alliance between England and France ensured the peace of
the world—and still more —when after the Russian war was
concluded, England let it be understood she had so far withdrawn from all interest in Europe, that whatever France might
do, so long as she did not invade us, we should not do more
than moralize and remonstrate, no matter what State was invaded by another; from that day all the great continental powers
have been maintaining vast military establishments, and the
continent has been agitated by a succession of wars which have
altered the map of Europe.

But, if we have abjured the doctrine of the Balance of Power,
France, in especial, has stedfastly maintained it as a fundamental
principle of her hereditary policy—taking care, of course, as was
natural to a power so eminent, that no continental power should
have heavier weights in the scale than herself. This is the true
reason, why in assisting the consolidation of Italy she deemed it
essential to her relative position to extend her frontiers and confirm her hold on the Mediterranean by the cession of Savoy and
Nice. And this is the true reason why she feels it necessary to
the maintenance of her relative position, and perhaps to the conditions of her very safety to check, while it is yet time, the
aggrandizement of a neighbour so near and so warlike as Prussia,
into the dominions of a Germanic Empire, with larger population and more ample resources than her own.

This consideration for her hereditary place in the Balance of Power may seem to an Englishman over sensitive, but he would certainly understand it as natural, and perhaps excusable, if he would put himself into the place of a Frenchman. And, on the other hand, if he would put himself into the place of a German, he would equally understand—why a German might consider that the sooner this battle was fought out the sooner the consummation of German unity might be effected—and why a Prussian statesman, sharing that opinion and courting this war, might yet desire so to control it that Prussia should be the challenged party and not the challenger, since Prussia could not, as the challenger, have united all Germans for the invasion of France, but as the challenged party, could unite all Germans in the defence of Germany.

Thus, my Lords, it seems to me that we might consider the true causes of this war, apart from the ostensible pretext of its outburst, with a fair and candid allowance for the national enthusiasm on both sides, and for the policy of the statesmen by whom the enthusiasm has been guided. And we might thus keep not only our actions, but even our minds, in the only genuine neutrality which could avail us if we are to become hereafter mediators—the neutrality of impartial sentiment and judgment. But this could only be, provided France—as, judging by all we know of the perfect loyalty with which the French Emperor has observed every engagement towards ourselves, we have a right to assume that she can and will—only provided France condescend to convince us that her Government never did propose, nor authorise to be proposed, any terms to Prussia of a treaty which comprehended the seizure and conquest of Belgium. For if England is left to suppose that at the very time France was bound to us by the most intimate alliance, a French Ambassador did, either with the authority or the privity of the French Government, suggest a measure so offensive to the honour of England, we might still maintain neutrality in point of action, but neutrality in point of sentiment would be impossible.

Meanwhile, I think, we may take this lesson from experience, that when other nations are armed to the teeth, it is penny wise

and pound foolish to discharge our seamen and disband our
soldiers, and I entreat the Ministers of the Crown to consider
that despite all their endeavours to avert so stern a necessity,
we may have to defend not only our honour but our empire—
we may have to defend from invasion not only the people of
Belgium, but the soil of Ireland, as the only spot in these kingdoms in which sympathisers with an invader can be found.

THE END.

PRINTED BY WILLIAM BLACKWOOD AND SONS, EDINBURGH.

www.ingramcontent.com/pod-product-compliance
Lightning Source LLC
Chambersburg PA
CBHW022257280326
41932CB00010B/891